FATHER PAUL OF GRAYMOOR

THE MACMILLAN COMPANY
NEW YORK · BOSTON · CHICAGO · DALLAS
ATLANTA · SAN FRANCISCO

MACMILLAN AND CO., Limited
LONDON · BOMBAY · CALCUTTA · MADRAS
MELBOURNE

THE MACMILLAN COMPANY
OF CANADA, Limited
TORONTO

Father Paul of Graymoor

By The Reverend David Gannon, S.A.

Father Paul

OF

GRAYMOOR

921
~~9929~~
CA

The Macmillan Company : New York

[1951]

Imprimi Potest

VERY REVEREND ANGELUS DELAHUNT, S.A.
Father General

Nihil Obstat

JOHN M. A. FEARNS, S.T.D.
Censor Librorum

Imprimatur

✠ FRANCIS CARDINAL SPELLMAN
Archbishop of New York

March 14, 1951

This Book is Gratefully Dedicated to

HIS EMINENCE
NICOLA CARDINAL CANALI

*Grand Penitentiary of the Holy Roman Church
and President of the Pontifical Commission for
the Government of the State of Vatican City*

In Memory of

RAPHAEL CARDINAL MERRY DEL VAL

Papal Secretary of State under Pope Pius X

Who Befriended the Society of the Atonement
and Brought It Safely into the
FOLD OF PETER

FOREWORD

THE ARCHDIOCESE OF NEW YORK is privileged to have within its confines several Religious Congregations which have been founded in the
Archdiocese by Americans under my predecessors—the Archbishops of
New York. These Religious Congregations are not only precious jewels
in the Crown of our Holy Mother Church, but they are also among
the important factors which contribute to the greatness of this noble
nation.

The Society of the Atonement at Graymoor is one of these Congregations which were founded by Americans, and the life and labors
of its Founder, Father Paul James Francis, are the subject of this
biography written by a devoted associate and fellow priest in Father
Paul's religious family—the Reverend David Gannon, S.A. In reading this biography one comes quickly to realize that the author knew
Father Paul intimately in his priestly as well as his personal life.
Father David Gannon gives us a comprehensive study of an extraordinary priest and at the same time writes an interesting and important
chapter into the annals of Church history in the United States.

Father Paul was a convert to the Catholic religion. And yet, as one
reads the account of his life, one wonders whether he was anything
else but a Catholic at heart even before his conversion. There are
many good and sincere men who are in the same position as Father
Paul was before his conversion. They are Catholic at heart, loving
and defending all the things that the Catholic Church loves and
defends. This is evident in many men in high places. It is seen in their
characters, their writings, their public addresses, their blameless lives.
It is seen in their sorrow as they lament the disunity of Christendom
in the face of the united forces of evil marching toward ultimate chaos.

Why then, we might ask, are these men who are seemingly at one
with the Catholic Church outside the One True Fold? The answer

to the question is that conversion rests primarily upon the Grace of God—"The Spirit breatheth where He will."

Father Paul prayed to God for light and his quest for truth and faith led him to the road that leads to Rome and eventually to the feet of the Vicar of Christ on earth. Father Paul did not find the road "home" an easy one to travel and his conversion to Catholicism was delayed because he hesitated to accept a decision made by the Pope concerning the question of the validity of Anglican Orders. The religious convictions of a lifetime are not easily overcome. But Father Paul received the Grace to accept the Catholic Faith in its entirety, and the Catholic Church graciously received him and his companions into her treasury of souls.

Two years before Father Paul entered the Catholic Church he founded a world-wide movement of prayer for the unity of all men in the One True Fold of Christ—the Fold of which Saint Peter and his successors have been appointed Shepherds by Christ Himself. This movement of prayer founded by Father Paul is known as *The Chair of Unity Octave*. Its object is to bring to fulfillment the prophecy of Our Divine Redeemer: "Other sheep I have that are not of this fold. Them also I must bring, and they shall hear my voice, and there shall be one fold and one shepherd."

The reunion of Christendom around the Chair of Peter and his successors at Rome was the primary work of Father Paul's life, just as it is the primary work of the Society of the Atonement today. The return of the "other sheep" has been of deep concern to the Holy See ever since the disunity of Christendom began in the religious upheavals of the sixteenth century. Never, however, has the need for a United Christendom been more urgent than in this our day when an evil ideology gnaws at the very foundations of Christian civilization. All "men of good will" see this materialistic, atheistic philosophy of life as a threat to the peace of the world. They see it for what it is—the destroyer of Christianity and all human freedom through the enslavement of freedom-loving peoples. Our bulwark against this world-wide threat is a reunited Christendom for which Father Paul prayed and worked so ardently.

The hope of the world is a Unity of Nations under the banner of the Cross of Christ. The world must make a momentous decision and quickly. Who then shall it be—Christ or Lucifer? What then shall come—Peace or Chaos? Whither shall we go—Bethlehem or Armageddon?

Father Paul was a follower of Saint Francis of Assisi who is the Saint of Unity. After the Founder of our Holy Religion Himself, the most successful and magnificent exponent of Christian democracy was Saint Francis. Our national principles of political equality are the fruition of the social gospel he first preached in Assisi which was afterwards propagated through Europe by his Brothers of Penance. The Christian Socialism of Saint Francis, as taught and practiced by the Church he loved and loyally obeyed, is the hope and guarantee of future prosperity, peace and happiness for the American Republic to which as a loyal son Father Paul was ardently devoted.

As the champion of human liberty and the deliverer of the oppressed, Saint Francis first reformed Assisi, his native town. But he was not satisfied with freeing the serfs and giving the franchise to every citizen of his beloved Assisi. His great desire was the emancipation of the whole human race. He saw and was saddened by the enslavement of the people under the feudal lords who kept them in a miserable state of subjection and frequently obliged them to wage wars.

Saint Francis broke the feudal yoke by the establishment of his Third Order, the Brothers of Penance. All who joined the Third Order took an oath to bear arms only in defense of Fatherland and the Church. Multitudes joined, and the Holy See gave them the protection of the Catholic Church despite the opposition of the feudal lords, and Christian democracy was born. Thus almost six centuries before the Declaration of American Independence Saint Francis proclaimed the principles of human freedom upon which it rests. The Brothers of Penance of Saint Francis spread the gospel of this new holy freedom from Italy into Spain and Germany and France and England. The common people everywhere, inspired by the Franciscan ideal of universal brotherhood, struggled to realize more of that liberty "wherewith Christ has made us free."

Through the centuries the spiritual sons of Saint Francis have left the imprint of their arduous labors on the vast lands of the Americas. The Franciscans were the first missionaries not only in areas of North America settled by the Spaniards but also along the northern coast discovered by Cabot under the English flag. Long before the Pilgrims landed at Plymouth, the intrepid Franciscan, Le Curon, had evangelized the Hurons and preached in the wigwams of the Mohawks. The Franciscan, Father Hennepin, was the first to explore the Great Lakes and gave to Niagara Falls the name of Saint Anthony. The Franciscan, Antony Margil, evangelized Texas; the famous monuments of Southern California were founded by Junipero Serra. The name of the City of the Golden Gate, San Francisco, tells the story of the labors of Franciscan Pioneers on the Pacific Coast.

To this illustrious roster of great Franciscans in America we may now add another name—Father Paul James Francis. He, too, was a Pioneer in a specific field—*The Reunion of Christendom*. Father Paul, in this our day, was a reflection of the Poor Man of Assisi—Saint Francis, the Saint of Unity. It is my prayer that all who read Father Gannon's biography of Father Paul of Graymoor may learn the lesson of its message, without which no man nor nation can long endure— the lesson of faith and unity and peace!

Francis Cardinal Spellman

ARCHBISHOP OF NEW YORK

January 22, 1951

CONTENTS

Foreword	Francis Cardinal Spellman	vii
Chapter I	Prologue	3
II	A Jesuit in Disguise	13
III	God Sends Another Son	22
IV	Given from Heaven	33
V	Enter Mother Lurana	41
VI	A Covenant Is Made	51
VII	Arrival at Graymoor	59
VIII	A Poor Friar Buys a Mountain	70
IX	He Finds a Leaking Palace	84
X	The Lame Man at the Temple Gate	91
XI	He Lights *The Lamp*	104
XII	Radicals Open the Pulpits	125
XIII	The Church Unity Octave	136
XIV	Pius X Prays for Graymoor's Conversion	150
XV	The Deluge of Grief	167
XVI	An Unquestionable Priesthood	191
XVII	A House Left Desolate	198
XVIII	Eventful Years	214
XIX	The-Union-That-Nothing-Be-Lost	221
XX	The Octave Extended to the Universal Church	256
XXI	"Willingly Do I Bear Witness"	284
XXII	The Mustard Seed Becomes a Tree	294
XXIII	The Brothers Christopher	302
XXIV	Life with Father Paul	313
XXV	Our Lady Receives a New Title	327
XXVI	The Friars on the March	342
Index		353

ILLUSTRATIONS

	Facing Page
Father Paul of Graymoor	(frontispiece)
The Reverend Joseph Newton Wattson, Father Paul's Father	52
Father Paul as an Anglican Clergyman	52
Mother Lurana Mary Francis, S.A.	53
Dimond House	84
St. John's in the Wilderness	84
The First St. Christopher's Inn	85
The Palace of Lady Poverty	85
St. Christopher's Inn Today	180
The Little Flower Memorial Building	180
The Wayside Shrine	181
St. Francis' Convent at Graymoor	181
Father Paul and a Group of Friars	212
A Group of Sisters of the Atonement	212
Sant' Onofrio al Gianicolo	213

PART ONE

The Anglican Years

PROLOGUE

Blessed are the Dead who die in the Lord . . . that they may rest from their labors. For their works follow them.

As HIS spiritual children slept on the Mount of the Atonement in the early hours of Thursday, February 8, 1940, the Angel of Death came unexpectedly into a humble monastic cell for the beautiful soul of Father Paul James Francis in the seventy-eighth year of his life. Awakened by pain preceding the fatal heart attack, he quietly called for the assistance of the lay Brother infirmarian who occupied the adjoining cell. A few minutes later he received from the hands of a Friar Priest the last rites of the Church. The resident physician of Graymoor was also in attendance, but despite all that medical science could do Father Paul was pronounced dead at 4 A.M. He died as serenely as he had lived. The Founder of the Society of the Atonement, the ardent Devotee of the suffering Christ, the magnanimous Knight of Heaven's Queen, to whom he gave a new title—Our Lady of the Atonement, the Founder of the Church Unity Octave,[1] the eminent Convert to Catholicism, the Co-founder of the Catholic Near East Welfare Association, the indefatigable Laborer for the world-wide missions of the Church, the loyal Defender of the Papacy, the tireless Worker for the reunion of Christendom, the great Lover of Poverty, the Champion of the poor, the Priestly Priest par excellence, now belonged to the ages. His life was one of deep faith, persevering prayer and efficacious penance; in his every word and act he strove to elevate the supernatural life of the world.

Numbed by grief, the Spiritual Sons of Father Paul, Friar Priests and Friar Brothers, knelt that morning outside his tiny cell in prayer. The full consciousness of what had so suddenly transpired had not dawned upon them. Only yesterday, Ash Wednesday, they

[1] The title of this prayer movement was later changed to The Chair of Unity Octave; see Chapter XX.

3

had heard him speak at the Ave Maria radio hour. The subject of his sermon was Purgatory. Last evening he had mingled with the Community during the recreation hour. As was his custom, he interrupted the joviality at the half hour to recite the De Profundis for the souls of the faithful departed. Now they were repeating the same De Profundis for the peace of his immortal soul.

The slow tolling of the Monastery bells awakened the young students in St. John's Seminary across the monastery quadrangle. Having heard the sad news, they made their way to the student chapel to pray for the soul of their Father, Friend and Benefactor. They loved this gentle Priest who graciously opened the doors of the Graymoor seminary to every worthy boy, however poor, desiring to become a priest.

The tolling of the bells awakened the Sisters of the Atonement in their Convent at the foot of the mountain. For their well being he had always shown a deep solicitude. With their Foundress, Mother Lurana, he had planned the Society of the Atonement. Before the altar on which daily he celebrated Holy Mass for them they, too, gathered in prayer.

The tolling of the bells awakened more than one hundred homeless men in St. Christopher's Inn, halfway down the mountain. For forty years Father Paul had given food, clothing and shelter to thousands of homeless men like the ones who heard the bells that morning. He called these hungry, shabby, weary, unwanted men Brothers Christopher (Christ Bearers); and with them, regardless of race, creed or color, he shared every spiritual and material gift the Giver of all good gifts gave to him. In the chapel of the Inn they prayed for this strange man who helped them and asked no questions. Many were the occasions when the Inn was taxed beyond its capacity. During the economic depression which began in 1929, and which deprived men of the opportunity of earning their daily bread, bills for food and fuel mounted higher each day; but no one was ever turned away. To a distressed bookkeeper he would say: "Do not worry; the never-failing Providence of Almighty God will take care of the bills." Father Paul kept faith with God and that faith was always rewarded. From one source or another the money always came to pay the bills. Every time he was told that there was a certain clique of professional "hoboes" abusing his charity, he said: "I would rather be fooled by a hundred men than run the risk of turning one worthy man away. Let God be the Judge of men's motives." The homeless men who heard the monastery bells tolling that morning, as Graymoor was steeped in sorrow, knew that they had lost a friend, an apostle of charity who could pierce through dishonored humanity and see the human soul with the indelible charm of Divinity upon it.

The Spiritual Sons and Daughters of Father Paul at the major seminary at Catholic University, Washington, D. C., and those laboring in mission fields, received the news of his death by telephone or cablegram. Houses of his Society were established in the South and Southwestern parts of the United States among the Whites, Negroes and Mexicans; in British Columbia among the Japanese, and in Northern Alberta among the Ukrainians. Friars and Sisters were also in Italy and Ireland. All of them felt the same poignant sorrow of a common great loss.

Four hours after the death of Father Paul, radio stations in America began broadcasting the news of his passing. One commentator relayed the news to the world in these words: "In the foothills of the Catskills at Graymoor, Garrison, New York, the Catholic Church in America has suffered a great loss. There, in a monastery, died a famous Franciscan Friar, Father Paul James Francis. He was an international leader in Church affairs. As the Founder of the Society of the Atonement his work among the poor was known throughout the world."

In the ensuing hours, days and weeks messages of condolence poured into Graymoor. His Excellency Amleto Cicognani, Apostolic Delegate to the United States, and many Prelates of the American Hierarchy sent warm messages of sympathy and pledges of Prayer. But it was not until the receipt of letters and cablegrams from Cardinals, Archbishops, Bishops, Priests, Sisters and Brothers all over the world—Europe, Asia, Africa and the Islands of the Sea—that the Friars of the Atonement realized the scope of their beloved Founder's work in Spreading the Kingdom of God upon the earth.

The Right Reverend Edward Hawks, himself a convert, wrote in the *Catholic Standard and Times* of Philadelphia:

Father Paul was the subject of controversy in every Episcopalian paper and circle. To a few, very few, he was a pioneer leading the vanguard of the most advanced Anglo-Catholics; for most he was a traitor to his own Church, tearing up the very foundations of its structure. Already he was editor of *The Lamp*, a provoking monthly which set all the staid Episcopalians by the ears. People denounced him without being able to answer him, or—and this was the most irritating—to ignore him. Seminary reading rooms tried to banish the publication from their tables, but it always came back. Month by month, in its pages, the message was reiterated: the Episcopal Church must return in a body to the Pope for history demands it, religion demands it, and common sense demands it. . . . Father Paul had already enlisted millions of Christians all over the world in a crusade of prayer which he called the Church Unity Octave. Dozens of Catholic Bishops had authorized the devotion; and Protestants of every kind co-operated, although the purpose was obviously definite—it was to bring all Christians into unity with the See of Peter. And all this had taken place long before Father Paul himself had any ideas of making an individual submission to the Pope.

The editor of the *Catholic Courier*, of the Rochester, New York, diocese, wrote:

With the death of Father Paul James Francis came the close of a career most interesting and most unique. So devoted to the ideals of the religious life was this man that he moved among the people of this generation as an almost mediaeval figure. He sought for the light, and he found it through God's grace. He heard the call of divine vocation and he answered it. . . . The Church Unity Octave, observed throughout the Church as a time of special prayer and devotion for the reunion of all Christians in the true faith, was the inspiration of Father Paul, and may be the accomplishment around which will center the most lasting memories of his life. . . . While we pray for the soul of Father Paul, let us try to match his zeal for the Church of God! We were born in the faith, he came to it through conversion. May his example inspire us to greater love for the Church and more active participation in its salutary work for the souls of men.

His Eminence Eugenio Cardinal Tisserant, Secretary of the Sacred Congregation of the Oriental Church, sent a most gracious letter to Graymoor from Rome, in which he wrote:

In my own name, and in that of the Sacred Congregation of the Oriental Church, I wish to convey to the Friars of the Atonement our sincere sympathy in the great loss you have suffered in the recent death of your Founder and Father General, the Very Reverend Father Paul Francis.

The fame of the Society founded by him and its accomplishments in the sphere of Christian charity has reached far beyond the limits of your own country. A feature of his work that I would single out for special praise is the providential and pious practice which owes its initiative to his zealous influence, namely, the Church Unity Octave of Prayer. Through the efforts of Father Paul it has spread throughout the world and has accomplished an immense good in awakening our Catholic people to a mission consciousness and to the need of interesting themselves in the conversion of those without the fold.

It is a source of satisfaction to me that in this very year, the last here on earth of this worthy religious, I was able to give an impetus to the spread of this pious practice in a circular letter to their Excellencies, the Bishops subject to this Sacred Congregation, in which the period of the Octave was suggested as a time of special observance of missionary endeavor and prayer. The fruit of the initiative of your lamented Father General will surely plead in intercession for him before the Throne of Divine Grace.

While my prayers and those of my associates are being offered in suffrage for this chosen soul, blessed with a lifetime of meritorious labor in the service of the Lord, it does not seem unfitting to entertain the pious hope that, from Paradise, Father Paul will continue even more efficaciously to further that Unity for which he strove so indefatigably during his mortal life.

Extending to you once again my heartfelt sorrow at your loss, and with prayer that your Founder's high ideals of spirituality and charity may be maintained and carried forward to still loftier heights of accomplishment.

In the same mail which brought this gracious letter from Cardinal Tisserant in Rome, came another from a member of his Hierarchy, under his jurisdiction, His Excellency, Bishop Calavassy of Greece, a friend of Father Paul for many years. From Athens, Greece, Bishop Calavassy wrote:

It is only today that I come to learn, reading the *Osservatore Romano*, the sad news of the death of our beloved Father Paul Francis.

This news was a heartfelt blow to me, as if I had lost my own Father. Was he not a good father and a sincere friend, the most sincere friend to me since the time I had the good fortune to meet him at Graymoor in

1917? He became since, not only my personal friend, but the best friend and benefactor of the Greek missions. Many of our organized works in Turkey and Greece are due to him; to his charity and to his zeal for the Cause of Reunion, to which our work, like yours, is devoted.

My seminary, my orphanage, my Sisters owe to him, to a great extent, their material existence and their establishment in Greece. For many years my clergy was practically supported by him, through Mass stipends he used to send me when he could afford them. He personally witnessed the result of his charity and his zeal when he gave us the pleasure of a stay with us in Athens in 1925.

You understand why all our communities here are today mourning his death.

I ordered all my priests to apply, as soon as possible, four Masses each of them for his soul, and all Sisters, Seminarians and orphans are praying for him.

I myself just said Mass for him, and I will continue to prove my gratitude to him in the same way in the next few days, although I am convinced that he does not need our prayers for himself, being already in possession of his deserved eternal joy in heaven.

I shall never forget the impression I had in visiting him for the first time at Graymoor. I was since then convinced that he was a man of God, a saintly Priest, a perfect Religious, full of the spirit of Our Good Lord Jesus Christ. By his poverty, his humility, his meekness and charity, his supernatural spirit and his extraordinary faith, he was giving the impression of a real saint. It was enough to visit his private cell in order to realize the degree of his mortification.

You know all this better than I do, but it must be consoling to you, I think, to know that your beloved Father, now in heaven, has his admirers far away in the missions and all over the world, because I am sure that all those who, like me, had the good fortune to make his acquaintance, had the same impression.

Let me now add that the death of our good Father Paul not only does not break the bonds which united us with Graymoor, but on the contrary it will strengthen them forever, since our gratitude to Graymoor will be eternal and since you all, I am sure, will never cease to honor his memory by your friendship and kindness to his old friends. I am sure that he now, from heaven, is observing with happiness our efforts toward the common cause to which he consecrated his life, and will bestow upon all of us the blessings of God for the full realization of that Cause "Ut Omnes Unum Sint" ("That they all may be one.")

In a more intimate sense the most consoling message which came to Graymoor was conveyed in a letter from His Eminence, Nicola

Cardinal Canali, Grand Penitentiary of the Holy Roman Church, to whom this biography is lovingly dedicated:

I cannot tell you, my dear Fathers and Brothers, how grieved I was to hear of the death of your beloved Father General, and my own personal and much esteemed friend. Not knowing that he was suffering in any way, and having heard from him recently, the news of his passing away was a great shock, as it must have been for all the members of your Holy Society. I informed His Holiness immediately, and he has graciously commissioned me to express his most heartfelt sympathy to all the Friars and Sisters. At the same time His Holiness imparts to each and every member of the Society his special Apostolic Benediction, assuring you that your beloved Father and Founder will be remembered in his prayers.

I am sure I need not remind you that dear Father Paul Francis has gained the esteem and sympathy of all who came in contact with him in Rome, and that, I think, was his well deserved experience everywhere. He was called to do a great work and he responded generously, so that we have reason to hope that this "good and faithful servant" is enjoying, or will speedily enjoy, a very great reward. His work has flourished marvelously, and now he and Mother Lurana, of holy memory, will continue to watch over their Society and procure for it still greater blessings than those already bestowed. I know the Friars and Sisters will make every effort to preserve the spirit of their holy Founder and Foundress, and that they may persevere and succeed in doing so will be my fervent prayer, and especially when praying at the tomb of the saintly Cardinal Merry del Val, who took such keen and practical interest in what he called the birth of your Society.

I commend myself to your prayers and send my special blessing to all the members of the Society, both Friars and Sisters.

With these messages of condolence from the highest dignitaries of the Catholic Church came others from sincere Protestants throughout the world, with whom Father Paul had kept in contact as he labored for the reunion of Christendom. Among these was a gracious message from an Anglican group in England whose aim is promoting Catholic Unity. The message read:

This Committee, representative of the Society for Promoting Catholic Unity, the Catholic League, the Priests' Sodality of the Most Precious Blood, the Confraternity of Unity and the Catholic Propaganda Society, offers to the Acting Prior and the Society of the Atonement its deep

sympathy in their bereavement of their beloved Founder, Father Paul
James Francis: and records its own sense of loss and its appreciation of
his inspiring work for the cause of Christian Unity, and its happiness in
the privilege of sharing with him in furthering the Divine purpose.

(signed)   REV. W. ROBERT CORBOULD
President

REV. G. S. DUNBAR
Honorary Secretary

With these letters from great and famous persons came thousands
of letters from the little people of the earth whom Father Paul
loved and served.

Ever conscious as he was of the dignity of human personality
and the sacredness of all human life, no person was unimportant in
his eyes. The charm and nobility of his character made the most
timid feel at ease in his presence. To him all men were the children of God, redeemed by the Atonement of Jesus Christ, and this
attitude toward all men constituted the greatness of his life.

As we look back over the years, those of us who lived with him
must admit that we never fully realized how truly great he was. The
amazing part of his phenomenal achievements in the fields of
Christian Unity and Charity is that they were accomplished solely by
Father Paul. For years his only companion was a lay Brother,
Brother Paul Jacob, a convert from Judaism, who entered the
Catholic Church with Father Paul and was then known as Brother
Anthony. But even then the religious life was lived in the lonely
Graymoor monastery as perfectly as if there were one hundred Friars
present. The Chapel bell was rung for morning meditation, the
Communion Service, the Angelus and the night prayers. Before he en-
tered the Fold of Peter, Father Paul rose at 2 A.M. to recite
Matins. Thirteen long years passed before he had the joy of seeing
his first Friar Priest ordained. This first priest, Father Francis S.A.,
was instrumental in causing the greatest sorrow in Father Paul's life.
The details of this affair are told in a later chapter. In the inter-
vening years he bore the heat and burden of the day alone. He
edited *The Lamp* magazine, built Graymoor's many buildings, took
care of the spiritual needs of the Sisters of the Atonement and. be-

fore his conversion, preached Christian Unity on street corners, the steps of New York's City Hall, and from every Episcopalian pulpit to which he could gain access.

His early life at Graymoor was practically a closed book to those who were admitted to the Society after St. John's minor seminary was built in 1913. Nor was there time to explore it, for a seminarian's day is spent in prayer, study and work. As Friars were ordained important work awaited them. They staffed the major and minor seminaries, the Novitiate, St. Christopher's Inn, the press, and the administration building into which thousands of letters poured each day from all parts of the globe. When the author of this book joined the Society of the Atonement in 1931 there were only nine Friar Priests including Father Paul. Two of them were in the mission fields of Texas. Is it any wonder that for years we were unaware of the greatness of our gentle Father! The greatness that was Father Paul and all his achievements were hidden in his deep humility. It was only when the restlessness of his noble soul was quieted in death, and the tremendous work he did fell upon the shoulders of others, that the vastness of that work was revealed.

For the past ten years there have been numerous requests for the written account of Father Paul's life. Hardly a week passed without the receipt of letters asking: "Has the life of Father Paul been published?"—"When will the life of Father Paul be published?" or, "Why hasn't the life of Father Paul been published?" The primary reason why it has not been written before this time is that, even with one hundred Friar Priests and fifty Friar Brothers, the Society of the Atonement still remains understaffed as it struggles to carry on the work of Father Paul. The writing of Father Paul's biography was begun as an avocation by more than one Friar since his death. But it was soon realized that compiling the salient facts of his life and work from bulging archives and from his prolific correspondence of fifty years was a stupendous task in itself.

On Monday, May 15, 1950, the author entered his cell after Vespers and found on his desk a letter from the Father General's office. It was the shortest communication he had ever received, and yet it was the most important one. It read:

DEAR FATHER DAVID:

I assign you to the duty of writing the life of our Father Founder.
Devotedly yours in Jesus and Mary of the Atonement,

ANGELUS DELAHUNT S.A.

To the author's knowledge no Friar of the Atonement had ever
received so important an assignment in so few words. His first reaction was to go to the Father General and plead incompetence. Then
he remembered how Father Paul so often in his instruction stressed
obedience. "Man," he said, "is never greater than when he stoops
to obey; the Catholic Church is admired, even by those who hate
her, because of the obedience of her members to constituted authority." For him the die was cast; the author began his work with
fear and trepidation. Each day as he passed Father Paul's tomb, in
St. Anthony's Shrine, on his way to offer the Holy Sacrifice, he
pleaded for Father Paul's prayers before the throne of Infinite Wisdom, that he might present the Founder of Graymoor to the world
as he really was with his human failing so greatly outweighed by
wonderful deeds; that in his excess of love he might not wander
into the fields of hyperbole.

May this account of the life of a great lover of God intensify
the reader's love for the Atoning Christ. May it strengthen your
faith in His Promises; may it help you to love your neighbor more,
animated as he is by the very Breath of God; and may it inspire
you to pray and work more ardently for the realization of Our
Lord's prayer on the night of His betrayal, which was the object
of Father Paul's whole life: "That they all may be one, as Thou,
Father, in me, and I in Thee; that they also may be one in Us."

Chapter II

A JESUIT IN DISGUISE

FATHER PAUL'S FATHER, Joseph Newton Wattson, was a recent convert from Presbyterianism to the Episcopal Church when he enrolled in the General Theological Seminary on New York's Chelsea Square in 1843. Within the walls of that venerable institution, "Tracts for the Times" which were being published by John Henry Newman and his associates at Oxford University in England had aroused an excitement totally foreign to the seminary's staid, conservative atmosphere. Despite the prohibition against them, these celebrated Tracts not only found their way into the seminary but they were read and studied avidly, however surreptitiously, by the students. Almost any conversation would invariably lead to a discussion of them. The tracts that were causing consternation and embarrassment to the Divines of the Church of England and to Episcopalians everywhere were rapidly converting the stronghold of Episcopalianism on Chelsea Square into another Oxford. Many of the students were men of intellectual brilliance—leaders in the academic world in which they lived. Quite naturally they resented the restrictions imposed on them by the professors of the seminary, who prohibited the reading of the tracts.

Imperceptibly, the Oxford tracts had opened a new world to the students of the General Theological Seminary; a world in which they could find no place for the theology of their textbooks. One day several students gathered in the room of Joseph Wattson, for what is known, in all halls of learning, as a "bull session." The topic of conversation was the usual one—the Tracts. They were in the heat of discussion when another student, by the name of Oliver Prescott, joined them. His contribution was what he called "a choice bit of gossip." "The rumor then going around the seminary," he said, "was that a number of Jesuit students in disguise were enrolled in the 'General,' and that once they had made all the converts possible they were going to lead them into the Church of Rome." Wattson, who had gained a reputation as a practical joker at the "General," thought the story was very humorous. He lowered his voice in pretended secrecy, and whispered: "Why, Prescott, didn't you know that?"

It proved to be a costly joke. From it arose a crisis in Wattson's life that was to affect his whole career. Prescott, a student much too serious for his own good, and with little sense of humor, reported the incident to the Dean. Unfortunately for Wattson his records showed that he was a convert from the Presbyterian Church. The Dean, already greatly disturbed by the influence Newman's writings had over the students, decided to act at once.

"This man is dangerous," he said. "On the record he is listed as a convert from Presbyterianism, but it could very well be a decoy to throw off any suspicion. Why, Wattson might even be *a Jesuit in disguise*. The student Donelly is also part of this plot; and, with that name, he could very easily be *a Jesuit in disguise*."

Ordinarily the whole affair might have been overlooked and allowed to die a quiet death. But, with conditions at the seminary what they were, the Dean could not afford to take the chance of overlooking the incident and thereby jeopardizing his own position. The Oxford tracts were causing so much excitement that the authorities of the Episcopal Church were preparing to make a thorough investigation of conditions at the seminary.

A prominent Episcopalian churchman of the time, writing his memoirs noted:

You have not yet heard of the regular conspiracy in the General Seminary to Romanize the Church. The students have formed a society, secret, with the watchword "C.U."—"Catholic Unity," and have been in communication with the Romish Bishop. They mean to colonize here that the work might go on simultaneously everywhere. The subject is now before the faculty in New York and a committee of three Bishops: Lee, Henshaw and DeLancey, has been appointed to investigate the matter. It is curious enough that this should come out after they had, by resolution, just whitewashed the Seminary.

With the Episcopal investigation under way, the Dean and the professors of the seminary suffered from frayed nerves and sleepless nights. Moreover, as always happens in the retelling of an already exaggerated incident, the "Wattson affair" assumed tremendous proportions. Something had to be done.

Finally, Joseph Wattson and James B. Donelly, who had been a Congregationalist before joining the Episcopal Church, were ordered to appear before the faculty council. The charge of being "Jesuits in disguise" was never mentioned; perhaps because these faculty members, intelligent as they were, saw, in a saner moment the ridiculousness of so unfounded a charge. However, Wattson and Donelly were accused of promoting Romish doctrines and their dismissal was recommended. An opportunity was given to them to defend their position, and they gave a good account of themselves in repudiating the charges. Their sincerity and truthfulness were so obvious even to the most prejudiced members of the council that they were exonerated. Nevertheless, they were asked to leave the seminary quietly, to avoid any further embarrassment to the authorities.

In fairness to the memory of these men, and in order to understand the situation in its true light, it is important to point out that *the Oxford Movement was not established to convert England to the Catholic Faith*, as so many have erroneously supposed. The primary purpose of the movement was to revive in the Church of England the teachings and liturgy of the early Christian Church. On August 31, 1833, John Henry Newman, in a letter to Frederick Rogers (Lord Blachford), tells of the object of the Movement:

. . . we have set up Societies over the Kingdom in defense of the Church. . . . They are already started (in germ) in Oxfordshire, Devonshire, Gloucestershire, Berks, Suffolk and Kent—the object being "*to make the clergy alive to their situation, to enforce the Apostolical Succession, and to defend the liturgy.*" We mean to publish and circulate tracts. I have started with four. We think of a quarterly magazine. . . . Everything as yet promises well—but we are merely talking about it as yet, and have got no rules even.[1]

[1] *Young Mr. Newman*, by Maisie Ward; Sheed and Ward, New York, 1948, p. 240.

The Oxford Movement began on July 14, 1833, when the Reverend John Keble preached on the "National Apostasy" in St. Mary's, Oxford. But John Henry Newman, more than any other man, was the personification and embodiment of the Catholic Revival in the Anglican Church.

Reading about the tumult caused by the Tracts at the General Theological Seminary over a century ago, one would suppose that the seminary authorities were disturbed because the place was flooded with Catholic literature, smuggled in by bona fide Jesuits in disguise. The truth is that the Tracts were written by the greatest luminaries of the Church of England at that time. And they were written not to further the cause of "Popery" but rather to apostolicize the Episcopal Church. What really frightened the authorities was that the Tracts were too "Romish" in doctrinal content—exactly what the learned sons of Ignatius Loyola would have written, so they thought.

They were smuggled into the seminary not by Jesuits but by students for the ministry of the Episcopal Church. The Dons of Oxford were the "Jesuits in disguise" only because the fruit of their intellects was worthy of a Jesuit's pen. The authorities feared the consequence of truth.

But the genius that was Newman could not gainsay the truth. As he dug into the cellars of antiquity, in his effort to establish in the Church of England the object of the Oxford Movement, he stumbled upon the terrible truth that what he sought for was the Catholic Church. It was inevitable. For, in the year 1834, a Canon of Lichfield Cathedral handed the first numbers of the Tracts to his cousin, the Roman Catholic scholar, Ambrose Phillipps de Lisle, who, after he had read Tract Number Four, on the Holy Eucharist, said: "Mark my words: these tracts are the beginning of a Catholic movement which will one day end in the return of the Church of England to Catholic Unity and the See of Peter." [2]

Newman had a difficult choice to make when the full realization of that truth was given to him. On September 29, 1843, he wrote to Maria Giberne, a dear friend: "I do so despair of the Church

[2] *Life and Letters of Ambrose Phillipps de Lisle*, by Edmund Sheridan Purcell; Macmillan and Co., Ltd., London, 1900. Vol. I, p. 199.

of England . . . . . and on the other hand I am so drawn to the Church of Rome that I think it safer, as a matter of honesty, not to keep my living (his parish). This is a very different thing from having the intention of joining the Church of Rome." [3]

The reason for the momentous step he finally took was given in a letter to the same person on January 8, 1845: "This I am sure of, that nothing but a simple, direct call to duty is a warrant for anyone leaving our Church. . . . The simple question is, can *I* (it is personal, not whether another, but can *I*) be saved in the English Church? Am I in safety, were I to die tonight? Is it a mortal sin in *me*, not joining another Communion?" [4]

Later that year, on October 8th, he wrote again to Maria Giberne: "Father Dominic, the Passionist, comes here tonight. He does not know of my intention—he comes to see my friend, Dalgairns, whom he received into the Church about a week since—I shall ask him to do the same charitable work for me." [5]

The day following, he wrote to T. W. Allies: "I am to be received into what I believe to be the one true Church and the one Communion of the Saints this evening, if it is so ordered. Father Dominic, the Passionist, is here, and I have begun my confession to him. I suppose two friends will be received with me.

"May I have only one-tenth part as much faith as I have intellectual conviction where the truth lies! I do not suppose anyone can have such combined reasons poured upon him that he is doing right. So far I am most blessed. . . ." [6]

John Henry Newman's disciples in the Oxford Movement who had the conviction and the courage received the same grace. Others ceased to follow the "Kindly Light" and were content with High Church Anglicanism, tenaciously defending the validity of Anglican Orders. That controversy was ultimately settled by Pope Leo XIII in the bull "Apostolicae Curae" of September 18, 1896, when Anglican Orders were declared invalid.

Newman's reception into the Catholic Church surprised the whole

[3] *Young Mr. Newman*, by Maisie Ward; Sheed and Ward, New York, 1948. p. 426.
[4] *Young Mr. Newman*, by Maisie Ward; Sheed and Ward, New York, 1948, p. 438. [5] *Ibid.*, p. 449. [6] *Ibid.*, p. 449.

of England: and well it might, for, in 1840, Newman occupied a
position in England that people of the present day can hardly realize. He was the idolized leader of a religious movement that stirred
Englishmen to the depths. To them he was the magnetic personality
who was to do great things for the Church of England. But five
years later, at the call of grace and conscience, he went forth
from his high place, leaving all things to follow Christ into the
Catholic Church.

When the doors of the General Theological Seminary closed on
Wattson and Donelly the gateway to the realization of their lifelong
dream and hopes closed also. They stepped out of the seminary
into a world of obscurity. The "joke" of the "bull session" changed
the course of their lives. The cloud of suspicion, which so suddenly
enveloped them that day, followed them to the grave.

As they passed the residence of the Catholic Archbishop of New
York, across the street from old St. Patrick's Cathedral, Donelly
suggested a visit to the Archbishop. "Wattson, the Episcopal Church
has treated us like a stepmother," he said, "let's go round the
corner and call on Archbishop Hughes."

But the idea did not appeal to Joseph Wattson. "Let's sleep over
the matter first," was his reply. As events turned out, the proposed
visit to Archbishop Hughes never materialized. Instead they parted, as
marked men in the Episcopal Church, never to meet each other
again. Had they called upon the Archbishop this book might never
have been written.

Donelly found a strong friend in Dr. Seabury, editor of *The
Churchman*—an influential Protestant paper—who was also the son of
the famous Bishop Seabury of Connecticut. Through influence, he
was able to have Donelly admitted to the ministry and also appointed
his assistant in the editorial office. But, as the story of Donelly's
dismissal from the seminary spread, he found it impossible to obtain
any worthwhile position in the Church. The last years of his life
were spent in a lonely West Virginia mission. There he died; a poor,
forgotten old man.

The fate of Joseph Wattson was not much better. After leaving the seminary he reported the incident to Alfred Lee, of Delaware, his own Bishop. Lee, who was an Evangelical, had little love for the Catholic Church; and still less for those clergymen within his own Church who espoused Catholic doctrine and ritual. His advice to Wattson was brief, and precluded any possibility of recommendation to the ministry by him. "Young man, go to Rome," he said; "for that is where you belong!" Wattson, who had never had the slightest desire to go to Rome, was stunned. Then began the search for a bishop who would support him.

The sympathetic William R. Whittingham of Baltimore, Maryland, was the one who finally admitted Joseph Wattson to the ministry. The Bishop told Wattson that he could not obtain a position for him, but only recommend him for one. He reminded Wattson that selecting the pastor was the special right which the vestrymen of each church enjoyed. Joseph Wattson knew that, under the circumstances, there was little possibility of his ever advancing far in the Episcopal Church.

For years he was the rector of small, wretchedly poor parishes, until at last he was offered the rectorship of St. Clement's at Millington, Kent County, Maryland. The church was built in colonial days of red clay brick which had been brought over from England. The only notable thing about it was a white "Communion table," a gift of Queen Anne. At St. Clement's Joseph Wattson found the only security and permanency he had known in all the years of his ministry. But it was no "plum," for even here he endured many hardships and trials through the twenty-five years of his rectorship.

Only once, during the years, was he offered a better position. The trustees of St. Luke's Episcopal Church, in Baltimore, invited him to be their pastor. But one of the more prominent members of the parish, hearing of their decision, objected: "Gentlemen, you certainly do not intend to call, as your rector, a man who was expelled from the General Theological Seminary in New York for being a Jesuit in disguise!" That ended the negotiations with the trustees; and again Wattson wondered what might have been his story if he and Donelly had gone to see the Catholic Archbishop of New York.

An interesting study, in contrast to the lives of Wattson and

Donelly, is the destiny of some of their associates at the General Theological Seminary who "went to Rome." They had the conviction and the courage to follow Newman's "Kindly Light," and like their guide, who became a Prince of the Church, they too distinguished themselves in the Church which generously received them.

The highly sensitive and deeply spiritual Edgar P. Wadhams was one of these students. As a convert to Catholicism his extraordinary ability was given full play. The Church recognized the genius in him. When the Holy See established the Diocese of Ogdensburg, in 1872, Edgar Wadhams was named its first Bishop.

Another student, during this period, was Clarence E. Walworth. He was an intimate friend of Wadhams, and with him embraced the Catholic faith in 1854. He entered the Congregation of the Most Holy Redeemer and made the acquaintance of Isaac Hecker, who was a Redemptorist at that time. These two men became fast friends. When Pope Pius IX directed Father Hecker to found a Congregation of Priests devoted exclusively to the work of the Conversion of America, Father Hecker gathered about him a group of men whose devotion to the cause of America's conversion was similar to his own. Father Clarence E. Walworth was one of these pioneer Paulists whose privilege it was to assist the saintly Isaac Hecker in the establishment of the Society of St. Paul the Apostle.

The most extraordinary character in the group was James A. Mc-Master. After entering the Catholic Church, he made a serious effort to live the religious life in the Redemptorist Congregation; but he did not persevere. Both he and his superiors accepted the fact that the religious life was not his calling. He left the Congregation in his novitiate year. Returning to the world, he became an outstanding figure in journalism, as the editor of the *New York Freeman's Journal*. His brilliant intellect and vast store of knowledge served the cause of religion well, as he brought honor and glory to the Church.

Joseph Wattson, living in obscurity by the waters of the Chesapeake, followed with interest the careers of his former associates. As he went about his humble duties among the simple people of Tidewater

Maryland, impoverished as they were by the conflict between the North and the South, we know that he often thought of a past so full of hope for a more abundant material life; he also thought of what might have been had he confided in Archbishop Hughes. This we can record with certainty from what we do know. But what his other thoughts were we do not know. If the author were to write further on the subject he would merely be recording the product of his own imagination. Father Paul, the son of Joseph Wattson, never mentioned, either in conversation or in his written word, any bitterness in his father's life. On the contrary he talked with tenderness of his patience, his sense of humor and his devotion to family life.

While Joseph Wattson never attained worldly prestige, there was reserved for him through the eternal years a far greater blessing. The suffering he endured through misunderstanding, loneliness, frustration and poverty, as he served God in the ministry of the Episcopal Church, was eminently rewarded. For his name will forever be remembered, chosen as he was by God to father, to train and to mould the character of one destined to accomplish great things— Father Paul James Francis.

[*Chapter* III]

GOD SENDS ANOTHER SON

CIVIL WAR was raging in the United States when Lewis Thomas Wattson, whom the world later loved and knew as Father Paul, was born on January 16, 1863. The bitter consequences of that war were felt by the people of the Eastern Shore of Maryland when the third son of the Reverend Joseph Wattson and his wife, Mary Electa, first saw the light of day. The God-fearing rector of St. Clement's and his devoted wife rejoiced that God had sent them another child, even though they knew that with this blessing came another burden. A few days later the child was baptized by his father, and was given the name of Lewis Thomas; but from then on he was known by his family and his friends as "Tommy."

Since few details are available of the early years of Joseph Wattson's nomadic ministry, as he moved from one pastoral charge to another, still fewer details are known of his wife, Mary Electa. He had met her almost by accident. The twice-widowed lady had been one of his parishioners who took an earnest interest in the activities of the parish. When their friendship had developed into a strong love, fully cognizant of the uncertain future which faced her, she nevertheless consented to be his wife. Until his appointment to St. Clement's, each day brought new hardships and trials to Joseph and Mary Wattson. But these generous souls accepted them as coming from an Almighty Father, Who knows what is best for each of us.

Mary Electa Wattson often told "Tommy" of those difficult early days. And though he never experienced any of the wretched poverty of his parents' early life, the story of that struggle was so vividly told that he never forgot it. A poor and struggling parish in Mississippi was the scene of their most trying days. Her eyes would light up whenever she recalled the day that her husband announced to her the good news that they would be moving shortly to a more com-

22

fortable rectory in Maryland, and that this was definitely the end of their wanderings. Part of the journey from Mississippi was made in an ox cart. As they crossed the muddy waters of the Yazoo River, they looked forward to a new life in Maryland, and they were not sorry to leave Mississippi, where they had suffered so much, behind them forever.

Lewis Wattson was, by nature, a quiet boy; and there was nothing extraordinary about him. He lived the life of the average American boy, being popular with his playmates and taking part in their games. But he preferred to go alone on long walks through the woods, or to fish in the creeks which were abundant in Kent County. He became a familiar sight on the country roads, with a straw hat carelessly worn on his head and a fishing pole over his shoulder. When parish duties permitted a few hours of relaxation, Joseph Wattson would join his son on these excursions, and these were Lewis' happiest hours. A strong bond of affection grew up between the elderly minister and his youngest son; it was so apparent that the parishioners of St. Clement's remarked how much alike they were.

Joseph Wattson was a great story-teller. He could entertain his family and his friends hour after hour with the reliving of the exciting events of his ministry. And while his father spoke, Lewis would sit spellbound. The story he liked the best was the one about the "Jesuits in disguise." It was always told with a tinge of humor. For Joseph Wattson, enjoying the blessings of the day, like all good men who have suffered unjustly at the hands of their fellow men, could look back on the cross of yesterday with a smile, knowing that bearing it without bitterness had made him a better human being.

One day, after returning from a parish sick call, Joseph Wattson and his son Lewis were sitting in the study of the rectory awaiting the dinner hour. The boy at that time was ten years old. But even at that early age he was displaying a keen interest in religion, disclosing a maturity far beyond his years. In moments such as this, the father and son often talked about the Catholic Church, her teachings and her ritual. And it was from his father that Lewis Wattson, even as a boy, learned to love the Catholic practices which he observed in later years in his own ministry. Since his days at the General

Theological Seminary in New York, Joseph Wattson had been a conservative High Church ritualist. So when the boy asked his father the question: "Father, have you ever been to a Roman Catholic service?" it came as no surprise.

"I was present once," the father answered, "in the Roman Catholic Cathedral of Baltimore, when Walworth, as a Paulist Father, addressed a vast concourse of men, which packed the building to the doors. It was not so much curiosity which prompted me to go in as something else. You see, Walworth and I were students together at the 'General.' I had heard that he had joined the Roman Church and had become a priest. When I learned that he was preaching in Baltimore I made up my mind that I would hear him."

He paused for a moment. Then he added, with an impressiveness which his son never forgot: "What we need in the Episcopal Church is a Preaching Order like the Paulists."

Deep within his soul, Lewis Thomas Wattson heard what he always believed to be the inspiration of the Holy Spirit. Clearly an inner voice whispered to him: *"That is what you will do some day; found a Preaching Order like the Paulists."*

It was the first intimation he had of his extraordinary vocation. He never doubted that inner voice which prompted him to undertake the great work of founding an order of "Preaching Friars." The full extent of his unique vocation, and what it would entail, developed in time; but the inspiration which motivated the work was given then, in his father's study. In all the remaining years of his life he never doubted its reality or its significance.

A new world opened to Lewis Wattson when he began his school days. The little rural school, which stood close to his father's rectory, was where he received his elementary education. His parents, like all the self-sacrificing parents of every age, decided Lewis should have every advantage of a good education; so they sent him for his secondary education to St. Mary's Hall, a private church school in Burlington, New Jersey. (The school has since become a private boarding school for girls.)

The carefree boy now became a serious student, interested only in acquiring knowledge. He was ever conscious of what the whispering voice had told him—it set the goal of his life before him—and he worked, studied and prayed the more intensely, knowing that his life was to be different from that of his classmates. Three generations later, he told his Friars that as a student he often wondered just how he was to accomplish the task of founding a preaching order, and in those times he assured himself that the voice, certain as he was of it, would show him the way.

After he was graduated from St. Mary's Hall, he entered St. Stephen's College at Annandale, New York. There he received his preparatory and college education. Scholastically he ranked highest among his classmates; his brilliant mind mastered the classics and the sciences without difficulty.

The autumn of 1882 found him enrolled among the students of the General Theological Seminary, his father's alma mater. In later years he told of the strange feeling that came over him as he passed through the portals of the ivy-covered buildings that the critics of another day had called "another Oxford." "I thought," he said, "that being the son of a man who had been asked to leave, because of his 'Romish leanings,' I would always be under surveillance." But almost two decades had passed, and no one seemed to remember the "Jesuits in disguise."

One of his classmates, after the death of Father Paul, described how he, as the young Mr. Wattson, looked and conducted himself at the seminary on Chelsea Square. He was short in stature, with light hair and delicate features. His eyes sparkled as he spoke. Like his father, he had a keen sense of humor, which is the secret of popularity in every school. His originality made him stand out as an independent thinker, whose opinions and ideas on most subjects were always refreshing and enlightening. In religious matters he was always a High Churchman, like his father before him—though far more advanced than his father ever dreamed of being.

The Reverend Joseph Wattson, now an elderly man, made many trips from Maryland to see his son at the seminary. Lewis was intensely proud of his father, who became well known to the students he met through his son. Among them there were some who, like

Lewis, later took the road to Rome, and distinguished themselves as converts in the Church. Harry R. Sargent, who became Dom Leonard O.S.B., one of the founders of Portsmouth Priory, was one of these. Before his conversion he was an important member of the Episcopalian Order of the Holy Cross. His conversion to Catholicism created quite a disturbance among Protestants. Another was William McGarvey, leader of a group of Episcopalian clergymen during the Open Pulpit crisis. McGarvey was an outstanding religious figure of the early twentieth century. His conversion, as well as that of some twenty associates, was an important development of what might be called the Oxford Movement in America.

In 1885 Lewis T. Wattson completed the three-year course of studies prescribed by the Canons of the Protestant Episcopal Church for candidates to the ministry. The Commencement exercises, at which the unusually large class of thirty students received their degrees of Bachelor of Divinity, took place during the week of Pentecost. On the Saturday before Pentecost the entire class gathered in St. Peter's Episcopal Church, which was located just a city block from the seminary, for the Baccalaureate Sermon. Taking as his text: "Ye have not chosen Me, but I have chosen you," Bishop George F. Seymour, of Springfield, delivered a masterful oration. The exalted character of their calling, and their duty to respond wholeheartedly to that call by manifesting a devotion to the service of the Church, was the underlying theme of the entire sermon. It fired the spirits of everyone in that class. For no one, however, did the Bishop's words mean more than to Lewis Wattson. For him those words were inspired. They were a challenge hurled at him from the pulpit to be up and about his business; a confirmation of his first call in his father's study; and with the confirmation came a further assurance that divine help would never be far off.

The graduation was also held in St. Peter's Church, which the students of another day had jokingly named "The Vatican." Lewis Thomas Wattson had the honor of reading an essay before the assembled faculty, students and guests. It was a proud day for him; but for the Reverend Joseph Wattson and his wife, seeing their son receive his degree, it was something more—an answer to their prayers and a reward of their sacrifices.

Shortly after his graduation he was made a Deacon of the Episcopal Church, on May 30, 1885. The ceremony took place in St. Paul's Church in Centerville, Maryland. Illness prevented Bishop Henry C. Lay, of Easton, Maryland, who should have presided, from carrying out the ceremony. He delegated Bishop Alfred Lee, of Delaware, to act in his place. And so it happened—Joseph Wattson presented his son for the deaconship to the very Bishop who, forty years before, had dismissed him from his service because of his expulsion from the seminary as "a Jesuit in disguise."

We do not have to imagine what the thoughts of the Bishop were as he received Lewis Wattson to the diaconate. On that day he expressed them. A dinner followed the ceremony, and Bishop Lee was among the guests of honor. The old man, now venerable with age, sat between the young deacon and his father. When he was called on to speak, tears coursed down his cheeks as he spoke of the incident which had taken place in his residence so long ago. He admitted how wrong he was when, to a bewildered and perplexed young man, he shouted: "Young man, go to Rome; for that is where you belong."

But the sand in the hourglass of Joseph Wattson's life was running low when he was finally and fully exonerated of the unjust charges which had hounded him for forty years. Men who had denied him a better livelihood had long since passed away when the Bishop, with moist eyes, told his story. It did not matter now to Joseph Wattson, for in those years he knew in his heart that he was innocent of any connection with Rome as a "spy," and therefore he could always speak of victory.

Immediately after his reception to the deaconship, because of the lack of ministers at that time, Lewis Wattson was given the care of St. James' Church in Port Deposit, Maryland. As a deacon he could not perform the Communion Service, but this duty was willingly assumed by his father. Five months later, young Mr. Wattson was given a city parish.

The vestrymen at St. John's Episcopal Church at Kingston, New York, had for a long time been seeking a new rector. This position was first offered to the elder Mr. Wattson, but he had already retired from the active ministry because of his age. However, he asked that this opportunity be given to his son, whom he recommended as an excellent preacher. He also assured them that he would assist his son until he could discharge the full pastoral duties upon his reception to the presbyterate. This plan appealed to the vestrymen of St. John's, and Lewis Wattson was invited to become its rector. He arrived in Kingston with his parents in the autumn of 1885, and there he remained for ten fruitful, happy years.

The parishioners of St. John's liked their young rector from the very start of his ministry among them. His extraordinary preaching ability, his dynamic personality, and his devotion to his parents made them realize how fortunate they were in having obtained his services. Moreover, the unique arrangement of the elder minister celebrating the Communion Service, while his son preached, attracted the people from all over the valley.

Lewis Wattson was made a presbyter the following year at the age of twenty-three by a special dispensation of his ecclesiastical superior, Bishop Henry C. Potter of New York. This special dispensation was necessary since the Canons of the Protestant Episcopal Church require that candidates for the ministry be twenty-four years of age.

Father Wattson, as he was now called, returned to St. John's after being made a presbyter by Bishop John Scarborough, of New Jersey, in Holy Trinity Episcopal Church at Trenton. And now the full burden of the rectorship fell upon his shoulders, for the years had taken their toll of Joseph Wattson's life. He died on July 4, 1887. "The Jesuit in disguise" now passes out of the pages of this volume, but his influence on the character of our hero remains all through it.

The fame of Father Lewis Wattson spread rapidly. He was in demand whenever any special occasion called for a notable speaker. Nor did he limit himself to the confines of the parish. He interested himself in the civic affairs of Kingston and served on many committees. The residents of Kingston soon realized that his endorsement of a project was not limited to a scrap of paper.

Father Wattson's pulpit oratory was the powerful magnet which drew ever-increasing crowds to hear him. His services, though often very ritualistic and following closely the Catholic rites, which he so admired, were well attended by Episcopalians of all leanings.

"I can see him now," wrote one of his parishioners of those days, at the time of his death in 1940, "as he would preach in his parish church, his wonderful voice touching all our hearts, his teaching appealing to us and making us better churchmen and churchwomen. He had a habit (probably you noticed it) while preaching, of grasping a black cross which hung around his neck, as much as to say, 'in the Cross of Christ I glory!'" A clergyman who later became a bishop in the Episcopal Church wrote: "I knew him as a preacher and I wish to say he had no equal in that particular."

Father Wattson was innately refined and cultured. Charm, integrity, kindness, sincerity and nobility were the essence of every sermon he ever preached. His eloquent and zealous preaching was but the expression of his deep spirituality. Moreover, his profound knowledge of the Scriptures and the writings of the Church Fathers put at his disposal a potent weapon with which to combat error and vice and to defend truth and virtue. He rarely wrote his sermons before delivery. They came from the abundance of his heart, and he always trusted in the Holy Spirit to inspire him. This habit which in ordinary men would be considered presumptuous was with him a virtue.

In May, 1894, he began the publication of *The Pulpit of the Cross,* which was originally intended to be a parish bulletin. However, its aims soon broadened to include within their scope the spiritual welfare of many others living far beyond the limits of the parish in Kingston. From the beginning of its publication *The Pulpit of the Cross* was a controversial paper. In explaining the object of the paper, in the first issue he wrote: "Our policy will be aggressive rather than defensive." The articles, for the most part, reflected the highly individualistic views of the editor. Looking through the files of this interesting periodical, one cannot help but be impressed with the very Catholic-sounding titles of its articles—"The Doctrine of the Real Presence"—"Extreme Unction"—"The Forgiveness of Sins" —"Confirmation"—"The Sacrifice of the Mass."

In his little parish bulletin, *The Pulpit of the Cross*, we find the enigma that was Father Paul before he became a Catholic. In his many articles he deplored the numerous divisions of Christianity and denounced them vehemently. "Evidently it was in the mind of the Divine Author of the Christian religion," he wrote in one edition, "to found on earth not many Protestant sects but one universal Church, and both the Old and New Testaments tell us the same thing."

However, when he was asked in the pages of his parish bulletin: "But what do you understand this one true Church of Divine Authority to be?" he answered: "I understand it to be that mighty Christian organism, which has come down to us from Jesus and His Apostles under the name of the Holy Catholic Church and which exists today in three great historic communions: the Roman, the Greek and the Anglican Communion, which last comprises all the English-speaking Christians throughout the world who are members of the Anglo-Catholic Church." He gave that answer in November, 1894. Eight months later, in July, 1895, he wrote in an editorial:

The Roman Church bases her claim to spiritual jurisdiction over the United States, along with the whole world besides, upon the doctrine of Papal Supremacy, which doctrine is that the Bishop of Rome is the Vicar of Jesus Christ on earth, the supreme ruler and head of the Catholic Church, and that it is necessary to salvation, for every human being, to acknowledge the Pope's authority and believe in his infallibility. Either the doctrine is true or it is false; if it is true, there is no Catholic Church apart from the Pope, nor indeed any Christianity. If it be false, every other argument which the Church of Rome might put forth in defence of her position is vitiated and made of no effect by this one gigantic error. . . . We appeal to history. . . . The argument from history as well as from Scripture is fatal to the Papal theories of the Church of Rome, and we cannot regard the Roman Catholic hierarchy in America in any other light than being the representatives of a foreign bishop, having no lawful jurisdiction in the United States.

In *The Pulpit of the Cross* Father Wattson defended his case for Anglicanism strongly and eloquently. But his ideas at that time on the Nature of the Church and her divinely constituted unity were a far cry from those he later defended and propagated. Three years after he wrote the above editorial, when Divine Grace flooded his soul, he made a complete about-face; not only did he repudiate what he had taught and written but, in the years which immediately followed the turn of the century, he became one of the most ardent defenders of the Roman Catholic Church and the Vicar of Christ on earth—the Pope.

But this was something of a future and gradual development. The Father Wattson of 1895 did not have the slightest intimation of what was to be a radical change in his way of thinking. Articles with titles such as "The Catholicity of the Church," and "The Essence of Church Unity" continued to appear regularly. Editors of other Protestant magazines read these articles in amazement. Secular newspapers also began to comment on some of the views expressed in *The Pulpit of the Cross.*

The *New York Sun,* noticing the extreme Catholic tendencies of the editor, remarked that he would, in the not too distant future, become a Catholic. Father Wattson, indignant at the observation, retorted that the New York paper was a good many years behind the times when it expressed such an opinion. "We were baptized into the Holy Catholic Church over thirty years ago," he declared emphatically, "and, please God, we expect to continue a Catholic until we die." To him the true Church of Christ was the Church of England and its American branch, the Episcopal Church. All other churches he regarded as Protestant sects, founded on rebellion and nurtured in heresy. The Roman Catholic Church he placed in the same category, despite the answer he gave to the correspondent in *The Pulpit of the Cross.* In this regard he was following in the footsteps of John Henry Newman who, before his conversion to the Catholic Church, believed that the Church of England had the Apostolical Succession; and that the doctrines of Rome were not held by the Fathers of the early Christian Church.

Father Wattson was following the "Via Media" of Newman—the Middle Road between Rome and Geneva (Calvinism)—firmly believing that Anglo-Catholicism was the true Religion of Christ. But there came a day when he, like Newman, became: "a man, who had written strongly against a cause, and had collected a party round him by virtue of such writings, who gradually faltered in his opposition to it, unsaid his words, threw his own friends into perplexity and their proceedings into confusion, and ended by passing over to the side of those whom he had so vigorously denounced." [1]

In both of these sincere men there was a lack of sufficient grace to see the truth; and, unless God's Grace illumines the intellect, confusion, error and contradiction will prevail. God, however, later gave to them the necessary Grace; and, responding to it, they became beacon lights guiding other men into the harbor of truth and light and grace—the Catholic Church—which they had found through that grace and which they so greatly loved.

[1] *Apologia pro vita sua*—Preface: John Henry Cardinal Newman

[*Chapter* IV]

GIVEN FROM HEAVEN

THE YEARS PASSED very quickly for the busy rector of St. John's Church at Kingston, without bringing him any closer to the realization of his ideal—the founding of a preaching order. In those years he had seen many changes. His work had expanded so much that he finally found it necessary to erect a mission church in another section of Kingston to take care of the ever-increasing numbers who looked to him for their spiritual needs. Devoted as he was to the Mystery of the Redemption, he dedicated the new church to the Holy Cross.

But through eight years of his ministry at Kingston he was ever conscious of a void in his life. Moreover, he knew that until the ideal of his life was realized this void would remain. The interior voice which he had heard so long ago pursued him unceasingly. It seemed to reproach him for his hesitancy; to blame him for having done nothing to accomplish the founding of an order of preachers "like the Paulists." Frequently he thought of retiring to some little church where he might begin the practice of a monastic life. His mission church of the Holy Cross appealed to him as the ideal place for that purpose. The adjoining house could easily be converted into a small monastery. This idea came to him again and again.

Finally, in 1893, he felt that he could postpone the beginning no longer. Why had he waited all these years? True, they were not wasted years, for he had accomplished much for his Divine Master; but never once had he been completely satisfied with himself. He had somehow to begin his life work *now* and overcome the dreadful sense of frustration under which he suffered. But how; in what way could he begin his life's work? It was then that he fell under the influence of St. Francis—the Poverello of Assisi.

The glorious story of St. Francis and of his absolute faith and confidence in God was what prompted Father Wattson not to abandon hope, but to seek further. The life of the Little Man of God so

33

completely fascinated him that he lived under its influence all the remaining days of his life. The almost unbelievable, Christlike life of
this thirteenth-century friar opened a new world to him—one which
he entered with holy joy and in which he remained forever. That
one could live and follow so closely the letter and spirit of the
Gospel he would never have believed possible were it not for the
overwhelming and incontestable proof of St. Francis' life. To him
St. Francis' life was the embodiment and literal fulfillment of the
Gospel, and proved that the living of it was not only possible but
practical. Furthermore, in reading the life of St. Francis, Father Wattson found an answer to his own perplexing problem.

He had thought the finding of a name for the preaching order he
was to establish would at least be the beginning he had so long desired. Devoted as he was to the Passion and Death of the Divine
Redeemer, he had decided that the name should be in some way associated with this Sublime Mystery. But seemingly every name connected with this phase of the life of Christ had already been chosen
by some existing religious order or congregation. But now he was no
longer non-plussed, for if St. Francis was able to obtain the Original
Rule for his friars by opening the Book of Gospels at random, could
he not find a name for his society in the same way?

So, on the 9th of July in the year 1893, Father Wattson celebrated the Communion Service with intense fervor. In prayer he
asked Almighty God that, if it be His Holy Will, the name which
he so ardently sought be revealed to him that day. After the congregation had left the church, the young rector took down from the
pulpit the King James version of the Bible, from which he had so
often read the Word of God to his people. He carried it to the
altar. Then, kneeling down, he invoked the aid of the Most Holy
Trinity. With great faith he opened the Sacred Scriptures three times,
and each time looked for the texts that would reveal to him God's
design in his future work.

The first text upon which his eyes lighted momentarily disappointed
him. There seemed to be no extraordinary sign contained in it, and
his hopes fell somewhat as he read in St. John 7: 37-39 [1]:

---

[1] King James version.

In the last day, that great day of the Feast, Jesus stood and cried, saying, If any man thirst, let him come unto me, and drink. He that believeth on me, as the scripture hath said, out of his belly shall flow rivers of living water. (But this spake he of the Spirit, which they that believe on him should receive: for the Holy Ghost was not yet given, because that Jesus was not yet glorified.)

Suddenly the full significance of the text dawned on him, and the disappointment of a moment ago passed away. Though the name was not explicitly mentioned in this text he saw in it what was more important—the Promise of the Holy Spirit without Whom the name would be of no avail. In this significant passage the power of a preaching order, the joy and inspiration of the religious life, were revealed. Again the Book was opened; this time his eyes fell upon the eleventh verse of the fifth chapter of St. Paul's Epistle to the Romans:

And not only so, but we also joy in God, through Our Lord Jesus Christ, by whom we have now received the atonement.

The last word of the verse seemed to stand out in the text with a vivid prominence; it was the answer to the prayer of the seeker. *The Atonement!*—that was what the new society should be called—the Society of the Atonement.

At the third opening of the Book he came upon St. Paul's description of the Institution of the Holy Eucharist, in the eleventh chapter of first Corinthians. So, from the Hand of God, came the name of the Society and its Spiritual Constitution. First there was to be the quickening, inspiring power of the Holy Spirit; then the crowning act of Redeeming Love—the Atonement upon the Cross of Jesus Christ—and, lastly, the Holy Sacrifice of the Mass, by means of which the Atonement of Christ is perpetuated. In this new Society the Most Holy Word of the Everlasting God would be preached by the Children of the Atonement everywhere through all the remaining ages.

Father Wattson, some years later, wrote to the Mother Foundress of the Sisters of the Atonement: "The moment my eyes rested upon the word 'Atonement' it seemed to stand out from that sacred page with a distinctness all its own and it flashed upon me, as I believe from Heaven, that the community God was preparing was to be called the Society of the Atonement."

The significance of the name and the unusual circumstances of its discovery so impressed Father Wattson that he was overwhelmed with sentiments of joy and gratitude. At first he thought it strange that some of the hundreds of religious communities already established had not appropriated this beautiful title; but later, as his work began to unfold itself, he realized more and more that no other name could so well designate his Society's vocation—the At-One-Ment with God of all the redeemed through Unity. For the theological definition of the term "Atonement" is, "the satisfaction of Christ, whereby God and the world are reconciled or made to be as one."

After he had received the texts, Father Wattson hastened from the church to the rectory, entered his study, and very carefully wrote down the three texts as he had received them. At the top of a sheet of linen note-paper he wrote the name of the Society, the verses which were now the "Atonement texts," and at the bottom of the sheet of paper he inscribed the full date. This precious manuscript is still in the Society's possession.

In the light of subsequent events it may be well to record here that Father Wattson experienced another intervention of Divine Providence that morning. As he was writing the texts an interior voice, similar to that which gave him the first intimation of a religious vocation twenty years before, inaudibly yet quite distinctly said: "You will have to wait seven years for this to be realized." The message came both as a surprise and a disappointment. It practically forbade the preconceived purpose of resigning St. John's and retiring to the mission church of the Holy Cross. However, keen as his disappointment was, he did not rebel against the manifest Will of God. The paper was carefully laid away, and the rector of St. John's went quietly on with his pastoral work as though nothing unusual had happened. Nor did anyone in the parish suspect that Father Wattson had undergone a most unusual experience.

The following two years were spent as the previous eight had been —in manifold parochial duties. A change came in the life of Father

Wattson in the summer of 1895 through the visit of a clergyman whom he found waiting for him on the porch of the rectory as he returned from a round of parish visiting. Introducing himself as the Reverend Irving P. Johnson, the visitor identified himself as a member of a group of unmarried Episcopal clergymen who were leading a semi-monastic life in Omaha under the spiritual direction of Bishop George Worthington of Nebraska. They called themselves the Associate Mission, and it was their aim to bring the message of the Gospel to people who were often without the services of a minister. The Reverend Mr. Johnson further stated that this group of clergymen were at present without a superior. Would he, Father Wattson, care to accept this position?

Before answering this most unexpected question Father Wattson asked for more information about the Associate Mission. From the Reverend Mr. Johnson he learned that the former superior, the Reverend Paul Matthews, had resigned, and planned to return to Cincinnati, his native city. Mr. Johnson was also leaving for, having entered into the married state he was automatically released from further service. Father Wattson had been recommended for the office of Superior by Dr. Sheldon M. Griswold, rector of the Episcopal church in Hudson, New York. This staunch friend of the Associate Mission was warm in his praise of the Kingston pastor. He had told the Associate Mission of Father Wattson's executive qualities as well as of his strong ascetical leanings, and had urged them to offer the superiorship to him.

As the Reverend Mr. Johnson talked, Father Wattson wondered if this offer was part of God's plan in the formation of the Society of the Atonement. Was Omaha to be its birthplace? So, before giving his decision, he felt obliged to tell Mr. Johnson something of his own plans for the future. First he admitted that the offer appealed to him. Then he disclosed all his hopes and desires. He told him of his boyhood inspiration, and of the unusual circumstances of the discovery of the name "Atonement." He also said that he saw in this move to Omaha the possibility of laying there the foundation of the society of preaching friars which he wished to establish. One might imagine that the Reverend Mr. Johnson would consider his host a visionary and be skeptical of his plans, but on the contrary he was impressed and encouraged him. Mr. Johnson even suggested that there might be some members of the Associate Mission who would be willing to join such an undertaking. It was a serious step for Father Wattson to take, especially since he had to care for his mother who was well advanced in years; but, as always, he placed the whole affair in the hands of God and accepted the offer.

It is a difficult and sometimes very sad experience for a pastor to bid farewell to people among whom he has labored and to whom he has been a spiritual father for years. When a pastor shares the anxiety and anguish of his people in times of trouble, sickness and death; when he shares his goods in times of unemployment and poverty; when he seeks them out in charity wards and behind prison bars, he unconsciously fashions a niche in their hearts which may be occupied by no other. There he remains enshrined until those grateful hearts turn to dust. The simple truth is that to his people no other pastor will ever be quite like him.

If, added to these Christlike deeds, they can further remember him for his deep spirituality, his love of children, his patience, his wonderful sermons, his gentleness and his sacrifices for their welfare, then, no matter what his faults may have been or how much more talented and gifted his successor may be, the good influence and the memory of that pastor will remain for generations.

Father Wattson, by such kindness and traits of character, had endeared himself to all the parishioners of St. John's at Kingston. In his farewell sermon before leaving with his mother for Omaha he told them that while he regretted leaving them he felt that at last he had found a work which could more completely satisfy the cravings of his spiritual nature. Forty-five years later, hearing of his sudden death, these same people were proud to say that he had once served as their pastor. One of them, testifying to his exemplary life, asserted: "Father Wattson was never quite satisfied with parochial life. Always he appealed to me as one who was fitted—one might say called—to the monastic life. His was essentially a spiritual nature, and unconsciously we all recognized the fact that his life was on a higher plane than the ordinary churchman."

Father Wattson arrived in Omaha in late September, on the feast of St. Michael the Archangel. Since his mother was well advanced in years, the directors of the Associate Mission graciously extended to her the hospitality of the house for the clergy. A private apartment was provided for her in a separate wing so that she might be able to maintain her independence. Her presence, therefore, in no way interfered with the disciplined schedule of the Mission clergy. Gradually Mrs. Wattson severed all connections with the world. Her greatest consolations were found in assisting at the daily services in the church adjoining the mission house, and in the cherished affection and devotion of her son. Two years after her arrival in Omaha she passed peacefully to her eternal reward.

Mary Electa Wattson was a valiant woman and a devoted wife and mother. She will ever be revered by the Friars of the Atonement as the mother of their saintly Founder.

Father Wattson immediately fell into the spirit of his new way of life. He found the work of the Associate Mission more satisfying than any other work he had done. The monastic character of the life at the mission house especially appealed to him. His subjects were all serious-minded men bound together in a common cause. "Mass, Matins and Mush," as one member put it, comprised the bulk of their daily schedule. However, study was also part of the daily routine. "We tried valiantly to keep up our reading of the Holy Scriptures in the original tongues, Hebrew and Greek," wrote one of them, "with some side reading of Church history and theology." The afternoons were devoted to missionary journeys. Each member was assigned a district, and it was his duty to visit the people of his jurisdiction regularly and to attend to their spiritual needs.

Under Father Wattson the field of action of the Associate Mission was greatly expanded. New mission stations were added to those already under their charge. The atmosphere of the mission house became more and more monastic, much to the displeasure of some of the residents who were not interested in becoming monks. But Father Wattson, completely oblivious of their dissatisfaction with his plan, gradually imposed a more rigid rule of life which included spiritual reading at meals and a rule of silence throughout the house. When some of the members of the Associate Mission protested to him that they were not Benedictines and, furthermore, had no intention of becoming such, Father Wattson bestowed on them a benign smile. He still hoped that among these men he would find the nucleus of kindred souls he was seeking for the establishment of the Society of the Atonement. In later years, as a Catholic Priest, he recalled, for his Friars' enjoyment, his difficult experience in trying to make monks out of men *who did not want to become monks.*

Father Wattson's first report to his ecclesiastical superior, Bishop George Worthington, was replete with progress, optimism and hope. It reported the remarkable successes among the people of the clergy of the Associate Mission, the number of conversions made, the new churches erected. The future held great promise, it went on to state, and the work of the Associate Mission would be a potent factor in the growth of religion in the vast territory of Nebraska.

Not long after his arrival in Omaha he revived *The Pulpit of the Cross,* his old parish bulletin of Kingston days. He was a born journalist and knew the power of the printed word. However, throughout his whole life, this talent was never used for any other purpose than for the extension of the Kingdom of God. He installed a hand-operated printing press in the basement of the clergy house and hired a skilled printer to operate it. His long hours of labor spent in the preparation of the bulletin were well rewarded, for the newsy little paper was given an enthusiastic reception by the people. Deeply gratified, its editor gave expression to his sentiments in one of its first numbers, when he wrote confidently of the future: "If God takes pleasure in *The Pulpit of the Cross* and the paper is ever true to its motto, 'Omnia pro Christo et salvatione hominum' (All things for Christ and the salvation of men), the Lord of heaven and earth will sustain it beyond a peradventure."

About this time, in the year 1896, he received a letter from a Sister belonging to a Diocesan Community established by the Right Reverend Bishop William Croswell Doane in Albany, New York. Her name was Lurana Mary White, and her letter brings us to another chapter in the extraordinary life of Father Wattson, later known as Father Paul James Francis.

Chapter V

ENTER MOTHER LURANA

LURANA MARY WHITE was a woman of rare talents and great spiritual qualities. From the earliest years she felt a desire to dedicate her life to God and to serve Him in His poor. One day, when she was twenty-three years of age, she heard a sermon which greatly helped her to decide her vocation in life. The powerful oratory of the preacher made a profound impression on her as he appealed to his hearers not to be ashamed of their religious convictions, but rather to live and practice them openly and courageously. "There may be before me," he said, "a young woman or a young man who secretly and half fearfully is worshipping the ideal of a wholly dedicated life, the oblation of herself or himself to God. I adjure you, be brave and bring that beautiful thing to the light and acknowledge it before God, to yourself and to others." From that day Lurana White thought only of the religious ideal of perfection. Writing under holy obedience, in her later years, she graphically describes this incident which was a crisis in her life.

"A very short time after this experience," she wrote in her *Memoirs*, "I knew that God was speaking to my soul more clearly than ever before; desires and ideals that I can best summarize in the word 'sacrifice' began to form somewhat chaotically but, notwithstanding, with partially definite shape, and I became conscious of two things: first, that my life was to be different from that of my girl friends, for I knew that I should not marry; and secondly, that I wished to do and suffer something worth while for God and for others."

To satisfy the desire to serve God in His poor, which now consumed her, she entered the Sisterhood of the Holy Child. From these Episcopal Sisters she had received her early education, and it was natural for her to return to them as she sought the fulfillment of her religious aspirations. After completing the required training, she was admitted as a member of the community. With the consent of her spiritual director she privately made vows of poverty, chastity and obedience. They were taken privately because Bishop Doane would not allow the Sisters to make the vows of Religion. However, he made no objection when Sister Lurana told him that she was making the vows privately. But, even then, Sister Lurana longed for something more which the Sisterhood of the Holy Child could not satisfy. Her great desire was to be part of a community which professed *corporate*, as well as *individual*, poverty. The Sisterhood of the Holy Child professed neither.

In the meantime she heard of Father Wattson, and of his work in Kingston and Omaha. With the permission of her superiors, she wrote to him to ask his counsel and, if possible, to place her future unreservedly in his hands. Her first letter, sent to him in 1896, asked the question, "Do you know of any community of Sisters in the Episcopal Church vowed to corporate poverty?"

In reply, Father Wattson sent the following letter:

> The Clergy House
> Omaha, Nebraska
> May 31, 1896

DEAR SISTER LURANA:

I am sorry that I cannot give you a satisfactory answer to your question. I am not sufficiently acquainted with the rule of the several sisterhoods in the Episcopal Church to tell you whether any of them practice strict corporate poverty. If there be such I am not aware of it. Yet I have no doubt that a goodly percentage of them have no endowment and live practically by faith. . . .

Worldliness is indeed the most serious hindrance now standing in the way of the Church's onward and upward progress in America, and a religious order either of men or women that would take Our Lord's precepts literally, as did St. Francis, and refuse to possess any property at all might serve as salt to preserve the lump.

> Yours very sincerely in Our Divine Lord,
> LEWIS T. WATTSON

This was the beginning of a correspondence which continued until these two chosen souls finally met in the autumn of 1898. During these two years of letter-writing each one learned much about the character and aspirations of the other. Father Wattson perceived in Sister Lurana a soul whose ideals were strangely similar to his own; and in time both of them recognized the fact that somewhere in the Divine Economy there was a reason for their spiritual relationship. But at first they understood very little of this plan. Father Wattson, however, did reveal to her his hopes of founding a religious community of men dedicated to the preaching apostolate and corporate poverty. He also suggested that possibly there could be established at the same time a community of women, who would constitute the second order of the Society of the Atonement. Sister Lurana found in this proposal of a Second Congregation the answer to her years of prayer for the perfect realization of her desires.

In June, 1897, accompanied by her uncle and aunt, she sailed for England. With the permission of her ecclesiastical superiors, who had released her from all obligations to the Sisterhood of the Holy Child, she planned to make a novitiate with the Sisters of Bethany, at Lloyd Square in London. She had discussed the matter with Father Wattson in their correspondence and he had strongly favored the plan. He advised her that, having once completed her religious training there, she would be well prepared to return to the United States to undertake the foundation of the Sisters of the Atonement. Before going to Lloyd Square she spent a few days at Oxford—so full of Franciscan memories—which she keenly enjoyed. With the consent of the Mother Superior and the Chapter of the Sisters of Bethany, who understood Sister Lurana's future plans, she was received as a postulant. She stayed with them a year. On the Monday following Low Sunday in 1898, Sister Lurana was clothed in a habit which was new in the Episcopal Church. It was a brown Franciscan habit with a gleaming white cord, having three knots symbolic of the religious vows of poverty, chastity and obedience. She then bade farewell to the kind and hospitable Sisters of Bethany. Anne White, her sister, had come from America to accompany her home; but before sailing they visited Rome and Assisi. While Rome, the Eternal City, impressed her with its timeless character and its uplifting spirit of Catholicity, it was Assisi that delighted her most. There she could almost feel the presence of the Little Man of God—Francis Bernardone. His spirit pervaded the Umbrian valley and, as she prayed at his tomb, she asked God for some of Francis' spirit, that her love for God might, like his, become more completely selfless.

While at Assisi Sister Lurana also visited Santa Chiara (the Church of St. Clare). There she remembered the Lady Clare who, after hearing Francis preach on God's love for the children of men, gave up the world to become like Francis. What transcendent joy would have filled the heart of Sister Lurana that day at Santa Chiara if she had known that the villa perched on the hillside would, thirty-three years later, be occupied by her own Sisters. That villa today is in the possession of the Sisters of the Atonement. It is a favorite stopping place for pilgrims from America, England, Rome and other countries when visiting the holy places of Assisi. The villa now known as St. Anthony's Convent and Hospice was, tradition says, occupied by relatives of St. Clare seven hundred years ago.

The prayer of Sister Lurana at the tomb of St. Francis was certainly answered by Almighty God. Leaving Assisi, she felt convinced that the ideal of poverty was what she had been seeking, and that now the quest was finished. Through all the remaining days of her life, her beautiful companion was what St. Francis loved to call his "Lady Poverty."

In her *Memoirs*, Sister Lurana tells an interesting episode in connection with her visit to Rome, which gives an insight into her devotion to the Vicar of Christ on earth, even in those days when she was an Anglican nun. She wrote:

On May 6th (Feast of St. John before the Latin Gate) we arrived at Rome. The next day I could hardly wait before setting out for St. Peter's. Here I was guilty of a pious act of duplicity. Upon entering the great basilica, we were surprised to meet, on the very threshold, two old friends from Warwick. It is unnecessary to relate that they were as amazed as we were! So we four went into the great Church of the Holy Apostle. Now I had made up my mind previously that I wished to venerate the great bronze statue of St. Peter in his Chair, that is, I wanted to kneel down and kiss his foot. But how to accomplish it before my two very Protestant friends? I could have managed it with my sister all right. This is what I did. I said to them, "Oh, have you seen that most interesting and beautiful statue over on the side altar, to the left, behind that row of pillars?" They said, "No," and started off; and I, feeling nearly frightened to death lest I should be separated from them permanently in that great wilderness of columns and arches, walked quickly toward the great bronze figure of the Prince of the Apostles, which I had already located. Reaching it, I knelt down and kissed the foot, making at the moment an interior act of devotion and allegiance to the Prince of the Apostles and his Successor, the reigning Pope, Leo XIII. My friends returned to me none the wiser regarding my little expedition. . . . It never occurred to me that I, an Anglican, would have any chance of obtaining a Papal audience, but I have since regretted exceedingly that I did not make the attempt.

When Sister Lurana and her sister returned in June of 1898 to their childhood home "The Terrace" at Warwick, New York, she wrote immediately to Father Wattson announcing her return. During her stay in London their correspondence had continued; and in that period of the correspondence the means which they would employ to bring about the establishment of the Society of the Atonement crystallized more clearly in their minds. Having sent the letter, she waited almost impatiently for an answer, which, she hoped, would contain further advice as to what she should do.

When Father Wattson received her letter he knew that Lurana White was now a mature woman. Education and travel had broadened her view and developed in her those qualities of mind and heart which were to make her the remarkable woman that the years proved her to be. Her keen, logical mind, her quickness of decision in which prudence reigned supreme and her devotion to duty, all combined to make her the ideal person to undertake a work, difficult as it was arduous—the foundation of a religious community.

These were qualities which Father Wattson perceived in her, and upon which he so absolutely relied through all the years of her life. There were few decisions which he made, affecting major community policies, without first consulting her. His confidence was never misplaced; for every counsel and direction she offered, through many years, considered first and foremost the interests of the Society of the Atonement. The fact is that the first few Friar Priests associated with Father Paul not only misunderstood, but also resented, the confidence he placed in Mother Lurana. It was this misunderstanding that led the very first priest ordained after Father Paul in the Society to inflict on him what he always said was the greatest sorrow of his life.

When Sister Lurana's letter reached Omaha, telling Father Wattson of her return to America, conditions had greatly changed there, through a new situation that had arisen.

Shortly after Sister Lurana's departure for England, Father Wattson began a careful and serious investigation of the Roman Catholic claims. He spent long hours in study, poring over numerous volumes which had been written on the question by Anglican scholars. But he carefully avoided looking into the problem from the Catholic viewpoint. One day, however, an incident occurred which changed the course of his whole life. It was an everyday occurrence in the lives of busy men—he missed a train for one of his mission stations, and the next train for his destination would not leave for several hours.

Instead of returning to the mission house, Father Wattson decided to pay a brief visit to a nearby Catholic church. As he entered the dim interior the flickering light of the sanctuary lamp, indicating the Real Presence, seemed to beckon to him. Like the star which led the Wise Men from the East to the manger throne of the Lord of Heaven and Earth, it brought this sincere Episcopal minister close to the altar on which Jesus Christ reposed in His Sacrament of Love. There he knelt and poured out his soul to God. His prayer was the plea of one asking for the light to see the truth and for the courage to follow it, even though he knows that the light may reveal as heresy what he believed to be truth. The visit refreshed him, and Father Wattson rose from his knees filled with a new determination to follow the truth, regardless of the consequences.

He returned home and retired to his study. From his library shelves he took down the books which he had often read before, and others which, up to this time, he had ignored. Then began a long period of reading. He reread from a new point of view Littledale's *Plain Reasons Against Joining the Church of Rome*, Gore's *Roman Catholic Claims*, and Puller's *Primitive Saints and the See of Rome*. The grace he had prayed for during his visit to the Eucharistic Christ was given to him, for now these books seemed nothing more than clever subterfuges aimed at preventing a sincere inquiry into the claims of the Catholic Church.

Then came the courage to follow the light; he opened up volumes he had not been able to touch in the past. He read Gibbon's *Faith of Our Fathers*, Murphy's *The Chair of Peter*, and Allies' *Peter, His Name and His Office*. He studied them carefully and, like his glorious patron at Damascus, the scales fell from his eyes. He saw what he had feared to see all his life. The claims of Rome *were true*, and communion with the See of Peter was the only way by which men could share in its divinely given Unity. Peace and joy flooded his soul and quite spontaneously he fell to his knees to recite the *Te Deum*. Little did he realize then that for the next twelve years he would be the most controversial figure in the Episcopal Church.

Facing the reality of the new situation in which he found himself, he decided to communicate with his ecclesiastical superior, Bishop Worthington. He also sent a letter to Sister Lurana. He explained the change that had come over him in this new religious experience. He also wrote that he felt obliged to admit that he was mistaken about his part in establishing the Society of the Atonement. He was convinced that the work should not be allowed to die, but he was equally convinced that its fulfillment should fall upon other shoulders. Therefore, he urged Sister Lurana to come to Omaha as planned, with the two Sisters (Sisters in religion, from the Sisterhood of the Holy Child) who were to join her in the new Sisterhood. Father Howard, who was succeeding him as the new Superior of the Associate Mission, was just as anxious about the proposed foundation as he was, and would give them a warm welcome.

Sister Lurana did not oppose the line of thought which Father Wattson had adopted. It was a matter of conscience with him, and she was in full sympathy with it. But to say that she was not disturbed by his decision would be to deny the truth. Actually she was shocked to learn that he had given up the idea of founding the Society of the Atonement. However, what disturbed her far more was a letter from Father Howard, imposing conditions upon her and her companions which she could not accept. He bluntly told her in his letter that he could not appreciate her ideas on poverty and, there-fore, felt compelled to restrict the Sisters in this matter. But Sister Lurana had sought too long and too earnestly for her beloved "Lady Poverty" to give her up now. So she decided against going to Omaha to make the Foundation of the Sisters of the Atonement.

Father Wattson did not fully realize what he was doing, in the confusion which flooded his mind after he had decided in favor of the Catholic Church. For twenty-five years he had kept the ideal of founding a preaching order constantly before him. He knew, dur-ing these years, that it was God's Will for him to bring about the realization of that ideal; yet now, after all that time, he was aban-doning it. Later he accepted it for what it was—a temptation. It *was* a severe temptation, but nothing like the intense one he was to un-dergo within a few months.

In later life he always jocosely referred to the devil, when speak-ing to his Friars, as "the Old Boy." The author can recall an in-cident of his novitiate days when three lay brother novices left the So-ciety in a comparatively short time. When Father Paul learned about their departures he informed the Community to pray fervently, "for," said he, "the Old Boy has gotten into the novitiate." And in re-ferring to the Omaha incident, as he often did, he would say, "Why, the Old Boy almost took the Society of the Atonement away from me in Omaha."

Priests who have been given the privilege of guiding highly in-telligent converts into the Catholic Church, and converts themselves, can deeply sympathize with Father Wattson's sad experience at that time. The forces of evil are ever at work in the world, sowing doubt and confusion and disunity in the minds of those souls whom the Divine Sanctifier is leading into the Elysian fields of more abundant Grace. He permits this doubt and confusion and disunity to assail the minds of those who desire to follow His Divine Promptings so that in their day of victory they may bear witness, not only to God's never-failing love for mankind, but also to that evil which ever seeks to destroy man's love for God—the Infinite Truth. So it was with Job, of whom, in the days of his great trials and sufferings, it was written: "In all these things Job sinned not by his lips; nor spoke he any foolish thing against God."

Father Wattson, in Omaha, was neither an Abraham nor a Job. He had not yet received the gift of their intrepid faith. When he received a letter from Sister Lurana, telling of her decision to remain at Warwick and await a further manifestation of God's Will, he agreed with that decision. Her defense of the ideal of corporate poverty had a reassuring effect upon him; and he realized how foolish he had been in doubting his vocation. Simultaneously with this realization came the vaguest outline of the peculiar vocation of the Society of the Atonement—to work and pray for the submission of the Anglicans to the authority of the Vicar of Christ. Of one thing he was now certain, his work lay in the East. It would be there that the Society of the Atonement would be called into being.

There was no need for further delay. His work at the Associate Mission was at an end. On the feast of St. Michael the Archangel, September 29, 1898, exactly three years after his arrival in Omaha, he resigned as Superior. Shortly after midnight he celebrated a private Communion Service in the oratory of the mission house. He always remembered his thanksgiving after that particular Communion Service. It was long and devout, because he felt the spirit of the Little Man of God very close to him. Sister Lurana's deep love of St. Francis and of poverty was beginning to take hold of him. Up to this time he was more the imitator of St. Paul than of St. Francis. He had imbibed the Pauline spirit rather than the Franciscan; and he thought of the Society of the Atonement as an order of great preachers, crusading as St. Paul did for the conversion of the world. Even though he was familiar with the life of St. Francis and was enamoured with the ideal of poverty, it was not until long after the correspondence with Sister Lurana started that his romance with "Lady Poverty" really began. The fire of love for poverty that later burned within him was lighted from the conflagration already burning in the soul of Sister Lurana. After it was kindled, his was the dual spirit of the preaching crusader and the lover of poverty.

One complemented the other, making him the unique character that he was.

Kneeling in prayer, he thought of the simple man who, though having nothing, yet possessed all things. He asked God for the Grace to be more like the seraphic Poverello, who had first inspired Sister Lurana with her deep love for absolute poverty. With God alone as his witness, he vowed to imitate as closely as possible the ideal of poverty which St. Francis had practiced. He resolved never again to touch money, but to place his entire trust in God, Who feeds the birds of the air and beautifully clothes the lilies of the field. Yet he knew that, in a world of materialism, such a heroic action would not be appreciated. He also knew that, if he were to keep this vow, the road ahead held many humiliations for him. But to him the action he took was not extraordinary for a follower of St. Francis. Throughout his future life such was the intensity of every act he performed for the love of God. If he decided to be poor then he would be totally poor; if he fasted then no food or drink would pass his lips; if a missionary appealed to him for aid he sent everything he had at the moment; if more homeless men sought his hospitality than he could provide for, rather than turn away the Divine Christ who might be among them, he would somehow manage to shelter them all. And this was the so-called imprudence that worldly men saw in him. But he gloried in the things that men called his infirmity. Living Christ was to him the practice of the theological virtue of Charity, by which he loved God above all things and his neighbor as himself for the love of God. So he was able to *bear all things, believe all things, hope all things, endure all things.*

Rising from his knees before the altar in the oratory, he left the Associate Mission and boarded the Overland Express for Chicago and the East, where he hoped the dreams of his life would come true.

Chapter VI

A COVENANT IS MADE

THERE IS SOMETHING lonely about a train speeding through the night. For a passenger who does not know what tomorrow will bring, and who has forgotten how to speak, or has never spoken, to God, the loneliness of a train speeding through the night is terrifying. The only thing Father Wattson had in common with such a traveler on that night train so long ago was that he did not know what the morrow would bring. He felt neither loneliness nor terror. For he had known how to speak to God since his youth; and in his communion with the Creator that night he prayed only for a strong faith in, and a deep love of, His Holy Promises. It was five years since he had received the "Atonement Texts." The voice had said there would be an interval of seven years before the Society of the Atonement would be called into being. What was he to do for the next two years? Perhaps after he had talked with Sister Lurana he would know.

On Saturday, October 1, 1898, he alighted from the train at Kingston, New York. The next day he preached at his former mission church, which he had built, to a large congregation of his former parishioners. Seemingly to these people he was now a failure. Three years ago he had told them that at Omaha he hoped to find what he had been looking for—the satisfying of the craving of his soul for a more intimate union with God. Now he was back, without a position and, apparently, without plans for the future. If only he had followed their advice and married while he was at Kingston how different life would be for him now! At least he would have had security. The one unpleasant feature of his former rectorship at Kingston was that his people constantly urged him to enter the marital state. They could not understand why he, the most eligible bachelor among them, had no desire to marry. The lack of a mistress in St. John's rectory was particularly conspicuous since all the other Protestant parsonages were blessed with them. The vestry-men of St. John's had, on many occasions, all but insisted that Father Wattson marry into one of the better families. They remem-bered now how he always smiled at their urgings; but now they were certain that he should have followed their advice. If only he had fallen in love how different things would be! Little did they real-ize that he was now intensely in love with a lovely lady, but one very much in the abstract—"Lady Poverty." Yet he could not tell them of her, because they would not understand. The people of Kingston would say of him what the people of Assisi, seven hundred years before, had said of Francis Bernardone, "Father Wattson is a fool, or else completely insane."

On the eve of St. Francis' Day, October 3, 1898, he left Kingston for Warwick, New York, to be a guest, for a few days, of Sister Lurana and her sister, Miss White, at the old mansion of the White family, "The Terrace." When he arrived it was evening, and the traditional hour of the death of the Seraphic Patriarch of Assisi.

Diaries, the written records of the events in the daily lives of people who keep them, have helped to send some men to prison; and they have also helped to raise others to the altars of the Church. Biographers bless the memory of their subjects when they have kept diaries, because these records substantiate the facts of which the historian writes. Diaries are also a blessing in another sense. They eliminate the necessity for the play of the biographer's imagina-tion, the product of which, however vivid, will always seem unreal to intelligent readers.

Sister Lurana kept a diary, and the author blesses her memory for this thoughtful consideration, as well as for the many others she showed to him during his early years in the Society of the Atonement. In her diary she preserved for posterity an account of her long-awaited meeting with Father Wattson:

Our Father Founder arrived in Warwick toward evening on October 3rd, the Eve of St. Francis' Day. On that memorable day we met for the first time. The future Father Founder told the story of his call and of his

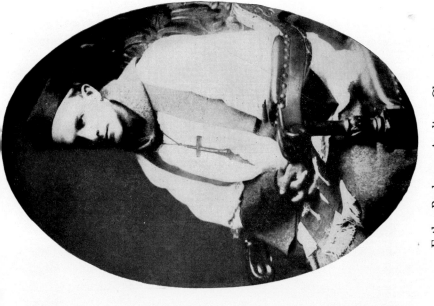

Father Paul as an Anglican Clergyman

Father Paul's Father:
The Reverend Joseph Newton Wattson

Mother Lurana Mary Francis, S.A.

hopes, and I told him of my search for St. Francis and corporate poverty. Then there came to us both the dawning realization of the oneness of God's call.

That evening they planned the future Society of the Atonement. They also decided to begin, in the morning, a triduum of prayer. In the Catholic Church a triduum is a period of three days' prayer as a preparation for the celebration of a great feast, such as that of Corpus Christi. When the Episcopal minister and nun planned their triduum of prayer they were, unconsciously, preparing for the greatest family feast day of the Society of the Atonement—Covenant Day.

During the three days' retreat which ended on October 7th in the quiet of prayer and meditation, the two chosen servants of God prayed that His Will in their regard be made manifest to them. Each morning Father Wattson celebrated a Communion Service in the little chapel which had been set up in one of the rooms. During the day he gave a series of spiritual conferences, directing attention to the one purpose of their lives—that God's Will be done. The many hours of peaceful solitude which each spent alone with God helped to make clear in their minds what He would expect of them in their founding a new religious community in the Episcopal Church. The three days of contemplation came to an end all too soon. They then made a complete oblation of themselves to God, which Sister Lurana describes very beautifully in her diary:

Then came October 7th and the end of the three days' retreat which we had kept together. Father blessed, and laid on the little improvised altar in the oratory, two crucifixes; one he gave to me and the other he kept for himself. The latter had been brought by me from Assisi, and I had seen it in the *Sacro Convento* lowered down by the Franciscan Father, our guide, until it touched the tomb of St. Francis. It was well understood by the Father Founder, and by me, that these same crucifixes represented the entire oblation of ourselves into the hands of God for the purpose of founding the Society of the Atonement.

Father Wattson and Sister Lurana left the oratory that morning in a state of great joy. As he descended the stairs to retire to his room, Father Wattson relived again the extraordinary chain of events which culminated that day in the act of oblation. Then suddenly, and without warning, he was plunged into a diabolical despair. He was assailed by doubts so strong that he began to wonder if the whole affair were not a delusion. Who was *he* that Almighty God should bestow on *him* so lofty a vocation? Was not, perhaps, the whole project of establishing a religious community a mad folly and doomed to failure at the outset; and what about this nun, Sister Lurana, how could he mislead her into the foolishness of founding a religious community? With what would they begin it? He had no money; had he forgotten that he had vowed never to touch money?

These were the temptations that assailed him shortly after he had been in almost an ecstasy of joy. His agony was intense. He felt that he was wrestling with Satan himself. And pounding relentlessly within him were the words: *"What you ought to do is to leave the Episcopal Church immediately, become a Catholic, and join the Passionists."*

Reaching his room, he knelt upon the floor. His soul groaned to God for divine assistance. He promised God to do whatever His Holy Will desired if God would only show him the way. He took up the Holy Scriptures, while he asked God to speak to him through His Holy Word. When he confidently opened the Book, his eyes fell upon the thirteenth verse, chapter six, of St. Paul's Epistle to the Hebrews. And there the Omnipotent God spoke to him with clarity and forcefulness.

For when God made promise to Abraham, because he could sware by no greater, he sware by himself, saying, *"Surely blessing I will bless thee, and multiplying I will multiply thee."* And so, after he had patiently endured, he obtained the promise.

For men verily sware by the greater; and an oath for confirmation is to them an end to all strife.

Wherein God, willing more abundantly to shew unto the heirs of promise the immutability of his counsel, confirmed it by an oath; that by two immutable things in which it was impossible for God to lie, we might have a strong consolation, who have fled for refuge to lay hold upon the hope set before us:[1]

[1] King James version.

In all the Sacred Scriptures more powerful words could not be found to calm, reassure and heal the anguished soul of Father Wattson. From that day he was the man of strong faith, and his faith in God was as unshakable as Abraham's. *Never, never* again did he entertain the slightest doubt about his vocation, or the special predilection of God for the Society of the Atonement. The "Covenant" which God made with him, through the medium of His Holy Word, was the assurance that God would never fail him or his community, even in the darkest days of its history which were yet to follow. Before leaving Warwick he informed Sister Lurana of what had happened. Father Wattson left "The Terrace" that day strong in faith and with deep peace of soul. He was the Warrior of God who, having passed through a great battle and conquered his enemy, could now enjoy the peace of victory: the sweet victory of Christ who conquered not only sin but Satan also.

At Warwick he decided to place himself in the hands of the Episcopal Order of the Holy Cross, at Westminister, Maryland, to be trained by them in the Religious life. Shortly after he arrived in Westminister he wrote a letter to Sister Lurana, evidently to strengthen her faith in the Covenant God made with him:

Perhaps on the score of Obedience, more than Poverty, will be the testing and trial of our patience; but God, having "confirmed" our vocation "by an oath," all things in heaven and earth which are needful for us are ours, and we have but steadfastly "to hold upon the hope set before us, which hope we have as an anchor of the soul, both sure and steadfast, and which entereth into that within the veil." Of all the gracious acts of Divine Providence which have been showered upon me from the day I was born, nothing has been more marvelous or exceedingly precious in my eyes than this wondrous message of the Divine Favor on the Society of the Atonement, and this solemn declaration on the part of the God of Abraham concerning "the immutability of His Counsel," divinely "confirmed by an oath" beyond the possibility of ultimate failure. Woe be unto us if, after this, we shall "fall away." Oh God, establish in us the truest humility and entire dependence on Thee, that our faith fail not!

Only those of us who were privileged to live in close association with the Founder of the Society of the Atonement can appreciate how strong his faith in God really was. Only those of us who can remember him, even as an old man, lying prostrate all night before the Blessed Sacrament, praying for his infant Society, can appreciate what he suffered as his faith in God was tested time and again. For even when he thought he was safe within the Fold of Peter, which he had defended so heroically and so long, he suffered from the opprobrium heaped upon him by those outside the Church, and from the suspicion and unjust attacks of those within. Men whom he thought sincere took advantage of his universal charity toward all; and, while enjoying his Franciscan hospitality, undermined the feeble faith of some whom he, the second Abraham, loved as other Isaacs; and in whom he saw the "multiplying" that God promised in His Covenant. Men lied to him, and he believed their word because his charity believed all things. Men fooled him, and he never became bitter. "Their treachery," he said, "will descend as hot coals upon their heads." Men said he would have been a genius in the world of business; yet many of his business ventures failed because he knew nothing of the shrewdness of a business world whose unethical philosophy is "dog eat dog."

There were many difficult days when it seemed that the Society of the Atonement would not endure. And many men, inside and outside the Church, "prophesied" that the Society would cease to exist at the death of its Founder. These reports came to him again and again, and his answer was always a benign smile as he continued to live serenely, working and praying to attain the goal that God had set before him.

The Society of the Atonement flourishes today only because it is built upon a strong rock; and the rock is the faith of Father Paul in God, which never faltered despite opposition, contradiction and frustration. And, in keeping faith with God, he never found it necessary to offer an apology for his life.

If storms should ever break again over the Society of the Atonement there are those who will remember how strong the rock is upon which the Society rests. They will calm the fears of young Friars who are afraid because they do not yet know how strong the rock is; but, once knowing it, they in their turn will calm the fears which might rise in the storm of another day. And so it will go until the end of time; for the faith of Father Paul will never die as his spirit lives again in each succeeding generation of his Friars.

The *Covenant Hymn* of the Society of the Atonement was written by Father Paul. In it he pours out his soul, and in it we find the faith and spiritual beauty of him who wrote it. It is sung by his spiritual children on every Covenant Day, which is always celebrated on October 7th. To them it expresses the heroic faith which they alone understand, because they alone know that God had spoken to their Founder through His Holy Word, saying, *"Surely blessing I will bless thee, and multiplying I will multiply thee."*

THE COVENANT HYMN

O God, Who makest Covenant,
Whose promise Thou wilt never break,
Make strong Thy servants militant
With faith and love no pow'r can shake.
Thy word prevail, when foes assail,
Lest we should fail, lest we should fail.

"Fear not," saidst Thou to Abraham,
"For I will multiply thy seed;
Thy shield and great reward I am,
Believe and thou art blest indeed."
Thine oath recall, when hosts appall,
Lest we should fall, lest we should fall.

The night in which He was betrayed
Our Lord took bread, gave thanks and brake.
Likewise the cup when He had prayed,
"My Body 'tis, and Blood, partake."
This food supply, nor us deny,
Lest we should die, lest we should die.

What Thou hast pledged to pass must come,
Thou shalt "repair the breach" of old,
The "other sheep" with those of Rome,
Shall constitute one only Fold.
This pledge recall, when hosts appall,
Lest we should fall, lest we should fall.

All glory, Lord, to Thee we pay,
To Father, Son and Holy Ghost.
Thy will let men on earth obey
That they may join the Heavenly Host,
Thy word prevail, when foes assail,
Lest we should fail, lest we should fail.

Amen

Chapter VII

ARRIVAL AT GRAYMOOR

GRAYMOOR today is known throughout the world as the Motherhouse of the Society of the Atonement. But how the Friars and Sisters acquired the property and where the name Graymoor came from are not as well known as the name itself. That story is a charming chapter of the Society's history; a history which can truly be called a divine romance, replete as it is with evidence of God's love for His new American Society.

During his visit to "The Terrace," Sister Lurana told Father Wattson of an incident which happened while she was at the convent in London. One evening during her stay there, she looked across the choir at Vespers and saw the large *cornette* of a strange Religious. That evening, through the kindness of the Guest-Mistress, the two nuns met. The other Sister was also an American, and a member of the Episcopal Sisters of St. Mary, Peekskill, New York. Her name was Sister Mary Angela. As always happens when two Sisters of different religious communities meet there was much "heavenly gossip" about their respective communities. After they returned to the United States, Sister Lurana corresponded with Sister Angela. In the correspondence Sister Lurana told the plans of Father Wattson for the Society of the Atonement; and it was in that correspondence that Sister Mary Angela pointed out the way to Graymoor in a fascinating story she told of an abandoned church.

Three pious Anglican ladies had discovered it. Two of them, the Misses Elliot, (one of these sisters later married and was known as Mrs. Nicholson) residents of New York City, had been in the habit of spending the summer months as guests of an old friend, Miss Julia Chadwick, whose home was at Garrison, New York, directly across the Hudson River from West Point. During their drives about the countryside, the three ladies came across a small deserted and desecrated chapel, which had not had a religious service in it for ten years. In that time it was used by tramps and cows, and the filth and dirt were appalling. The good ladies were horrified to find a House of God so profaned; and with their own hands they began to clean it.

When they had restored the small church to some of its original cleanliness and order, the three ladies reported the matter to the rector of the Episcopal church in Garrison. The whole affair, which shocked the three ladies so much, did not disturb the rector, for he had known of the abandoned church. If anything did disturb him it was the nuisance these ladies were making of themselves in trespassing upon the realm of ecclesiastical authority. However, the necessary permission for them to use the church for services was finally granted. They then persuaded an Episcopal clergyman from New York to rededicate the church to St. John the Baptist, to whom it was originally dedicated. With their own money they hired a chaplain to conduct an occasional service for the people of the surrounding countryside. It then became known as St. John's-in-the-Wilderness, and was used as a chapel of ease.

Not long after the rededication, the church and the tiny piece of property on which it stood was offered to the good ladies who had restored it. They called the place "Graymoor" after the two persons who were most closely associated with its early days: Doctor Gray, onetime rector of the Garrison church, who had built the chapel; and a Mr. Moore, a professor at Columbia University, who had been the chief benefactor. Since they now had the full responsibility of caring for the church, the ladies humorously called themselves "the vestry" of St. John the Baptist Church.

The Finger of God is seen in all things by those who cooperate with Him in the Divine Plan of Man's Redemption. It is seen not only in great movements but also in insignificant happenings. Nothing is more evident in the fifty years of Graymoor's history than this pertinent fact—the Finger of God directing souls, sometimes without their being aware of it, to bring into being His Design in the work that Graymoor was destined to do. By a strange coincidence, these three Anglican ladies were lovers of St. Francis just as Sister Lurana was; and they found St. John's in 1893, the same year that God gave the "Atonement Texts" to Father Wattson.

The story of how St. Francis had restored the Church of San Damiano inspired them to restore St. John's. Almost every country church in America is painted white, but St. John's received a coat of brown paint in honor of the Poverello. As the ladies worked to restore the church they often said how nice it would be to have some group of nuns following the Rule of St. Francis take care of the church permanently.

Sister Angela, at near-by Peekskill, knew of their hopes; and hearing from Sister Lurana the story of the new Society pleaded with her to accept the place. "I only hope Father Wattson may not discourage this idea," Sister Angela wrote, "but it is all being directed and ordered for you, no doubt, and I must trust it to the only One Who knows what is best for you and for His Glory."

The story which Sister Lurana told to Father Wattson about Graymoor captivated his heart. In her writings she tells about his enthusiasm, and his first visit to Graymoor:

At the conclusion of the retreat, our Father decided to visit Graymoor, to see what were the possibilities of the place. Leaving Warwick on Friday, immediately at the close of the retreat, he spent Sunday at Kingston, and the following day set out for Garrison; eventually reaching that part of the township now known as Graymoor. He found it an undulating valley nestling among towering hills, with but few inhabitants, and decidedly solitary; yet, withal, an excellent place wherein chosen souls might prepare themselves, by prayer and the practice of the evangelical counsels, for either contemplation or active mission work, as God might dispose.

Father Wattson arrived at Graymoor on October 10, 1898. He wrote to Sister Lurana of his visit, and his letter reflected the great joy of his heart. For the remaining years of his life he loved Graymoor with a great love; for him no other place was quite so beautiful as the place God reserved for the Friars and Sisters of the Atonement. In later years he traveled extensively in his work for Christian Unity. His letters home were always filled with nostalgia for his companions, and the natural beauty in which they lived. On arriving home, he told his spiritual children, time and again, that nowhere did he find a spot equal to the home of the Society of the Atonement in the Highlands of the Hudson. "Surely they may exclaim," he said, "those happy souls whom God has called to this lovely place: 'I have a goodly heritage, my lot has fallen unto me in pleasant places,' for theirs is the 'hundredfold' promised even in this life to those who leave all to follow Christ."

So it was with every gift God gave; to him it was always the best. God could do no less because of His great love for the Society of the Atonement. If the Friars were fortunate enough to have steak for dinner, that, too, was the best; though we, who had to eat it, knew it was far from the best. On one of the great feast days of the Church, not long before he died, when steak and talking during the meal were two privileges of the day, Father spoke across the room to one of the Friar Brothers. "Well, Brother Philip," he said, "how is the steak?" The answer he received, though true before God and man, really shocked Father Paul, in its apparent ingratitude to God. "It is as tough as shoe leather, Father General," replied Brother Philip. Whereupon the good Brother ate the rest of his steak kneeling on the floor. To the Founder of the Society of the Atonement all God's gifts were good. If they appeared otherwise it was only because a human hand had trembled in fashioning what God intended to be beautiful and good.

Once he had visited and had seen for himself the natural beauty of the place described by Sister Angela to Sister Lurana, Father Wattson would think of no other place to make the foundation of the Society of the Atonement. It was an ideal retreat for a religious institute, far enough removed from the din and noise of a busy world, yet near enough to maintain the necessary communications. Nor was there any need for further delay since Sister Lurana was eager to make the foundation. Shortly after Father Wattson's visit to Graymoor, she wrote him saying that she was ready to go, and that there was an Episcopal clergyman—Father Davis—at Graymoor, to take care of her spiritual needs. "The girl, of whom I told you here, will go with me, and the others would just as well come a little later. The other day, in New York, I had a most interesting visit with Miss Elliot. Her sister, Mrs. Nicholson, and a friend, who is Sister Mary Angela's cousin (Miss Redmond) had quite a meeting and everything is most satisfactory. It must be God's Will. He is so wonderfully shaping things. Ask Him to give me more self-confidence, or, rather, less of self. When I am most glad in the thought of the future, that utter sinking of heart comes."

When the Society of the Atonement entered the Catholic Church, some ten years later, Miss Elliot and her sister, Mrs. Nicholson, united with the co-trustees of the Episcopal church at Garrison in a lawsuit to take back the property of St. John's from the Sisters of the Atonement. The litigation lasted through eight long years, the details of which are told in a later chapter. However, it is a story with a happy ending; for, many years later, Miss Elliot and Mrs. Nicholson died as Catholics in the Graymoor convent; and their remains rest peacefully beside the remains of the Sisters to whom they brought much suffering.

Sister Lurana received a letter in answer to hers, within a few days, from Father Wattson, telling her to begin the work at once. "Your letter of December 5th just received," he wrote. "Surely it is the Holy Spirit Who prompts you to go to Graymoor at once, and with gladness I bid you Godspeed. The time of waiting is past. God's Advent message to you is 'Go forward,' and your joy is in Obedience. . . . 'May He send His angels before thy face to guide thee in all thy ways'!"

Mother Lurana, as she was now to be known, left "The Terrace" on December 15, 1898, the Octave Day of the Feast of the Immaculate Conception. She was accompanied by her sister, Miss Annie White; and a poor girl, a godchild of hers, Viola Carr. The journey to Graymoor was made by railroad to Newburgh, then by ferry across the Hudson to Beacon, then again by railroad to Garrison. From Garrison to Graymoor the journey was made by horse and sleigh, for the snow lay deep upon the ground. It was evening when Mother Lurana arrived at Graymoor to make the foundation of the Sisters of the Atonement. Her sister, Miss White, stayed only until the next day, and then left for the West in order to reach her mother in California in time for the Christmas holidays.

The scene which confronted Mother Lurana on that cold and dreary winter day was devoid of all cheer. The evening shades, which had already descended, added to that frigid atmosphere. Gone was the autumnal beauty which had captivated the heart of Father Wattson. For Mother Lurana there was only cold and snow and loneliness, but her heart was warm with the fire of a great faith. All that mattered to her was that the Society of the Atonement, for which she and Father Wattson had worked and prayed so long, was a reality at last. The temporary convent which the good God provided was a farm cottage called the "Dimond House," said to be more than a century old. It was a rickety old building which had never received even one coat of paint, and was situated about three-quarters of a mile from the small, brown-coated church of St. John's-in-the-Wilderness. In many places the icy winds penetrated the crevices. When Mother Lurana entered that house, no bright fires burned upon the hearth, nor were there the smiling faces of friends to bid her welcome; nor did these discomforts disturb her, for she was a pioneer to whom God gave great strength and courage for the work she was to do. Being the practical woman that she was, she began immediately to make the old house more liveable. She lighted a fire, and then set up a temporary chapel in one of the small rooms. For supper they all shared a loaf of bread which had been given to her by a poor woman in Warwick that very morning as she was leaving.

That night, as Mother Lurana knelt in the cold chapel, she poured out her heart in thanks to God. She saw no ugliness in the poverty which surrounded her. It was what she had wanted all her life, and it was a companion she would always treasure. So it was that the ideal of Father Wattson and Mother Lurana came into being. It is a day which is always observed by their spiritual children as Foundation Day; a day in which festivity reigns supreme, and the story is recalled of the courage and devotion of a man and a woman whose faith in God could make dreams come true.

It is a sad and tragic spectacle to see so many in the world— among whom, unfortunately, are many of our Catholic people— seeking pleasure, and filling their minds with the make-believe doings of fictional characters who never existed, when they have at their disposal the reading of the lives of flesh-and-blood heroes who were, and are, the real saviors of the world. It is particularly sad and tragic when what they read pollutes the mind, which God Almighty gave us as a glorious gift in order that man might always seek and know the truth. What a tragedy it is! The great St. Augustine, after he had obeyed the admonition, "take up and read," understood the depth of the tragedy, and in anguish his soul cried out to God: "Too late have I known thee, oh Beauty, so old yet ever new." No reading is more engrossing than the lives of men and women who loved God and served Him in the face of great suffering, as they spread His Kingdom upon the earth. Mother Lurana was such a soul. She was a highly cultivated, charming woman, who might have become a queen in Society; but, wounded as she was with the exquisite dart of Divine Love, she chose poverty instead. When she arrived at Graymoor, the world took no notice of her coming because the event was too insignificant; and yet she was enkindling a lasting spiritual fire upon the earth; she was, by her sacrifice and suffering, delivering the key-note address for perhaps the greatest crusade in the history of the Church—the Reunion of Christendom.

The first winter at Graymoor was a hard and difficult one. The cold blasts of wind which blew down from the hills penetrated the crevices of the old building so that it seemed colder inside than out. Every winter, Graymoor is swept by high winds and heavy snow: even with the centrally heated buildings now in use, it is never what city dwellers would call comfortably heated. This has been one of the hardships of Graymoor winters and the cause of serious illness in many cases. How even the valiant Mother Lurana and her companions were able to endure that winter, in the barely heated Dimond House, and the still less heated St. John's, has always been a mystery to her spiritual children. But she was to be the Spiritual Mother of those who were to bear the choice name of the "Atonement"; and she knew that, once given that exalted vocation, to complain of hardships would be sheer hypocrisy.

The building of a new convent before the next winter set in was an urgent and serious problem which she had to face. During the winter she received a letter from Miss Elliot, who was in New York, which gives us some idea of the hardships the noble women at Graymoor were enduring. "The thermometer went down to zero here yesterday," Miss Elliot wrote. "I really shudder to think what it must have been at Graymoor. . . . Would it be against your rule—when the Society is organized—to own the little church? There is every likelihood of my living, some day, in the far West, and before that comes into the question I would like to have the future of St. John's secured." This letter is important not only because it gives us an insight into the living conditions of the first winter but also because, in the light of what followed, it brings into focus the complete about-face Miss Elliot took when the Society became Catholic. In answer to this letter, Mother Lurana wrote back that as a Franciscan Religious she preferred not to own the property.

The first Christmas spent in the Graymoor wilderness by Mother Lurana was different from the one spent in London the year before. Then she had been with the Sisters of Bethany, and the solemnity of the Savior's birth had been observed with many lights, flowers, incense and glorious Christmas music before a great, magnificent white altar. She thought of the spacious chapel in Lloyd Square, as she and her few companions trudged along the country road, piled high with snow, to the rustic church of St. John's-in-the-Wildnerness. Inside, the building itself was bare and cold, dimly lit by the few candles she could afford to buy for the occasion. There was no music swelling from a grand organ, and there were only a few voices to fill the church with the *Glorias* of the Christmas season. Yet she felt a peace she had never known before. The memory of last year brought no regrets. She knew this was the life she had been seeking, and this was the Will of God for her. To those who give up all things to follow Him, Christ gives the gift of His Peace; and in the possession of that Peace they possess all things. Mother Lurana kept the Peace of Christ in her soul always, even through many turbulent days. It made her the calm, strong woman that she was, great in faith and good works.

In the spring, ground was broken for a new convent, adjoining St. John's Church. It was a happy day for Mother Lurana when she wrote to Father Wattson, who was then in Westminister, Maryland, making a novitiate with the Episcopalian Holy Cross Order, that the cornerstone of the new frame building would be laid on the feast of St. John the Baptist, June 24, 1899. It was to be dedicated to her beloved Poverello—St. Francis of Assisi.

Though he greatly desired to be there, his being "a prisoner in spiritual bonds" prevented Father Wattson from being present at Graymoor for this auspicious occasion. In lieu of his presence, he wrote a letter to Mother Lurana, in which he expressed his regrets and told of his great love for the Society of the Atonement, and also his many hopes for its future. In the vast correspondence which passed between these two chosen souls, most of which is carefully preserved in the archives of the Community, this letter is the most outstanding and remarkable of them all. It reveals the soul of a man who was motivated by a strong faith in all that he did, and who showed a willing obedience to the manifest Will of God in doing a work which so many of his fellow Episcopalians denounced as visionary and impractical. The letter reads:

Holy Cross House
Westminster, Md.

WELL BELOVED IN THE LORD, GREETINGS:

For the love I bear the Society of the Atonement, and that I may the more wisely direct the children God hath given and will give me in it, I have, as you know, placed myself in the hands of the Order of the Holy Cross to be trained by them in the Religious life. Being, therefore, a prisoner in spiritual bonds, I may not be present at Graymoor to unite with you in the laying of the cornerstone of the Convent of St. Francis. But my heart and soul are with you in joyous faith and most fervent prayer.

It is Our Divine Lord Who said, "except a corn of wheat fall into the ground and die it abideth alone, but if it die, it bringeth forth much fruit." The religious act, which you at Graymoor on the feast of St. John the Baptist perform is nothing less than the planting of a seed, which will take root downward and bear fruit upward; increasing and multiplying until a thousand valleys in the world's great harvest field will, "stand so thick with corn that they shall laugh and sing." If in prophetic vision your eyes could be supernaturally opened to gaze forward along the vista of the Church's future to the end of time, and it were given you in that vision to sum together all the blessed fruitage, which shall hereafter spring from today's seed planting, I doubt not that even the elect Mother Foundress of the Sisterhood of the Atonement of Jesus would find her most sanguine hopes surpassed by the marvelous fecundity of God's grace, imparting its fruitfulness to the sacrifices and entire oblation of themselves, which she and Sister Martha have made in obedience to the Divine Call.

Jesus said, "The Kingdom of God cometh not with observation." When He, the Lord of that Kingdom, even the Catholic Church, was born the angel heralds proclaimed it not in the streets of Jerusalem, but only to a few shepherds on the outskirts of Bethlehem, "the least among the thousands of Judah." So, on this birthday festival of John the Baptist, no double-leaded headlines in the *New York Herald* proclaim to the millions of the American metropolis that a Religious Order is being cradled at Graymoor, a place so obscure that a letter addressed to it would be forwarded to the dead-letter office at Washington, as unknown to the postal authorities. No paper, secular or religious, we imagine, will report the laying of the cornerstone, and yet the Great God of Heaven, "Who holds within the Hollow of His Hand all worlds, all space," looks down with Fatherly approval on this religious act; His Son, Our Lord, and His Virgin Mother, rejoice, and all the holy angels and saints rejoice with them. Yes, and devils too look on and gnash their teeth in rage, foreseeing in this humble convent, and what it shall bring forth, another extension of the primal prophecy, "the seed of the woman shall bruise the serpent's head." The undertaking of two defenseless women to build a house in this sparsely settled region of the Highlands, without money enough on hand to finish the building they have begun, much less to furnish and provision it when completed, must seem to be, from the viewpoint of the worldly wise, sheer madness. What can come of such folly save starvation, or else a return of these foolish women to their senses! But these two heroic souls (or, if you will, "fools for Christ's sake") wearing the brown habit of St. Francis, and wedded like him to Holy Poverty, know well that He, in Whom they have put their trust, will never let them be confounded. They are sure His promise cannot fail: "Seek ye first the Kingdom of God and His righteousness, and food, raiment and shelter and all else that is needful will be freely added unto you."

"The lions do lack and suffer hunger, but they who wait upon the Lord shall want no manner of thing that is good." But why should the pious women come like John the Baptist into so solitary a place to take up their abode, when there is so much practical good they might do by establishing themselves in New York? The answer is not far to seek. John the Baptist did not always remain in solitude, but when the hour ordained by God arrived he appeared on the banks of the Jordan and mightily prepared the way for Christ. Nor will the Sisters of the Atonement always remain cloistered at Graymoor. When in retirement the Holy Ghost shall have sufficiently taught and trained them for this work, we believe He will send them forth into the slums of the city; and their brown habit shall then be seen where the poor are crowded thickest together and vice and misery are most strongly entrenched. But let none think that in this sequestered retreat from the turmoil and bustle of the Great City, fifty miles away, that the poor Sisters of the Atonement will have no influence in the world outside and beyond the Graymoor Highlands. In the convent of St. Francis, an altar and tabernacle are to be erected to the worship of the Triune God. Upon that altar (the Lord willing it) the all prevailing Sacrifice of the most hallowed Body and Blood of Jesus Christ shall be daily offered: and within the tabernacle the Blessed Sacrament will be perpetually reserved. Consequently Emmanuel will ever abide in this house, and as the Graymoor nuns kneel in loving adoration before Him, interceding for all mankind, He will hearken unto their requests. So these holy women, through their power with God in the Most Holy Sacrament, shall bless with the benediction of prayer the very ends of the earth.

It was the voice of one man praying at Babylon which moved God to promise that He would bring again the people of Israel to their own land and "turn the captivity of Sion as the rivers in the South." And who shall compute the mighty host of captives who are snatched from Satan's greedy clutch by the prayers of Holy Virgins, keeping watch before the Tabernacle of their God! It has been said that St. Theresa converted more souls by her prayers than the great Francis Xavier did by his missionary labors.

The motto of the Sisters of the Atonement is *"Non nisi te Domine"*; "Naught but Thyself, O Lord!" And to this they have added: "as having nothing and yet possessing all things: as poor yet making many rich." So long as they are unswervingly true to Jesus Christ, the Spouse of Virgins, and to the principles of poverty which He inculcated both by precept and example, the powers of hell shall not prevail against them. They will "flourish like a palm tree planted by the waterside." They will "spread abroad like the cedars in Lebanon." And the good they are destined to accomplish will never perish from the earth.

Faithfully in Our Lord and His Atonement,

Lewis T. Wattson

The author feels incapable of commenting on this magnificent letter. Any added words of his would detract from the greatness and the power of the letter itself. Fifty years after the letter was written every prediction it contained was fulfilled.

Chapter VIII

A POOR FRIAR BUYS A MOUNTAIN

FATHER WATTSON was thirty-five years old when he requested the Episcopalian Order of the Holy Cross to allow him to enter their monastery for his religious training. They understood his intention of remaining only until such time as would be needed for him to learn the principles and practices of the monastic life. The request was an unusual one, for religious communities, as a rule, do not favor such arrangements. However, the evident sincerity of Father Wattson impressed the superior and founder of the Holy Cross Order, Father James Huntington. He called a meeting of the community chapter and proposed to them that they accept Father Wattson to prepare him for his work as a religious founder.

One of Father Wattson's classmates at the General Theological Seminary was Henry R. Sargent, who had since become a monk in the Order of the Holy Cross. It was this man who became Father Wattson's novice master. In religious communities a novice master is appointed to that position because of his prudence, charity, deep piety and religious observance. It is his responsibility to train in virtue and in the observance of the Rule, men who aspire to become members of that particular community.

Religious sometimes speak of the "Spirit" of their particular community, which, of course, is an anomaly, since the "Spirit" of every Religious Order or Congregation is *the Spirit of Jesus Christ*. Generous souls who give up the world to follow Christ, and enter monasteries, convents or diocesan seminaries, all have the one common motive—to pray, sacrifice, work and suffer to fulfill what is wanting of the sufferings of Christ, and thus work for the sanctification of their own souls and the redemption of the souls of others. This motive was the secret source of the heroic patience of the Saints, and it was their "Spirit." However, individual Religious

Communities do have certain traditions, customs and unique work which can be called the "Spirit" of the Community. So, if the author writes of the spirit of any community, let it be understood in this light.

The Spirit of the Episcopalian Order of the Holy Cross is certainly not the Spirit of the Society of the Atonement; and for Father Wattson to place himself under this group for training was a great act of humility in the first place. When he entered the Catholic Church there was no question as to the need of a canonical novitiate for him, just as there was no question raised as to the orthodoxy of his theological beliefs. If there were, he would not have been ordained a priest so quickly. His classmates at Dunwoodie Seminary, who are today pastors and prelates of the Church in the Archdiocese of New York, have given testimony to this truth. But, like the humble Mother of Christ, who needlessly submitted herself to the Rite of Purification in the Temple, he submitted himself to this religious training because he felt it was expected of him. And it was an extremely difficult thing for Father Wattson to do, knowing that his novice master was a former classmate of approximately the same age, and that he possessed as strong a personality as his own.

A novitiate is a religious house where the soul of a novice is put through a refining process which remolds his character, enabling him to live the new life he has freely chosen. The one who has the responsibility of reshaping the character of the novice is the novice master. Sometimes the method he uses in testing the patience, obedience and humility of the novice is seemingly devoid of all common sense, as far as the novice is concerned. But if the block of marble could rationalize it would think the same way about the great sculptor who, with hammer and chisel, is seemingly chipping it to bits as he strives to produce a masterpiece of art. The sculptor and the novice master have a common motive; both labor to produce a masterpiece—one in gleaming marble, the other in divine grace.

When Father Wattson went to Westminster, Maryland, it was mainly to study and learn the fundamentals of the Religious Life, for the establishment of the Society of the Atonement. Yet he sub-

mitted himself to the life of a novice under the Rule of the Episcopalian Order of the Holy Cross. And Father Sargent treated
him as a novice of that order. There were the usual tests of patience, humility and obedience, of course. But on these the novice
master heaped the daily humiliations of deriding Father Wattson's
aspirations. When Father Wattson confided in him his plan for the
three congregations of the Society of the Atonement in the Anglican
Church, Father Sargent derided his plans, and told him that he did
not even have a religious vocation, not to speak of founding a religious community.

After leaving their novitiate, Father Wattson made every effort to
establish amicable relations between the Episcopalian Order of the
Holy Cross and Graymoor, and also to continue friendly relations
with Father Sargent. But the attitude of some members of the Holy
Cross Order toward the Society of the Atonement became so an-
tagonistic and unbearable that the Graymoor Founder was compelled
to write the following letter:

St. Bernard's Day
August 20, 1909

DEAR FATHER SARGENT:
I was glad to accept your invitation, and much enjoyed our visit together at the Clergy House last Wednesday afternoon, but I feel constrained to tell you that it must be the last time I can either visit or
write to you until the Order of the Holy Cross has recognized its inex-
cusable attitude towards the Society of the Atonement and returned the
advances which I have made on several occasions towards the establishment of proper religious relations between the two communities.

The breach of Christian charity, and I may say of common courtesy, is
so flagrant that I need not enlarge upon the subject. You will, I am sure,
appreciate how much I feel my portion of our personal loss, but your
sense of the proprieties of the situation are too keen for me to entertain any fear that you will misunderstand my motive, or fail to justify my
action in placing the honour of the Society of the Atonement above my
private friendships.

With sincere regrets that such a communication as this should be necessary, I am as always,

Your attached friend and brother in Christ,
PAUL JAMES FRANCIS, S.A.

Perhaps the hardest cross Father Wattson had to bear during his novitiate was Father Sargent's strong disapproval of Father Wattson's correspondence with Mother Lurana. However, he found a sympathetic friend in Father Huntington who, perhaps because he was a founder himself, could appreciate the difficulties and trials Father Wattson was undergoing. Father Huntington not only approved the correspondence with Mother Lurana, over the protest of Father Sargent; but also gave Father Wattson permission to leave the novitiate whenever his presence was necessary at Graymoor. Had Father Huntington agreed with Father Sargent, the greatest letters written by the Founder of Graymoor would not have been penned. Today they are among the richest treasures of the Graymoor archives, carefully preserved by the Sisters of the Atonement. For this, the Friars of the Atonement will ever be grateful to their sisters in religion.

This valuable practice of filing all correspondence was done at the request of Father Wattson who, on June 27, 1899, wrote to Mother Lurana:

. . . Surely a book of remembrances ought to be written for the spiritual children, who come after, of all the wondrous providences and supernatural dealings of these days, when God is so near to manifest this good will towards us. Let us, therefore, keep on file all letters that record anything of God's marvelous dealings, that in time to come the data may be at hand for some historian of the Society of the Atonement to tell the story of God's unfailing love and care for those whose whole trust and confidence is in Him, and Him alone.

Much of the correspondence with Mother Lurana is taken up with suggestions and advice on community affairs. He also confided in her his own plans for the Friars, the First Congregation of the Society of the Atonement, which had not as yet been established. Time and again he asks her counsel, her opinion on some matter, and in large measure he relied on her prudent judgment. During this time he wrote a letter to Mother Lurana, revealing his soul:

I see things with a much clearer vision now. Of ourselves we are dust and ashes, God is all power and grace. He is the Creator of the Society of the Atonement, not I. Moreover, God, with Whom a thousand years are but as one day, does not measure time as we do. The hardest lesson I have to learn is patience. "Thou must be as a child under tutors and governors, differing nothing from a servant until the time ordained by the Father has fully come." This seemed to be the Holy Spirit's message to me as a result of the retreat, and I am glad and thankful to obey. After the almost incessant work of nearly fourteen years of ministerial service it is indeed a joyous thing to retire into the desert with St. John Baptist and learn the A.B.C. of the contemplative life. I feel that "bonds and imprisonments await me" when I again put forth into the world to grapple with Satan in the stronghold of pride and rebellion against God. And, oh, I do need to get down to the very roots of pride and self-will in my own nature and learn the truest and most profound humility, lest in the hour of temptation I fail and Our Lord be disappointed in me.

Among the matters which he considered at this time was the question of heavenly patrons for the Society. The Blessed Mother of God was forever to be its Queen. But he also desired to have particular patrons for the three congregations. He was modeling the Society after the pattern set by St. Francis in his three Orders; the Friars Minor, the poor Clares and the Third Order. As the special protector of the First Congregation—the Friars—he chose the Apostle of the Gentiles, St. Paul. St. Francis was to be the heavenly patron of the Sisters of the Atonement—the Second Order. As the patron of the Third Order of the Atonement he chose St. John the Baptist. In a letter to Mother Lurana he wrote:

St. John the Baptist most fittingly belongs to the Third, especially as the Third will doubtless serve to prepare the way for the advent of not a few into the First and Second Orders. Then, too, St. John Baptist emphasizes repentance by confession and amendment as the royal road to obedience just as St. Francis emphasizes poverty and St. Paul emphasizes chastity, or the love of Jesus only.

Again he writes:

I have this morning completed the first draft of the rule for the 3rd Order and after having offered it to Jesus, our Divine Lord, and laid it before Him on His altar throne—I next, before all others, submit the draft to you—for to you under God, the Holy Spirit, I owe whatever of inspiration I possess for the establishment of St. Francis Tertiaries in the American Church.[1]

He also wrote to Mother Lurana about the matter of a habit for the Friars of the Atonement. It seems a strange question since the Sisters were already wearing the brown habit of the Poverello. But quite evidently the Franciscan vocation of the whole Society of the Atonement had not yet become quite clear to Father Wattson's mind. And again he was guided by the counsel of Mother Lurana, the Anglican nun who had so deep and so remarkable a love for St. Francis. When he wrote and asked her the question: "What do you think of white as the habit of the First Order, as making more emphatic our witness for the celibate priesthood?" she answered immediately and explained what she believed to be the Franciscan vocation of the Society of the Atonement. There was no doubt in her mind whatsoever. Not only should the Friars and Sisters of the Atonement strive to acquire the spirit of St. Francis, but also conform themselves to the Order even in the way of dress and custom. The rough, brown robe of the Little Poor Man, therefore, should be their garb also, symbolic of their spiritual kinship with him whom they lovingly called "Our Holy Father Francis." Mother Lurana's decision prevailed, and both the Friars and Sisters of the Atonement have followed the Franciscan way of life since. The Sisters made the first brown habit worn by their Father Founder, and they made every other one he wore—even to the grave.

During Father Wattson's novitiate, Father Howard, at Omaha, decided to give up the Associate Mission. Writing to Father Wattson, he said:

I have definitely decided that I have no vocation for the religious life. Last week I wrote to Bishop Worthington that when my three years are

[1] Father Wattson, as an Anglican, was planning his Society along the lines of the three original rules of St. Francis for the Friars Minor, the Poor Clares and the lay Tertiaries.

When the Society of the Atonement entered the Catholic Church and became affiliated with the Franciscan Order, the Friars and Sisters of the Atonement followed the rule of the Third Order Regular of St. Francis, and the Third Congregation of the Society adopted the rule of the Third Order Secular of St. Francis.

up on November first, I would retire from the Associate Mission. What the bishop will do with this big house I do not know, and I am most sorry that I feel it my duty to leave it, and thus leave him to wrestle with the problem alone. But I could no longer be happy or contented in this work.

Father Wattson was unhappy to see the Associate Mission close, and in writing to Mother Lurana he said:

Please pray that the Associate Mission may not perish, and that Father Howard may not degenerate into a married priest, trundling a baby carriage.

In a letter written at Pentecost, in 1899, he writes with sorrow of the tragedy of the Anglican Church:

As to loving our Anglican Mother—that shall be rightly measured by the extent we spend and are spent in her service, by how much we suffer in her behalf. If tomorrow we could restore to her all that she has lost of Catholic faith and worship and holy living—would we hesitate to go to the stake for her? God sustaining us, I believe we would gladly become martyrs for her sweet sake. In will and intention have we not already offered ourselves a living sacrifice to God to help bring again from Babylon the captive Daughter of our people? "Greater love hath no man than this, that he giveth his life for his friends!" May such be our love through the blessed Atonement of Jesus, the Prince and Bridegroom of the Catholic Church.

When Father Wattson placed himself in the hands of the Episcopalian Order of the Holy Cross to be trained in the principles of the monastic life, before he was to found the community of Friars at Graymoor, his intention was to remain at Westminster, Maryland, through the regular period of the Novitiate, which lasted two years. However it was understood that if in the judgment of the Superior, Father Huntington, the needs of the Sisters of the Atonement required his presence at Graymoor before the end of the two years, he was to go to minister to them.

Towards the end of September, 1899, the Sisters' chaplain accepted a call to another sphere of work, and the services of another chaplain could not be obtained. Father Wattson, after conferring with Father Huntington and obtaining his approval and consent, went to Graymoor to act as chaplain to the Sisters. Despite many difficulties, the time he had spent at Westminster had been of the greatest spiritual benefit to him. He was edified by the manner in which the members of the community observed the rule. These men have always been regarded by many as the greatest ornament of the ministry of the Episcopal Church of America. Father Wattson left Westminster on October 2, 1899. He was then thirty-six years old.

Instead of going directly to Graymoor, he visited the famed Franciscan monastery in Washington—Mount Saint Sepulchre— founded by the late Father Godfrey Schilling, O.F.M., as the American Commissariat for the Holy Land. In his entire life, Father Wattson had never seen or conversed with a Franciscan Friar, though he often desired to do so. To fulfill this desire was the purpose of his visit to Mount Saint Sepulchre. When he arrived at the monastery he was cordially received by Father Matthew Fox, the acting Superior in the absence of Father Godfrey. Father Matthew extended every possible courtesy to the Episcopal clergyman, and he assigned one of the young Friars as his guide to show him all the noted shrines and chapels in the monastery church and gardens. On that visit he made the acquaintance of Father Paschal Robinson, O.F.M., who later became Papal Nuncio to Ireland, and remained a loyal friend of Graymoor until his death.

Father Wattson was invited into the refectory to have dinner with the community, and he was seated at the right of Father Matthew as the day's guest of honor. Later Father Matthew and Father Wattson walked through the spacious grounds of the monastery. In a grotto where the scene of St. Francis receiving the stigmata was portrayed, Father Wattson told Father Matthew of his vocation and what he hoped to do at Graymoor. The Friar Minor listened attentively and with deep interest. Only the day before in the garden of the Anglican monastery at Westminster, Father Wattson had tried to convince Father Sargent, for the last time, of the reality of his call to found the three congregations of the Society of the Atonement on the rule of St. Francis; only to receive the rather scornful reply: "I don't believe you have a vocation to found one Franciscan Order, much less three." But Father Matthew, as a true son of St. Francis, was kind and sympathetic. When Father Wattson knelt in the grotto of the Stigmata and asked Father Matthew to bless him and his work, the Friar Minor gave him the blessing of St. Francis with his whole heart. This Franciscan love was shown to the Graymoor Founder all the rest of his earthly pilgrimage by the great men of the Friars Minor, among whom were: Father Edward Blecke, O.F.M., Father Stanislaus Woywod, O.F.M., the Most Reverend Paschal Robinson, O.F.M. and Diomede Cardinal Falconio, O.F.M.

Father Wattson arrived at the Garrison station late in the afternoon of October 3, 1899, the eve of St. Francis' Day, as destitute of worldly possessions as the Poverello of Assisi. It was exactly one year after he had met Mother Lurana at Warwick. While walking the four miles from the Garrison station to the Sisters' convent on the Albany Post Road, he was overtaken by a man riding in a buckboard. The man was Mr. Joseph Davis, who had erected St. Francis' House, which was to be dedicated by Bishop Coleman of Delaware the next day. Mr. Davis offered a ride in the buckboard, which the Founder of the Society of the Atonement gratefully accepted.

Then followed a lively conversation in which he learned much from Mr. Davis about the history of the region and its people. In the course of the conversation he asked Mr. Davis if he knew of any cave in the near-by hills which might be converted into a hermit's cell. Mr. Davis regretted that he could not tell him of any such cave but promised to find out if there were one before winter set in. In almost the same breath he volunteered the information that there was a magnificent river view from the summit of the hill that skirted the Graymoor valley to the east. "A river view," said Father Wattson, "why, that was the one thing which I thought Graymoor lacked to make it the ideal place for the establishment of a religious institute." On his arrival at Graymoor he waited only long enough to greet the Sisters, and then started off with Mr. Davis to climb the side of the hill to the summit. Reaching the top, he was not disappointed. There it was in the distance, the majestic

Hudson, winding its way through the highlands, like a lake in Scotland or Switzerland.

To Father Wattson this was it—the home of the Friars of the Atonement. God would somehow give it to them. "Upon this mountain," he enthusiastically cried out, "will rise the monastery home of the preaching Friars. From these heights the prayers and works of reparation of countless Friars of the Atonement shall daily ascend to the throne of the mighty Lord of heaven and earth, beseeching His mercy and clemency upon a sinful world." Then, kneeling down upon the earth, he raised his arms and dedicated the mountain to the service of God, giving it the name by which it is now known throughout the world—the Mount of the Atonement.

We may liken this man of faith to a dutiful son who tells his friends, "Because my father loves me and I love him so much, he gives me everything I ask of him." And the father, hearing the words of his son, and overwhelmed by his great love says, "His love is so precious to me that I can refuse him nothing." Such was the relationship between this man of faith and the Heavenly Father he loved so well. Dedicating a mountain which he did not own was an insane act according to the standards of the world, but he believed in his heart, "The earth is the Lord's and the fullness thereof." Unless the reader understands Father Paul as a man of faith whose rule of life was the practical and literal interpretation of the Gospel, much of his life's work will be incomprehensible. However, once the reader understands this important fact, he will find a consistency running through all Father Paul's life which is in perfect accordance with the perfectly sane principles of the Gospel of Jesus Christ.

From Mr. Davis he learned that the whole mountain could be bought for the modest sum of three hundred dollars. But if it could have been bought at that moment for ten cents he would have lost the bargain, since he did not possess even that small amount. However, there were no sleepless nights over the matter, for he knew God would somehow provide the necessary funds. The way God brought that about is still another beautiful story, which we will record from the writings of Mother Lurana. In the story she speaks of herself in the third person. The scene is the ship's deck on which she returned to the United States from England after her stay with the Sisters of Bethany.

Upon the ship's deck, she [Mother Lurana] found her steamer chair placed alongside an English lady, Miss Buxton, coming to America to visit her sister, who was the wife of an Englishman in the government service at Washington. Before the ocean voyage was ended, something far deeper than an ordinary acquaintance was established between them.

Miss Mary Buxton had been brought up in the Low Church school of Anglicanism, but through the influence of Mrs. Humphrey Ward's writings, and her own studies of East Indian cults, she had allowed the pendulum of her religious thought to swing to the extreme of Unitarianism. She no longer accounted herself an orthodox member of the Church of England.

Mother Lurana was reading, at the time, the life of St. Francis of Assisi, and passed it over to her companion. To the latter it had the force of a new revelation. She saw how impossible the Existence of such a life was on any other hypothesis than that Jesus Christ was the son of God. Her faith in Christianity having fallen into ruins, with the help of St. Francis and the Franciscan nun by her side, she began to build it up again; but this time on a Catholic and not a Protestant foundation.

Before her return to England the following year, Miss Buxton came to Graymoor and spent a few days as the Mother's guest in St. Francis' House. It was during this short visit that she was introduced to the Mount of the Atonement, ascertained the price at which it could be purchased, but said nothing of her purpose.

Another sister of Miss Buxton had married Doctor John Taylor, a distinguished surgeon of Birmingham, England. Doctor Taylor's father had been an English clergyman who belonged to the school of Keble, Pusey and Liddon. Doctor Taylor himself was in spirituality and Catholic mindedness one of the very best products of the Oxford Movement in England.

It was into the sympathetic ears of Doctor and Mrs. Taylor that Miss Buxton, upon her arrival in England, poured the story of her recovery of faith, the meeting with Mother Lurana on the steamer, her visit to Graymoor, and her cherished desire to purchase the Mount of the Atonement for the Society as a thank offering for her conversion.

The good Doctor claimed the privilege of sharing in the offering, both for himself and his wife, and the consequence was that he enclosed a draft of sixty pounds ($300) in a letter to Graymoor, stating that it was a joint gift of himself, Mrs. Taylor and Miss Buxton for the purchase of the Mount of the Atonement, in order that upon its summit might be erected a monastery wherein Holy Religion would always be faithfully observed.

This important letter reached the hands of Father Wattson on the morning of the Feast of the Invention of the Holy Cross, May 3, 1900, just as he ended a retreat of seven days in St. John's Church.

So reads the record, written by Mother Lurana, of how God sent the funds to purchase the Mount of the Atonement. There is, however, a very interesting sidelight to this beautiful story, and that is that Miss Buxton later entered the Catholic Church in England shortly after the Society of the Atonement was received into the Catholic Church. She returned to America and entered the Graymoor Convent as Sister Mary Clare, S.A. She died in 1933, and is buried among Graymoor's beloved dead. That chance meeting with Mother Lurana, and the reading of St. Francis' life, changed the whole course of her existence.

When Father Wattson received Doctor Taylor's letter he immediately consulted a legal adviser to clear the title and to secure a deed for it in the name of the Society of the Atonement. The deed transferring the tract of twenty-four acres of mountain woodland to the Society was executed on Ascension Day, May 24, 1900. That afternoon the Sisters climbed to the mountain top, where they united with Father Wattson in an act of fervent thanksgiving to Almighty God for the priceless gift of Graymoor's Holy Mountain.

Father Wattson took possession of the property on June 14, 1900, which happened to be the Feast of Corpus Christi. For the third time he climbed to the summit. This time he carried a heavy, rough cross, which he had fashioned out of a tall cedar tree at the foot of the mountain.

In the Graymoor cemetery there is a grave over which is a cross marked, Brother George Geare, T.S.A. He died in February, 1930, at the age of seventy-nine, and was the first member of the Community to be buried at Graymoor. Brother George was one of Father Wattson's first companions. He was a clergyman of the Church of England, and was known then as the Reverend John Holwell Geare. Because he found it impossible to share the austere life of

Father Wattson, he did not remain long when he first came. Many years later he returned to Graymoor and applied for admittance as a lay Brother, but he was past the age limit. However, he became a Third Order Brother and worked in the Administration Building of the Society. He was an educated, cultivated man with a keen sense of humor and a cheery smile. Every morning, as he arrived at his desk, he would invariably say to his co-workers, "Good morning, may God save the King!" To which greeting, Brother Philip, S.A., another Englishman, would respond with a profound, "Amen."

Brother George often told the story of what happened the day the cross was erected on the summit of the mountain. Father Wattson first cut down a large cedar. From this tree he fashioned the huge cross and, placing it on his shoulder, carried it to the top. On the way up, the Reverend John Geare recited prayers from the Anglican *Book of Common Prayer*. They were accompanied by a young man, Ferdinand Wallerstein, who was a convert from Judaism to the Episcopal Church. (We shall learn his interesting history in the following chapter). When the cross was erected more prayers were said by these three devout souls. To this day that cross stands where the Founder of the Society of the Atonement erected it; and all who know Graymoor call it, "The Corpus Christi Cross."

Two years later, while still an Anglican, Father Wattson wrote the following on the back of the original deed to the Mount of the Atonement:

s T a

The Feast of the Presentation
of the Blessed Virgin Mary
November 21, 1902

I, Paul James Francis [Lewis T. Wattson], Minister General of the Society of the Atonement, do affirm before God, Our Lady, St. Francis, St. Paul, and St. John Baptist and these witnesses, that I hold the property named in this deed, being the Holy Mount of the Atonement, only as a Trustee until that day when the Anglican Communion shall have been reconciled to the Vicar of Christ and received back into communion with the Holy Roman Church; and I will command my successors in the office of Minister General of the Society of the Atonement so soon as that happy "repairing of the breach" is consummated to place this deed at the feet of St. Peter's Successor, as a token of the fealty, obedience and devotion of the Children of the Atonement to the Roman Pontiff, sitting in the Chair of Blessed Peter and exercising his authority as the divinely appointed Shepherd over the whole flock of Christ and His vicegerent over the Holy, Catholic and Apostolic Church.

(signed)

PAUL JAMES FRANCES, S.A.

(Lewis T. Wattson)

Witnesses

Lurana Mary Francis, S.A.

Paul Jakob, S.A.

This was certainly not a true legal procedure; but it does prove Father Paul's spirit of detachment and generosity, as well as his love for the Catholic Church and the Vicar of Christ, even when he was yet an Episcopal minister.

Chapter IX

HE FINDS A LEAKING PALACE

WHEN St. Francis' Convent was nearly completed, Mother Lurana, in the spirit of obedience which characterized her whole life, wrote to Bishop Henry C. Potter, Episcopal Ordinary of the Diocese of New York, asking him to preside at the dedication which she so greatly desired should take place on the feast-day of the Poverello— October 4th. A very cordial note came from Bishop Potter, in answer, telling her that he would be pleased to preside at the dedication if Mother Lurana would designate some other day than October 4th, since that day, for him, was filled with appointments.

Mother Lurana replied that were October 4th any other day than St. Francis' Day she would gladly do so. In that letter she asked Bishop Potter if he would be willing to delegate the Bishop of Delaware, Bishop Leighton Coleman, to dedicate the convent. Bishop Potter sent a gracious note in answer, giving his consent; and in due time a letter of acceptance was received from the Bishop of Delaware. All this seemingly unimportant data is *very* important in order fully to understand what transpired ten years later, when the authorities of the Episcopal Church instituted legal proceedings for possession of the Graymoor property—after the Society of the Atonement entered the Catholic Church. But even before this time, apparently enraged by Father Paul's pro-Roman crusade, in a bitter attack on the Graymoor foundation, the *Church Standard* of Philadelphia, an Anglican weekly now extinct, called the Friars and Sisters of the Atonement—"Ecclesiastical squatters."

Bitterness, prejudice and bigotry cause men to make statements that are untrue, absurd and irrational; and frightful sins are committed every day in the world in the name of love—love for a cause, an ideal, or a person. Christ told His followers: "These things I have spoken to you that you may not be scandalized. They will expel you

Dimond House

St. John's in the Wilderness

The First St. Christopher's Inn

The Palace of Lady Poverty

from the synagogues. Yes, the hour is coming for everyone who kills you to think that he is offering worship to God. And these things they will do because they have not known the Father nor me."

If the *Church Standard* had not been blinded by the jaundice which warped its judgment at that time, and had investigated the history of Graymoor, it would have come to the logical conclusion that Bishop Henry C. Potter, Episcopal Ordinary of New York, would certainly never delegate Bishop Leighton Coleman of Delaware to dedicate the convent home of "Ecclesiastical squatters."

The historical records of the Graymoor archives prove that Father Wattson obtained the original permission of Bishop Potter for the foundation of the Sisters at Graymoor in 1898. They further prove that Father Wattson was careful to seek and obtain Bishop Potter's written permission to succeed the Reverend Mr. Davis as chaplain to the Sisters; and that later he received Bishop Potter's permission for Bishop Coleman to act as Visitor to both the Friars and Sisters of the Atonement. To make the relationship with Bishop Coleman the more intimate, he secured his canonical transfer from the Diocese of Omaha to the Diocese of Delaware. So that, up to the time he entered the Catholic Church, he was subject to the jurisdiction of Delaware even though he resided in the territorial boundaries of the Episcopal Diocese of New York.

Although St. Francis' Convent was dedicated by Bishop Coleman on the feast-day of the Poverello, October 4, 1899, the Sisters did not take possession until October 18th. In the meantime, Father Wattson luxuriated in the unfinished convent. When it came time to make way for the Sisters, he looked for a cave in the surrounding hills, but found none. Mr. Davis, the Sisters' builder, solved the problem of permanent shelter for the balance of the autumn and winter by placing at Father Wattson's disposal an old paint shop, which was situated more than a mile north of Graymoor.

Father Wattson gratefully accepted it from Mr. Davis, and joyfully named it "The Palace of Lady Poverty." The roof leaked, and when it rained he said the midnight office holding an umbrella in one hand and the breviary in the other. The "Palace" was illuminated by a candle. To keep the cold blasts of wind out, he stuffed the broken windows and gaping crevices with paper and rags. An overcoat and top boots helped to keep him warm.

But he never complained of its poverty. Like Mother Lurana, it was what he wanted—the foundation of the Society of the Atonement—and his soul was at peace. Fortunately, the first winter was mild, and by repairing the roof and windows he made the shack livable. "The Palace of Lady Poverty," in which the Founder of the Society of the Atonement spent his first winter, has been preserved, and is now incorporated into the beautiful chapel of St. Elizabeth of Hungary at Graymoor.

During that winter, Father Wattson was invited by the Reverend William Harman Van Allan, Rector of Grace Church, Elmira, New York, to preach a mission there. Ten years later the Rector of Grace Church became involved in the controversy over the Graymoor property. During that mission, on January 10, 1900, Father Wattson wrote to Mother Lurana at Graymoor:

The mission has begun most happily. The congregations are large and the people seem most seriously disposed to accept the message of God, which I have been sent to deliver to them. The children's mission is a special joy. There must have been two hundred and fifty present at the children's service yesterday afternoon, and the interest of the little ones is beautiful in our eyes. . . . Father Van Allan I find to be of most brilliant attainments, coupled with the graces of holy chastity and true devotion to the souls of men. The possibilities of twelve days preaching in this wicked and worldly city of forty thousand people are incalculable—increase the fervency of your intercession.

In this letter he discussed again the question of the habit for the Friars of the Atonement:

May God make His Will perfectly clear in regard to the habit—nothing would distress and grieve me so much as to take any such grave step without the certain approval and direction of Our Divine Lord. My mind is by no means clear as to the Will of God in the matter, and I will not move forward unless the Pillar of Fire goes before. When the time for advance arrived heretofore, God invariably pointed the way in a manner that left no room for hesitation and doubt. I look to Him for the same direction now; and if He withholds it I will simply refuse to budge until the direction comes.

When he returned to Graymoor, the question of the habit to be worn by the Friars of the Atonement was settled in his mind. On January 25, 1900, the feast of the Conversion of St. Paul, Father Wattson assumed the habit of rough gray-brown material which had been made for him by Mother Lurana. Since there was no one of authority in the Episcopal Church present, Father Wattson officiated at his own investiture. The evening before, he placed the habit on the altar of the convent chapel, where the ceremony was to take place on the following morning. He spent almost the entire night in a lone vigil before the altar. He wrote a few days later:

It was with much fear and a sinking heart that I at last put on the habit about which I had so long dreamed. During that time of preparatory prayer and meditation a vision of what it meant to follow the Crucified was given to me. It was a foreshadowing of Gethsemane, and my poor heart and soul shrinks from the ordeal that lies before me. But I am very happy about it, nevertheless. Each day I am growing to love my habit more and more.

Much care had gone into the making of this habit which was to be the distinctive garb of all future Friars of the Atonement. The habit of the Graymoor Friars is very much like the robe worn by the Friars Minor. The tunic is the same. The cowl differs somewhat. Instead of a short cape hanging from the shoulders it has a shield-shaped scapular which reaches to the waist, front and back; this is lined with serge material of a deep red color, symbolic of the Precious Blood of the Atonement. The waist is girded by a white cord, having three knots symbolic of the vows of religion. To the white cord is attached the seven-decade Franciscan crown. A crucifix suspended from a blood-red cord, also symbolic of the Precious Blood of the Atonement, hangs around the neck. In addition, after a Friar makes the three vows of Religion perpetually, he wears an emblem in the front center of the cowl consisting of the six-pointed Star of David, symbolizing Hope; the heart of Charity, and the five-pointed star symbolizing Faith.

From the day he assumed the Franciscan habit until after he had entered the Catholic Church, when religious obedience required that he conform to the usual clerical attire when traveling, Father Wattson never wore anything but his habit wherever he went. In a letter written a month after he assumed the habit he wrote:

I have been to New York, Brooklyn and Jersey City in my habit, creating no special sensation, nor arousing any unpleasant demonstration, so that now I am quite well satisfied that I can go anywhere in these United States without being a target for jibes and boisterous ridicule. I am beginning to feel quite at home in monastic dress and the strange feeling I had at first is quite worn off.

The Graymoor Friar now became a familiar sight preaching in the cities of the Hudson Valley and beyond. In New York City he usually preached from the steps of City Hall. His fiery sermons always succeeded in attracting crowds of people around him. The medieval-looking Friar in a modern world background was a picturesque sight in itself.

The progress of Graymoor was—at least in the beginning—regarded with interest by the Episcopal Church; perhaps because Graymoor had adopted the Franciscan rule of life and had chosen St. Francis as its model and patron. The Poverello of Assisi has always exercised a strong appeal to the Episcopalian mind. So, a benevolent attitude was taken towards the Society of the Atonement in the Episcopal Church, which lasted until Father Wattson openly and unequivocally committed the Society to the work of Christian Unity.

Numerically the growth of the Society of the Atonement was slow and discouraging all through the years that it remained in the Episcopal Church. Many young men and women applied for admission into both communities, but few of them persevered. However, life at Graymoor was very rugged in those early days and it required courage and stamina to survive the wretched poverty and the unsettled conditions within the Society. At Father Paul's death, a lifelong friend of his wrote to the Friars: "You ought to have seen Graymoor in the early days! No one in the world but Father Paul could have started 'from scratch,' without a nickel, and built up the glorious institution that now is a model for the Church." Yet, through all the hardships, the faith of Father Paul and Mother Lurana never wavered, for they had perfect faith in God's Covenant with the Society.

On July 27, 1900, seven years after he received the "Atonement Texts"; and had been told that he must wait that long, Father Wattson was professed in Religion. He made the vows of Poverty, Chastity and Obedience before the Right Reverend Leighton Coleman, Bishop of Delaware. Because there was no friary at the time, the ceremony took place in a canvas tent, erected for that purpose on the very summit of the mountain, close to the Corpus Christi Cross. The ceremony was described by Mother Lurana as follows:

The Friar who is making the triple vows of Poverty, Obedience and Chastity is the Reverend Lewis T. Wattson, who from this hour ceases to be Father Wattson and becomes Father Paul James of the Atonement; for this new name in religion takes the place of the old to emphasize the irrevocable nature of the step thus taken, just as in marriage the bride loses her maiden name to bear the one that comes as a dowry from her husband.

After the profession, Father Paul, as we shall from now on call him, celebrated the Communion Service. Then, with the permission of Bishop Coleman, he addressed these words to the small gathering: "My children in the Blessed Atonement, I have just been given the name of James (the name was the Bishop's choice); now James means Jacob, and I am going to ask all the members of the Society present to come and kneel before me, as the Patriarch Jacob asked his sons to do, that I may give you my blessing." By a strange coincidence, the number of the Society at that time equalled the number of Jacob's sons—twelve. Several weeks later, Father Paul asked and received the Bishop's written permission to add Francis to his name. From then on it was the family name of the Society of the Atonement.

During his visit to "The Terrace" when Father Paul first met Mother Lurana, she introduced him to a young Jew whose name was Ferdinand Wallerstein. He had been born in Germany, the son of devout orthodox Jews, and had come to the United States at an early age. He made his home in Warwick, where he worked as a barber. Having become acquainted with Mother Lurana, who was then Miss White, he confided many of his religious problems to her. On one occasion he showed her a prayer which he had composed, addressed to the God of Abraham, Isaac and Jacob, asking for light to know whether Christ, Whom the Christians worshipped, was indeed the Messias.

Father Wattson and he had a long conversation in Warwick, the result of which was the baptism of the young Jew. In the spring of 1900 he arrived at Graymoor to enter the new Society. That summer he was clothed as a lay brother in the Atonement habit by Father Paul and given the name of Paul Jacob. He, being the "first-born among the Friars," as Father Paul said, always held a very special place in the heart of the Founder of the Society. And rightly so, for he was Father Paul's only companion for years, devoted and loyal through joy and sorrow. He entered the Catholic Church as the only other Friar with Father Paul, and then assumed the name Anthony. He died on his feast day, June 13, 1939, just eight months before Father Paul himself died.

[*Chapter* X]

THE LAME MAN AT THE TEMPLE GATE

THE TRUTH that Jesus Christ established only one Church, which is in no way divided, and that the one Church of Christ is the Catholic Church, first came to Father Paul in Omaha, after he visited a Catholic Church and returned to his study to prove that truth to himself from the writings of Anglican and Catholic scholars. Later, in the solitude of Graymoor, he prayed for more light as he further studied the Roman Catholic claims. The results of that prayer and study were that he became firmly convinced of these claims, and of the unique vocation of the Society of the Atonement. His conviction was that the Graymoor Religious were to repair the sixteenth-century breach of the Church of England with Rome.

In a conference which he had with Mother Lurana in the summer of 1900, he outlined what he now recognized as the vocation of the Society. That vocation obliged the members of the Society to point out to Anglicans, whenever and wherever an opportunity presented itself, that they were put in a false position by the breach with Rome; and that Anglicans should now endeavor to be again *Corporately United* with the Holy See.

Mother Lurana, who knew Father Paul better than any other living person, was not surprised to hear him say what he did. She had expected it for a long time, and she was absolutely one in faith and conviction with him. However, wanting to be certain that he understood the consequences of such an undertaking, she asked him: "Do you realize to what persecutions, ostracism and peril of annihilation you will be exposing the Society of the Atonement by undertaking such a propaganda?" "Yes," he answered, "I think I do realize quite clearly what a wild and foolhardy proposal it is from the standpoint of worldly prudence. As far as I know, I am the only Anglican ecclesiastic in thirty thousand who holds these views; nevertheless, if

91

our witness is from God, sooner or later it will prevail, though the whole world be against us."

And so, as Father Paul so beautifully explained their new position: "With eyes wide open, therefore, to the consequences, and putting present popularity behind them, the joint Founders of the Graymoor Institute determined to plant their feet firmly on the Rock of Peter and courageously face the storm, which they felt morally certain would sooner or later overtake the infant Society of the Atonement." In this prediction they were not mistaken.

Shortly after this conversation with Mother Lurana, the Reverend William Van Allan of Grace Church, Elmira, New York, and another High Church clergyman of New York City, paid a visit to Father Paul at Graymoor. Dr. Van Allan was so gratified with the results of Father Paul's preaching in Elmira that he called to invite him to preach again the following October. After showing the two visitors St. John's Church and the new convent, Father Paul invited them to walk with him to the top of the mountain, which was still in a wild state. The conversation of the three clergymen gradually drifted into a discussion of Anglo-Catholicism and the question of the Reunion of Christendom. Father Paul said that after all Anglican controversialists had done to build up a system of Catholicism with the Pope left out; the study of Holy Scripture, the Fathers and Church history had convinced him that the Papacy was truly *Jure Divino*, that the Anglican position ever since the Reformation, so called, was a wrong one, and that it could never be right again until the Anglican Church made her submission to the jurisdiction of the Holy See.

Dr. Van Allan and his companion were shocked. All the way down the mountain Dr. Van Allan poured forth a torrent of arguments against the Papacy. From that time, the zeal of Dr. Van Allan for Graymoor rapidly declined and his attacks upon the pro-Papal position of the Society of the Atonement in the public press became notorious.

It was on the feast of St. Simon and St. Jude, Sunday, October 28, 1900, that Father Paul officially committed the Society of the Atonement to its vocation of Christian Unity. With the members of the community gathered before him in St. John's Church, he delivered a fiery sermon in which he proclaimed the unique vocation of the Society. The text was appropriately taken, in part, from the Catholic Epistle of St. Jude, whose feast day it was. "Dearly beloved, I beseech you to contend earnestly for the Faith once for all delivered to the Saints."

"*That Faith*," Father Paul said with great emotion, "*is the Faith of the Holy Roman Church, and the Chair of Peter at Rome is the divinely constituted center of a reunited Christendom.*"

After the sermon, he called all the members of the Society into St. Francis' Convent, and there asked them to subscribe their names to a profession of faith which he had drawn up, and which embodied the main points of his sermon. To the members of the Third Congregation living in the world he sent the same profession of faith, for their signatures. The names of members who refused to sign were automatically dropped from the membership lists of the Society.

The period of popularity which the Society of the Atonement had enjoyed in the Episcopal Church was now at an end. But Father Paul was not greatly disturbed by the new situation which had arisen. He remembered another incident which had happened almost nineteen hundred years before at Capharnaum. Our Divine Lord had revealed the sublime mystery of the Eucharist to those who followed Him. The truth of Christ's words was too much for many of them to bear, and so they said, "This is a hard saying. Who can listen to it?" St. John relates that, "From this time many of His disciples turned back and no longer went about with Him."

Two months prior to the time Father Paul committed the Society to the vocation of Christian Reunion—on August 26, 1900—he wrote to an aspirant who was planning to enter the Convent:

Probably by the time you reach St. Francis' House, you will find the carpenters putting up an addition, which, God willing, will more than double the size of the Convent. The little community has trebled in a year, and some of the postulants and novices are sleeping in the garret, so that an addition is absolutely necessary if accommodations are to be provided for you and the others who are coming.

But just as soon as the Christian Unity message of Graymoor became known, the membership of the Society began to dwindle, and the enlargement of the convent was postponed for several years. There was plenty of room in the convent for those who remained faithful after the proclamation by Father Paul on Papal Infallibility and Supremacy on that last Sunday in October, 1900.

During the previous summer Mother Lurana received a legacy which had been left to her by her grandmother. She gave this to Father Paul so that he and Brother Paul could have a roof over their heads. So, on September 8, 1900, the feast of the Nativity of Our Lady, ground was broken for the erection of a small wooden friary on the Mount of the Atonement.

The friary was finished three months later, and Father Paul invited the Society's ecclesiastical superior to dedicate it on the feast of the Immaculate Conception, December 8th. Bishop Coleman accepted the invitation and came to Graymoor to officiate at the ceremony. Just before the ceremony began Father Paul announced to all those present for the dedication that the friary would be dedicated in honor of the Dogma of the Immaculate Conception, and that the building would bear the name of St. Paul. Although the Bishop afterwards declared to Father Paul that he did not personally accept the dogma, he proceeded with the dedication without protest.

However, while driving the Bishop to the station after luncheon, Father Paul informed him of the strong Catholic position which the Society of the Atonement now held. He told the Bishop of their belief not only in the Immaculate Conception of the Blessed Virgin but also in the Primacy and Infallibility of the Pope, whom they recognized as the successor of St. Peter and the Vicar of Christ. Though Bishop Coleman was visibly distressed he made no decision then. He told Father Paul that he would reserve his judgment until he had further time to reflect and pray over the matter. In a few days a letter came from Bishop Coleman in which he stated that, while he did not believe in the dogmas of the Immaculate Conception of the Blessed Virgin and the Infallibility of the Pope, he did not see any reason why he should withdraw from his position as Visitor of the Society of the Atonement.

To a Catholic, trained to regard any compromise with relation to dogmatic truth as intolerable and not to be entertained for a moment, this decision on the part of the Anglican Bishop of Delaware must seemed almost incredible. However, the bishops of the Episcopal Church are so trained in the school of doctrinal comprehensiveness peculiar to the Anglican system, and such latitude is allowed the individual as to what he chooses to believe or disbelieve, that in the same diocese today there are those who deny the Virgin Birth, and others who, in their zeal for reunion with Rome, profess belief in the whole of Catholic doctrine.

Up to the beginning of November, 1900, Father Paul was invited to speak in many pulpits of the Episcopal Church because he had become a renowned preacher. He had always been cautious in expressing his views, trying not to offend anyone. Now his tactics changed, as he threw caution to the winds. Fearlessly and boldly he proclaimed the message of Christian Unity. His favorite and most frequent theme was the *De Jure Divino* supremacy of the Bishop of Rome in both honor and jurisdiction. He was a modern Peter the Hermit, preaching the necessity and urgency of the new crusade. In every conversation the subject inevitably veered to the topic of reunion; and before very long his reputation as a strong pro-Roman ecclesiastic was firmly established in the Episcopal Church. The unpopularity of Father Paul increased daily among his fellow clergymen. Men who at one time were close friends and sympathetic admirers of his work as a Religious Founder now openly disavowed any connection with him.

A staunch supporter of the Graymoor position on the reunion of Christendom was the Reverend Father Barnes, Rector of St. Barnabas' Church (Episcopal) on Bushwick Avenue in Brooklyn. During the summer of 1901, he invited Father Paul to preach on Sunday nights in St. Barnabas' Church. Not content with preaching indoors, Father Paul went into a public square near the church on Sunday afternoons to preach the message of Christian Unity to the people assembled there.

The secular press was beginning to take notice of Father Paul's preaching. One newspaper, the *Brooklyn Citizen*, devoted three columns to a feature article about Father Paul, in its issue of September 2, 1901. The headline read:

The Minister General of the Society of the Atonement Declares that the Pope Is the Supreme Head of the Church, and Calls upon the Anglican Communion to Repudiate the Doctrine of the Reformation which Denied the Divine Right of the Roman Pontiff to Rule over the Christian Church as the True Vicar of Christ.

The article went on to say that:

The open air preaching of Father Paul James Francis, the Minister General of the Society of the Atonement, at the corner of Myrtle and Knickerbocker Avenues on Sunday afternoons lately, has attracted wide attention. It has seemed like a return to the times before the Reformation to see a Friar in the habit of St. Francis of Assisi preaching to a crowd in the streets. When Father Paul has collected a sufficiently large audience he leads the people into Saint Barnabas' Protestant Episcopal Church at Bushwick Avenue and Grove Street.

Quoting Father Paul, the article continued:

The Church Must Have a Head

There is scarce a band, or company of creatures in God's universe, from the denizens of the beehive to the choirs of angels in heaven itself, who do not possess one of their number to act as leader and preserve unity. In legislative bodies not so much as a committee of three can discharge its functions unless one of the three presides in a chair of unity. It is a madman's dream to contemplate a united church on earth without a visible head. If every parish must have its rector, and every diocese its bishop, and every province its archbishop, how could the whole Catholic Church throughout the world exist as one fold without having one supreme or chief shepherd over all? Did, then, the Divine Founder of the Catholic Church in its original constitution provide for a permanent head and universal shepherd over His flock, to feed the sheep the sound doctrine and protect them from the wolves of heresy? The Society of the Atonement believes that He did when He said to Simon Peter, the "Primate" (St. Matt. X:2) of the Apostles: "Thou art Peter, and on this rock I will build My Church, and the gates of hell shall not prevail against it. And I will give unto thee the Keys of the Kingdom of Heaven (i.e., the Catholic Church), and whatsoever thou shall bind on earth shall be bound in heaven; and whatsoever thou shalt loose on earth shall be loosed in heaven. (St. Matt. XVI:18). I have prayed for thee that thy faith fail not, and when thou art converted strengthen thy brethren. (St. Luke XXII:31) Feed My sheep—feed My lambs—feed My sheep." (St. John XI:16).

Supremacy of Pope Recognized

The Society further believes that the See of Peter is to this very day the city of Rome; and that Leo XIII, the Roman Pontiff, sitting in the Chair of Peter, is the Vicar of Christ and by divine right the Universal Shepherd over the Flock of Christ.

This being so, Christian Unity can only be realized by all the Bishops of the world acknowledging the supremacy of the Bishop of Rome as the successor of St. Peter and being reconciled with him.

The Mountain of Difficulty

A great mountain of difficulty stands in the way of such reconciliation, and only the exercise of the most sublime faith, coupled with the greatest charity, can remove the mountain and cast it into the sea. Yet, with God all things are possible, and the Society of the Atonement believes it can and will be accomplished.

Reading the press notices of the year 1901, one would imagine that the Society of the Atonement was a large group of Franciscans. The fact is that the First Order consisted of Father Paul and Brother Paul Jacob only; and the Second Order, the Sisters, outnumbered the First by just a few.

On the Feast of the Most Holy Rosary, October 7, 1901, the third anniversary of Covenant Day, Father Paul and Mother Lurana established *The Rosary League of Our Lady of the Atonement*. The organ of the league was a tiny periodical entitled *Rose Leaves from Our Lady's Garden at Graymoor*. The Rosary League was "formed to pray and work for the restoration of 'Mary's Dowry' (England) to Our Virgin Queen, the Holy Mother of God."

Rose Leaves was the precursor of *The Lamp*. It ceased publication in December, 1910. That small periodical was instrumental in bringing a great blessing to the Orient—the establishment of a Catholic university in Tokio. The very interesting story of the university is recorded in the following chapter.

Rose Leaves was another medium established by Graymoor to bear witness to Papal Supremacy and the urgency of the Reunion of Christendom. In the first issue the editor wrote:

May we hope that *Rose Leaves from Our Lady's Garden* will be treasured by those who receive the little paper, not only because of the witness it bears to Catholic truth and the honor of the Mother of God, but also because it is a monthly visitor from Graymoor, the Beulah Land of the Atonement.

In the meantime, Father Paul continued his street preaching. Wherever he could gather an audience he pleaded the cause of Christian Unity. Up and down the Hudson Valley he moved, preaching in the cities of Newburgh, Beacon, Kingston and Poughkeepsie. Always his topic was *Corporate Reunion*.

Father Paul during his lifetime told his spiritual sons many interesting stories of his Anglican days. One in particular stands out prominently in the minds of all those who lived with him, among whom was the Author of this biography. This chapter is entitled "The Lame Man at the Temple Gate" because it is apropos to the famous story. There was, at first, the temptation to entitle it "Father Paul Hurls a Thunderbolt," for that is how the incident struck his hearers when it happened. It is the story of the parting blow he struck when he was invited to preach at one of the meetings of the Episcopalian Archdeaconry of Long Island. He would never have received this honor had it not been for a college chum of his, the Reverend Charles A. Jessup, at whose church in Greenport the meeting was to be held. Father Paul had roomed with Charles Jessup both at St. Stephen's College and at the General Theological Seminary, and the association of years had drawn them together in strong bonds of mutual friendship. Differences of opinions or views were not allowed to affect this relationship; and so it was when Charles Jessup invited Father Paul to preach.

As the time for the Archdeaconry meeting drew near, Father Paul wrote to his friend intimating that he would preach on the Reunion of Christendom and the Chair of Peter. This letter filled the Reverend Mr. Jessup with consternation and dismay. Such a sermon at the opening of the Archdeaconry meeting was a dreadful thing to contemplate. So Charles Jessup had a conference with the Archdeacon, who also had been a college and seminary friend of Father Paul. The two of them then outlined a plan by which the dreaded sermon on the Pope would be side-tracked.

On the day of the meeting, September 10, 1901, Father Paul, not knowing of the plan of his friends, boarded a Long Island train in New York, which his friend, Charles Jessup, was to meet. When about halfway to his destination, the Archdeacon got on the same train and, with a cordial handshake, took the seat beside his old college friend. "By the by," he said, "I hope you do not intend preaching anything very High Church tonight. The people of Greenport are quite Low, and it would be very unfortunate if the sermon gave offence to anyone." To the remark Father Paul made no answer, but he debated with himself internally. When they arrived at the parish house, the Archdeacon again brought up the subject of the sermon, and ended the conversation by saying, "Preach them a spiritual sermon."

That evening, after the clergy had entered the church in procession, "Evening Prayer," according to the Anglican prayer book, was begun. Such a service as this is usually divided into as many parts as possible, because the greater the number of visiting clergy taking part, the better pleased they are; and the people also.

A feature of the Anglican evensong, which is Archbishop Cranmer's substitution for Catholic Vespers, is the reading of two "lessons"; the first "lesson" is taken from the Old Testament, and the second one is taken from the New. That night, the man chosen to read the first "lesson" was a clergyman of Low Church tendencies from the North of Ireland. With a trumpet-like voice, he read from the second chapter of Ezechiel: "Son of man, stand upon thy feet, and I will speak unto thee . . . whether they will hear, or whether they will forbear (for they are a rebellious house), yet shall know that there hath been a prophet among them. And thou, son of man, be not afraid of them, neither be afraid of their words, though briers and thorns be with thee."

That settled the internal debate which had been going on in the soul of Father Paul since he had met the Archdeacon on the train.

He would obey God, follow his conscience, and preach the sermon he had prepared on the Pope. During the singing of the hymn before the sermon, he knelt in silent, earnest prayer for wisdom and strength; and then ascended the pulpit steps.

In his opening remarks he said that he had been requested to speak on the "Spirit of Missions"; and so he would base his sermon on the description, contained in the Acts of the Apostles, of Saints Peter and John going up into the Temple at Jerusalem; and how they saw a man sitting at the Beautiful Gate of the Temple, who had been a cripple from his mother's womb. Father Paul declared that this man made bold to ask an alms from the Vicar of Christ; and Peter said to him: "Silver and gold have I none, but such as I have I give unto thee, in the name of Jesus Christ of Nazareth rise up and walk." And he took him by the hand and lifted him up and immediately his feet and ankle bones received strength and he, leaping up, entered with them into the temple, walking and leaping and praising God.

In this lame man outside the temple, Father Paul said that he saw the figure and type of Anglicanism; that special form of ecclesiasticism which had been the product of the so-called English Reformation. Anglicanism, in fact, had always been lame from its birth; and unto this day lay prostrate just beyond the door of entrance into the Catholic Church, its hands always outstretched for alms.

"Why this constant lament every year over a deficit in the funds of the Foreign and Domestic Missionary Board?" he asked. "And why such paucity of converts to show for the sums already expended? How could the Anglican communion cease being such a sorry failure in the missionary conquest of the world for Christ? Who was there on earth to give strength to her feet and ankle bones, and make the Episcopal Church one of the mightiest missonary forces on the face of the earth? The answer is not far to seek; there is one man alone who could speak the word of divine power and work the spiritual miracle that is necessary. That man is the Pope of Rome, the Successor of St. Peter and the Vicar of Christ, now reigning on the throne of the Fisherman.

"If we but fix our eyes on him, and ask the favor of *corporate admission* into the temple of Christian Unity, from which Henry and Elizabeth Tudor expelled the English people, the Anglo-Saxon race would become the mightiest missionary power in Christendom.

"In pre-Reformation times, when English missionaries took their commission from St. Peter's Successor at Rome, as, for example, Wilfred and Willibrod and Boniface, they converted most of Northern Europe to Christianity. The English and American missionaries might do the same today for Asia, Africa and the Islands of the Pacific, if once again they took their marching orders from the Vicar of Christ."

The congregation, especially the clergy, grew more tense with each word Father Paul uttered. Finally the North of Ireland presbyter, who had read the lesson from the Prophet Ezechiel, could endure the sermon no longer. Rising and approaching the Archdeacon, he said, "You cannot allow that man to go on preaching such popery: *you must stop him.*"

The Archdeacon, who sat stunned by the effrontery of the preacher rose to his feet with the help of his cane, and limped forward to the center of the chancel; then mounted the altar steps. He had been maimed for life in a railroad accident, and the figure of the lame man, halting upon his cane, made the whole scene all the more suggestive. Facing the congregation, as he held the collection plate in his hands, the Archdeacon shouted: "Let your light so shine before men that they may see your good works and glorify your Father which is in Heaven." This is one of the so-called "offertory sentences" of the Episcopal Church. When it is said, during a service, the wardens or vestrymen understand it as a signal to take up the collection. The last words Father Paul said, as he was interrupted by the Archdeacon, were, "The Chair of Peter."

That night, in the seclusion of his hotel room, he felt very much at one with the unpopular Prophets Ezechiel and Jeremias. But, like them, he knew the consolation which comes to a man who has done what he knows God wants him to do, even though he also knows that "briars and thorns" will be henceforth his daily lot. The next morning, on his way to the business meeting of the Archdeaconry, Father Paul met a lady whom he knew. This lady had always had a deep affection for him. She looked at him with pity in her eyes, and then said, "Oh, Lewis, how could you?" She then walked away. It was another parting with still another friend.

The business meeting was called to order, and Father Paul sat alone in the back seat. The Irishman who had read the lesson from Ezechiel the previous evening asked for the floor. He then proceeded to read a set of fiery resolutions, condemning in no uncertain language the sermon of the preceding evening. He denounced Father Paul as disloyal—one who had incurred ecclesiastical censure. In order to prove to the Episcopal Church at large how completely the clergy of the Archdeaconry repudiated such popish sentiments, he moved that a copy of the resolutions be sent for publication to the leading church papers. However, there was another Irishman present, who possessed the proverbial Irish sense of fair play. He was a missionary of indefatigable zeal, and his herculean labors commanded the respect and admiration of the entire Archdeaconry. This tall, commanding figure spoke in defense of Father Paul with captivating Celtic eloquence. He said that the resolutions just read were an outrage, surpassing anything of the kind he had ever heard. "We of the Archdeaconry," he said, "have invited a brother clergyman, of another diocese, in good canonical standing, to preach before us; and forthwith we proceed to indict the preacher as a *heretic* without the semblance of an ecclesiastical trial, and brand him before the Church at large as a *traitor*; and all because he has advocated our reunion with the Mother Church of Rome, *from which we were separated in an evil hour.* Mr. Chairman, I move you, sir, that these resolutions be laid on the table." And they agreed with him, just as the elders of the Sanhedrin had agreed with Gamaliel when he said: "Keep away from these men [the Apostles] and let them alone. For if this plan or work is of men, it will be overthrown; but if it be of God, you will not be able to overthrow it. Else perhaps you may find yourselves fighting even against God."

Though Father Paul often told this story to his spiritual sons in a spirit of mirth, it was certainly not humorous when it happened. Upon the heels of this incident came the Bishop's threat to depose him from the ministry of the Episcopal Church. But in later years he always looked back upon it with humor. He told it often. Once, when through the gracious charity of Patrick Cardinal Hayes he was permitted to seek subscribers to *The Lamp*, he told it from the pulpit of St. Patrick's Cathedral in New York; much to the amusement of the thousands who attended the Masses that Sunday.

The last time he told the story of the Archdeaconry meeting was a few weeks before he died in 1940. He had been invited to speak during the observance of the Church Unity Octave in the National Shrine of the Immaculate Conception, on the campus of the Catholic University of America. His Friar Sons agreed that he was at his best that night. He spoke for an hour to a capacity crowd which filled the spacious crypt, telling them of his ideal and its fulfillment. In the following month that magnificent sermon became a precious memory.

Some years after the Archdeaconry meeting, Father Paul founded the "Anglo-Roman Union," and the clergyman who had defended him became a member of the Executive Committee. His name was John Manning.

Throughout his whole life, Father Paul loved the Anglicans. They were his good people. And, loving them, he prayed, worked, sacrificed and wrote with his gifted pen for their conversion to the Catholic Church. He wanted them to share with him the happiness he had found at the feet of Peter. Until he died, he looked with sorrow upon the Anglican Church, just as Peter looked with pity upon the lame man at the Beautiful Gate of the Temple. Father Paul's great desire was to repair the breach, and bring, "the lame man at the Temple gate" within the Temple itself.

Chapter XI

HE LIGHTS *THE LAMP*

THE WHOLE Archdeaconry affair came out in the press; and the aftermath was the closing of practically every pulpit in the Episcopal Church to Father Paul's preaching.

The *Living Church*, staunch voice of the Protestant Episcopal Church in the United States, commenting on the sermon in its issue of October 5, 1901, stated:

Whether there ever can be again . . . a universal Primacy on the part of the See of Rome may be an abstract question upon which men may legitimately differ. It is at present of the practical value of the celebrated problem as to who killed Cock Robin. We regret that an esteemed one of our clergy should have taken this unfortunate position which cannot fail seriously to mar his influence. We feel that he stands absolutely alone in his position, and that it is wholly inconsistent with the ecclesiastical allegiance which he owes to his bishop and the national Church. . . . The whole Anglican communion is unanimous in repudiating absolutely the doctrine of Papal Supremacy, which the earnest but erratic priest of Graymoor has preached.

All his fellow clergymen, however, did not abandon him as an ecclesiastical leper to be shunned. A few came secretly, like Nicodemus, to tell Father Paul that they inwardly agreed with his religious convictions.

Although almost every pulpit was closed to him, he continued his street preaching. The theme of all his sermons was Reunion with the Holy See, but he always stressed *Corporate Reunion*. "Every individual conversion to the Church of Rome," he said, "was a disloyalty to the general welfare of the Anglican Church."

When two of his friends, who had become Catholics, visited him at Graymoor and urged him to follow their example. he defended the principle of *Corporate Reunion* by saying: "You tell me to go to Rome. My father was told to do the same thing. The Oxford men were told to do the same thing. If they had taken the advice given to them there would be no Catholic Revival in the Episcopal Church. If *they* had gone to Rome you would not be here today advising me to follow you. There must be something more than a conviction that Rome is right. There must be a conviction that it is right for me to go to Rome now. *I have no such conviction.* To me it seems that there should be a *Corporate Reunion*, and this is being delayed by individual conversions."

The words of the clergyman, which had abruptly ended Father Paul's sermon at the Archdeaconry meeting—"Let your light so shine" —kept haunting him. At first he wondered why; and then it suddenly came to him. Since he could no longer give his message from church pulpits, he must use some other method to reach Church people. His light must shine before men in the written word. He, therefore, took up his pen and lighted *The Lamp*.

The years proved it to be the greatest impetus of all to his Christian Unity movement. The first issue of the magazine appeared on the feast of Candlemas in February, 1903. Father Paul's editorial for the first number is a masterpiece of exposition. It is important for us to print it in full here so that the reader will understand Father Paul's mentality for the next six years of his life; and also to understand, if that is possible, the untenable position he held. That untenable position was the acceptance of the completeness of Catholic truth with the exception of the invalidity of Anglican orders. Pope Leo XIII had declared them invalid on September 18, 1896, seven years before *The Lamp* appeared. And yet Father Paul held to their validity until he received from God that fullness of grace which led him into the Catholic Church in 1909. Above the very first editorial he quoted from Isaias LXII:1, which again gives us a glimpse of that restlessness of soul which was his as he worked for the reunion of Christendom.

For Zion's sake will I not hold my peace, and for Jerusalem's sake I will not rest, until the righteousness thereof go forth as brightness, and the salvation thereof as a lamp that burneth.

Editorial

"Glory to God in the Highest and on earth Peace to men of Good Will." This was the song of the angels when the Prince of Peace was born. To preach the same message of Peace to those who have the good will to receive it, and to give glory to God in the Highest, this is the mission of *The Lamp*. May it never be untrue to the purpose of its being.

We place *The Lamp* under the special protection and patronage of Our Immaculate Lady Mary, Queen of Heaven, and her Seraphic Knight, St. Francis of Assisi; the Saint par excellence of Church Unity.

Candlemas, the beautiful Feast of the Purification, when she who was "the Lamp of Burnished Gold" came into the Temple bearing the Light of the World, marks the first appearance of *The Lamp*. We have lighted it as a witness to the Old Faith as taught by the English Church before a wicked King severed her from the Center of Unity. We believe that not only does Our Blessed Lord wish us to pray, but also to work, for Unity; and instead of magnifying differences between ourselves and Rome we ought to minimize them, and thus prepare the way for that peace which we all long for as Christians. We intend by God's grace to let the full, clear light of Catholic Truth, "whole and undefiled," shine in the homes and hearts of our readers. We ask for *The Lamp* the cordial support of all Catholics who look forward to the day when the Ecclesia Anglicana shall be completely reconciled with the appointed Head of the Church on earth, the occupant of St. Peter's Chair.

We believe all that the Catholic Episcopate in communion with the Apostolic See of Rome believes, the Dogmas of the Immaculate Conception and Papal Infallibility not excepted. *But we also believe in Anglican Orders and the perpetuity of the Anglican Church.* The breach with Rome is going to be repaired in God's good time and the same relations re-established between the Vatican and the Ecclesia Anglicana which existed prior to the Sixteenth Century. Meanwhile it is our duty to witness to the truth and to do our utmost within the Anglican Communion to prepare and make ready for Corporate Reunion. This we propose to do by keeping in the front rank of that great Catholic Movement, which began at Oxford seventy years ago. The advance which this movement has made since 1833 has all been in one direction, the direction which truly Catholic movements of necessity take, the direction which leads to Rome; for there is the Chair of Peter, and as it was in the days of St. Jerome so it is now and ever shall be until the end. "*Where Peter is, there is the Catholic Church.*"

If anyone shall be so illogical as to maintain that the Church of England is the same Catholic, Apostolic Church that was in England for nine hundred years before Henry the Eight's day and "yet accuse us of disloyalty because we believe in the Pope," we would just remind such an one that the greatest friends and champions the Church of England ever had in any age believed with their whole heart and soul that the Pope was the Vicar of Christ and the Supreme Shepherd over the Catholic Sheepfold. St. Augustine, the first Archbishop of Canterbury, had more to do than any man with the founding of the English Church, but he would never have set foot with his forty companions on English soil had not a Pope sent him. The Church of England never had a better friend than Thomas à Becket, who became a martyr in her defence; *but, oh, what a Papist he was!* And what devoted sons of the Holy Father at Rome were St. Dunstan and St. Anselm and Archbishops Warham, Peckham and Arundel. It is because we refuse to recognize Archbishop Cranmer and Henry the eighth, as safer Prereformation Divines of the English Church, *that we would rather go to the block* with Sir Thomas More and Bishop Fisher than deny that the Bishop of Rome is the Successor of St. Peter and the head of the Catholic Church.

In later years, when referring to his Anglican years and the untenable position he held, Father Paul always said, *"but never for a moment were we in anything but good faith."* This is proved by the advice given to him by Cardinal Gibbons of Baltimore, whom he consulted prior to his entry into the Catholic Church. The Cardinal advised him not to take any definite steps towards submission to Rome until all his doubts concerning Anglican Orders were resolved. "You are in Good Faith," the Cardinal said, "be patient and follow the leading and guidance of the Holy Spirit."

Father Paul became a minister of the Episcopal Church in 1886 and, for ten years, until Pope Leo XIII in the Apostolic Letter, *Apostolicae Curae*, stated: *"We pronounce and declare that Ordinations carried out according to the Anglican rite have been and are absolutely null and utterly void,"* he believed himself to be a validly ordained priest. He was steeped in the writings of Anglican scholars and many of these, even after the Letter was published, did not regard the Pope's decision as "perpetual, final and irrevocable." The *Anglo-Roman Review* of Paris, whose attachment and submission to the Holy See had never been questioned, followed the same line of thought and used exactly the same words. But in a brief to the Archbishop of Paris, dated November 5, 1896, Leo XIII said that he was deeply grieved at this. "We have deemed it opportune," he wrote to Cardinal Richard, "to communicate these things to you, because they aim chiefly at the *Anglo-Roman Review*, which is published in your diocese. Among the editors are men who, instead of supporting our constitution as they should, weaken it by their tergiversations and discussions. Care must be taken then that nothing appear hereafter in this review that be not in full accord with our intentions. It is certainly better that it desist and observe strict silence rather than that it raise an obstacle in the way of our designs and of the excellent object that we are pursuing." He then refers to Anglicans who did not receive his decision as final, and says that, as far as Catholics are concerned, it would be a transgression and an inconvenience for them to lend themselves to the designs of these men and to favor them in any way whatsoever.

The *Anglo-Roman Review* was founded chiefly to promote conversions to the true Church. Upon the receipt of Pope Leo's letter to Cardinal Richard, the editor suspended publication and made a complete submission to the Pope's decision.

However, a document, written in Latin, from the Primates of the Anglican hierarchy appeared on March 8, 1897, with the title: "Reply of the Archbishops of England to the Apostolic Letter of Pope Leo XIII on Anglican Orders." The reply was divided into twenty chapters and attempted to refute the Pope's arguments against the validity of Anglican Orders. But this document, signed by the Archbishops of Canterbury and York, avoided that part of the Bull in which are pointed out the profound changes made in the Edwardine Ordinal in regard to the rite of Ordination.

Father Paul was fully cognizant of what was transpiring between England and the Holy See. He knew of the efforts of the illustrious English statesman, Mr. Gladstone, and of Lord Halifax, to bring about a settlement of the important question of Anglican Orders. And he was just as disappointed as they were when the final decision was made declaring them null and void. But the reply of the English hierarchy gave him the hope, as it did them, that the matter was not finally settled. They hoped that the "whole controversy" would be further considered, despite the Pope's decision; or, at least, if closed now, opened up again at a future time. The Pope's decision was a most difficult one for the Anglicans to accept. In their reply to Leo XIII they admitted that the letter "Apostolicae Curae"—"tended to overthrow their whole position as representing the Church."

Such was the state of affairs when *The Lamp* appeared. As far as the Catholic Church was concerned the question of Anglican Orders was once and for all time settled. For some Anglicans, among whom was Father Paul, it was not. The Anglicans who accepted the decision were glad that it was settled, and at that time there were many conversions to the Church; among whom was the brilliant Anglican, the Reverend Basil Maturin, who was an Irishman, and wielded great influence at Oxford. Many in England, who had queer ideas of the conditions Rome would lay down should there be a reunion, were happy to know that to become a Catholic one might remain an Englishman, but not an Anglican.

Furthermore, Father Paul was immersed in non-Catholic historical writings, the authors of which had "poisoned the wells of history" so far as Catholic truth was concerned. This is proved from the quotation already given from *The Pulpit of the Cross*, in which he wrote, "The argument from history . . . is fatal to the Papal theories of the Church of Rome." This he wrote only fourteen months before Pope Leo declared Anglican Orders invalid. Father Paul also had a hazy notion of the true meaning of the Dogma of the Infallibility of the Pope. He was under the impression that the Pope was infallible only when defining in conjunction with an Ecumenical Council of the Church. He did not understand Papal Infallibility for what it is, something personal to the Pope in virtue of his apostolic authority, and independent of the consent of the Church. Father Paul did not fully understand the findings of the Vatican Council in 1870 which declared "it to be a dogma of divine revelation that when the Roman Pontiff speaks ex cathedra—that is, when he, using his office as shepherd and teacher of all Christians, in virtue of his apostolic authority, defines a doctrine of faith and morals to be held by the whole Church—he, by the divine assistance promised him in blessed Peter, possesses that infallibility with which the divine Redeemer was pleased to invest His Church in the definition of doctrine on faith and morals, and that, therefore, such definitions of the Roman Pontiff are irreformable in their own nature and not because of the consent of the Church."

Even though Pope Leo's Apostolic Letter, "Apostolicae Curae" declared that it was a final pronouncement of Anglican Orders, Father Paul, misunderstanding the Dogma of Papal Infallibility, believed that an Ecumenical Council in the future could, as new facts came to light, set aside the pronouncement. This, of course, was a great mistake. For in the second to the last paragraph of the letter the Pope declares:

That these letters and all things contained therein shall not be liable at any time to be impugned or objected to by reason of fault or any other defect whatsoever of subreption or obreption or of Our intention, *but are and shall be always valid and in force*, and shall be inviolably observed both juridically and otherwise, by all of whatsoever degree and pre-eminence; declaring null and void anything which in these matters may happen to be contrariwise attempted, whether wittingly or unwittingly by any person whatsoever by whatsoever authority or pretext, all things to the contrary notwithstanding.

In the very first issue of *The Lamp* Father Paul had an article on: *A True Conception of Papal Infallibility*, in which he quoted from the *Ave Maria*—a Catholic paper—giving the meaning of the definition of Papal Infallibility. In quoting from the *Ave Maria*, he put in bold type the words: "HE (THE POPE) IS VERY RARELY INFALLIBLE." Father Paul took further consolation from the same article, which read:

. . . All it (Papal Infallibility) means is that the Pope can never mislead the world in regard to what Christ taught and commanded. It is not held that the Pope is infallible in governing the Church. As a Ruler he may fail; as Supreme Teacher he cannot err because of Our Lord's promise.

Father Paul found consolation in these words because, like many other Anglicans hoping for *Reunion*, he did not regard the Apostolic Letter of Leo XIII on Anglican Orders as an ex cathedra pronouncement. The thought of accepting a decision which declared his "orders" invalid was unthinkable. While Father Paul, as an An-

glican clergyman, agreed with Newman that the definition of Papal
Infallibility was what every Catholic held as the logical necessity of
Revelation which would be worthless unless we had some sure means
of knowing what it is that is revealed, yet he did not agree with
Leo XIII. For years he had celebrated a service which he called
"the Catholic Mass." He reserved in his chapel what he thought was
the Blessed Sacrament. To accept it now as something which was not
"real" was too overwhelming a proposition for this sincere man to
accept.

The author of the article in the *Ave Maria*, which Father Paul
quoted as an authority in *The Lamp*, was a minimizer of the real
definition of Papal Infallibility. This definition has both a primary
and secondary object. The primary objects are the doctrines of
faith and morals. The secondary object refers to any truth the declaration of which is necessary for the support and substantiation of a
revealed truth.

Father Paul continued to exercise his ministry sincerely believing
that he could. Many there were who attacked his position, declaring
it unsound. Others questioned his motives and still others doubted his
sincerity. And so the storm raged all the more furiously around him,
but he remained undisturbed as he sent out issue after issue of *The
Lamp*. Following the dictation of his conscience, he asserted that he
could not embrace the Catholic faith at that time no matter what
accusations were hurled at him.

While the storm of controversy raged around Father Paul on the
seemingly double-allegiance stand that he took, he was literally bom-
barded with mail from Catholics and non-Catholics alike. In the
June, 1903, issue of *The Lamp* he wrote: "A distinguished Jesuit
Father, in the *Sacred Heart Messenger* exclaims, 'How any one can
pretend to obey the Pope and remain an Anglican is more than we
can understand.' " Father Paul quoted in the same issue an Episcopal
clergyman who wrote, "Your position is absolutely untenable. It is
neither Anglican or Roman, and I am positive, therefore, that it cannot be Catholic."

In answering these and similar charges, Father Paul wrote articles
on "Our Divided Allegiance" in two issues of *The Lamp*. In the

defense of his position there is an unmistakable lack of grace in seeing the truth objectively but on the other hand there is a positive
sincerity on his part. He wrote:

> In all good conscience before God, we conceive our spiritual allegiance
> to be a divided one; not, we hope, through any grievous fault of our
> own but because, long before we were born, two things which God has
> joined together man, in the violence of self-will and evil passion, unlaw-
> fully put asunder. When father and mother quarrel and separate, the
> children are of necessity confronted with a divided allegiance . . . there
> being schism in the household the children, in a measure, become a law
> unto themselves and balance their allegiance to either parent as wisely
> as they may. . . . Our spiritual Mother (the Anglican Church) and the
> Father of Christendom were alienated from one another three hundred
> seventy years ago; as dutiful children of both we desire to render to
> each the love and obedience which our conscience, enlightened by the
> Holy Spirit, dictates. Herein lies at the same time our peace and our
> tribulation. . . . Terribly crippled as the Church of England is by reason
> of heresy and schism we do most lovingly confess and acknowledge her
> to be our spiritual mother. Yes, and we are sure God, our Saviour, loves
> her too with a love fathomless as the ocean, deathless as Himself, and
> all the while He is leading her back, step by step, patiently, tenderly,
> through the long night back to the Father's House.
>
> And we, the sons and daughters . . . will cling to her always. . . .
> When the mother, pardoned and reconciled, dwells once more in the
> Father's House we will dwell there too, most gladly, most joyfully; but
> we would rather be with her in the desert, fighting her battles and
> helping our Lord bring her on the homeward way, yes, to die in exile
> by her side, than disowning her to herd with Peter's sheep, though it
> were in the greenest pasture and to "lie down beside the still waters of
> comfort."

Those words of Father Paul lay bare his own soul and his manner
of thought in the days before he became a Catholic. Inconsistent as
they are in the light of logical thinking, they were the substance of
all his writings and sermons for many years. He clung to a Mother
(the Anglican Church) and at the same time berated her for her
infidelity to the Father (the Catholic Church). Father Paul prayed
and worked to reunite them in a manner that was already declared
impossible by the Father—*Corporate Reunion* with the acceptance
of the validity of *Anglican Orders*. When he was reminded that for-

mal schism is a mortal sin, his answer was: "As an Anglican, I may be in schism, but I am not the one who makes the schism, therefore I am not a schismatic." It was only when God gave him the grace to accept the fulness of the Catholic Faith that he could see through the fallacy of his arguments in the position he held for so long. Until then he always prefaced his arguments with the words: "In all good conscience before God."

There are some ostensibly sincere Anglican clergymen who, like Father Paul in his Anglican years, are convinced of the Papal Claims, but who remain outside the Catholic Church and defend their position on Father Paul's *early* theory of *Corporate Reunion*. Since this is so, it is important that this volume should explain just what Father Paul understood by *Corporate Reunion*; why he held such a theory and how his mind was changed in the matter.

Father Paul understood the term *Corporate Reunion* in its strict etymological sense. That is, the coming together again of two bodies, which were formerly one, in such a manner that all parts of both bodies merge into one body again. This is how Father Paul understood *Corporate Reunion* in his Anglican years.

The reasons he believed that the Anglican Church could be corporately reunited with the Holy See were, first; because, *at that time, he firmly believed in the validity of Anglican Orders*; secondly, there was the historical proof that Catholic Bodies in the Oriental Church had been received back *Corporately* by Rome after a period of schism. His line of reasoning was that if it had happened with these Catholic Bodies of the East, it could happen with what he termed "the Anglican Branch of the Catholic Church."

The fallacy of this argument was that while the Eastern Bodies were in schism, mainly through disciplinary matters, they maintained an inviolable, valid priesthood which kept intact the full deposit of faith handed down from Apostolic times, *and the Church of England did not*. They possess these powers because, unlike the Anglicans, they have never changed, tampered with or destroyed any part of the original rite and intention in conferring Holy Orders.

Father Paul, in his tireless work for the submission of Anglicans to the Holy See, proclaimed: "If the devil is powerful enough to take the whole of England out of the Catholic Church, then God by the Omnipotent Power of His Holy Grace can bring them back corporately again." To this man of faith it was as simple as all that.

Father Paul changed his position on *Corporate Reunion* when he received the necessary grace to enter the Catholic Church. He then quickly saw that the Apostolic Letter of Leo XIII, declaring Anglican Orders null and void, abolished forever the possibility of a *Corporate Reunion* of Anglicanism with the Holy See. And, seeing this, he realized, in its true light, the tragedy that is England. Then, knowing of the invalidity of Anglican Orders and seeing the disunity in the beliefs and practices of Anglicanism, he agreed with the scholarly Cardinal Vaughan, Archbishop of Westminster, who, on January 19, 1896, wrote:

I have no confidence in the prediction of a conversion en masse. It is not in that way that a people like the English is converted. A convert needs much instruction before his conversion is thorough. A conversion en masse might easily end in confusion en masse. But the conversion of souls individually, exactly as they enter into the world and leave it to present themselves before their Judge, is the result I expect from prayer and devotion to Our Lady.

These are the reasons why Father Paul held the position he did on *Corporate Reunion* as an Anglican, and why he changed his position when he became a Catholic. The Anglicans who contend that he held to "the corporate principle" even after he entered the Fold of Peter have pointed to *The Lamp* of December, 1909, which was published about a month after the Society's conversion. In that issue he wrote:

Shutting their eyes to Rome's method of employing the Corporate method of conversion in treating the Uniate bodies of the East, men have consistently said that Rome would admit of no other but the individual process of submission to her jurisdiction, as far as Anglicans and other non-Papal bodies of the West were concerned. *The Lamp* is now in a position to assert the contrary. A *pusillus grex*, a society of Anglicans numbering but a score of souls, has asked for the privilege of a corporate submission, and reception, and received from the Holy See an affirmative answer. Though this little cloud on the horizon be but the size of a man's hand, it is the prophecy of an abundance of rain and index of what Rome will do when the corporate movement toward the center of Catholic Unity has gathered momentum and brought not a score but scores of thousands to assemble before the door and knock for admission to the Catholic Church.

At first glance this statement seems to be a reiteration of what he had been preaching as an Anglican—the *Corporate Reunion* principle. But the very fact of his own conversion proved that he no longer believed that the *Corporate Reunion* of the Anglican Church was possible. For when the Society of the Atonement was *Corporately* received into the Catholic Church, each member was called upon to make an *individual* Profession of Faith. After his conversion, when writing on *Corporate Reunion*, he meant small groups such as the Society of the Atonement. Whereas he previously considered individual conversions as disloyal to the *Corporate Reunion* of Anglicanism in the same editorial of December, 1909, he wrote:

We must not deprecate or seem to disparage the individual process of convert-making. We are much too grateful for our own admission to the Fold of Peter not to stretch out a loving hand to every individual soul, who is contemplating the same step, with a glad cry of help and encouragement. We want all our dear old friends and Anglican brethren to know that wide open arms and a heart brimful of joyous welcome awaits every one of them who, now or hereafter, turns toward Graymoor seeking us as a medium of entrance into Peter's ship.

This statement is a complete reversal of the stand which he had taken in regard to individual conversions when he was still an Episcopal clergyman. It proves how quickly he adopted the Catholic Church's attitude on the question of conversions.

Since the Society of the Atonement was *Corporately* received into the Catholic Church there have been other groups received in the same manner. Among these are the Benedictine Monks of Caldey, the Benedictine Nuns of Milford Haven, South Wales; the Religious Brotherhood in England who are known as "The Servants of Christ the King"; the Sisters of the Love of Jesus, in Canada; the Bethany Congregation of Jacobite Monks under Archbishop Mar Ivanios of India; and the Jacobite Sisters, under Mar Theophilos, also of India. It is important, however, to point out here that while the Benedictine

Monks of Caldey, like Father Paul, were received into the Catholic Church as *laymen,* and later ordained to the priesthood, since they did not possess valid orders; Mar Ivanios and Mar Theophilos, who were in schism, were neither reordained as priests or reconsecrated as Bishops since they already possessed valid orders.

When Father Paul spoke and wrote of *Corporate Reunion* after he entered the Catholic Church, it was *Corporate Reunion* with qualifications that he meant. For then he knew that faith is an individual intellectual act.

Those clergymen of the Anglican communion who remained loyal friends after his conversion to the Catholic Church knew that Father Paul's mind had been changed on the matter. Among these was the Reverend John J. Staunton, Jr., a zealous missionary of the Philippine Islands.

He eventually entered the Catholic Church and, after teaching philosophy at Notre Dame University for a number of years, was ordained a priest in the seventieth year of his life. Father Staunton, before his conversion, held the principle of *Corporate Reunion.* He was saddened to see Father Paul enter the Catholic Church. Five years after Graymoor became Catholic, he wrote the following letter:

Mission of St. Mary the Virgin
Sagada, Philippine Islands
October 2, 1914

DEAR FATHER PAUL:

Mrs. Staunton and I always think of you with a great deal of affection. I was not among those who discontinued subscription to *The Lamp* when you followed the leading of your conscience. . . .

I hope that you sometimes remember us in a kindly way, though outcasts. Under present developments I am heartily in sympathy with "reunion," and with the Holy See, though I fully realize that Rome could not recognize "the Anglican Church" or any part of it as at present constituted; and I do not pretend to have arrived at an understanding of, or belief in, what seems to be included in the word papalism. My personal "unbelief," however, aside, it appears to me that Rome loses much more than it gains with every individual convert—with yourself as a notable exception—which it draws from the ranks of the Anglican Catholics. Where they go to they count for nothing; where they come from they count for much towards the ultimate result.

But probably these ideas do not interest you, as you are at work on the other theory.

Always affectionately yours,

JOHN J. STAUNTON, JR.

In a thesis of his, published five years after he entered the Catholic Church, Father Paul wrote:

We do not expect a corporate submission of *all* Anglicans to the Apostolic See, in either this or any other subsequent generation, but we *do* anticipate the home-coming of the Catholic Remnant. How extensive the numbers will prove to be God alone knows![1]

To England will come a "second spring" but it will not come by the Corporate Reunion of Anglicanism, which in its disunity on religious beliefs and practices does not bespeak the Spirit of Holiness, as we shall see in the following chapter.

In the first editorial Father Paul said that *The Lamp* would be a messenger of good will. It achieved the opposite effect. If there was any heat engendered by its lighting it was the heat of anger and opposition. But in publishing *The Lamp*, the idea of arousing passionate controversies was certainly not Father Paul's intention. In fact, in explaining its peaceful mission, he wrote:

To make more plain the mission of *The Lamp* and that it may never depart from its original aims until the goal is reached and the prize is won, the Savior's words "Ut omnes unum sint" (that all be one) will be printed as the headline of every page.

The *Church Standard*, Anglican weekly of Philadelphia, under date of March 23, 1903, stated:

We have before us a copy of a periodical called *The Lamp*. . . . It purports to be published at Graymoor, Garrison, N.Y., but it is otherwise strictly anonymous. . . . Honest and honorable High Churchmen justly resent the charge that they are "Romanizers," and among the advanced High Churchmen of our acquaintance are some of the most

---

[1] *Beyond the Road to Rome*, by Georgina Pell Curtis; B. Herder, St. Louis, Mo., 1914, page 216.

learned and intelligent opponents of Papal usurpation and doctrinal nov-
elties whom we have ever known. Anonymous supporters of the Papacy
cannot be numbered with such men. They have no honest standing in
any school or party in the Anglican or any other communion. . . . The
only name that can be applied to them, because the only one which
etymologically defines their purposes, is that of Papists. That there is
such a faction is beyond dispute; and this anonymous periodical is a
proof of it. Anonymous traitors to the Church at whose altars they serve
must be left to their own secret devices.

As the storm raged around Father Paul, he received a letter from
the Reverend Charles Le V. Brine, Rector of Christ Church,
Portsmouth, New Hampshire. When he wrote the letter this clergy-
man of the Episcopal Church was an advocate of the Reunion of the
Church of England with a schismatical Oriental Church of the East.
The letter read:

I beg to return this sheet [*The Lamp*]. I wish to have no part with
such base unpardonable disloyalty. I utterly repudiate your avowed purpose and I brand you a dishonourable and dishonest son of Mother
Church—without honour and without shame.

Father Paul wrote in answer, in *The Lamp*:

. . . he should tell us plainly why he esteems it noble, honourable and
honest to champion the cause of Reunion with Constantinople, but the
part of a shameless, "dishonourable and dishonest son of Mother
Church" to edit a paper advocating Corporate Reunion with Rome.

Many read the magazine to stir up their indignation and then heap
insults upon its editor. Monsignor Edward Hawks, a distinguished
convert from the Episcopal Church and an ardent admirer of Father
Paul, whom we have already quoted in the prologue, in another
letter describes the havoc *The Lamp* caused in Nashotah, an Anglo-
Catholic seminary in the West.

For five years Father Paul's magazine, *The Lamp*, had been causing a
wild controversy in High Church circles. It advocated the return of the
Episcopal Church to the obedience of the Pope. It did much more than
this; it gave convincing reasons for such a step. It brought to Episcopa-

lians the arguments which they had never seen because they had never read Catholic books. The first copies that reached the reading room at Nashotah were torn up and the students were furious. I remember the occasion very well, for Bourne and I were then in residence. My dear friend, Father James Richey, then an Episcopal minister, expressed the opinion that Father Paul ought to be thrown out of the ministry. Little did he suppose that he, himself, was one day to become one of the editors of *The Lamp*.

The Father Richey, of whom the Monsignor writes, became a close friend of Father Paul. He came to live at Graymoor and assisted in editing *The Lamp*. After his conversion to the Catholic Church he studied for the Priesthood and was ordained. Bourne also entered the Catholic Church and was ordained a priest. Only "The Book of Life," of which Our Divine Lord speaks, has the complete record of all those who entered the Catholic Church through the influence of Father Paul and his struggling little magazine, *The Lamp*. Persons entered the Church because of his writings in defence of her claims while he, himself, remained outside her holy portals.

There were few paid subscribers to *The Lamp*. To keep it rolling off the printing presses required faith and courage. But Father Paul was not interested in profits. He had a work to do—to spread abroad the message of Christian Unity—and, in doing it, he knew that he was being faithful to the vocation God gave him. Such generosity, however, on the part of a penniless Friar could not continue without having repercussions on the struggling Graymoor community. The members were obliged to sacrifice and endure the extremes of poverty so that *The Lamp* could appear regularly. Even then, it appeared late some months because the printer could not be paid on time. That is to say, it did until the resourcefulness of the valiant Mother Lurana settled the serious problem.

The devotion of Mother Lurana to *The Lamp* was second only to that of Father Paul. After the pulpits of the Episcopal Church were closed to Father Paul, she understood how dear *The Lamp* was to him. He certainly did not find on street corners the people he was trying to reach, therefore, street preaching was limited in its scope.

The only life-line open to him for the accomplishment of his work of Christian Unity was *The Lamp*. It had to continue lighted, throwing forth the rays of truth which were dispelling the darkness of unbelief, schism and heresy everywhere. If necessary they would beg on the streets for the money to pay the printer.

So, when the emergency arose, Mother Lurana sent her Sisters, few as they were at that time, on begging tours into all the neighboring cities and towns. Out into the brickyards of Haverstraw and Beacon, and down into the streets of New York they went, holding out their tin cups for the alms of the passers-by. In the cold, snow and sleet of winter days, and in the heat of summer months they stood in their appointed places, like soldiers upon whom rests the safety of a city, begging in order that men might know the truth.

Father Paul never forgot the loyalty, sacrifices and devotion of the Sisters. He knew how difficult it is to beg, for everywhere he went he begged as the need to do so arose. Therefore the Sisters always occupied a special place in his heart to the very end of his life. In times of prosperity it is quite easy to forget those who befriended us in our times of need. Ingratitude has brought much sorrow into the world. The ingratitude of His people wounded the human heart of Christ; and so He could say, "Jerusalem, Jerusalem! thou who killest the prophets, and stonest those who are sent to thee! How often would I have gathered thy children, as a hen gathers her young under her wings, but thou wouldst not!" But Father Paul always showed his gratitude to the Sisters. In later years, when the Society of the Atonement was a Catholic community and the charity of the faithful would not allow it to suffer any want, he divided the alms which came in the mails to Graymoor between the Friars and the Sisters. This was one of the many ways in which he showed his gratitude to them.

He did it in countless other little ways. He located his office as Father General in the Sisters' convent and each day, while saying the Rosary, would walk down to it at the foot of the Mount. When he became an old man this was exertion for him. But he realized how much it meant to the Sisters to have his presence in St. Francis' convent at least part of the day, and so he never disappointed them. It would have been more convenient for him to have had his office in the Friary; just as it would have been easier to assign a young Friar Priest as the Sisters' Chaplain, but he was a grateful soul and in these ways he tried to pay back a great debt. Each morning after meditation and Divine Office in common with the Friars, he would leave the chapel to go to the convent, a custom he observed to the very day of his death. During his life he urged his Friars to continue, after his demise, to pay the debt to their spiritual sisters who had sacrificed to keep *The Lamp* burning brightly.

With each new issue of *The Lamp* Father Paul gained more prestige. He became the acknowledged leader of the pro-Roman minority in the Episcopal Church; and *The Lamp* was their voice. The authorities of the Episcopal Church were embarrassed. They had underestimated his influence. The *Living Church*, which is the official spokesman of the Episcopal Church, no longer looked upon him as an "erratic priest of Graymoor."

Now it was a different story. Father Paul and *The Lamp* could not be ignored; so, month after month, the *Living Church* took issue with him. The correspondence carried on by the editors of both magazines appeared in their respective publications. While neither editor was influenced by the correspondence their readers certainly were. Father Paul's arguments for Reunion with the See of Peter became the platform of the pro-Roman group within the Episcopal Church.

The storm of criticism aroused against Graymoor as it became more aggressively pro-Roman, and the pressure brought to bear against Bishop Coleman by certain ecclesiastical opponents of Father Paul, among whom was Doctor Van Allan, caused the Bishop of Delaware not only to resign his position as Visitor, but also to institute proceedings to depose Father Paul as a heretic. The little band who had planted "their feet firmly on the Rock of Peter" now felt the real fury and violence of the storm.

The *New York Herald*, on April 20, 1903, carried a half-page article on Father Paul under the startling headline:

COURTS MARTYRDOM TO HELP
REUNITE THE
ANGLICAN CHURCH WITH ROME

The subtitles were:

Father Paul, Episcopal Monk, to be Tried
for Declaring Reformation a Mistake

Leo XIII Is Supreme

Insists that Rome Will Extend to English
Church Privileges Given Eastern Rites

The article read in part:

In his mountain halidom . . . Father Paul James Francis . . . waits for the head of the Protestant Episcopal Church of the diocese of Delaware, the Right Reverend Leighton Coleman, to cite him to trial. To the charge which will be made against him he pleads guilty in advance, for he will be accused of teaching that the English Reformation was a mistake and that the Anglican Church should ask to be taken back into the Roman Catholic fold. . . . "This is the Corpus Christi Cross," said he, "and here Bishop Coleman and I stood three years ago. Yonder was the tabernacle and within it was the altar where I knelt. . . . Here to this quiet spot I came as a witness to a great truth and I am ready for anything—for trial, for martyrdom if need be. Ostracized by the clergy, insulted by many and often reviled, I believe that some day, perhaps not in mine, all the Christian Churches will be united under the guidance of the Bishop of Rome."

Father Paul consulted a Canonist of the Episcopal Church and then wrote Bishop Coleman a letter. He informed the Bishop that he would stand trial for heresy. He further chided the Bishop that this would be a new kind of heresy trial, in which the accused would be charged not with the denial or corruption of any article of faith of the Anglican Church, but only with believing more than was strictly required by the Anglican formularies, namely; the Immaculate Conception of the Blessed Virgin Mary and the Infallibility of the Pope. The force of this argument seemed to have impressed

Bishop Coleman. The trial for heresy never took place, but the threat of deposition remained as Father Paul boldly continued to preach and write on Anglican submission to the Holy See.

The penalty of deposition, which Father Paul expected every day and which was never imposed on him, actually came to one of the first contributors to *The Lamp*. But Almighty God Who can bring good out of evil rewarded the one who suffered unjustly by allowing him to see a great blessing come to mankind because of his suffering. That blessing was the establishment of a Catholic Univerity in Tokio, Japan, through the personal invitation of the Emperor. The story is a most fascinating one.

When *Rose Leaves* was published by Graymoor in 1901, Mother Lurana sent a copy of the tiny periodical to the Reverend Arthur Lloyd in Tokio. This clergyman was then president of St. Paul's College, and second in authority to the Bishop in the Anglican missionary jurisdiction of Tokio. The small magazine with its pink cover fascinated the scholarly missionary, and he wrote to Mother Lurana thanking her for sending it. This letter led to further correspondence with Mother Lurana and Father Paul, and soon the Reverend Arthur Lloyd became a convinced advocate of *Corporate Reunion*.

Professor Lloyd was an Englishman by birth and a graduate of Cambridge University. In Japan he was serving under the American Mission Board. When he became President of St. Paul's College its enrollment was small. During his tenure of office he increased the enrollment five times the number it was when he took office. It then attained a rank of importance quite above any other educational institution of the American Episcopal Church in the Foreign Field.

In the second issue of *The Lamp* Professor Lloyd made his debut with an article entitled: "How It Looks to a Missionary." In that article he not only declared his belief in the Primacy of the Holy See as "the consistent witness to the Unity of Christ's Church," but he also made the statement: "I have taken to the periodical payment of Peter's Pence, as an outward and visible sign of the desire of my heart."

When the Episcopal authorities at the "Church Missions House" in New York read the article of Professor Lloyd in *The Lamp*, they immediately cabled to Tokio ordering the resignation of the offending clergyman. Later, when the Emperor of Japan learned of the resignation of Professor Lloyd, he invited him to become one of the professors of the Imperial University. The Imperial Family also comissioned him to translate their poems into English. These were published in 1905 as "Imperial Songs." Professor Lloyd became President of the Asiatic Society and remained at the Imperial University until his death.

On the occasion of sending his periodical offering of Peter's Pence to Pope Pius X, at the close of the Russo-Japanese War, Professor Lloyd suggested that the Supreme Pontiff write a letter to the Emperor of Japan, thanking him for the considerate treatment which the Catholic soldiers had received from the Emperor during the course of the war.

Pope Pius X, in his humility and zeal for souls, accepted the suggestion and commissioned Bishop William O'Connell (later Cardinal and Archbishop of Boston) to deliver the letter to the Emperor. Bishop O'Connell was graciously received by the Emperor, and the direct result of the embassy was the establishment of a Catholic university in Tokio. And so the existence of this university, which is destined, God willing, to bring many of the Japanese people into the True Fold, can be directly traced to Graymoor's first publication, Rose Leaves.

When Professor Lloyd was forced to resign the presidency of St. Paul's College, he suffered a nervous breakdown which was brought on by the persecution he suffered for defending the Holy See. During that illness, his distraught wife sent a letter to Mother Lurana saying: "Send to my husband no more of those little pink tracts." But the Reverend Arthur Lloyd endured his suffering, and in doing so he made the world a better place to live in.

The Rose Leaves from Our Lady's Garden at Graymoor, which Father Paul and Mother Lurana scattered in the Kingdom of the Rising Sun, by their fragrant messages of love brought into being a great university. The Lamp, which is the successor to Rose Leaves, outshone its predecessor in an almost endless chain of similar glorious accomplishments.

Chapter XII

RADICALS OPEN THE PULPITS

THE *Corporate Reunion Principle* in which Father Paul so firmly believed, and for which he so ardently prayed and worked, received a death blow in the year 1907. Up to that time he sincerely believed that Anglicanism was part of the Catholic Church, and that it could be corporately reunited with Rome; but what happened in 1907 convinced him that the *Corporate Reunion* of Anglicanism with Rome was hopeless.

In October of that year the General Convention of the Episcopal Church which met in Richmond, Virginia, passed an amendment to Canon XIX of their code of law. Before this amendment was passed the Canon read:

No Minister in charge of any congregation of this Church; or in case of vacancy or absence, no Churchwarden, Vestryman or Trustees of the Congregation, shall permit any person to officiate therein, without sufficient evidence of his being duly licensed or ordained to minister in this Church; provided, that nothing herein shall be construed as to forbid communicants of the Church to act as Lay Readers.

The convention at Richmond amended this Canon so that the pulpits of the Episcopal Churches were opened to any minister of another sect who might be invited to preach, with the permission of either the rector or the bishop. This action officially introduced Modernism into the Episcopal Church.

The heresy known as Modernism first appeared in the beginning of the twentieth century. "Its foundation is an agnosticism—the teaching that God can in no way be the object of certain knowledge; and in Immanence—the teaching that the foundation of faith must be sought in an internal sense which arises from man's need of God. From these principles, allied with various evolutionary doctrines, Modernism sets out to demolish dogmas (which it calls variable symbols), sacraments (which it reduces to faith-nourishing signs), the authenticity and genuineness of the Scriptures, the Church, and ecclesiastical authority and discipline. It reduces Christ to human dimensions, and makes inspiration a common gift of mankind.[1]

Modernism was first noticed among the younger Catholic clergy of Italy. It was denounced by several Bishops in the years 1905 and 1906; and it was formally condemned by the decree of the Holy Office, "Lamentabili," in July, 1907; and by the papal encyclical, "Pascendi," in September of the same year.

In the encyclical, "Pascendi," Pius X describes Modernism as the synthesis of all heresies; a collection of heresies destructive not only of Catholicism, but of all supernatural religion and even of Theism. It implies an independence of dogma and of authority quite irreconcilable with fundamental Catholic principles. If accepted it would destroy Catholic teaching in every department—Philosophy, Theology, Scripture and the History of Religion.

Most of the persons affected by the condemnation within the Church (many of them of blameless life) submitted to the authority of the Church; but others refused to conform, among whom were the outstanding scholars: Loisy in France, Tyrell in England, Minocchi and Murri in Italy.

Fundamentally the aims of the "Open Pulpit" movement and Modernism were the same. With the passing of the amendment of Canon XIX, men who rejected whole sections of the Bible, and others who even denied the Divinity of Christ, now had access to the pulpits of the Episcopal Church. All that was needed was an invitation to preach, from a rector of a church or the bishop of a diocese.

The results were havoc and confusion among the ranks of sincere Episcopal clergymen who viewed the new legislation as the betrayal of a trust and a deathblow to their church. The majority of the High Church party deplored it; but for the Broad Church, as well as the Low Church party, which had allied itself to the supporters of the movement, it was a major victory.

---

[1] A *Catholic Dictionary*: General Editor, Donald Attwater, The Macmillan Company, New York, 1941, page 347.

The groups mentioned above are what constitute Anglicanism to-day. The High Church party believes almost the whole of Catholic doctrine; the adherents of the High Church carry out all the rites and ceremonies as they are found in the Catholic Church. The Low Church party rests its position on the Bible and does not stress rites and ceremonies. With the Broad Church party almost anything is tolerated, for there is no rule of faith. Then there are the "Prayer Book Anglicans," who follow, in varying degrees and interpretations, the official formulas of the different Books of Common Prayer. Anglicans are better known as Episcopalians in the United States.

The Pope's condemnation of Modernism was the signal for the liberals in the Episcopal Church to renew their efforts to purge Episcopalianism of the Catholic dogmas and practices which had been revived by the men at Oxford; and to reassert its essentially Protestant character. They denounced Pius X as reactionary, and called upon Protestants and "liberal" Catholics to unite against papal aggression and domination. The Broad Church party took the lead in this movement, and succeeded in enlisting the support of most of the Low Church party, whose anti-Catholic prejudices were too strong for them to resist the invitation to join forces. Many of the clergy who belonged to the High Church party were undecided and their ranks eventually split.

The initiative taken by the Broad Church party assured them a dominant role in the work of preparing the program for the General Convention of 1907. In the months preceding the meeting the ground was made ready for the introduction of certain measures which, if passed, would serve to emphasize the liberal character of the Episcopal Church. Among these was included the amendment to Canon XIX, which has become known in the history of the Episcopal Church as the Open Pulpit canon.

When the General Convention opened in October all attention was focused on Richmond, for everyone realized the importance of the deliberations. From the opening sessions, the news coming from the Convention was most disconcerting. Everyone could easily understand from the news that the Broad Church party was in power. The first unwelcome news was the defeat of the proposal to deny the recognition of divorce in the Episcopal Church. This news increased the apprehension of those who were concerned about the passage of the amendment to Canon XIX.

When word did come that the Broad Church party had been just as successful in obtaining the approval of the General Convention on this proposal as in all of their other liberal measures, sincere Churchmen of the Episcopal Church were stunned. They could hardly believe that their representatives had betrayed the high trust placed in them by falling in line with the program of the Broad Church party. But the truth that the Amendment to Canon XIX was passed by a huge majority could not be denied. When it was submitted to the House of Bishops, that body gave its approval almost unanimously, after making a few unimportant changes in the original proposal. However, the real shock came when it was learned that even the High Church bishops, clergymen and laymen had supported the measure. The truth is that had it not been for them the Broad Church party would have had a difficult time winning their point, and the amendment might never have received the required vote. But, as it turned out, the High Church party had, all unwittingly, betrayed the very cause for which it stood.

The repercussions were strongest among the Anglo-Catholic element in the Episcopal Church. This group bitterly deplored the action taken by the General Convention, and even denounced it as the first step to apostasy. Nashotah Seminary, in Wisconsin, and St. Elizabeth's Church, in Philadelphia, were especially violent in their reaction. From these two places there began a steady stream of conversions to the Catholic Church almost immediately after the opening of Episcopalian pulpits to clergymen of other Protestant denominations. The "Open Pulpit" legislation was the occasion—but not the cause, as some critics have tried to insist—for this exodus. By the end of 1908, no fewer than twenty ministers, and hundreds of lay people who were influenced by their example, had been received into the Catholic Church. At their head was William McGarvey, the Rector of St. Elizabeth's Church in Philadelphia. He was the leader in the "secession" from the Episcopal Church; and to him must be given the credit for much of its success. Mother Edith, who for twenty-five years had been the Superior of the Episcopalian sisterhood of St. Mary at Peekskill, New York, was under McGarvey's spiritual direction. She also embraced the Catholic faith in 1908, and then entered Mother Drexel's community of the Sisters of the Blessed Sacrament.

Before he entered the Catholic Church, McGarvey was the Superior of a religious community known as the Companions of the Holy Savior. This Society was formed on June 15, 1891, when seven young men met in the rectory of the Church of the Evangelists. Its real purpose, although it was not generally known, was to promote the ideal of celibacy among the Episcopal clergy. A simple rule of life was agreed upon, and at the first election, which was held on September 18, 1891, William McGarvey was chosen for the office of Superior. At first there was no thought of an organized religious order, but in the course of time the Companions of the Holy Savior came to be recognized as such.

It was through this medium that William McGarvey exercised his greatest influence. At one time more than fifty ministers were enrolled in the Society either as actual members or as associate members. Many of the Companions lived in community at St. Elizabeth's Church, under the immediate direction of McGarvey. Others were scattered throughout the country. A strong group existed at Nashotah Seminary, which was composed of both professors and students. By means of letters and by occasional personal visits, McGarvey was able to maintain a close contact with all who were interested in the purpose of the Companions of the Holy Savior. His influence increased as the years went on, and many looked to him for direction. It was not surprising then that so many turned to him after they recovered from the shock of what had happened at the General Convention in Richmond.

No one was left in doubt very long as to what course of action McGarvey would take. The news had stunned him but it did not paralyze his brilliant mind.

The effect of the "Open Pulpit" movement at Nashotah was much the same. One of the professors, Edward Hawks, came east to see McGarvey. He explained the difficulties which the Open Pulpit legislation had created for him and James H. Bourne and Sigourney Fay; all of them on the faculty of Nashotah. McGarvey counseled them to wait a few months before taking any definite step, and to do, in the meantime, what he and the Companions were doing—pray fervently.

The period of indecision came to an end on February 20, 1908, when Edward Hawks and James H. Bourne were received into the Catholic Church. In Philadelphia, the Companions acted as a body. On May 3, 1908, William McGarvey wrote his resignation as rector of St. Elizabeth's to his ecclesiastical superior, Bishop O. W. Whitaker. A few days later he wrote a letter to Archbishop Ryan of Philadelphia, asking for an interview. The result of that meeting was that on May 27, 1908, the Feast of the Ascension, seven of the Companions were received into the Catholic Church. Six of the seven— McGarvey, Cowl, Hayward, McClellen, Bowles, Gromoll, entered the Seminary and were later ordained Priests. And all were outstanding in their Priesthood, bringing honor and glory to the Catholic Church.

In the months that followed there were many other conversions to the Catholic Church. Not all were clergymen, nor were all famous personages. The aftermath of the "Open Pulpit" legislation in the Episcopal Church was the loss of much prestige, and, what was still more important, the loss of some of her best men.

Father Paul, on the Mount of the Atonement, was greatly disturbed by the results of the General Convention at Richmond. In a long editorial entitled "The Episcopal Commons," published in the February, 1908, edition of *The Lamp*, he expressed his mind on the matter. Though he did not realize it at the time, he was then definitely on the road to Rome. The editorial read, in part:

. . . Until very lately . . . Episcopalians, like Roman Catholics, held themselves aloof. Their Church, they said, was founded by Jesus Christ and not by Luther or Calvin or John Knox; and whereas they had a charitable feeling towards all who professed and called themselves Christians, they could not recognize the ministers of the Protestant Denominations, however successful in a popular way they might be. . . . In other words, the Protestant Episcopal Church in the United States was a "garden enclosed," "a vineyard with a hedge planted about it."

Since the General Convention at Richmond the claim of the Episcopal Church to Catholic exclusiveness has been cast to the winds and by the unanimous vote of the House of Bishops and the overwhelming majority of her clerical and lay deputies she has committed herself to a new policy. . . . A spurious Catholicity, called *Comprehensiveness*, has been adopted as a substitute for that genuine Catholicity which Newman, Pusey, Keble, Neale, Wordsworth and Forbes with a great multitude of godly teachers after them sought to introduce into the Anglican measure of meal until the whole was leavened. In the amendment of Canon 19 our own bishops have "broken down" the Church's hedge and "all they that go by (may now) pluck off her grapes." And we shall presently see the fatal havoc which must follow, when "the wild boar out of the wood doth root it up; and the wild beasts of the field devour it."

Out of the mouth of our own bishops we must henceforth judge the Episcopal Church and alas a chorus of them are shouting from the very housetops that the glory of Anglicanism is not its unflinching fidelity to Catholic faith and practice but its universal toleration and its all inclusive comprehensiveness. . . .

A fountain that is poisoned at its source cannot but bring forth poisoned waters and that our Episcopate is certainly tinctured with the deadly poison of this bogus catholicity, commonly called Anglican Comprehensiveness, grows increasingly apparent from month to month. Something like a mania to decatholicise the Episcopal Church in the interests of Protestant Christianity seems to have gotten possession of the Anglican Episcopate the world over.

This was a long editorial. In reading it one can see that Father Paul was disillusioned by what had happened at Richmond. He knew now that the *Corporate Reunion Principle* was impossible of fulfillment, yet he did not admit it even then. But the fulness of the light had not yet come. He was still almost two years away from the Portals of the Holy See.

In the editorial he took issue with the *Church Standard* and the *Churchman* which week after week were bringing "a painful revelation of the state of the Episcopal Church" to their readers by advocating "Protestant Federation." But what disappointed him more was "the way the *Living Church*," was, "proving itself a broken reed to those who would lean on it for support."

The *Living Church* was editorially supporting the "New Catholicism" which Dr. Newman Smyth, a prominent Congregational minister, declared to be impending, by stating:

There is coming and to come a new Catholicism for our Protestant faith. The signs of its presence are such as these: One is the growth of a common Christian conscience. For us now no one church, no single church in existence, is big enough to hold a big Christian man.

Father Paul, answering Dr. Smyth in the editorial, wrote:

If not one of the Churches already in existence is big enough, not even the Holy Roman Church, to contain one of "the big Christian men," who are going to embrace it then? May the good Lord deliver us Lilliputians from their company lest we be crushed by their huge bulk.

Concluding the editorial, Father Paul wrote:

Rude as the awakening has been, it has come none too soon. If the Anglican Communion is not the Catholic Church, and is not even a vineyard securely hedged about, or a garden enclosed, then it is in plain English an Episcopal Commons, where the wild boar out of the wood and the wolves of heresy are to be allowed to roam at will and the Lord's sheep can look for no adequate protection from the shepherds, who claim to derive from God their authority to rule over and feed them and lead them in the way everlasting. . . . They may yet repair the broken hedge. But will they? Otherwise how shall they keep their sheep?

Father Paul's answer to the Richmond Convention was the formation in February, 1908, of the *Anglo-Roman Union*. The membership was composed of Episcopal clergymen and laymen who had denounced the "Open Pulpit" Canon. The most outstanding of these men was the Very Reverend F. E. Aitkins, Dean of the Episcopal Cathedral at Michigan City, Indiana.

On the night of February 10, 1908, this group, headed by Father Paul, met quietly for dinner in New York. It was the desire of the organizers to avoid all publicity until the Union had acquired sufficient strength to withstand the opposition it was bound to provoke. However, the *New York Sun* was notified by someone of what the dinner was about, with the result that, just as the meeting, which took place after the dinner, was closing, several newspaper reporters arrived. The following day the New York newspapers carried an account of the meeting, naming the men who had been elected and also the principles of the *Anglo-Roman Union.*

Though Father Paul never mentioned in *The Lamp* the names of those who attended that meeting, the secular newspapers did not hesitate to do so. On February 23, 1908, the *New York Herald* carried a half-page article on Father Paul and the Anglo-Roman Union. The headlines read.:

*Pro-Roman Episcopalians Unite to Hail
the Pope as Primate*

One of the sub-titles read:

Remarkable Movement led by Father Paul to unite Anglicans and Catholics is gaining ground in the United States and is now in full swing

The article read, in part:

Organization in this city . . . of the Anglo-Roman Union composed of Protestant Episcopal clergymen and laymen who seek reunion with the Roman Catholic Church by recognizing the primacy of the Pope, draws attention to a remarkable situation. . . . Its development . . . is largely due to the indefatigable work of Father Paul James Francis, a clergyman of the Protestant Episcopal Church, who since 1901 has devoted himself to the realization of the ideal of unity for which he has worked more or less since boyhood.

He lives in a weather-beaten friary on the top of a mountain near Garrison, N. Y., from which he issues a magazine devoted to the propaganda and sends literature throughout the country. Occasionally, sandaled and tonsured and wearing the habit of a Franciscan monk, he goes forth into the world preaching of his hope of unity and then returns to his mountain retreat, there to pray and to work for the dawn of the day of a reunited Christendom.

A dreamer of dreams some call him, and churchmen who believe in the immutability of all things religious speak of him with a smile, yet this Episcopal-Franciscan has sent forth an influence which has a far-reaching effect. Evidences of a trend toward his teachings are said to have appeared in half the Episcopal dioceses of the United States. The work has been carried on without display, and even now "Father Paul," as he is usually called, deplores the publicity which his plans have gained.

The newspaper then gave the array of prominent names who were elected officers at the meeting:

. . . The President of the Union is W. M. Cammack, a financier of Philadelphia; its vice-presidents, the Rev. Dr. Theodore M. Riley, rector of Christ Church, Hudson, N. Y., and formerly a professor in the General Theological Seminary, and W. A. Buchanan of Philadelphia. On the council are Father C. P. Burnett and the Rev. Father B. J. Fitz, of this city, and the Very Rev. F. E. Aitkins, of Michigan City, Ind., for the clergy, while the lay members of the council are George Hazelhurst of Philadelphia; Dr. H. M. King of Liberty, N. Y., and E. L. Prior of Jersey City. The secretary of the Union is the Rev. Father Augustine Elmendorf, rector of Holy Cross Church, Jersey City, and the treasurer, J. W. Barney of the same church.

The *Anglo-Roman Union* ceased to function shortly after the Society of the Atonement entered the Catholic Church. Some of its members followed Father Paul into the Catholic Church; among whom were Carlton Strong, a prominent Pittsburgh architect, Ernest L. Prior of the Wall Street firm of Frame & Company, and John W. Barney of the *Wall Street Journal*.

On February 10, 1916, Father Paul wrote to a friend:

This is the 8th anniversary of the formation of the Anglo-Roman Union . . . in New York and I am celebrating it by writing you this letter. I rejoice at the many signs which go to show that although the Anglo-Roman Union itself, like John Brown's bones "lie mouldering in the grave" the cause of Reunion goes marching on.

The author has incorporated this chapter on the "Open Pulpit" movement into this volume for the purpose of showing the disunity of Anglicanism, and further to prove the impossiblity of *Corporate Reunion* of the Episcopal Communion with the Holy See. A Catholic who today would hold to the principle of *Corporate Reunion*, in view of the Apostolic letter of Leo XIII on Anglican Orders, would be treading on dangerous ground.

The Society of the Atonement prays many times each day the prayer of Christ: "That they all may be one; as Thou, Father, in Me and I in Thee." In that prayer Anglicans are included; but as obedient children of our holy Mother—the Church—we pray not for *Corporate Reunion,* since that is not possible; but rather for "an abundance of rain"—of which Father Paul wrote—a great multitude of individual conversions. For it is our prayerful desire to see England "merry" and glorious again. A nation is only as great as its people. The greatness and the glory that was England were men like Edward the Confessor, Anselm, Thomas à Becket, Thomas More and John Fisher.

Father Paul, after receiving the grace of the Catholic Faith, extended an invitation to all who sought "A medium of entrance into Peter's Ship" to come to Graymoor, "now or hereafter." The Graymoor Friars know what the "stumbling blocks" are to some conversions. The breaking of lifelong ties of friendship, and the economic insecurity of the future, especially for married clergymen, seemingly are the greatest. But only *The One Friend* is really necessary. And as for the fear of economic insecurity, Christ says: "But if God so clothes the grass of the field, which today is alive and tomorrow is thrown into the oven; how much more you, O you of little faith!"

The Founder of the Society of the Atonement never permitted gates to be erected around the Graymoor Monastery, fearing that some soul, seeking the aid of the Friars, might, at some time, find the gates locked. So it is today—a monastery without barricades— open to all the world who would seek its peace; and so it shall ever be. Father Paul is no longer here to greet those who come, but his spiritual sons are here; and everything is still the same, for his spirit is the Spirit of Graymoor: and Graymoor is Father Paul.

Chapter XIII

THE CHURCH UNITY OCTAVE

WE NOW COME to that period in Father Paul's life in which his ideas for the reunion of Christendom crystallized in a world-wide movement of prayer. In that period his fondest hopes were realized far beyond anything that he, himself, had imagined. Through this prayer movement he became known in all parts of the world, even to the sacred confines of the Vatican itself. The amazing part of this chapter of his life is that he accomplished it alone by co-operating with God's Grace. Through the mediums of his gifted and prolific pen and *The Lamp* magazine, he spread the Graymoor fire upon the earth, inspiring people everywhere, Catholic and non-Catholic, to pray for a miracle of Grace—the reunion of Christendom.

About the turn of the century Father Paul began a correspondence with an English clergyman by the name of Spencer Jones. He was one of the leaders of the Reunion movement in England, and had published a book entitled *England and the Holy See*, the preface of which was written by the late Lord Halifax.[1] In his book the Reverend Mr. Spencer Jones defended the claim of the Holy See with a forceful argument, the logic of which no one dared challenge. He called upon Anglicans to accept every doctrine and practice of the Catholic Church, and quite bluntly declared that this was the only reasonable course to follow because the Catholic Church alone was the living expression of the full Christian tradition. It was a masterly defence of the Primacy of the Holy See; but, unfortunately, it discouraged individual conversions by calling upon Anglicans to work for *Corporate Reunion*.

Father Paul popularized the thesis of this book through the pages of *The Lamp*. He wrote an editorial review on the "Introduction" to

---

[1] Father of the present Lord Halifax, who was at one time Ambassador from the Court of St. James's to the United States.

England and the Holy See, by Lord Halifax, in the first issue of
The Lamp, which read:

Perhaps the most practical and sensible book on Church Unity which
any Anglican Divine has written since the great 16th century Schism, is
the Rev. Spencer Jones' Essay towards Reunion—*England and the Holy
See.* . . . No less notable than the book itself is the introduction by
Lord Halifax. It shows a marvelous change of temper on the part of
English Churchmen towards the Bishop of Rome that such a book should
be tolerated.

The correspondence Father Paul began with the Reverend Mr.
Spencer Jones developed into a lifelong friendship between the two
men. Their mutal efforts in promoting the cause of Unity won many
new adherents for the movement both here and in England. In
1907 they further collaborated in writing a book which they published under the title of *The Prince of the Apostles.*

It was a small volume but it created quite a sensation in the
English-speaking world. The conservative Anglicans were astounded
at its effrontery, and some of the pro-Roman Anglicans realized for
the first time how very Catholic-minded some of their confreres had
become. The thesis propounded was so orthodox and faithful to
Catholic teaching on the subject that it might have been taken, word
for word, from a Catholic Textbook on theology. The Reverend
Vincent McNabb, a priest of the Dominican Order, in his review
of the book in the *American Ecclesiastical Review* of March, 1908,
wrote:

The book under review is not professedly a work of pioneers. It is not
so much a discovery as a creed. The most significant fact is not what is
said, but *who* have said it. We set even more store by the authors than
by the scholarship. And, if we may be allowed the phrase, we find the
title-page the weightiest page of the book. From the first to last there is
hardly a phrase to jar the ears of the most convinced Roman Catholic.
Most of the matter is familiar to Catholic students who have made the
acquaintance of the treatise *De Ecclesia.* Some of the matter is unfamiliar; yet fresh and apt. But all the doctrine, whether familiar or unfamiliar, has the ring of true Catholic dogma. And the book is published
not by a professor of Oscott or Stonyhurst, but by an Anglican vicar in
the Cotswolds and the head of an Anglican brotherhood in the United
States.

The Prince of the Apostles was published by The Lamp Publishing Company. Although the authors were named on the title page as the Reverend Paul James Francis and the Reverend Spencer Jones, Mother Lurana was in reality the inspirational spirit behind the book. She proposed that a series of articles treating of St. Peter and the Holy See, which had appeared in *The Lamp*, be re-edited jointly by Father Paul and Spencer Jones, and published in book form. The first chapter, entitled "The Open Mind" was largely written by her. She also had much to do with the arrangement of the chapters.

The chief purpose of the book was to emphasize the divine-right character of the primacy of the Holy See. The greater part of the book, as was noted by Spencer Jones in the "Preface," was written by Father Paul. Only five of the chapters were written by Spencer Jones. The dedicatory words read:

> To the honour of the illustrious
> Archbishops
> St. Anselm and St. Thomas of Canterbury
> We dedicate this volume
> in
> Thanksgiving for their Example
> And in the
> Hope of their Intercession

In the book Spencer Jones argued:

Let this be carefully weighed, the Church of England today claims continuity with the Church of England before the Reformation; and the Church of England before the Reformation was in conscious dependence in spirituals upon Rome from A.D. 597 to A.D. 1534. And if this was so then why should it not become so now? If it was not wrong to contemplate the change *away* from Rome, why should it be wrong to contemplate the change *toward* it? You may say "It is impossible." But that is a question of fact and not of principle. And you cannot say it is dishonest, though you may think it vain to contemplate it.

The man who wrote these words died in the Anglican Church many years later.

It is interesting, if not amazing, to see the tremendous effect

Father Paul's writing and preaching had upon the clergy and laity of the Episcopal Church. This effect can best be gauged by the *Living Church*. In 1901, the editor had assured its readers that the Reunion Movement was confined to one "erratic priest"—Father Paul. Two years later the *Living Church* assured its readers that the Reunion Movement amounted to only a "triumvirate"—Father Paul, the Reverend Spencer Jones and the Reverend Arthur Lloyd in Japan. But in the October 26, 1907, issue, in a four-column editorial on *The Prince of the Apostles* and *The Lamp*, the *Living Church* stated:

> There are not wanting indications that the pendulum can no longer be held at the extreme anti-Roman end. When men differing from each other as radically as Lord Halifax and Dr. Briggs are agreed in saying that the common view of Rome is at least an unbalanced one, it is hopeless to attempt to hold the pendulum back from swinging. . . . It is not strange that there should have arisen an avowed pro-Roman party in the Anglican Communion . . . it is the party now in advance of the pendulum in its inexorable backward swing. It is going to swing; the only question for us to determine is: How far?

In further comment on the authors of *The Prince of the Apostles*, the editor of the *Living Church* stated:

> In the first place it is the veriest nonsense to reply by charging disloyalty against these writers. . . . We hasten to add that we have a large sympathy with these dreamers of iridescent dreams and a mirage does represent a far distant reality. The dreamers are the prophets of better times to come when men of other generations shall be able to realize what these could only dream of.

Father Paul was now someone to be reckoned with. He and his pro-Roman movement could no longer be branded as "erratic." Too many brilliant men of the Episcopal Church were influenced by him to warrant such an appellation. The world-wide mission of *The Lamp* was illustrated by the fact that its contributors included Dr. Spencer Jones of England and Dr. Arthur Lloyd of Japan.

In a letter which Father Paul received from Spencer Jones in 1907, he suggested that one day each year be set aside as a day of special prayer for Christian Unity and public sermons on the Pope.

He proposed St. Peter's Feast Day, June 29th, as an appropriate day for this purpose.

The idea appealed to Father Paul, and from this "seed-thought," as he called it, he conceived the idea of the *Church Unity Octave*. To Father Paul one day of prayer was not enough. The Reunion of Christendom to the Holy See was a tremendous work, therefore his plan was for an octave, eight full days of prayer. He chose the time between the Feast of St. Peter's Chair at Rome (January 18th) and the Feast of the Conversion of St. Paul (January 25th). The official prayers to be used during the Octave were drawn up in the liturgical form in which commemorations are made in the Divine Office. They consisted of an antiphon, a responsory, and an oration. The former he took from Sacred Scripture; and the oration he chose is the prayer found in the Canon of the Mass immediately preceding the Communion. It is the Catholic Church's own daily prayer for the preservation of her divinely given peace and unity. The Octave's prayers are:

Antiphon   That they all may be One, as Thou,
Father, in me and I in Thee; that
they also may be one in Us; that
the world may believe that Thou
hast sent me.
V. I say unto thee thou art Peter.
R. And upon this rock I will build My Church.

Prayer

O Lord Jesus Christ, who saidst unto
Thine Apostles: Peace I leave with
you, My peace I give unto you; regard
not our sins, but the faith of Thy
Church, and grant unto her that peace
and unity which are agreeable to Thy
Will. Who livest and reignest God forever and ever, world without end. *Amen.*

Once the idea of the Octave was clear in his mind, Father Paul worked to spread knowledge of it during the latter part of 1907. *The Lamp* carried the announcement that the first observance of the Octave would take place in January, 1908. He contacted many

Anglican clergymen and also some Catholic priests and prelates. From England and the United States came letters of congratulation from Anglicans who were pleased with this new effort for Reunion. The same enthusiastic response came from a number of outstanding Catholic prelates and clergymen. The late Archbishop of Boston, William Cardinal O'Connell, gave it his whole-hearted approval. He supported the Octave even in the days when it was still under Anglican auspices, and continued to do so until his death. In his first letter to Father Paul he wrote:

I have received your note of January the 6th, and you may rest assured that I, myself, and my clergy and people, will join their prayers with yours for the holy purpose outlined in your note.

The same approving comments appeared in the editorials of prominent Catholic magazines; one of these, the *New York Freeman's Journal*, observed:

The Lamp carries on an earnest, intelligent and laudable crusade for unity with the Church of St. Peter, which must be productive of great grace and great success in the direction aimed at, even though not wholly in the way the promoters hope for. A re-united Christendom is a good and great intention for the suffrages of the faithful. . . . As Catholics we may join—during these eight days as well as every day— with the Holy Father, whose constant prayer is that the day may hasten when there shall be but "one fold and one shepherd."

Another, the *Ave Maria*, enthusiastically urged its readers to participate in the *Church Unity Octave* and concluded with the statement:

We hope that all Catholics who sympathize with the Anglican heirs of Newman—what true Catholic does not?—will offer fervent prayers that the movement inagurated by "Father Paul" may be abundantly blessed.

The heart of Father Paul was filled with joy at these favorable reactions. They more than recompensed him for all the trials and difficulties he had endured since he began the crusade for Reunion. The favorable reception of the Octave was an incentive for him to redouble his efforts in the cause of Unity. His great desire now was to make each succeeding Octave more widely and more fervently observed. Hardly had the echoes of the success of the first observance of the Octave died out than he was already engaged in long-range planning for the 1909 observance.

The founding of the *Church Unity Octave* was almost his last work in behalf of Reunion as an Anglican clergyman. Not long after the close of the observance in 1909, he began negotiations with Catholic authorities which led to the submission of the Society of the Atonement to the Holy See in October of that year. It seems almost providential that he instituted this movement of prayer so close to the end of his career as an Episcopal minister. For, after his entrance into the Catholic Church, the Octave remained the sole link which bridged the two periods of his life. Through it Father Paul was able to maintain an effective contact with those in the Anglican Communion who continued to work and pray for Reunion. In the realm of prayer he could still remain one of them in the great objective toward which they mutually aimed.

However, with the inauguration of the Octave, the scope of his work for Reunion broadened. The intentions of the Octave prove this. They are:

January 18th (The Feast of St. Peter's Chair at Rome)—The return of the "other sheep" to the One Fold of Christ.

January 19th—The return of Oriental Separatists to Communion with the Apostolic See.

January 20th—The submission of Anglicans to the Authority of the Vicar of Christ.

January 21st—That the Lutherans and other Protestants of Continental Europe may find their way back to Holy Church.

January 22nd—That Christians in America may become One in Union with the Chair of St. Peter.

January 23rd—Return to the Sacraments of lapsed Catholics.

January 24th—The Conversion of the Jews.

January 25th (Feast of the Conversion of St. Paul)—The Missionary conquest of the World for Christ.

Father Paul's work for Reunion now included every soul not in communion with the Apostolic See. The Octave became universal "when," as he so often expressed it, "the Society of the Atonement was linked to the Dynamo of Rome." How the Octave became universally observed, and the results of its observance will be told in a later chapter.

However, there are two objections to the Octave that have, more than once, been hurled at the Society of the Atonement, which must be answered here. The first objection was to Father Paul's being the Founder of the Octave. This came from Anglicans, as we might expect. The second objection was that since there already existed an Octave of Prayer for Unity in the Catholic Church there was no need for its being adopted by the Church when the Society of the Atonement became Catholic. This came from Catholics who should know better.

The author answers the first objection because it impugns the veracity of one he greatly loved—Father Paul. He answers the second to make more known and to throw more light upon the wonderful life and work of Blessed Vincent Pallotti, Founder of the Pious Society of Missions, who was also the Founder of the Octave of the Epiphany at Rome: and also to show the difference between the two Octaves of prayer.

After Father Paul entered the Catholic Church, each year literature was sent from Graymoor to England. The Anglicans, in return, kept Father Paul informed of their efforts for Reunion, and sent samples of the literature they were distributing. In January, 1928, he received literature from the Catholic League, an Anglican group, which prompted him to write the following letters, copies of which are in the Graymoor archives.

January 25, 1928

Reverend C. R. Beresford, Hon. Secy.
24 Lime Grove
London, W.12, England

REVEREND DEAR DOCTOR BERESFORD:
I have read with much interest your Church Unity Octave literature lately received. I am glad to know that it is so widely observed among you.

Permit me, however, to call your attention to a misstatement of the first page of the folder, doubtless arising from lack of knowledge of the facts. It is stated, "It owes its origin to an Anglican priest, Father Spencer Jones, was promoted in America by the Friars of the Atonement since 1908, and has now spread throughout the world."

The facts are these: in 1907 Reverend Spencer Jones wrote me a letter in which he made the excellent suggestion that a sermon on the Petrine Claims be preached in Anglican churches on the Feast of St. Peter the Apostle, June 29th. After prayer and consideration, the thought of the Church Unity Octave came to me very strongly, and I wrote that I intended to begin a Church Unity Octave from the Feast of the Chair of St. Peter, January 18th to the Feast of the Conversion of St. Paul, January 25th, this to consist of eight days of prayer for the Reunion of Christendom. You will see, therefore, that the name, the object and the time originated here at Graymoor. Reverend Spencer Jones thought it an excellent idea and later on, I believe, was able to put it into operation in England, but from the beginning it was well taken up here and has developed until, as you know, it is now of practically universal observance.

I am sure, now that you know the facts, you will next year correct the statement above referred to.

Under separate cover I am sending you some of the latest of our Church Unity Octave literature. I am sure you will be interested to see how it has been extended.

With every good wish for you and the work of the Catholic League, believe me,

Very sincerely yours in Christ,

FR. PAUL, S.A.
Superior General

January 25, 1928

Reverend Spencer Jones
　Moreton-in-Marsh
　　England

MY DEAR FRIEND:

I am enclosing a copy of a letter which I have just sent to the Honorable Secretary of the Catholic League.

I am sure that you will assist me in this matter, for it is necessary during my life to have the origin of the Church Unity Octave clearly established.

Moreover, and I am sure this will appeal to you, this undue claim on the part of the Catholic League is really hampering the extension of the Church Unity Octave in some quarters. I do not need to say any more, for you will understand this.

With every good wish, believe me, as always,

Very fraternally and faithfully

yours in Christ,

FR. PAUL, S.A.

Superior General

The Reverend Spencer Jones, who was a perfect Christian gentleman, in reply sent the following letter, the original of which is also on file in the Graymoor archives. It is being published for the first time here with the hope that the controversy as to who founded the Octave will be now and forever closed.

The Rectory

Moreton-in-Marsh

England

February 6, 1928

DEAR FATHER:

Thank you for your letter. Of course the Church Unity Octave is your child and its marvelous development and success is due entirely to yourself under God. My recollection of my relations with you in the matter is as follows:

1. I wrote you in the first instance about twenty years ago, suggesting that St. Peter's Day should be observed as a day of special intercession and preaching in behalf of Church Unity.

2. In reply to me you said in substance, "Would not the Octave—St. Peter's Chair to St. Paul's Conversion, be better for this purpose?" I've no doubt that I said "Yes," though I cannot remember precisely what I did say. But certainly I do think it much better.

Thus a proposition that the special effort for reunion should be identified with St. Peter—indicating the "Roman" direction in which you and I already—quite independently of one another—pointed in 1900-1902, was broached by me. And you in reply, and in substance said, "Good, but I think I know something much better, viz. C.U.O."

No credit attaches to me for work on this side of the water even, for all the hard work of organizing the observance each year has been undertaken and carried out by our brethren in London, which is 91 miles distant from me. And this explains how the misunderstanding must have arisen, for the circular is drawn up by them and not by me, and I scarcely ever attend any of the committee meetings, owing to my distance from town. But it is careless on my part not to have corrected the form of the statement; nevertheless it is no fault of the present secretary, who has come on the scene only in quite recent years, and who no doubt has referred to former circulars and reproduced them in the main. I ought to have called his attention to it, but my not having done so has not been intentional of course. I have always been all these miles away when the committee was drawing up the circular, and no doubt if any reference at all be made in the future to *me* it will be made clear that C.U.O. is yours entirely in every aspect of it as such, and not mine in any wise.

With all kind wishes and with a deep appreciation of the really extraordinary work you have done in promoting an enterprise of your own inauguration, I am,

Sincerely yours in Christ,
Spencer Jones

In reply to the Reverend Spencer Jones' letter, Father Paul closed the question with the following letter:

February 27, 1928

Reverend Spencer Jones
  The Rectory
    Moreton-in-Marsh
      England

My dear Friend:

I am afraid that I gave you a great deal of trouble in my last letter *in re* the origin of the Church Unity Octave. As I am sure you know, personally I was not at all disturbed about the matter, but it seemed best during my lifetime to clear up any inaccuracy. Your letter has certainly done that for me. Thank you ever so much.

May I add that, of course it never occurred to me that you were in any way responsible for the mistake that had, through a combination of circumstances, erroneously circulated.

With every good wish, as always I am

Fraternally yours in Christ,
Fr. Paul, S.A.
Superior General

In the Graymoor library there is a mimeographed manuscript of the life of Blessed Vincent Pallotti, Apostle and Mystic, who was the Founder of the Pious Society of Missions. It is a translation by the Reverend Joseph De Maria, P.S.M., who is a spiritual son of Vincent Pallotti. Though Father De Maria does not state the fact, it is evidently translated from the German language, since the original author is Reverend Eugene Weber, another spiritual son of Blessed Vincent Pallotti. On page 122 of the mimeographed manuscript the origin of the Octave of the Epiphany at Rome is given:

Despite the many demands upon their charity the society (the "Catholic Apostolate") deemed it advisable to hold a celebration in the very first year, an event to occur yearly which would require considerable financial help from the friends of the Society, especially from the wealthy nobility. This event is none other than Pallotti's original and much admired celebration of the Epiphany. It is uncertain how this idea of the solemnization of the Epiphany originated with him. It is probable that he borrowed the idea from a practice then observed at the Propaganda College. It was a very old custom in this institution to keep a day during the Epiphany, making it the occasion of a many-language entertainment. A select audience, composed of local and foreign persons of distinction, would listen to speeches and verse delivered in some fifty different languages by as many representative students hailing from all parts of the earth. The thought which upheld this feast of tongues was the Universality of the Catholic Church illustrated in such a diversity of tongues into one common faith. From the same idea and also for reasons of prudence on the part of the Western Church, developed the custom to let the members of the Oriental Churches, otherwise feeling themselves excluded and slighted, celebrate the sacred mysteries in their own rites and in their proper liturgy on the Feast of the Epiphany.

These two elements which Pallotti found at the Propaganda were to be fused by him into a more intimate and magnificent union. The Venerable (now Blessed) may also have known of the private revelation which had been made to the Venerable Maria Maurizi which represented the Feast of the Three Kings, or Magi, celebrated in great pomp. But we know not whether this influenced his institution of the special solemnity and, if it did, to what extent. We can definitely claim that his mystic union with Christ had a great share in his devotion to the Feast of the Epiphany. The festive occasion of the Propaganda, more esthetic in nature, was now transferred into a more directly religious event.

His idea of a Universal Apostolate naturally broadened the meaning of the festivity so as to embrace both home and foreign missions. Pallotti's Catholic Apostolate ever laid stress upon the double function of missions and of the rekindling of faith and charity at home. The celebration was to symbolize in one church and during one week that which he desired ardently to take place in every church of the Catholic world for every week of the year.

His magnanimity transcended the bounds of time and space. Therefore the different nations so well represented in Rome were to be offered the opportunity of hearing the message of faith and charity announced in their own language. The Oriental rites as celebrated in the Propaganda were now to take on the lavish solemnity with which their native orientalism can invest them. When the great efforts for ecclesiastical unification and centralization during the past century be considered Pallotti's idea achieves a remarkable success insofar as it granted the Oriental rites such a unique opportunity to display the beauty of their liturgy.

It was also part of his plan thereby to give bolder relief to the Universality and Oneness of the Church. Whence it was his wish to have all classes of the secular and regular clergy in Rome, as well as the different national colleges, represented at the service during the Epiphany week. The solemnity was to be an assembly of the peoples of the earth.

This was possible in the eternal city. In a few years Pallotti's Epiphany feast has won a place among the popular religious celebrations of Rome, ushered in on the vigil with the noisy trumpeting of children who would parade in bevies blowing the Befana.

However flurishing Pallotti's Epiphany observance proved at Sant' Andrea della Valle (in Rome) it did not effect the results elsewhere which he aspired to. According to his design the Epiphany Octave was also to signalize a week given over to foreign missions and missions at home in the local churches. As often was the case with him, his ideal here likewise exceeded the powers of a mere mortal.

This Octave which is described above by Father De Maria was founded by Vincent Pallotti in the year 1836. It is observed each year at Rome in the beautiful Theatine Church of Saint Andrew of the Valley. The *Catholic Encyclopedia*, under "Pallotti," states:

It was Venerable (now Blessed) Pallotti who started in 1836 the special observance at Rome of the Octave of the Epiphany. Since then the celebration has been faithfully maintained. Pallotti's chief desire was to make this observance a means of uniting the dissenting Oriental Churches with Rome.

The Octave of the Epiphany, unlike the Octave Father Paul founded, is not universally observed. Moreover, it has as its *one* and *only aim* the Reunion of the Oriental Churches in schism. It is observed in Rome only, by the celebration of the different Oriental Rites in Communion with the Holy See, and by sermons during the

Octave of the Epiphany. However, the Pious Society of Missions observes the Octave by special prayers wherever its houses are established throughout the world.

Father Paul's Octave is more universally known and observed, and it embraces every soul outside the Catholic Church.

The extent of its influence is evidenced in the leading article of the international quarterly review, *Unitas* (October–December, 1950). *Unitas*, the official organ of the Unitas Association of Rome, is edited by Father Charles Boyer, S.J., Prefect of Studies and Dean of the Theological Faculty, Gregorian Pontifical University, Rome. *Unitas* writes:

> The Missionary Union of the Clergy, which has now become a vast organization, solidly established in more than fifty nations, and numbering over 340,000 priests among its members, held its third international congress at Rome in the Pontifical Gregorian University in the month of September (1950). One of the principle themes discussed was the problem of the return of all separated brethren to the one true Catholic Church.

The following resolution was formulated:

> *Opera multiplicentur ut Fratres separati redeant ad unicum ac veram Christi Ecclesiam, et ut oves quae perierunt de domo Israel ad fidem perducantur; in omnibus paroeciis celebretur Octavarium pro Unitate (a die 18 ad diem 25 mensis Januarii); insuper in Seminariis hebdomeda aut saltem dies pro Oriente Christiano.*
>
> (Let efforts be multiplied that our separated brothers return to the one and true Church of Christ, and that the sheep that are lost of the house of Israel be led back to the faith; let the Octave for Unity—from the 18th to the 25th of January—be celebrated in all parishes; moreover let a Week or at least a Day for the Christian Orient be celebrated in the Seminaries.)

The above resolution emphasizes the significance of the Octave as bearing upon the Church's missionary endeavor, and is in perfect accord with the intentions of Father Paul Wattson, S.A. who founded it. By virtue of his gigantic faith and tremendous vision, Fr. Paul saw in this Octave a vessel for the ultimate achievement of Christ's Kingdom.

Chapter XIV

PIUS X PRAYS FOR GRAYMOOR'S
CONVERSION

THERE ARE some Catholics and Protestants who, at one time or another, have said that Father Paul remained a Protestant at heart until he died. Perhaps what they saw in him was his great love for the
"Other Sheep," and to them that was "the Protestant" in him. This
strange statement has been made by some men who never had the
privilege of meeting Father Paul.

Not many years ago a Sister of the Atonement in Ireland called at
a parish rectory seeking alms for the poor. In giving her an offering the priest said, "Your founder was a great man but he remained
a Protestant at heart until he died." Inquiring further, the Sister
learned that the good Soggarth had never been to the United States,
nor had he ever met Father Paul elsewhere.

Today, quite logically, a Protestant is one who adheres to the beliefs of Protestantism; which is a generic term for those forms of
Christianity derived from the teachings of those who revolted from
the Catholic Church in the sixteenth century, and for any sect
deriving from them. However, the Anglican Communion, for the
most part, reject the designation as applying to them. Certainly Newman and the men of the Oxford Movement rejected any connection
with what they called the "Motley Protestantism" which, to them,
had disfigured the Church of England, and obscured her essential
Catholicity.

When the *New York Sun*, ten years before Father Paul entered the
Catholic Church, observed that he would in the not too distant future become a Catholic, he indignantly replied: "We were baptized
in the Holy Catholic Church over thirty years ago, and, please God,
we expect to continue a Catholic until we die." So even before he
became convinced of Catholic claims, he called himself a "Catholic."

And after he became convinced of the Primacy of the Holy See he was certainly Catholic in mind and heart. His writings in *The Lamp* and his actions while still an Anglican give proof of his Catholic mentality. After his conversion, his love for the Church, his devotion to the Holy Father, and his missionary zeal ranked him high among the greatest Catholics of his time.

Nothing, however, proves his Catholicity more than the custom he instituted at Graymoor in the year 1904, while the Community was still Anglican. One cent out of every dollar the Friars and Sisters received was sent to the Holy Father in the form of a Peter's Pence donation. In doing so, he was following the example of the Reverend Arthur Lloyd of Tokio. Even though the offerings sent to Graymoor in those days, when a raging storm of controversy engulfed them, were small, Peter's Pence were sent to Rome faithfully twice each year: on the Feast of St. Peter's Chair at Rome (January 18) and on the Feast of St. Peter in Chains (August 1). And, without fail, they were courteously acknowledged by the Holy Father, Pius X, through his Secretary of State, Cardinal Merry del Val. The first letter of acknowledgement, under the date of March 20, 1904, read:

I have duly received the contribution of $10.00 in the name of your associates. His Holiness wishes me to express his sincere appreciation of this generous initiative on your part, and to assure you of his good will.

His Holiness prays that God may grant you light and strength to soon enter the true fold of Christ and expressed his benevolent feelings in your regard.

Yours faithfully
R. Card. Merry del Val

Mother Lurana also sent Peter's Pence to Pope Pius X as an expression of the love she and her Sisters had in their hearts for the Father of Christendom. The first acknowledgment read:

His Eminence Cardinal Merry del Val presents his kind regards to the Superior of St. Francis' House, Graymoor, and begs to acknowledge receipt of the letter of December 20th and the offering sent by her to His Holiness. His Eminence duly communicated the contents of her letter to the Holy Father and he is deeply touched by the act of generosity. His Holiness writes to express his thanks and trusts that God will give light and grace to each and every one at Graymoor House and lead them to the faith in the one true fold.

There were many other manifestations of the Society's deep love and veneration for the Vicar of Christ, particularly in *The Lamp*. Yet it continued to remain in the Anglican Communion. Not until the inauguration of the Octave of Prayer did the members of the Society begin to think of making their submission to the Holy See. The first overtures of the Society with the view of submitting to Catholic authority were made in the Spring of 1909. Father Paul often said that only when he began to doubt the validity of his Anglican Orders was he prompted to consult Catholic Ecclesiastics concerning the position of the Graymoor community. This serious doubt disturbed his peace of mind profoundly and he was most anxious to have it solved. He decided to visit Monsignor C. G. O'Keeffe, the Catholic pastor of Highland Falls, New York, who was a friend of the Graymoor Community, and a subscriber to *The Lamp* from its first issue. Mother Lurana first advised Father Paul to "wait a little while until we can more fully understand God's wishes and our own position." But later, after consultation with him, she took the first step toward Rome.

Mother Lurana wrote to Archbishop John Farley, of New York, for an interview; which he granted. The Archbishop received her kindly but the interview produced no tangible results. The Archbishop could see no possibility of a corporate approach to the Holy See. He suggested that each Friar and Sister make an individual submission, and that the Society be dissolved. The Society of the Atonement, at that time, was so small and insignificant that its corporate reception into the Catholic Church did seem like a wild, extravagant dream. What Father Paul and Mother Lurana sought had never happened before to serve as a precedent.

On February 5, 1909, Father Paul received a letter from a Catholic correspondent to whom he had revealed his difficulties, urging him to visit James Cardinal Gibbons, and ask his advice. Accordingly Father Paul wrote to the Archbishop of Baltimore, asking for the privilege of an interview. The meeting was arranged for Friday, March 5, 1909.

Wearing the brown habit, the Founder of the Society of the Atonement arrived at the old colonial mansion in Baltimore at the appointed time, and was presented to Cardinal Gibbons in his private study. The Cardinal was vested for a Pontifical Requiem Mass, which was about to begin in the Cathedral, and he could talk with Father Paul only a few minutes before the Mass began.

Father Paul told the Cardinal about the Church Unity mission of the Society of the Atonement, and then briefly told of his position on Anglican Orders. The advice which the great American Cardinal of his day gave to Father Paul was a distinct disappointment to him. "You are in good faith," the Cardinal said, "be patient and follow the leading and guidance of the Holy Spirit." Then the Cardinal rose, bade his visitor farewell, and hastened into the Cathedral. Father Paul had hoped that the learned Cardinal would clear up all the doubts he had as to Anglican Orders, and suggest an immediate submission to the Apostolic See.

When he returned to the office of the Cardinal's secretary, Father Paul expressed his disappointment at the outcome of the interview. In reply the Cardinal's secretary said: "The man you ought to see is the Apostolic Delegate, Monsignor Falconio. I was his secretary before I came here. . . . He not only receives *The Lamp*, but he reads it every month upon its arrival. You know he is a Franciscan; and I have heard him say that he could see no reason why those Franciscans at Graymoor who held the full Catholic faith might not be received corporately into the Catholic Church."

After leaving Cardinal Gibbons' residence, Father Paul returned to Graymoor and immediately wrote a letter to Monsignor Falconio, asking for an interview. A reply from the Apostolic Delegation informed Father Paul that His Excellency Monsignor Falconio was on his way to Rome, but that he would be glad to see Father Paul immediately upon his return to Washington some time in August.

In the meantime a letter came from the new Episcopal Bishop of Delaware, Dr. Frederick Joseph Kinsman, to Father Paul, inviting him to Delaware and instructing him to bring a report of affairs within the Society of the Atonement. Dr. Kinsman had succeeded Bishop Leighton Coleman, who died in 1907. In his conference with Bishop

Kinsman, Father Paul was frank in telling him of his theological position and the position of the Society of the Atonement in matters of Reunion. The Bishop told him that he was grateful for his open statement and that, after prayerfully considering the matter, he would send his decision to Graymoor. The Bishop's decision was received in a letter dated July 5, 1909. Of that letter Father Paul often said, "this was one time when the Anglican Clarion sounded no uncertain note." The letter read:

MY DEAR FATHER PAUL JAMES FRANCIS:

Since your visit here in May, I have carefully considered all that you have told me of your own convictions in regard to the Church, with the result that I have not changed or modified the opinion expressed in talking with you; or in the letters written before your visit, when of necessity I spoke tentatively, as not being absolutely certain that I understood your position. I wish now to repeat what in substance I have said already as expressing my deliberate judgment in the matter.

You will remember that in talking with you I said that I understood you to hold the following propositions, and that you assented to them as rightly defining your position.

(1) That the Catholic Faith is the faith as now defined by the Roman See;

(2) That the Papacy was established "jure divino" as the necessary bond of unity in the Church.

(3) That Anglicanism is properly represented by the Church of England in pre-Reformation times and in the reign of Queen Mary: and yet

(4) That Anglican Orders are valid notwithstanding the papal condemnation of them.

This would seem to resolve itself into the single proposition that you accept the whole teaching of the Roman Church save the single detail of the repudiation of Anglican Orders. I must repeat that this proposition is an impossible one for a clergyman of our Church.

My advice is that, in the interest of single-minded honesty and devotion to duty, you make the choice between the two Churches. You cannot serve either the Papal Church or the Protestant Episcopal Church well if you try to serve both at the same time. Either give up belief in a divinely established Papacy and in Roman dogmas as the one complete expression of the Christian faith, as one must do who is a consistent and contented Anglican; or else give up Anglican Orders, make an unqualified submission to the Latin Church, and be a good Roman Catholic. I have no hesitation in saying that if I were in your position

I should choose the latter alternative. This would seem to be the natural outcome of the line of development you have adopted. For your own peace of mind and for the effectiveness of your work you ought not to try to discharge an impossible dual loyalty.

The Episcopal Bishop, Dr. Kinsman, who wrote the above letter, entered the Catholic Church ten years later, in 1919. He wrote the story of his conversion in a book entitled *Salve Mater*. Dr. Kinsman lectured at Graymoor after his conversion, and remained a staunch friend of the Society until his death on June 19, 1944, as a Catholic layman. When he left the Episcopal Church, the *Living Church* paid him the following tribute:

Bishop Kinsman was one of the finest characters who have adorned the American episcopate. His leadership was always welcomed. His learning we always respected. Scarcely a person withdrawing from the communion and fellowship in which he played so fine a part could administer such a blow as he, could wrench the ties of affection so effectively.

When Father Paul received Bishop Kinsman's letter he was convinced that the only road that the Society was now to take was the one which led to Rome and the Vicar of Christ. On August 13, 1909, he left for Washington to keep an appointment with the Apostolic Delegate. Monsignor Diomede Falconio, who was a Friar Minor, received him with extraordinary kindness. Father Paul was then forty-six years old. In telling his story to this kind prelate, he went back to that day in his father's study, thirty-six years before, when an interior voice had spoken to him. He told of his father's hard struggle to earn a livelihood because he was branded as "a Jesuit in disguise"; he told of the years he faithfully served God in the Episcopal Church in good faith, believing that he was a validly ordained priest; he told of the "Atonement Texts"; he told of the grace he received when he paid a visit to the Eucharistic Christ in a Catholic church of Omaha; how, in responding to that grace, he found that the Papal Claims were true; he told of Mother Lurana and the Covenant promise; of Brother Paul Jacob and the Sisters; of the beauty of Graymoor and its river view; of the Archdeaconry meeting and the closing of the pulpits; of his preaching on Unity and the Papal Claims; and of the storm that raged around him. And then he humbly asked that the Society of the Atonement be admitted *corporately* into the Harbor of truth and grace and life and light and love—the Catholic Church. Monsignor Falconio listened, deeply moved. His advice was simple; and though he promised nothing his words were filled with hope. Father Paul was to return to Graymoor and draw up a letter to him, incorporating in it those petitions he desired to make of the Holy See. The Apostolic Delegate would be more than happy to forward the letter to Rome. And so the following letter was written on August 19, 1909:

Your Excellency—In accordance with your wish permit me to place in writing, as simply and concisely as possible, the substance of what I said to you last Friday morning.

Through Your Excellency I desire to approach the Holy See in the attitude of a suppliant, asking, not for myself alone, but for the Society of the Atonement and certain others associated with it, admission to the Fold of Peter.

It is as a Society we ask for this admission, and our appeal is to the Holy Father for his sanction, protection and governance, in order that the Name and Institute (Society of the Atonement), which we believe we have derived from Our Lord Jesus Christ, may be confirmed to us by His Vicar.

Your Excellency will remember my telling you certain things concerning my own vocation and that of the Reverend Mother Lurana Mary Francis explanatory of the strong and deep faith we have regarding the same, and I will not now attempt to repeat any of these things; but should Your Excellency desire me to commit them in writing I will joyfully comply with your command.

Briefly and concisely stated, the things we ask of the Holy See are these:

(1) the acceptance of the Society of the Atonement in its entirety to submission and Catholic communion;

(2) the confirmation of the Society's Name and Institute;

(3) our reception as members of the Third Order of St. Francis;

(4) the acceptance in trust as the "Caput et Mater" of the Society; St. Francis' House, Graymoor (which we call our "Portiuncula") and of the adjoining Mount of the Atonement and of St. Paul's Friary, a property of extraordinary beauty, twenty-four acres in extent;

(5) the commission of our members, both the Friars of the Atonement and the sisters of the Atonement, for work of (1) reconciling sin-

ners unto God through the precious Blood of the Atonement, (2) the winning of Anglicans and other non-papal Christians to the obedience of St. Peter, (3) the conversion of the heathen.

In conclusion we wish to assure the Holy Father, through Your Excellency, that God has already graciously bestowed upon us the gift of supernatural faith in every dogma of the Holy Catholic and Roman Church, and we abhor and detest all heresies—especially Modernism—contrary to the same.

From the very commencement of our Foundation at Graymoor, as far as we have been given the understanding and power to do so, we have served the Holy See and borne witness (particularly by means of *The Lamp*) to the "jure divino" Primacy of the Roman Church. And now, should Divine Providence open the way for the admission of the Society of the Atonement into the Sheepfold of Peter, we will endeavor therein to serve to the utmost the interests of Our Lord Jesus Christ and His Vicar, the Father of Christendom.

Mother Lurana relates in her diary that after the letter was posted there followed "a little profession of faith in which Father (Father Paul) declared that we had already received the supernatural Gift of Faith in every dogma of the Catholic and Roman Church and that we abhor all heresies which she abhors, especially Modernism."

On August 24th, Monsignor Falconio wrote a note saying that he had received the letter, and that it was now on its way to Rome. Then followed weeks of waiting. However, Father Paul's soul was at peace. The uncertainty which had weighed heavily on him for so long had vanished. He was completely resigned to the Will of God. "Well, Mother," he asked one day in September, "when do you think the answer from Rome will come?" The great lover of the Poverello said, "Why, it will come on St. Francis' Day, October 4th, of course."

Father Paul predicted that the Holy Father's answer would come on "Covenant Day," October 7th. "The letter," he said, "will come on that day as a further manifestation of God's love for the Society of the Atonement and as another seal upon the Covenant He made with us." St. Francis' Day came; but the letter did not come on that day. Some of those associated with Father Paul at Graymoor became anxious. Their anxiety was well founded since they had no idea of what disposition Pius X would make of the Society.

On October 7, 1909, exactly eleven years after God, through His Holy Word, had promised him, "Surely blessing I will bless thee; and multiplying I will multiply thee," Father Paul received the long-awaited letter as he had predicted. In a voice overcome with emotion, he read its contents to his spiritual children:

REVEREND AND DEAR SIR:

I take pleasure in informing you that I am in receipt of a letter from His Eminence, Cardinal Merry del Val, in regard to your plans, which I have made known to the Holy Father.

His Eminence directs me to inform you, in the name of the Holy Father, that His Holiness is much gratified to learn of your resolution and that of your Community, and that he hopes and prays for the happy outcome of your good dispositions.

With regard to your Community there will be no objection to its continuing in the same way, even after its union with the Catholic Church. It is necessary, however, that it, like all other Communities which are established in the Church, conform to the rules laid down for such proceedings by the Canon Law. Hence the Community must come under the jurisdiction of the diocese in which it is established, the Bishop of which will see that everything is in accordance with the regulations of ecclesiastical law.

In the future when the Community shall have given proofs of its utility to the Catholic Church, steps may be taken to have it approved by the Holy See—provided everything proceeds regularly and successfully.

Praying that God may assist you and the Members of your Community with His holy grace,

I remain,

Very sincerely yours in Christ

D. FALCONIO

Apostolic Delegate

Through the Everlasting Goodness and Mercy of God, the Graymoor Community would now be Catholic. The grace of two observances of the Octave for Christian Unity fell in abundance upon it as the Spring rain. It was welcomed by that Rock of Faith, Father Paul, and that lover of Poverty, Mother Lurana; they thanked God for the rain of grace as the husbandman who, standing in the downpour with uncovered head, thanks God for the rain falling on his parched crops, for now he knows that his children will have the food of life.

It was *The Lamp*, with its crusade for the Reunion of Christendom and its defense of Papal Claims that became the providential instrument of the Society's *Corporate* submission to the Holy See. Had *The Lamp* never existed, Monsignor Falconio would not have become acquainted with Graymoor; and, not being acquainted with its activity, he too might have rejected the request for *Corporate* submission as unprecedented. For otherwise why should so extraordinary a favor be granted to a group of non-Catholics, insignificant in numbers, who had been repudiated and ostracized even by their own Church?

Fifteen years later, Father Paul was a guest of Cardinal Merry del Val at his residence in Rome. Taking Father Paul into his private study, the Cardinal told him the story of what happened when his letter reached Rome. After the Holy Father had read the letter, Cardinal Merry del Val pleaded the cause of the Graymoor Friars and Sisters. "Holy Father, let them in," he said. And the great and saintly Great White Shepherd of the sheep of Christ said: "Yes, we will let them in."

Together with Monsignor Falconio's letter conveying the message of the Holy Father, instructions were sent as to the procedure to be followed in the *Corporate* reception. The Apostolic Delegate came almost immediately to New York and notified Father Paul to meet him at the residence of Archbishop Farley on Wednesday, October 13th. There Father Paul was received by the two Prelates who were soon to become Cardinals of the Holy Roman Church.

Monsignor Falconio presented Father Paul to Archbishop Farley and informed him of the action which the Holy See had taken in the case of the Graymoor Community. Then the details of the *Corporate* reception were happily arranged.

Archbishop Farley gave Father Paul the privilege of choosing a priest who would instruct the Community prior to their reception into the Church. Father Paul chose Monsignor C.G. O'Keeffe, whose parish was across the Hudson River from Graymoor.

Monsignor O'Keeffe was gracious and kind to the Graymoor Community for years. Father Paul and Mother Lurana were greatly devoted to him. A humorous story was told by Father Paul of a visit the Monsignor made to the convent during the summer of 1909.

He was a man of physique similar to G.K. Chesterton. When he arrived at the convent he was arrayed in a satin cassock with red piping and red buttons, wearing slippers and red stockings. An orphan girl, whom Mother Lurana had adopted, answered the door. The poor child was overwhelmed by the Monsignor's splended appearance and, after showing him to the reception room, she rushed upstairs in great excitement, shouting: "Reverend Mother, the Pope is downstairs!"

Archbishop Farley also delegated an old friend of Graymoor, Monsignor Joseph Conroy, who was Vicar General of the diocese of Ogdensburg, to officiate at the ceremony in his name. Monsignor Conroy was later consecrated Bishop of Ogdensburg. Until his lamented death on March 20, 1939, he maintained a loving and fatherly interest in the progress and affairs of the Society of the Atonement. Before his death he saw to it that houses of both the Friars and the Sisters were firmly established in his diocese. He often said that any diocese having the Sisters of the Atonement working in it was greatly blessed by God.

The date of the great occasion—the reception of the Society of the Atonement into the Catholic Church—was designated by Archbishop Farley. It was Saturday, October 30, 1909. Monsignor O'Keeffe recommended that the instructions be prolonged, but Monsignor Conroy had no sympathy for such a plan. The Archbishop followed the advice of Monsignor Conroy. On October 28th two Friars Minor arrived at Graymoor to make arrangements for affiliating the community with the Franciscan Order. One of them was the late Father Edward Blecke, the Provincial of the Holy Name Province. He remained a loyal and true friend of the Society until his death. The other was Father Paschal Robinson, who later became an Archbishop, and died as Papal Nuncio to Ireland. He too became a close friend to Father Paul. These two great Franciscans graciously welcomed the Society of the Atonement into the family of the Seraphic Patriarch.

The day before the reception of the Society into the Church, Archbishop Farley sent a large box of gifts to Graymoor; in which were five sets of vestments and all the linens necessary for the celebration of the Holy Sacrifice of the Mass. His secretary, Monsignor Patrick Hayes (later Archbishop and Cardinal) sent a gold chalice and paten and a missal and missal stand. It was the beginning of many manifestations of deep affection which the Archbishop showed to the Society. After the reception into the Church he sent gifts of money to see them through many difficult days.

On the morning of October 30th, the Friars and Sisters who then constituted the infant Society of the Atonement, together with some lay associates, assisted at the Holy Sacrifice of the Mass offered by Monsignor Conroy in the convent chapel of Our Lady of the Angels. There were seventeen in the little group which made its Profession of Faith into the hands of the personal representative of the Archbishop of New York later that morning. Mother Lurana, in her diary, lists them as follows:

Very Rev. Paul James Francis, S.A., and Rev. Brother Paul Jacob, S.A.

Rev. Mother Lurana Mary Francis, S.A., Sister Amelia Evans, S.A., Sister Edith Lester, S.A., Sister Clara Francesca Pellitzer and Sister Isabel Baxter, novices.

Florence Elliot Locke (afterwards Sister Mary Francis, S.A.), Mary Margaret Cree, Edward Ignatius Baker, Ernest John Prior and Emma Louise, his wife; Mallam and David Prior; Elizabeth Monica Gibson, Miriam Irene Joseph (afterwards Sister Miriam, S.A.), and Marie Venard.

The news of Graymoor's conversion did not come as a surprise to the thousands of Catholics and non-Catholics who had followed its activities for so long, wondering how they could hold so untenable a position. In *The Lamp* for November, 1909, it is surprising to read in how simple a manner Father Paul announced the fact; he wrote:

The present issue of *The Lamp* has been held back in order to make the following announcement: On Saturday, October 30th, in the Chapel of Our Lady of the Angels, Graymoor, the Right Reverend Joseph Conroy, Vicar General of the Diocese of Ogdensburg, acting under faculties from the Most Rev. John M. Farley, Archbishop of New York, received into the Holy Catholic and Roman Church all members of the Society of the Atonement resident at Graymoor or who could conveniently be present from a distance. Msgr. Conroy was assisted in the ceremonies incident to the reception by the Rev. Paschal Robinson, O.F.M., distinguished among the Friars Minor as one of the greatest living authorities in the field of Franciscan literature, and by the Rev. Patrick Drain, pastor of the Church of Our Lady of Loretto, Cold Spring, in whose parish Graymoor is situated. Not to go into details, suffice it to say that previously application was made to Pope Pius X through the Apostolic Delegate at Washington, Monsignor Falconio, to take the Society under his "protection and governance" and to preserve its "Name and Institute." On October 7th the answer was returned by His Excellency, the Apostolic Delegate, in the affirmative. During the ten days previous to the reception of the Society the Right Rev. C.G. O'Keefe, pastor of the Church of the Sacred Heart, Highland Falls, N.Y., several times visited Graymoor to examine the members of the community preparatory to their admission. It is the wish of the ecclesiastical authorities that the publication of *The Lamp* should continue.

The secular newspapers were not quite so modest as *The Lamp* in announcing the great event. The ultra-conservative *New York Times* carried almost a full page on Graymoor's reception into the Catholic Church, in its issue of November 14, 1909. Seven pictures of Father Paul and scenes of Graymoor appeared with the article, under the title:

THE CONVENT THAT CHANGED ITS FAITH

The sub-title read:

Convent of the Society of the Atonement, Formerly an Anglican Institution, Joins the Church of Rome—Why this Conversion is Unprecedented in Church Annals

The article read, in part:

Such a transference is absolutely without precedent. The Church of Rome has always opened her doors to converts to her doctrines, whether they returned to her from the Anglican Church, which was once an integral part of herself, or turned to her from some other than the Christian denominations. But such converts have without exception made their professions of faith as individuals and have been received as individuals into the Church. There is no single instance of a corporate body having entered into the Roman Church as a body, and there has been a settled conviction that such an entrance was impossible. The reception of the convent and the Society of the Atonement by the Church under special dispensation from Pope Pius X on Wednesday last has established a new order of procedure, which, in all likelihood, will be followed by other corporate religious bodies heretofore deterred by fear of their dissolution from application for entrance into the Church of Rome. . . .

For the past nine years their most effective aim for the restoration of the Church as it was in the day preceding Luther and the Reformation has been *The Lamp*, a monthly magazine issued by the friars, devoted to the preaching of Church unity. This little publication has naturally had many battles to fight and many obstacles to meet, as it advocated its doctrine. For nine years Father Paul had patiently replied to objections, arguments and ridicule, steadfastly pointing to the efficiency of the Church united as compared to the waste of energy of scattered denominations. The November issue contains the following statement:

> With the writings of Macaulay, Green, Dixon and Gairdner before us, not to mention a long array of other notable historians and religious novelists, who have treated of the Reformation period in English history, it is plain as A.B.C. that the root reason why the Church of England lost her hold upon the masses of the English nation was the repudiation of Henry VIII of Papal supremacy and the substitution therefor of the royal supremacy. And unless that root cause of her constitutional weakness is removed by a return once more to the proper relations with the Holy See, the story of Anglican failure and incapacity to rule and lead religiously, one of the greatest and most masterful races on the earth will continue to repeat itself from generation to generation.

Father Paul is confident that the success of the order will be greater as a Catholic than as a Protestant institution.

"It has always been urged," he said, in an interview, "that the Church of Rome would refuse to accept the submission of a corporate body. Pope Pius X has accepted this body, which represents in its friars, sisters and tertiaries but a very small number of persons. Unquestionably a larger body would receive a more ready admittance, and unquestionably other Anglican bodies, following this example, will make their submission to the Roman Church. The men to whom we minister are mainly Catholic. The 'Brother Christophers' who come to us are mainly Catholic. The efficacy of our ministrations to those who are in need will be immeasurably increased since we are now in the same church. It is our hope as we grow stronger to send our missionaries both in America and in other countries to urge the return to the mother church."

The action of this handful of men, widely known for their lives of self-sacrifice and devotion to their cause, has come as a thunderbolt upon Protestant denominations. Without a doubt the consequences of the controversy thus aroused will be far-reaching. But while ecclesiastics wrangle the brotherhood will work on, following the bell, which for nine years has called them at the appointed time, ministering to the needy with increased zeal, happy in the belief that they have advanced a step in their mission. And while the storm of criticism and indignation and even ridicule which is certain to be aroused by so unprecedented a departure breaks, hundreds of men and women in the valley beneath the Mount of the Atonement will cry a blessing upon their heads.

Yes, Graymoor was "home" at last. Their cup of joy was overflowing. Father Paul and Mother Lurana with their spiritual children had turned their faces to the dazzling light of God's Grace, and it blinded them to the sorrow and tears that were still to come. God in His Infinite Mercy deemed it so, and for the moment it was better that way. Peter, James and John were blinded by the glory of light on Tabor; but it was on Calvary, and not Tabor, that the work of Man's Redemption was consummated and the infinite love of God for man was revealed.

The souls of Father Paul and Mother Lurana were transfigured on the "Tabor" of October 30, 1909; but soon after they were following Christ to Calvary; it is the lot of all who would spread His Kingdom upon the earth. For pain is the touchstone to all progress in His Vineyard; and those who labor in it commiserate only with those who suffer in ignorance of the ultimate usefulness of all suffering. So let us follow them, as they carry heavy crosses, through the following pages and listen to the false charges of the "high priests" and the rabble; and witness the frightful betrayal of one they loved.

PART TWO

In the Fold of Peter

Chapter XV

THE DELUGE OF GRIEF

THE SOCIETY of the Atonement was welcomed into the Catholic Church by many of her priests and by members of the Catholic Hierarchy. One of these wrote: "Do not give up your work for Reunion. You have only changed the base of the battle. You can do a work which no one else can do. Do not lose your sympathy for your old friends who remain behind. They need it more than ever." Many asked that the magazine be continued no matter what the sacrifice. "Surely, with a very little readjustment," wrote one of these, "*The Lamp* can be carried with you across the spiritual river, and set up, with much of the old attractiveness, and a new authority, in the true watch-tower of the Lord. I vehemently hope so."

The *Boston Pilot*, official organ of the Archdiocese of Boston, stated:

A corporate reunion, such as that of the Anglican Community of Graymoor, might serve as a splendid solution for the difficulties which are exercising other Anglican bodies. It is conceived in the true Catholic spirit, and is evidently the directing of divine grace.

The Lamp's readers among the Anglicans were especially concerned about the fate of the magazine. To them the message of Christian Unity found in its pages month after month was like a beacon guiding them to a safe harbor. Now they pleaded that its light be not allowed to go out. One of the most gratifying letters received read:

It is an increasing pleasure to receive *The Lamp.* I have not in the past entirely refrained from criticizing your position, as I did not understand it, nor indeed do I think that you have understood it yourself in the last three or four years as you do today. If I understand you, you have for a long time entertained hopes which you no longer possess, at least in the same way. It takes a pretty big measure of hope to cover all the anomalies of the Anglican Communion today. Your change is not surprising, neither is it to be condemned, because made in all sincerity. Your object too is a great and good one and you are pursuing it along a wise course and, I hope, can do much toward its attainment in the Roman communion which you could not do outside of it. There is much misunderstanding of Rome and this you can help clear up. There is also much which the Roman Catholic Church can consistently do to make it easier for the scattered sheep to be gathered into the One Fold of visible Unity, undiminished faith and recognized authority.

However, not all the letters which poured into Graymoor following the Society's conversion were written in this glad vein. Many letters of condemnation were also received. The editor of one Anglican periodical felt that Father Paul had become a traitor to the cause of *Reunion*. He was particularly annoyed that so little explanation of the Society's action had accompanied the announcement in *The Lamp*. He wrote:

As we understand it, the one reason for the existence of *The Lamp* has been the hope of corporate reunion between the Anglican and Roman communions, for which of course we all wait and pray. The paper still advocates corporate reunion while the editor has set an example of particular reunion and he does not seem to think that his action calls for any kind of explanation.

Such misunderstandings were to be expected and since the Society of the Atonement could not, and did not, suffer any real harm from them, they were ignored by Father Paul. But then a really vicious charge was hurled at him which he could not ignore. The charge was that he had accumulated money and property under the guise of being a loyal Episcopalian. This charge had to be dealt with since it was a question which affected the sincerity of his motives, his life's work, as well as any future work of the Society of the Atonement. It further placed in jeopardy the small holdings of the Friars and Sisters at Graymoor. The whole controversy evolving from the charge against the Society was based on the question whether the property of the Society rightfully belonged to it, or whether in justice it should revert to the Episcopal Church, since the Society of the Atonement was now Catholic. Some within the Episcopal Church charged that

Father Paul and the Sisters had built their modest dwellings at Graymoor from donations given to them only by Episcopalians.

Moreover, it was asserted that these offerings would never have been made if there had been even a slight doubt about Graymoor's loyalty to the Episcopal Church. Just two weeks after the Society made submission to the Catholic Church a letter appeared in the *Living Church*. It was entitled "The Seceding Community at Graymoor." The letter was written by the Rector of the Church of the Advent, Boston, Mass., the Reverend William Harman Van Allan. It read, in part:

An interesting moral question arises in connection with the secession of the Rev. Lewis T. Wattson (Father Paul James Francis) and his immediate followers to the Roman obedience. When the Society of the Atonement was forming in 1900, Fr. Wattson preached several times in Grace Church, Elmira, New York, of which I was then rector; and appealed for funds to support his new work. One of the declarations he repeatedly made was that all the property of his society would be vested in his Bishop, so that absolute poverty would not be an idle profession. He gave this as an illustration of what he meant: "Our rule requires Reservation. Should the Bishop object to that, he can at any time turn us out of house and home, since it will all belong to him." I know that many gifts made to him were influenced by this positive promise. If he kept his word, of course all the buildings and equipment at Graymoor will remain in the hands of the Bishop of Delaware, his diocesan. If, on the other hand, he presumes to retain possession of the property now, it will be only as he breaks his promise and convicts himself of obtaining money under false pretences. The late Bishop of Delaware told me that he had striven to hold Fr. Wattson to this promise of his, but that he always evaded its fulfillment.

In a reply sent to the Editor of the *Living Church* Father Paul stated:

In the winter of 1900 I preached a mission in Grace Church, Elmira, and in the following October conducted a week's conference. In both cases my services were entirely gratuitous. As far as I can remember the amount of money contributed in Elmira to the building fund of St. Paul's Friary was less than fifty dollars, most of which came from two persons as a thank-offering for blessings received during the mission. A woman of the congregation placed a small stained-glass window in the

Friary Chapel, as a memorial of her husband. She may have it at any time.

The Sisters' Convent was built and dedicated before I went to Elmira.

I deny in toto that I ever made any promise to the late Bishop of Delaware to vest the property of the Society of the Atonement in his hands or of the diocese; consequently he never wrote or spoke to me of the subject.

The clamor as to the morality of the Society of the Atonement's holding the property it possessed as Episcopalians became louder among the ranks of some Episcopalian bodies, and particularly in the pages of the prominent Episcopalian magazine, the *Living Church*. Father Paul found all this extremely painful. To him much more than the Graymoor property was at stake. He was reluctant to say or do anything which might give rise to bitterness and distrust among his former co-religionists. He realized that his work for Unity would be most effective if he could continue to enjoy their full confidence and if they continued to regard him as a sincere friend, entirely devoted to their welfare.

In the early days of the Catholic Church, when the Apostles were being persecuted by Saul, and they prayed for the strength to cope with his "threats of slaughter," their prayer was answered by God in the conversion of Saul, who then became the great Apostle Paul. His sudden conversion so amazed the early Christians that, at first, they could hardly believe it. When the Lord instructed Ananias to seek Saul in "the street called Straight," he answered: "Lord, I have heard from many about this man, how much evil he has done to Thy saints in Jerusalem." And the Lord answered: "Go, for this man is a chosen vessel to me." In the trying days when Father Paul suffered so keenly from these false charges, Almighty God touched the heart of Father Paul's greatest enemy, and converted him to become Graymoor's best friend in an evil hour. That man was the Reverend J. A. M. Richey, who was formerly an instructor at Nashotah Seminary in Wisconsin.

Almost from the beginning of his crusade for Unity, the Reverend Mr. Richey had been one of Father Paul's strongest opponents. When copies of *The Lamp* reached the reading room at Nashotah, he would denounce its editor and the magazine's contents. At times his rage became so great that he would tear *The Lamp* into bits. He read it merely to vent his anger upon Father Paul. More than once he vehemently called for the expulsion of Father Paul from the Episcopal Church. The Reverend Mr. Richey went so far as to say that *The Lamp* was lighted from the fires of hell.

However, Richey's sense of decency and propriety was outraged by the bitterness of the property controversy. He came to the defense of Father Paul, as he himself said, "out of the spirit of broadmindedness, as well as that of simple justice and fairness." In November, 1909, he sent Father Paul a copy of a letter which he had sent to the *Living Church*. In a short note which accompanied the copy of the letter he wrote: "I must make the same request of you that I did of the *Living Church*, that if you use my response to the letters appearing in that journal against you, you will use it in its entirety." The letter read:

To the Editor of the "Living Church:" In justice, please suffer me to reply to the "moral question" raised by Dr. Van Allan and which he says still requires an answer. . . . He (Father Paul) was always outspoken for the cause of Catholicity, in spite of the fact that it is not the most propitious mode of tickling the purse-strings of our people at large. . . . Now, if Father Paul is not legally entitled to the property in question why not take it from him? But if he is legally entitled to it he is also morally entitled to it, for he ever spoke for the Catholic cause and for Catholic Unity. With others who have gone to Rome, he believes that himself and his Community at large can only and truly be what they professed to be, or accomplish the purpose which they ever strove for, by joining the Roman Church.

To take down the buildings, sell the pieces and give back the dimes and dollars to the individuals who donated them would be impossible; whereas, to turn the property over to our diocesan authorities would be, in every probability, to divert the property from the expressed intent and purpose of the donors and builders. If it is legally theirs it is also morally so, and for Father Paul to give it back under his new convictions and relations would be, so far as I can see, a perversion of justice to the rest of his community, and of intent in general. From our standpoint they are Catholics still and the Society of the Atonement continues. If they think, now, that we, really, are not Catholics, the more reason why they should guard a property which was acquired for Catholic uses solely.

A letter dated December 4, 1909, came to Father Paul. It was signed, "Presbyter," and it expresses the mind of many men in the Anglican Church who recognized the sincerity of Father Paul in regard to the Graymoor property. It read:

To THE EDITOR OF "THE LAMP". The last copy of the *Living Church* has just come to hand, in which is published your last reply to the Rev. Clairborne, and although I have not been particularly interested in this controversy, I am nevertheless inclined to sympathize with you, and am frank to state that as it appears to me you have decidedly the best end of the argument. Possibly you will appreciate this the more when I tell you that, being what is known as a "broad" Churchman, I am of course not at all inclined toward the Roman Catholic Faith. By this I do not mean to condemn you in the step you have recently taken. On the contrary I commend you for following, as I believe you did, the leadings of your conscience in the matter. In other words you were honest with yourself.

This honesty and integrity is, in my opinion, a most high and desirable accomplishment. That you are honest and sincere is to me apparent from your letter. What your particular opinions are is a matter of indifference to me, but that you are an honest, true man, a great loving soul, is indeed a matter of great joy to me and an occasion for congratulation.

In spirit, then, I extend to you the hand of brotherly love and assure you that there are those who do understand and appreciate you. When we come to the higher worlds above us, it will be no surprise to me to find that you have been faithful to the Light and are a Child of Light. I expect to find you crowned with light and glory because you have been faithful to the Light.

The letter of the Reverend W.S. Clairborne to which "Presbyter" referred was the end of the controversy, for at the bottom of it the editor of the *Living Church* wrote: *"The discussion of this subject is now at an end."*

Father Paul's letter, dated November 27, 1909, answering the Reverend Mr. Clairborne, read:

To THE EDITOR OF THE "LIVING CHURCH":
Permit me to reply to the question put to me by the Rev. W.S. Clairborne in your current issue. I have not "accumulated" any property as

"a minister of the Protestant Episcopal Church in the United States of America"; on the contrary I long ago parted with every penny I possessed. In 1900 the Society of the Atonement was given twenty-four acres of land by three good friends in England (and therefore not members of the Episcopal Church). Upon this land was built St. Paul's Friary, the money for which was given, with the exception of a small amount, by our Reverend Mother Superior. Let me say that the above mentioned benefactors are not at all disturbed by our recent step, as the Society of the Atonement, to which they gave, retains its corporated existence and its superiors remain the same.

As to the second question, were we not supported by the contributions of the faithful (of the Episcopal Church) "given largely because of the endorsement of (my) brothers in the ministry?" Emphatically, No; for had we attempted to live upon such contributions we would long since have starved to death. The Society was supported by the alms given our Sisters when they went begging each week, and those who bestowed them were overwhelmingly Roman Catholics, and this notwithstanding the Sisters let it be clearly understood that they were Anglicans.

All this is very painful to me. Some day those whom I still count my brethren will, I believe, understand that I am not, as they seem to consider me, an enemy.

The Reverend J. A. M. Richey, having become convinced of the sincerity of the "erratic priest" of Graymoor, now lent him his every support. When the controversy was at an end he became not only an ardent admirer of Father Paul, but also one of his closest friends. He became a Catholic not many years after the property incident. After his conversion he came to Graymoor and lived with his family in a cottage adjacent to the monastery. The strangest part of his life's story is that he became one of the editorial staff of *The Lamp*, a magazine he once bitterly condemned. After his wife died he began his studies for the priesthood and was ordained. His daughter became a Sister of Charity in New Jersey. His son studied for the priesthood at Graymoor but did not persevere.

We also mention here, incidentally, that the January issue of *The Lamp*, 1910, announced the conversion to the Catholic Church of the Reverend Henry R. Sargent, Father Paul's novice master at the novitiate of the Episcopalian Order of the Holy Cross. Quoting the *American Catholic* (Anglican), the notice read:

The Reverend Henry R. Sargent has joined the Roman Communion. We will not pretend to minimize the fact that here we have sustained a great and serious loss, and we sympathize most deeply with the Order of the Holy Cross in the departure of so important a member of their community. The loss must be felt all the more from the fact that it is the first time that any one of the Fathers has left the ranks of the Order for the Roman obedience.

When the fury of the controversy about the Mount of the Atonement has seemingly subsided, it was discovered that, in clearing "the Mount" of the violence, it had descended upon the Sisters of the Atonement in the Valley, like an avalanche. And, of course, here the Episcopal Church had something more tangible to work on. When one of those involved in this unhappy incident—Mrs. Nicholson— lay dying, as a Catholic, in the Graymoor convent forty years later, she learned that Father Paul's biography was being written. Her request was that the author "be merciful in relating the facts of my foolishness." That request will be honored here; only the facts will be given, without any attendant emotion.

It was in March, 1910, a few months after the corporate reception of the Society of the Atonement into the Catholic Church, that the Wall Street firm of Messrs. Zabriskie, Murray, Sage and Kerr began legal action as lawyers for Dr. Arthur Lowndes and co-trustees to secure possession of the three-quarters of an acre of ground at Graymoor on which stood St. John's Church and St. Francis' Convent, which had been occupied by the Sisters of the Atonement since October 18, 1899. The co-trustees uniting with Dr. Lowndes were Miss Alice Elliot and her sister, Mrs. Nicholson. The only other living trustee named in the procedure was Miss Julia H. Chadwick who, throughout the litigation, which lasted over a period of eight years, was to take the side of the Sisters of the Atonement.

Mother Lurana, during the early days, could easily have obtained a transfer of this property to herself in legal form, but in her Franciscan idealism she chose to occupy it without owning it. Such was the arrangement made between her and the three other ladies actually interested in the mission. This small piece of land was to be the site of the motherhouse and the permanent home of the Sisters of the

Atonement. In compensation for the gift of the ground and St. John's Church, the Sisters gladly undertook to relieve the ladies of the financial burden they had hitherto borne in carrying on the mission. But when the Society became Catholic certain persons, who were never friendly to the Society even in its Anglican days, prevailed upon Miss Elliot and her sister, Mrs. Nicholson, by appealing to their loyalty to the Episcopal Church, to join with the Reverend Arthur Lowndes in a lawsuit to evict the Sisters. The whole story of what happened up to the time of the litigation was graphically told by Miss Chadwick in the following letter, which she sent to the *Living Church*:

MISS CHADWICK'S LETTER

May I ask the courtesy of your columns for a word on a matter anent which much that is erroneous and exaggerated has already appeared, the time seeming to me now ripe to let fall a few drops of cold fact into the seething cauldron of recrimination and misrepresentation as to the mission and convent of Graymoor?

During the incumbency of the Rev. A. Z. Gray as rector of St. Philip's, at Garrison, some time in the seventies, a piece of land, about half an acre in extent, in the heart of the hills some three miles from Garrison, was given to him by its owner, a farmer of the neighborhood, with the understanding that a "Union" chapel for the use of Methodists, Episcopalians, etc., was to be erected on the site. Mr. Gray built, at his own expense, a small chapel, seating about fifty people, where he held services until he left the parish. Then the work of St. John's was taken up by the Rev. Mr. Seabury of Fishkill (the parish of St. Philip's even then taking no interest in the work) and continued until his death. After Mr. Seabury's death the chapel remained closed for ten years, during which no attempt was ever made to hold service there.

In 1893 I returned to Garrison after a long absence, and was told by a devout member of Mr. Gray's congregation of the state into which the chapel of St. John in the Wilderness had fallen, and, on visiting it, I found that it was being used by tramps as a lodging house (it is on the main road to Peekskill), the doors having been broken down, the carpet pulled up to make a bed near the stove, the ends of the pews and the stuffing of the hassocks burned in the stove. The roof was full of holes, the plaster fallen down, and over a hundred panes of glass were broken.

Moved by the wreck of the building which had once been used for Divine service, I appealed to two friends who were occupying my mother's house at Garrison, and together we cleaned the chapel with our own hands (its condition was so filthy that we could not hire anyone to do it), and repaired it at our own expense, except that a bill for re-shingling and plastering was generously paid by the Rev. Walter Thompson.

We asked permission of the then rector of St. Philip's to open the chapel for Sunday school. He held that the parish of St. Philip's was not, and never had been, responsible for St. John's, which was, to use his own words, a private possession, or "chapel of ease" of the Rev. Mr. Gray. He held also that the Methodist Church was the best church for the country people; but he, not acknowledging jurisdiction over St. John's, did not feel that he could forbid our doing what we wished.

We accordingly reopened St. John's with a religious service, for which a friend volunteered, and held Sunday school ourselves for some months. I think it was the second summer that we secured the services of a clergyman, who came regularly from Peekskill, we paying him a stated sum for each service, and for several years we raised this sum by our own efforts, and so supported the services at St. John's, with neither help, sympathy, counsel or countenance from St. Philip's as a parish, such money contributions as we received from residents of Garrison be-ing given to us out of friendship and admiration for the earnest and persevering enthusiasm of the two friends mentioned. So far as I know, no incumbent of St. Philip's ever set foot in St. John's to hold service during this entire period; we hired and paid for every service held in the chapel, except a few voluntary ones by friends from New York.

About ten years ago Father Paul Wattson and the Rev. Mother Lurana of the Society of the Atonement were introduced to one of my friends and we were more than glad to accept their proposal to relieve us of the heavy burden we had borne for so many years (having failed to arouse any interest in the work in the parish of St. Philip's), and very happy to install them (the Sisters of the Atonement) at Graymoor, where they spent their first year in a farmhouse which they hired, about a mile from the chapel.

From that day to this they lived and worked in this wilderness, having built themselves a modest home on part of the original half acre, the other property held by the Society of the Atonement in the vicinity having been purchased later with funds supplied by their friends. Dur-ing this time they have been, for the most part, ignored by the parish of St. Philip's and its incumbents, until the recent event of their reception into the Roman communion, which has aroused the storm to which your columns bear witness.

During the years when we were supporting the chapel the largest congregation of which we have any record was twenty odd persons; in summer fourteen was occasionally the number, in winter it sank to three or four, but the average for the year was six or eight. The late Bishop Potter refused to recognize the work or to confirm there, as he held it was not a strong enough mission.

At present, with the large number of men on the Aqueduct work, many of whom have brought their families and live in the vicinity, the chapel is crowded at every service. Putting all prejudice aside it would seem that the law of supply and demand might be applied even to the case of a mission chapel in an isolated mountain district, and that (the Episcopalians having had their innings of some twelve years without much success) given a total absence of Episcopalians and a plethora of Roman Catholics in the immediate neighborhood, it would be more sensible to have a Roman Catholic Chapel, which is needed, than an Episcopal mission which is neither needed or wanted. This, however, is an argument which, I am well aware, carries no weight where religious prejudice is concerned, else the offer of the society to purchase the stony acre would have been accepted, as a solution of the problem more in accord with common sense as well as with dignity, and a regrettable Church scandal might have been avoided.

The present state of affairs gives but too tempting occasion for the foes of all churches to quote, but with a difference, the old phrase: "See how these Christians love one another!"

Very respectfully,

JULIA HALSTED CHADWICK

One year after the litigation started, Mother Lurana sent the following letter to the lawyers for the plaintiffs:

MESSRS. ZABRISKIE, MURRAY, SAGE & KERR
ATTORNEYS FOR THE PLAINTIFFS IN THE
ST. JOHN'S CHURCH PROPERTY SUIT

Graymoor, N. Y.
January 26, 1911

DEAR SIRS:

As the Defendant most gravely concerned in the suit brought by the Plaintiffs for whom you are attorneys, I, Mother Lurana, Superior of the Sisters of the Atonement, desire to state, first:

That I am permitting the case to go by default, not because I am indifferent to the very painful consequences that will result to us, or because I do not believe in the validity and equity of our right to remain in possession of this property, and our ability to prove the justice of our claim in the Courts. The reasons are by no means such, and difficult as they are to express, I feel in justice bound to you and the Honorable Court, as well as to myself, to attempt the explanation, or better yet, simply to make a statement as follows:

We are Franciscans, and our holy Founder, St. Francis of Assisi, away back seven hundred years ago, told his first children in the Order that they should *not offer resistance*, in other words, that they must obey literally our Lord's words in the Holy Gospel: "If any man sue thee at law and take away thy coat give him thy cloak also."

My second reason is: That the special work of the Society of the Atonement is Church Unity, a work to which we have given our lives, and I would rather that our little band of Sisters were homeless than that we be the means of a legal battle that could not but help stir up uncharity and strife between the Catholic Church and Anglicans (Episcopalians). I know this sounds very academic, if not fanatical, in a twentieth century law office, but the issue is a downright practical one, and I dare not take any other course than the present one. I will not deny that there has been to me personally a very real temptation to fight it out, but, as I said above, I dare not, on conscientious grounds.

The third thing I wish to state is: It is our earnest hope that your clients, having achieved a legal victory and having had this, our home, handed over to them, will then meet us in some reasonable financial settlement. This we have since the suit began, and before, more than once expressed a desire for, but only to be refused.

It may not be law, but I wish your plaintiffs might realize in some slight degree what is the heavy suffering and strain that they have brought upon a little community of Sisters, who exist only to do all the good they can, and in their work here at Graymoor to fulfill what I believe are the conditions of your trust deed, "to minister to people of the neighborhood." Yesterday one of my young sisters was found with her head on her arms crying bitterly, her unfinished work beside her. No, this is not law, but it may count in another Supreme Court.

But this is a digression. Allow me to state in addition, as briefly as I can, certain facts that appear to justify to us our belief that we are in justice and equity the lawful owners of this property. And first, to clear the issue:

It was *the Sisters* who were invited to come to Graymoor by Miss Elliot, representing the Trustees; it was *with the Sisters* that the arrangements were made, and Rev. Father Paul (Rev. Lewis T. Wattson) acted as our Chaplain, coming in that capacity to reside here after the Sisters had lived at Graymoor nearly a year. Let it be a clean-cut issue: —It is the Sisters of the Atonement who are to suffer, a little band of women. Father Paul has his own property about a mile distant, which is in no way involved, and he lays no claim to this property.

The Sisters, as stated above, having been invited to Graymoor in 1898 and living all the winter and into the summer in the old "Dimond House," a half mile distant down the road, the experience of that blizzard winter, which cannot be described, made it desirous, if not imperative, that a house through whose siding daylight might not be seen, should some way or other be built, for us. About then I received a letter from the above-mentioned Miss Elliot, dated February 10, 1899, which I quote: (I have this letter in my possession.) "The thermometer went down to zero here (N.Y.) yesterday.

"I really shudder to think what it must be at Graymoor . . . . . . Would it be against your Rule—when the Society is organized—to own the little church? There is every likelihood of my living some day in the very Far West and before that comes into the question I would like to have the future of St. John's secured." Then I built our little Convent— built it with a small legacy left me by a grandparent and all that I had; the Episcopal Church, as has been stated, did not contribute to the building, but Miss Elliot gave us about $500 toward it, a very small part of the building's cost, and this amount has been expended many times over in the care and furnishing of the church, in Rev. Father Wattson's ministrations and our own work, for all of which no remuneration was received. We continued for over ten years in sole possession, bearing all expenses and the Trustees were never heard of.

Many years later, after vainly striving to make Episcopalians of the few scattered inhabitants, and our Rev. Chaplain preaching to empty benches, the Sisters forming principally, at all times and most frequently, the sole congregation, we, the Society of the Atonement, became convinced of the divine claims of the Catholic Church and resolved to make submission. We became Catholics, and that while a negotiation was pending looking toward giving me the long-promised quitclaim deed of this place.

We could have waited until it was in our hands, but feeling that such a proceeding would not be honorable, I met Miss Chadwick, one of the Trustees and an Episcopalian, in New York and told her of our impending reception into the Church. I also wrote to Miss Elliot (another trustee) of our intention, but continued my request for a settlement. Miss Chadwick wrote me that she would use all her influence toward our having as far as possible a good legal title to the property of which for so many years we had held entire possession. She also wrote me that she had received a letter saying that Miss Elliot agreed that even in the case of our becoming Catholics the right thing was for us to have a deed and that in consideration of $100, a nominal sum, she would agree to give it. A short time after I received the following letter from Miss Chadwick:

"Since I wrote you there seems to have been a change in Miss Elliot's feelings and intentions, much to my regret, as I certainly supposed the matter was settled by her letter to me, agreeing to accept the offer you made. I am more sorry than I can say that there should be a hitch in the matter. I assure you that under no circumstances will I consent to St. Philip's, Garrison, getting hold of the Chapel, but beyond refusing my signature to anything which would give it to them I fear I am powerless. The quitclaim was never recorded, I now learn. Perhaps if your lawyer were to consult Mr. E. D. Dinsmore he might get some light on the legal force of that document. . . . I am much mortified to find myself in the embarrassing position of being obliged to seem to fail to keep my word, which I supposed was given with Miss Elliot's in my letter to you accepting your offer. I know you will hold me guiltless in the matter, for you know I wish you to retain the Chapel as well as the Convent built by you."

We became Catholics on October 30, 1909; in March of the following year we received notice of the action to be brought against us.

This Church of St. John Baptist was built "to minister to the people of the neighborhood"; no record remains of its ever having been consecrated to the worship of the Episcopal Church. The property was offered years before to the Episcopal Bishop of the Diocese (Bishop Potter) who refused it on the ground that there were not enough Episcopalians in this neighborhood attending the church to make it worth while for the Diocese, or Archdeaconry, to shoulder its expense. It is on record in the minutes of the Vestry of St. Philip's Church, Garrison, (in whose parish the mission of St. John's was then situated), that they, the Vestry, also refused it for the same reason. But now, please consider, the population of this vicinity is overwhelmingly Catholic (while there are no Episcopalians), and it is only by St. John's remaining a Catholic Church that it can fulfil the original intention and express condition of "ministering to the people of the neighborhood." We have, to the best of our ability, carried out this trust. Several years ago when the shafts of the New York City aqueduct closed down in our vicinity and the laborers were starving, the soup kettle was not off our kitchen stove for months and as many as forty men were fed by us twice a day. One of our Sisters died that year, ministering to a starving Italian woman to whom she went on an icy day when ill herself. She took a heavy cold and in three days was dead. Again I say, these things may not be law, but I do believe they will count in another Final Hearing.

This place was a heap of weeds and stones when we took possession; no

St. Christopher's Inn Today

The Little Flower Memorial Building

The Wayside Shrine

St. Francis' Convent at Graymoor

grass would grow and the Sisters removed with their own hands thousands of these same stones and weeds and from a practically valueless property we have, in our poverty and little by little, made it a garden-spot of beauty and the church (which is very dear to us) from an old wind-racked building into a beautiful house of God, filled with the poor who love it, and worship there. And may I ask, if a congregation changes its faith may it not in law have the right to carry its church building with it? We were the sole congregation in those old days, as I said above. In a court of law does it not also count that a woman, relying upon the word and good faith of the Trustees, put her all in a little house on the land they promised to give her; that she and those with her worked faithfully to fulfil their trust, and just because they became Catholics are turned out of the little home built by themselves, the place over which they have been in control and of which they have borne all expenses for twelve years?

I commend these considerations to the honorable Court, the plaintiffs in this suit, and you their attorneys.

In the meantime the case was prevented from going by default through the intervention of Miss Chadwick. She contested the petition of the Plaintiffs on the ground that she had faithfully discharged her duties as a Trustee; and that the Sisters, having assumed the responsibility of carrying on the mission and ministering to the spiritual needs of the people of Graymoor had faithfully discharged their contract and in no way merited a dispossession. In testifying before the court she stressed the points that there were no longer any Episcopalians in Graymoor: and that St. John's Church was completely filled every Sunday since the Society entered the Catholic Church.

These were sad and difficult days for the Sisters of the Atonement. In *The Lamp* of November, 1917, Father Paul wrote:

As we were preparing the last copy for this issue of *The Lamp,* word came to the Sisters from their lawyer, Mr. James Dempsey of Peekskill, that Judge Tompkins of the Supreme Court of the State of New York had rendered judgment in favor of the plaintiffs in the suit which they began over seven years ago to dispossess the Sisters of what has come to be known as the *Graymoor Portiuncula,* that little portion of ground, less than one acre in extent, which had been given to them by Divine Providence, nineteen years ago in somewhat the same way as the Portiuncula of Assisi had been given to St. Francis.

Plaintiff's Lawyer Refuses Settlement

The latest word as we go to press is that Mr. Zabriskie, attorney for the Plaintiffs, has informed the Sisters of the Atonement through their lawyer that they will not consider any financial settlement, and that 60 days will be the outside limit within which the Sisters must vacate the premises. The law allows the defendants the right to appeal the case, but this the Sisters are unanimously resolved not to do. It was with the greatest reluctance, and only in defense of a sacred trust, that they have defended the case in Court for the past seven years, and it would be the reversal of their original resolve if by their own volition they became the aggressors and carried the case into the higher courts. The only appeal they make is to the Court of High Heaven, and they have already begun to move out as peaceful lambs from their shelter.

Again in *The Lamp* of December, 1917, he tells of the sad plight of the Sisters:

When the Sisters first received word that Judge Tompkins had given them over unconditionally into the hands of the "Trustees," with thirty days in which to move out, ten of those thirty days had passed by and it was a physical impossibility to have a shelter prepared for the Novices, (Our Lady's Hostel is only large enough for the Professed Sisters) and to get their belongings out of the Convent in twenty days. So it seemed for the moment that the only thing to do was to appeal their case to the Appellate Court, if only to gain time. But this was but a momentary thought, for in reality the Sisters were unanimously against it, and they preferred any hardship to such a course. And so the Mother wrote to their lawyer the letter given below:

Dear Mr. Dempsey:

In approaching, tomorrow, the Plaintiff's Attorney on our behalf, I request that you announce as our decision, not holding it out as an alternative, *that we will not take our case to the Court of Appeals* (unless the ecclesiastical authorities of this Catholic Archdiocese should insist). As I made clear in the beginning of the litigation, it was most reluctantly and forced by circumstances that I became a defendant. I cannot, therefore, in conscience, at this point continue such litigation by·what would be the first aggressive action on our part. We are Franciscan Religious who desire only to live out our brief life in this world, according to the principles that govern our work for Church Unity, and in obedience to the precepts of peace and non-resistance laid down in our Rule by the Holy Founder of our Order, Saint Francis of Assisi. We carry our final appeal to another Court and another Judge. I will be glad, however, if you will again, as you did in the beginning of this case, ask our opponents if they will consider a financial settlement. If not, we beg to know at the earliest moment possible what length of time is given us in which to remove from our dear Convent home.

Thanking you for all your kind offices, I am,

Very sincerely yours,

LURANA MARY FRANCIS, S.A.

Graymoor, Garrison, N. Y.
October 28, 1917

In reply, the following letter was received, giving the result of the interview with the Plaintiff's attorney:

DEAR MOTHER LURANA:—In compliance with your express request, I promptly conferred personally with Mr. Zabriskie, at his office, in New York City, on the subject of a settlement or compromise, if possible, of the litigation without further activities on our part, and to whom I submitted for precise consideration the following propositions in substance:

(1) Would he (Mr. Zabriskie) consider any terms now for a settlement on any financial payment by us? To this Mr. Zabriskie promptly responded in the negative absolutely.

(2) That if the Mother and her Society promptly vacated the premises without further resistance and surrendered all their rights to the buildings and improvements as made at their expense and by their sole efforts, would he not consider the Society's rights to an award or rebate on the basis of the value of such improvements? Mr. Zabriskie again replied in the negative, but consented to submit it with the first proposition to his clients, although I believe the plaintiffs will be practically controlled entirely by the attitude of their said counsel.

As I personally emphasized to you, the advisability of an appeal is indispensable, as you have everything to gain thereby and practically nothing to lose, except perhaps the expenses in amount as I have indicated, and which are insignificant as compared with the full value of the property in controversy in its present condition.

The Appellate Division, which is the first appellate tribunal, is constituted of five judges at each session, and who on a printed record of the whole case, including exhibits, could and undoubtedly would give more thoroughly of their time and consideration to an analysis of the legal and equitable aspects of the subject in controversy and the respective rights of all those involved, and render an opinion of some length accordingly.

I take occasion also to reiterate that your right of appeal once lost is gone forever, and the judgment as rendered in the trial court, however unsatisfactory or disappointing to the unsuccessful side, by reason of the omission of any opinion, becomes absolute and beyond any prospect of amendment, and I would again urge your very serious consideration within the allotted time and for the proper protection of your rights and interests, and those vitally associated with you, to consider not alone the expediency, but the advisability, if not the necessity of preferring an appeal for the purpose of obtaining not only a thorough review of all disputed questions, but a final adjudication on the merits of the case as a whole, including specifications, as desired, of the rights and exact status of the various parties and interests as affected. At any time during the pending of an appeal any compromise if arranged for could be effected and the appeal forthwith discontinued.

Very respectfully yours,
JAMES DEMPSEY

Peekskill, N. Y.
November 1, 1917

A week later the Sisters' attorney sent the following letter to Mother Lurana, which he had received from Mr. Zabriskie:

ZABRISKIE, MURRAY, SAGE & KERR
COUNSELLORS AT LAW
49 WALL STREET
NEW YORK

November 5, 1917

DEAR MR. DEMPSEY:

After our interview the other day with regard to Graymoor, I communicated to my clients the purport of our conversation. From what they say I have no reason to suppose that overtures on your part for a settlement on either of the lines which you suggested will be acceptable to them.

If your clients submit to the judgment and quit the premises, my clients, as I anticipated, would wish to give them whatever time may be fairly reasonable in which to remove. You said that you thought that your clients would need as much as thirty days, but not more than sixty days for this purpose. We should have no objection to this.

Yours truly,
GEORGE ZABRISKIE

This was the state of affairs when on November 8, 1917, Father Paul met the Honorable Hamilton Fish on the street in Garrison. Mr. Fish's father had been Governor of New York State and he, himself, had presided over the Assembly in Albany three times. Hamilton Fish was a prominent Episcopalian, being the Senior Warden in the Church of St. Philip's at Garrison. When he heard from Father Paul the sad plight of the Sisters, he not only expressed his sympathy with the Sisters in their trouble, but also his strong disapproval of the whole affair.

The result of that conversation was that he called upon Mother Lurana, and volunteered to champion the cause of the Sisters. Not long after, a petition was drawn up by the people of Garrison and Philipstown. Hamilton Fish, whom Father Paul called "another Daniel," was the first to sign it; and through his efforts others signed it.

The Petition read:

A Memorial and Petition

Addressed to

The Right Reverend David H. Greer D.D., Bishop of New York; Mr. George Zabriskie, Attorney for the Plaintiffs, and to the Trustees of St. John's Church, Graymoor: namely: Miss Alice May Elliot, Mrs. Sarah Nicholson, Plaintiffs, and Miss Julia H. Chadwick, Defendant.

We, the undersigned, being residents of Garrison and Philipstown, wish to express our earnest desire that an agreement may be promptly arrived at, by which the Sisters of the Atonement be not evicted from the Convent built by themselves and twice added to at large expense. As the judgment now stands—the Sisters refusing to appeal the same for Religious reasons—they will in a few days be forced to leave the home so dear to them, built by their own efforts and, with the exception of six hundred dollars ($600.00), by the money gifts of Roman Catholic citizens.

If agreeable to all parties, we would suggest some such settlement as the following. The Sisters to pay to the Plaintiffs in the suit the sum of two thousand dollars ($2,000.), being a valuation or rebate as follows:

One thousand dollars ($1,000.00) for the 3/4 of an acre of ground, with its Church and open shed, that is the property in its unimproved condition when the Sisters were asked by the Trustees to take over its charge and built their Convent thereon; also six hundred dollars ($600.00) being the amount of a gift from Miss Elliot toward the building of the original Convent, and lastly four hundred dollars ($400.00), which is interest at 5 per cent on the valuation of the property of one thousand dollars ($1,000.00) for the eight years the Sisters have been in possession as Catholics.

In return for the above payment the Sisters should, of course, receive from the Trustees, and also the Gray heirs, as clear a title as possible, and the good will of both parties just named, for their future peaceable possession.

Bishop Greer, after receiving the petition, called a meeting of the Trustees and their Counsel, Mr. Zabriskie. Mr. Fish, who was a member of the Standing Committee of the Episcopal diocese of New York, also attended. Encouraged by Bishop Greer and Mr. Fish, the Trustees expressed their willingness to make a settlement with the Sisters. However, Mr. Zabriskie would not hear of it. Incidentally his obduracy was due to the fact that besides being the Counsel of the Plaintiffs he was also Chancellor of the Episcopal Diocese of New York.

Mr. Zabriskie contended that the judgment handed down by Justice Tompkins, of the Supreme Court of New York, was unalterable; and that the Plaintiffs had no power to give the Sisters a quitclaim deed, even if they desired to do so.

Then, as Father Paul poetically described it, "Mr. Fish played the part of Portia, and to the consternation of Shylock declared that he would prepare and introduce a bill into the State Legislature making the transfer of the property lawful."

Judge Morgan J. O'Brien, of New York City, volunteered to serve as Counsel for the Sisters. The bill was introduced into the State Legislature on March 13, 1918, and passed the Assembly. The Governor of New York signed it on March 21st.

During this time of great trial, Catholic people everywhere came to the aid of the Sisters, so that they were able to acquire the adjacent property and erect better buildings. And through it all their great and loyal friend was the late Right Reverend Monsignor Lavelle, Vicar General of the Archdiocese of New York.

This tragic chapter has a very happy ending. Miss Julia Halstead Chadwick spent the last years of her life in her villa outside the city of Florence, Italy. There she was received into the Catholic Church; and there she died, fortified by the Sacraments of the Church, on the vigil of the Immaculate Conception, December 7, 1936.

The plaintiffs in the case also became Catholics. They died at

Graymoor and are buried in the Sisters' cemetery. Miss Elliot died in 1930; and her sister, Mrs. Nicholson, passed away in 1949. When Miss Elliot died, Father Paul wrote a beautiful memorial which tells of their conversion and Miss Elliot's happy death. It also shows the magnanimity of Father Paul, whose beautiful soul could never descend to anything ungenerous. The memorial read:

ALICE MAY ELLIOT—A MEMORIAL

The Foundation of the Society of the Atonement at Graymoor will always be associated with the name of Alice May Elliot, whose mortal remains were laid to rest in the Sisters' "God's Acre," St. Joseph's Cemetery, on the western slope of the Mount of the Atonement, upon the Eve of St. John Baptist Day, June 23, 1930 . . . Thirty-seven years before, on the very same day the Church of St. John the Baptist at Graymoor was reopened for religious worship after it had been closed for years. Miss Elliot herself was present as a happy participant in that Evensong service on the eve of the Patronal Feast. She, assisted by her sister, Mrs. Nicholson of New York City, and Miss Julia Chadwick of Garrison, all three devout Anglicans, had labored for weeks in repairing and renovating the church so that it might once more be dedicated to the worship of Almighty God. During the time of its abandonment, tramps passing up and down the highway had converted it into a wayfarers' inn, and performed within its walls many sacrilegious acts. The roof had to be reshingled and out of devotion to St. Francis the church had been painted brown. In fact it was after Miss Elliot had read the story of St. Francis restoring St. Damien's in Assisi, that she was inspired with her two companions to undertake this work of restoration.

Surely God must have moved them to undertake this charitable work because at the very time the Founder of the Society of the Atonement was receiving the name and texts of the Institute in Kingston, forty miles to the north on the opposite bank of the Hudson River. He little dreamed at the time that they were preparing a Bethlehem at Graymoor for the Atonement Institute.

It was in October five years later that the Mother Foundress of the future Sisters of the Atonement, in retreat at her home in Warwick, received a letter from Sister Mary Angela of the Anglican Community known as the Sisters of St. Mary, whose Mother house is at Peekskill, New York, telling her about Graymoor and the desire of Miss Elliot and her companions to have a convent of Franciscan Sisters attached to "St. John's in the Wilderness," as it was then called. This led to further correspondence and all things were arranged for the Sisters of the

Atonement to make their Foundation at Graymoor. It was accordingly on December 15, 1898, the Octave of the Feast of the Immaculate Conception, that Sister Lurana left her home at Warwick, New York, with one companion and came into the Graymoor Valley to make her Foundation. The convent *pro tem* was a farm cottage a quarter of a mile distant from St. John's Church, called the "Dimond House," said to be more than a century old, through the siding of which snow easily drifted. The building of St. Francis House close by the church occurred during the ensuing summer, the corner-stone being laid on St. John the Baptist Day, 1899.

Not long afterward Miss Elliot accompanied her sister, Mrs. Nicholson, to the far West where the Nicholsons had a ranch. Years went by. The corporate reception of the Society of the Atonement into the Catholic Church took place in 1909. This step deeply grieved and disappointed both Miss Elliot and her sister, who in the meantime had returned to New York City. Impelled by influences brought to bear and their own conscientious scruples at allowing St. John's Church to become a Roman Catholic house of worship, they became plaintiffs in an eight-year litigation instituted to evict the Sisters of the Atonement from possession. Mr. Hamilton Fish's intervention and how it all ended happily has been frequently told, and can be found in the historic copy of *The Graymoorian*.

But, "God moves in a mysterious way his wonders to perform." In 1928 Mrs. Nicholson visited Assisi and at the tomb of St. Francis she was converted to Catholicism. On her return to New York both she and Miss Elliot were received into the bosom of Mother Church. In the meantime Miss Elliot had become ill. By slow degrees the disease that was to prove fatal crept over her. She had to be taken to the hospital. Then Mrs. Nicholson wrote to our Father General and to Mother Lurana telling of her conversion as well as that of her sister, likewise of the latter's illness. Two Sisters of the Atonement were despatched at once from St. Clare's Mission in the Bronx to St. Francis Hospital to call upon Miss Elliot and to invite her in the Mother's name to come to Graymoor, where at Our Lady's Hostel she would find a home and tender loving care in her illness. She gladly accepted the invitation. The Sisters' car went down to the hospital door and very comfortably the journey "home" was made. Her return to Graymoor after long years of absence took place on January 15, 1929. Months went by during which time she needed constant attention and skillful nursing, which the Sisters most lovingly gave her and she learned to love them ardently in return. When she would sometimes gently protest at all the "luxury" surrounding her in Our Lady's Hostel on the Convent grounds, the Sisters would answer

that they were trying to repay the great debt they owed her—*Graymoor!*
On St. John Baptist Day, 1929, Miss Elliot was received into the Third
Order of St. Francis and took the name of Sister Elizabeth. From time to
time her old friends and relatives at Garrison (where much of her girl-
hood had been spent), visited her, and her room at the Hostel was
kept well supplied with beautiful flowers from their conservatories.

The sister whom she loved so intensely, Mrs. Nicholson, was able to
come very frequently from New York to see her, sometimes bringing
with her her daughter or her son, both also so dear to their aunt. Every
Sunday morning and on all the greater Feasts she received Holy Communion in her room, and by degrees she grew into a deep knowledge
and appreciation of the Catholic Religion, and her heart was indeed full
of gratitude to Almighty God for the supernatural gift of Faith. She
had always been an intensely loyal Anglican of the advanced type, and
things Catholic were, therefore, less difficult for her to grasp. Always a
devout woman, her spirituality mellowed and deepened during the long
illness which she bore with the greatest fortitude and sweetness. When
the end came it was without great suffering and she literally fell asleep
in the Lord on Friday, June 20th. On Sunday afternoon her body
was brought into Saint John's, clothed in the Tertiary habit. With the tall
lighted candles about her a watch was kept by the Community until the
Mass on Monday morning, June 23rd.

How fitting that every honor of a Founder should have been shown
her in the very church which she had rescued from desecration and prepared for the coming of the Atonement Friars and Sisters to Graymoor.

The Requiem Mass was one of the most beautiful the writer has ever
had the privilege of attending. The procession from the Convent to the
cemetery of the Sisters was very impressive. One of the students with
acolytes on either side led the way bearing aloft the crucifix. The lay
guests at the Hostel and the Tertiary Sisters followed. Next came the
little oblates distinguished by their light blue veils. After these the
Postulants in black, then the Novices in white veils. Then the professed Sisters. After them the students in black cassocks; the Friar-
novices and the professed Friars; then automobiles of her friends from
Garrison, the Priests and lastly the funeral car. The body of Alice May
Elliot, Sister Elizabeth T.S.A., was lovingly laid to rest under the
shadow of the large Crucifix and close by the graves of six Sisters of
the Atonement who have already received the Master's call and been
added, as we trust, to the number of those Religious who in the New
Jerusalem "follow the Lamb whithersoever He goeth." It was a perfect
day. The sun beamed gloriously from a cloudless sky and all nature
seemed to rejoice that one who had been God's instrument in prepar-

ing Graymoor for the coming of the Friars and Sisters of the Atonement should herself receive the habit of the Third Order, and find her last resting place in the Nuns' cemetery, while she herself having received the Kiss of God's Peace had passed within the Veil to be numbered with the Children of the Atonement in Glory Everlasting.

Chapter XVI

AN UNQUESTIONABLE PRIESTHOOD

WHEN Father Paul made his submission to Catholic authority, he realized that he would enter the Church without ecclesiastical rank of any kind. After his conversion the once prominent Episcopal minister became a Catholic layman. His vows taken as an Anglican Religious had no legal binding or recognition in the Catholic Church. Before he could attain the status of a Religious in the Church he would have to pronounce them again—this time by authorization of and into the hands of the Archbishop of New York, or one delegated by him. However he continued to wear the religious habit. In the meantime, Father Paschal Robinson, O.F.M., graciously remained at Graymoor, and acted as the unofficial Chaplain of the Society until such time as the Archbishop would appoint one.

He offered Holy Mass each day at Graymoor and attended to the spiritual needs of the community. The pastor of the Catholic Church at Cold Spring, a few miles away, in whose parish the Graymoor community was situated, also helped whenever he could. The problem of obtaining the services of a permanent chaplain was a painful problem for the Society of the Atonement after they entered the Catholic Church. Archbishop Farley assigned one priest after another, but often the choice of a chaplain proved most unhappy. The reluctance of these priests to stay at Graymoor is understandable. Life for them at Graymoor was lonely, and these priests, for the most part, were secular priests unaccustomed to loneliness and poor food. So it was no easy task that the Archbishop gave when he assigned one of his priests as Graymoor's chaplain. They could not even look forward to the ordinary comforts and conveniences of the most modest rectory. Eventually it became a matter of sending anyone who could be prevailed upon to go. More than once a priest came as chaplain who was totally unsympathetic to the community. This sort of thing caused the members of the Society added grief at a time when, being new in the Church, they needed and expected guidance and understanding. There were periods of three or four days when they were deprived of the consolation of Mass and Holy Communion.

It is heart-rending to read the record of these early days in Mother Lurana's diary. Time and again she wrote to the Archbishop telling him that they were without a chaplain. The first one sent to them was an old priest who stayed one day and then left, saying that he had some business to attend to in New York. A few days later he sent a note saying that he could not stand the life at Graymoor, that the loneliness of the wilderness filled him with terrified homesickness, that he had no vocation to be a hermit, and that he feared the cold of the coming winter.

The next one was an Italian priest. The letter from the Archbishop's secretary informed Graymoor that he spoke English "pretty well." He stayed a week and then departed with the excuse that his rheumatism would not permit him to walk from the Friary on the top of the Mount to the Convent in the valley each morning for Mass. His successor was another Italian priest who remained two weeks. Then, while on a visit to Mt. Vernon, he fell off a trolley car and was injured. In her diary Mother Lurana wrote: "The poor Archbishop, he must think Graymoor a howling wilderness where no living priest can exist." And so the chaplains came and went. The problem was never completely solved until the Society of the Atonement had its own priests to take care of the community's spiritual needs.

On November 10, 1909, Archbishop Farley paid a visit to Graymoor. Among others, the matter of a chaplain was to be discussed. He arrived in the morning and after inspecting the Friary and the Convent, he confirmed the members of the Society. There were thirteen confirmed that day—two friars, five nuns and six lay associates. Father Paschal Robinson, O.F.M., representing his Provincial, received them into the Third Order of Saint Francis.

That afternoon Father Paul and Mother Lurana spent hours in conference with the Archbishop. They saw him for the first time as he really was—affectionate, charming, patient, and intensely interested in their many problems. The many details which had to be settled before anything like a regular monastic routine could be put into effect at Graymoor were discussed. The Archbishop advised them to proceed cautiously in the management of the affairs of the Society of the Atonement. Knowing how unfamiliar they were with the canonical procedure of the Catholic Church, he counseled them to turn to him for direction rather than risk making a mistake that might hold back the progress of the Society for years.

The important matter of Father Paul's training for the priesthood was also settled. Point by point the Archbishop went through the business at hand patiently. Father Paul and Mother Lurana never forgot the kindness of Archbishop Farley that day. At the close of the conference he told Father Paul that it was his wish to see *The Lamp* continue its crusade for *Unity*. To make sure that lack of funds would not prevent its publication, he left a generous donation. Mother Lurana also received a substantial donation to see the Sisters through any emergency that might arise.

In a few days the Rector of St. Joseph's Seminary, Yonkers, New York, announced to the Seminarians that Archbishop Farley was sending the convert-founder of Graymoor to make his theological studies with them, before ordaining him to the priesthood. The news was received with joy by the students for he was by no means unknown to them. Even before his conversion, he and his Episcopal monastery on the Hudson were often the topic of conversation. When the news of his submission to the Church became known they surmised that the Archbishop would eventually ordain him as a Catholic priest.

The arrangements made by the Archbishop were that he was to spend four days each week at the Seminary and the other three days at Graymoor. It would give Father Paul from Thursday evening until Sunday afternoon to take care of matters which had to be taken care of at Graymoor. In addition to his regular classes, he was given the personal assistance of one of the seminary instructors for after-class work. With this arrangement Archbishop Farley hoped to be able to ordain Father Paul as soon as it was possible to do so, without his having to stay at the seminary for the full four-years course of theology.

So, on the Sunday following the Archbishop's visit, Father Paul left Graymoor for Yonkers. He was dressed in a second-hand suit of clothes which Archbishop Farley gave to him in his need. From that day he traveled in the dress of a Catholic clergyman prescribed by the ecclesiastical laws of the Catholic Church in the United States. Until the day of his death the clothes he wore were of the poorest —purchased from the push-cart dealers on upper Park Avenue in New York City by the Sisters. The day he left Graymoor for the seminary, Mother Lurana wrote in her diary: "It was dreadful to see him out of the dear brown habit. One of the Sisters cried."

"Brother" Paul, as the Archbishop instructed he should be addressed, was well received by the professors and students at St. Joseph's Seminary. Despite his advanced age, he immediately adjusted himself to the daily routine of the seminary. During the course of his studies at St. Joseph's he was never obliged to take a written examination; and at no time was he called upon to speak in class. The only occasion on which he was subjected to a test was an oral examination at the completion of the term.

The students themselves regarded him almost with veneration. His fame awed them, and the stories of his ascetical life had deeply impressed them. Many of these students are pastors and prelates in the New York archdiocese today. The author has spoken to several of them during the writing of this biography, and they have been helpful in throwing more light on that period of his life. While he associated more with the professors—since he was so much older than the students—he, nevertheless, enjoyed recreating with the students. They remember him especially for his great devotion to the Holy Eucharist. While walking on the grounds he never passed by the chapel without kneeling down to offer a prayer. Many times they saw him there praying with outstretched arms. He had a genius for making friends, and rarely was he seen on the campus, either between classes or during recreation, when he was not surrounded by a group of students. The students often bought his railroad ticket to Garrison, since he carried no money on his person. Always he volunteered to reimburse them in postage stamps, but of course these were never accepted by the students of St. Joseph's.

The weeks passed into months and Father Paul adhered to his weekly schedule of four days at the seminary and three days at Graymoor, with clocklike regularity. Invariably a heavy correspondence awaited him when he returned to the Friary each Thursday. *The Lamp* also had to be edited; and it was published month after month without fail. These activities were interesting and stimulating, but the legal dispute over the Sisters' property, in which he had to deal with lawyers and Episcopalian Trustees, drained his physical strength.

While the property of the Friars was in no danger since Father Paul possessed a clear deed to it, he was gravely concerned about the welfare of the Sisters. He felt personally responsible for them and whatever affected them was of vital concern to him. It was for this reason that he undertook to handle the details of this distasteful business for them. From one law office to another he went, consuming precious time and energy that could have been used more profitably in other matters. He particularly dreaded the task because of the possible psychological reaction it might produce in the minds of his former Episcopalian co-religionists, whom he had no desire to offend. He was the soul of charity and patience in his dealings with lawyers and the Episcopalian Trustees of St. John's; for, under no circumstances, would he allow his effective work for the *Reunion* of Christendom to be destroyed.

Throughout his whole life Father Paul was loved for his transparent zeal and charity. The theme of every sermon he gave and every article he wrote on *Unity* was that Charity is the foundation-stone of a *Reunited Christendom*. As an Anglican, Father Paul corresponded with Father Robert Hugh Benson after his conversion to the Catholic Church. Father Paul was edified by the charity and courtesy which Father Benson—whose own father at one time was Archbishop of Canterbury—showed to his former associates in the Church of England. After Father Paul's conversion he, too, extended the same charity and courtesy to his former friends. In pleading for understanding, in the pages of *The Lamp,* he quoted Father Benson, who in a lecture before the Catholic Truth Society of Liverpool, in October 1907, stated:

At that time I believed that we had the true priesthood, and we practiced Catholic doctrine. We had what we believed to be the Mass, we observed silence during the greater part of the day, we wore a certain kind of habit with a girdle, and some wore a biretta. We used the Anglican Book of Common Prayer, supplementing it with a great part of the Catholic Breviary and I for months—I might say years—before I became a Catholic, recited my Rosary every day. We taught the doctrine of Confession, and I can tell you that at the conclusion of the missions which I conducted as part of my public work I used to hear far more confessions than I have heard as a Catholic priest. People came perfectly naturally to confession, and I thank God that I am able to say with certainty that most of them made true acts of contrition. I cannot bear those people who say that the Anglican Church is a mockery. It is not true, and to call it a mockery is almost as much as to say that its clergy were playing a hypocritical part. We were not. We believed that we were true priests, and I may say that we kept the seal of confession exactly as it is kept by Catholic priests. On practically every point except the supremacy of the Pope we believed the teaching of the Catholic Church, taught most of her doctrines, as thousands of Anglican clergy are doing today, and it is this High Church teaching that is building the bridge over which Anglicans will come into the true fold.

Father Paul was one in mind and heart with Father Benson, which explains the keen suffering he endured during the Graymoor property controversy as he strove to combat bitterness with love.

Every moment he could spare during the week ends at Graymoor he gave to the formation of the Rule and Constitution of the Franciscan Friars of the Atonement. He knew that until these were drawn up to the satisfaction of the ecclesiastical authorities there was little possibility of the Society's being approved. Father Paschal Robinson, O.F.M. and Father Edward Blecke, O.F.M. assisted the Graymoor community. These priests assumed most of the work. Their knowledge of Cannon Law and their rich experience, which they placed completely at the service of Father Paul, saved him many hours of labor. To these two devoted friends, as well as to Father Stanislaus Woywod, O.F.M., another outstanding scholar and Canonist, who at a later date rendered the same invaluable service to the community, the Society of the Atonement owes a great debt of gratitude.

As the seminary term drew to a close in the spring of 1910, Father Paul was informed by the rector that he would be promoted to the sub-deaconate and the deaconate. He also advised him not to entertain any hopes of being ordained to the priesthood that year. The rector told Father Paul that Archbishop Farley considered it inadvisable to advance him to the priesthood until he had at least another year of theology.

Father Paul resigned himself to the Archbishop's decision. The same unhappy conditions in regard to a permanent chaplain still prevailed at Graymoor, so the news came as a disappointment to the Sisters. They immediately began a Novena to Our Lady of Perpetual Help to obtain the favor of an early ordination for Father Paul. Under date of June 8th, 1910, Mother Lurana wrote in her diary:

A letter from Father Paul tells us the wonderful news that Archbishop Farley will ordain him on June 16th, in the Seminary chapel. . . . Wonderful to relate, the 16th is the Feast of Our Lady of Perpetual Help, she to whom we have prayed for this intention.

When the great day of his ordination arrived there were just a few of Father Paul's intimate friends present for the ceremony. Mother Lurana and Sister Amelia went down from Graymoor. Father Paschal Robinson was present, as he was for so many other notable occasions in the early days of the Society. Father Solanus, O.F.M. Cap., from the Capuchin monastery in Yonkers, was also present. He had already been invited to preach the sermon at Father Paul's first Solemn Mass. That day Mother Lurana recorded the event in these words:

I cannot describe the wonderful ceremony any more than I can describe the dignity of our Father, nor the look upon his face. A true son of St. Francis in his gray-brown habit and white vestments and white linen alb, embroidered in blue with Our Lady's monogram and lilies. Ah, now, no one can question his priesthood, a priest forever, forever!

Chapter XVII

A HOUSE LEFT DESOLATE

THE PAGES of the history of the Catholic Church are reddened by the blood of persecution. The very fact that she endured the frightful slaughter which resulted in a huge multitude of martyrs, disaster of all kinds, confiscation of property, schism and heresy is proof of her divine establishment and the indwelling of the Holy Spirit. Decius, the Roman Emperor, decreed the destruction of Christianity in the same words that Cato, the Roman Senator, had decreed the destruction of Carthage four hundred years before—"Delenda Est." However, in this struggle it was the Roman Empire and not the Church that was destroyed. Graymoor's early history is replete with evidences of the never-failing Providence of Almighty God. Were it not protected by Divine Providence it could never have endured, as being the whim of a mere mortal, in the face of all that did happen to destroy the Society of the Atonement. So far in the life of Father Paul we have told of the great trials which came to him through the persecution of his fellow Anglicans. That record is closed now, for he is safe from their thrusts within the Fold of Peter, and they can no longer harass him. But coming into the Catholic Church, the crosses he carried became heavier in another way, and were it not for the sustaining Grace of God he could not have, humanly speaking, carried them. What makes this chapter of his life almost unbelievable is the undeniable fact that his persecutors were not Anglicans but Catholics; one of them was the first priest ordained in the Society after Father Paul. Some of these attacks on Father Paul cannot be revealed in this volume since they involve persons still living.

In later life Father Paul never spoke of these trials. The only written evidences of them are the veiled allusions to them in the

early editions of *The Lamp,* and in documents on file in the Graymoor archives.

Many knew of the new storm that engulfed Graymoor after its
conversion. They knew of it either because they had instigated it, or
because they had become part of it. Father Paul discussed it only
with the Ecclesiastical Authorities of the Archdiocese of New York
with whom such matters remain inviolate. His deep sense of loyalty
to the Society of the Atonement would not permit him to discuss its
affairs, especially its family problems, with anyone whom it did not
concern. Yet through all these trials the Society of the Atonement endured because it was founded by, "a wise man who built his house
on a rock. And the rain fell, and the floods came, and the winds
blew and beat against that house, but it did not fall because it was
founded on rock." And the rock was the faith of Father Paul in
God's promises. That faith never faltered even while he carried a
heavy cross, which was most of his life. For when he was not carrying a cross he lived in the shadow of one, until he entered into
"that rest which remains for the people of God."

God's answer to those whose decree for Graymoor was "Delenda
Est" was the same one He gave to Decius; for as the early Christians multiplied and spread over the earth under the very eyes of
Decius, so too the spiritual children of Father Paul multiplied and
spread under the eyes of his persecutors. Some, realizing their mistake,
later became loyal friends of Father Paul. The rest he left to God.

Before the reception of the Society of the Atonement into the
Catholic Church there were always a few at the friary "trying out
their vocation." After the "first fervor" had worn off and they settled down "to live the life" which Graymoor's rule imposed on
them, they found it too rigorous to endure. So one after another
packed his belongings and left. And, month after month, the story
remained the same. Father Paul and his one faithful Friar-Brother remained the only permanent inhabitants on the Mount of the Atonement. In his preaching engagements, when he spoke so ambitiously
of the Society of the Atonement and its great vocation, no matter
what grandiose thoughts were conjured up in the minds of his lis-

teners, he himself knew only too well that he spoke of a dream yet to be fulfilled.

When the Society became Catholic there were many within the Church, among whom were some priests, who, for some unexplained reason, had no desire to see the Society continue as a Catholic community. These persons wondered how long it would be before ecclesiastical authority would suppress it. Had they reserved their opinions to themselves no harm would have been done. Unfortunately, however, this was not the case, and a cloud of suspicion hung over Graymoor for years. Father Paul suffered keenly from this opposition as he struggled bravely to establish the Society according to the laws of the Catholic Church. A few years after the Society's conversion he was able to erect a small minor seminary on the Mount—the story of which will be told in a later chapter.

There were not a few—particularly the ones who pretended to be "in the know"—who would glibly predict one fate or another for the community, none of which was very pleasant. These self-styled prophets caused untold harm to the Society of the Atonement, and held up its progress for years. Aside from the anguish inflicted on Father Paul, the havoc these reports worked within the community left lasting scars. A student would spread the news among his fellow students that he had heard that Graymoor was to be closed down soon; or certainly it would be as soon as Father Paul died. The reason it was not already closed was because the ecclesiastical authorities did not wish to hurt Father Paul. And so, rather than chance an uncertain future, many students left from year to year.

This devastating gossip went on for years. The author distinctly remembers being told this very story when he arrived at Graymoor in 1931. It was told to him by students who later left the community, and by several laymen who were taking advantage of Father Paul's hospitality at that time. In a conference with Father Paul, in which the author related what he had heard, Father Paul made no comment on the story whatsoever, but merely told him about the Covenant Promise.

More than one boy who wished to become a priest in the Society wrote telling Father Paul that he could not come because his pastor was opposed to the idea, and had refused him a recommendation. In *The Lamp* of August, 1914, Father Paul made a mild protest:

We have lost many vocations up to the present time because aspirants desiring to come to Graymoor have been counseled against doing so by priests who did not believe that the Society of the Atonement was going to prove a success. It is time, we think, when the clergy who have doubted the permanency of the Society of the Atonement should alter their opinion.

The discriminatory practice continued even after this, and in a later issue of *The Lamp* the complaint was repeated:

We have been disappointed in the coming of several young men to begin their studies in the preparation for the priesthood in our First Congregation, and again the influence that dissuaded these young men from coming has been traced to the same source. We rely upon those of the clergy who have a better opinion of us to offset by their good offices in our behalf this unfortunate want of faith on the part of others.

Apart from these two protests in *The Lamp* he made no attempt to vindicate the Graymoor position, no matter how freely the rumor about its instability circulated. He went about his duties placidly, and gave no indication of interior agitation. Some of the stories which came to him were so fantastic that there was no point in answering them. Even what seemed plausible was difficult to refute. His great consolation was found in prayer. After a busy day he would spend whole nights lying prostrate in prayer before the Most Blessed Sacrament, praying for the fulfillment of God's promise to him.

The effect of this campaign against Graymoor was that after being in the Catholic Church for ten years the Friars of the Atonement consisted of Father Paul and two priests ordained in 1920. Brother Paul Jacob, who since his conversion was known as Brother Anthony, was still the only Friar-Brother. Others had come, aspiring to be Brothers, but they left for the same reasons that prompted the exodus of the students.

In the book in which Father Paul recorded the clothings and professions of the first members of the Society, the very first entry reads:

In the year of Our Lord 1912, on the feast of the Conversion of St. Paul the Apostle, January 25th, in the Chapel of St. Francis on the

Mount of the Atonement, Graymoor, Garrison, N. Y., I, (Fr.) Edward Blecke, O. F. M., being authorized by Cardinal Farley, Archbishop of New York, received to the Profession of life vows in the 1st Congregation of the Society of the Atonement of the 3rd Order Regular of St. Francis, Paul James Francis, S. A. (Lewis T. Wattson) Priest, and Anthony Paul (Ferdinand Wallerstein) Brother. On the same day and in the same place I gave the habit of the 1st Congregation of the Society of the Atonement to Paul Francis, giving him the name of Brother Francis. In testimony whereof I sign my name

FR. EDWARD BLECKE, O.F.M.

Brother Francis was professed in religion and was ordained to the priesthood in St. Joseph's Seminary on May 17, 1913. Father Paul rejoiced that there was now another priest to assist him establish the Society on a sound basis. After his ordination Father Francis was appointed novice master. This priest brought the community closer to the brink of complete ruin than any other previous misfortune had. Only the providential intervention of several devoted friends of Father Paul among the clergy, who stood high in ecclesiastical circles, averted the disaster of closing Graymoor. Father Francis was never loyal to Father Paul, and he was completely influenced by those who predicted Graymoor's suppression. Father Francis was a brilliantly intellectual man, who thought Father Paul was incapable of governing a religious community. Moreover, he had illusions of grandeur in which he saw himself "in control" of Graymoor after Father Paul would be deposed as Superior. Furthermore, he thoroughly resented the confidence Father Paul placed in Mother Lurana in regard to the affairs of the Society.

In justice to Father Francis' memory we may say that perhaps Father Paul made a mistake in placing too great a responsibility in the hands of an inexperienced priest. At that time Father Paul was perhaps the most eminent convert in America; besides he was a renowned preacher. He was in constant demand from many sources. And he saw in all these engagements to preach and speak an opportunity for furthering his work for the Reunion of Christendom. Besides all these engagements, he had to leave Graymoor often on affairs of business. And, in leaving the monastery, he did not leave behind him a well-ordered community. For all practical purposes ev-

erything was suspended until he returned, for Father Francis was anything but a good disciplinarian. And, laboring under the delusion and
the fear that Graymoor was to be suppressed, he did not care what
happened.

As novice master, Father Francis had as his assistant a member of
the community who was known as Brother Pascal. He was far from
being an exemplary religious, and Father Paul wished to dismiss him.
However, Pascal was a particular friend of Father Francis, who was
ever ready to defend him.

In all religious communities within the Catholic Church "particular
friendships" are discouraged because the Church, after almost two
thousand years of experience in human affairs, has found that such a
friendship constitutes one of the greatest obstacles to spiritual prog-
ess. But Graymoor was a new community within the Church at that
time, and there was still much to be learned. A sudden tragedy is like
a flash of lightning which, in a split second, illuminates the landscape
hidden in darkness and reveals the pitfalls to be avoided. The tragedy that came to Graymoor through a particular friendship taught
Father Paul a great and valuable lesson. Until his death he remained
the relentless foe of particular friendships within the Graymoor community. It seemed as though the wounds inflicted on him through a
particular friendship of two of the early members of his community
had never really healed.

Affairs at Graymoor became so intolerable for Father Paul in the
early part of March, 1915, that he consulted the Auxiliary Bishop of
New York, the Most Reverend Thomas F. Cusack. (Archbishop Farley had appointed Bishop Cusack to watch over the infant Society of
the Atonement.) The Bishop's advice to Father Paul was immediately
to dismiss Brother Pascal. That evening Father Paul notified Pascal to
leave the community the next morning. Pascal's answer was: "I refuse
to do so. We are under instructions from Bishop Cusack to remain
until he directs otherwise." Father Paul then told him of his visit to
Bishop Cusack, and of the Bishop's desire for him to leave.

That night, after the community had retired, Pascal walked to
Peekskill and contacted Father Francis, who was staying in New
York, prior to his leaving for a monastery where he was to make a re-

treat. Pascal's story to Father Francis was that he had been turned out of the monastery.

The following day Father Francis returned with Pascal, who had met him at the station in Garrison. They arrived at Graymoor with taxicabs and a truck for luggage. Father Francis stormed into Father Paul's office, protesting Pascal's dismissal. In the meantime Pascal was rounding up the students and novices for a quick departure in the taxicabs. They left under the impression that they were acting under orders from Bishop Cusack. At the appointed time, Father Francis got into a taxicab with several students and drove off. Only two students remained loyal to Father Paul and refused to go.

Father Paul, in recording the tragic incident of the students' departure, wrote:

. . . not one of them being allowed by the conspirators to say one word to me, not even good-bye. I have now learned that this attempt to ruin our Institute has been going on in secret for weeks. In his interview Father Francis (before his departure) showed me a telegram from Bishop Cusack (of New York) authorizing him to investigate the affairs at the Friary and report to him the same afternoon. This was the telegram that had frightened the students into their sudden departure. When I saw Bishop Cusack a few days later, to my amazement, he informed me that Father Francis had not been near him; neither had he, the Bishop, sent him any telegram.

On that day, March 6, 1915, Mother Lurana wrote in her diary: "This day will ever be remembered in the annals of our First Congregation, for this day—'The strong man armed, the destroyer of souls,' assaulted the holy place." Then follows a long account of what happened that day, which she concludes with the words: "I cannot write any more of this pitiful thing. My pity and my heartache is for the priest who still wearing the habit of the Society could do such a deed; come like a destroyer to tear down with his own hands what he, himself, had worked so hard to build up. Truly the devil is hard on his dupes."

Through his great trial Father Paul found consolation in the devotion and loyalty of Brother Anthony, the Sisters and Mother Lurana. He did not "tread in the wine-press alone." Sixteen years before, when he was in the novitiate of the Episcopalian Order of the Holy Cross, he wrote a beautiful letter asking Mother Lurana to pray that he would have the courage and faith to endure the suffering which he knew must come:

The fact that we should be so entirely of one heart and one soul in our spiritual vision is a striking proof of itself that our inspiration and illumination comes from the same Divine Source. Especially as no one fully understands either of us save God and I trust our patron saints. We are being drawn into the deeper recesses of the Sacred Heart and I feel that the Holy Spirit is revealing to you perhaps more clearly than He is to me, *what that means.* "Are ye able to drink of the bitter cup that I drank of and to be baptized with?" We cannot be in the highest, divinest sense one with our Lord without being one with Him in His Passion and Martyr death. Under the fervor of a sudden spiritual impulse two or three times lately I have cried unto God and said— "O Father in Heaven, Thou didst not spare Thy only begotten Son, spare not me!" And then when the voice of the Beloved has seemed to answer—"You know not what you have asked"—I have stood aghast at the awful significance of such a prayer. I have offered myself to God to be a victim for the sins of my brethren, as well as my own, in union with His Son. I have put forth my hand to the plough, I cannot turn back; I must follow Him, Who set His face as a flint to go up to Jerusalem to die.

I believe He has accepted the free will oblation, I believe I shall taste of His bitter cup; I believe I shall know something of His baptism of blood; but there is one phase of His Passion I shrink back from with a nameless dread, and that is the "treading of the winepress alone," the exceeding bitter cry—"My God, my God, why hast Thou forsaken Me?" So long as my soul is filled with the consolations of the Comforter—so long as my heart is like the burning bush flaming with the delicious presence of Jesus to drink even gall would be sweet—but, oh, to be left alone, in the darkness with the wild beasts of hell all about me and the solid ground sinking from under my feet, no sweet consolations, no sunshine of heaven, no arm of Omnipotence to lean on—oh, could I follow my Lord even then. Oh, pray for me that my faith shall never fail even for an instant—that whatever suffering or anguish or crucifixion, even to literal martyrdom I may be called upon to undergo I may endure cheerfully and even joyously for the love wherewith I shall be consumed for Jesus Christ and the souls of men.

Several weeks after Father Francis left Graymoor, Father Paul received a letter from his good and loyal friend Father (now Monsignor) Edward Hawks, who was a priest in St. Edward's Rectory, Philadelphia, Pennsylvania. In the letter he refers to one of the students who had left St. John's Seminary. (Here we shall call this student T.M.) The letter read:

St. Edward's Rectory
Philadelphia, Pa.
April 30, 1915

DEAR FATHER PAUL:

Enclosed is a document that I think you will find useful. I discovered who was the originator of the rumor here. It was T. M. His pastor sent him to me and he of his own free will wrote and signed the enclosed. I must say in justification of him, that the rumors were very much "improved" upon when I heard them. He denies that he said anything further than is contained in this statement. He spoke in the highest terms of Graymoor. He also denies that he took any part in plotting against the community. He believes himself a victim and sees now that he acted with great imprudence. . . .

He tells me that for several weeks before he left he was conscious that something was wrong. Father Francis practically took no classes at all. . . . T. M., however, was so carried off his feet by the apparent truth of what was told him that he never used any proper precautions to test the real state of affairs. He wanted to go home and he took this opportunity of going without proper thought. Directly he left Graymoor he began to see the mistake he had made. He is very sorry now for everything, and very fearsome lest he be prevented from further study for the priesthood. He seems to be a very nice young man—but very unsophisticated. Just the kind of person who would be easily influenced. . . .

I hope you will be pleased with the results I have obtained. Can I do anything further?

Yours very sincerely
EDWARD HAWKS

The statement of T.M. was as follows:

To whom it may concern—I wish to state of my own free will that I left St. John's House of Studies at Graymoor because I thought Father Francis was authorized to close the house, Brother Pascal having informed me that the Cardinal of New York had sent Father Francis to Graymoor for that purpose. I know nothing whatever derogatory to the

character of Father Paul James Francis, S.A., whom I have always regarded as a saint.

I was astonished when Brother Pascal informed me that things were
not as they should be, and although he gave no proofs of the scandalous
things that he stated, yet I believed him and Father Francis to be sincere
when they told me of these alleged scandals. Brother Pascal took me
and B. S. and K. H. into a room by ourselves and read us a copy of a
letter which he stated had been sent to the Bishop. This letter contained
serious charges against the Superior of the Community (Father Paul)
and also charged him with exceeding his authority in the governing of
the Community.

I now believe that this letter was never sent and was only used as a
means of persuading me and other men to leave Graymoor. I left Graymoor in an automobile with Father Francis, Brother Pascal and several
others, thinking that I was obeying the mandate of Bishop Cusack. Although I never asked to see the document, trusting entirely to the sincerity of Father Francis and Brother Pascal. On the way to Garrison I
was astounded to hear Brother Pascal remark that it would be a good
thing to lay the state of affairs before the *Menace* and get a fortune of
several thousand dollars out of the scandal.

I now understand that I have been the victim of a conspiracy which
was made between Father Francis and Brother Pascal to injure Father
Paul and if possible to ruin the community. I think they did this for
revenge when they realized their inability to 'control' the community. I
am very grateful for this opportunity of doing anything in my power to
repair whatever damage has been done. I have a letter dated the 21st
of March written by Father Francis. I wish to quote this extract from
it—which goes a long way to explain the intention of Father Francis. It
read: "I returned on Tuesday (to Graymoor) and was there long enough
to pack my trunk and come back to New York. All the boys were there
we left behind, and they were certainly a very sick looking crowd."

The words prove that Father Francis had wilfully deceived me when
he said that the Bishop had authorized him to close the house. I have
also received letters from Mr. G., Mr. H., Mr. S. and Brother Pascal. The
first two wrote letters which were outrageous in their lack of decency in
speaking of Graymoor, and I tore them up in disgust and burned
them. . . . I repeat what I have already said, that I never saw anything
at Graymoor which could give any grounds for scandal. I found the life
there hard and felt that I was unfit for it. I intended to leave at the end
of the scholastic year. I only left when I did because I unwisely believed the revelation that Father Francis and Brother Pascal made to
me.

                                    Signed—T. M.

These infamous things and this frightful opprobrium was heaped upon Father Paul by a man he loved and trusted. Years later, Father Francis wrote to Father Paul, asking favors. And, in granting them, Father Paul ended his letter with the words: "With *prayerful good will* for your future, I am—Sincerely yours in Christ—Paul James Francis, S.A."

Satan, in trying to destroy Graymoor, had seemingly done his work well. And it behooved him to try, for Graymoor was raised up by God to "repair the breach" which he had made by his diabolical machinations. But he did not know that he reckoned with another Job, whose faith in God was just as strong. "And the Lord said to him (Satan): 'hast thou considered my servant Job, that there is none like him in the earth, a simple and upright man and fearing God, and avoiding evil?' And Satan answering said, 'Doth Job fear God in vain . . . stretch forth thy hand a little and touch all that he hath: and see if he blesseth thee not to thy face.' Then the Lord said to Satan: 'Behold all that he hath is in thy hand; only put not forth thy hand upon his person.' " And when Satan had destroyed all that Job had: "Job rose up . . . and fell down upon the ground and worshipped [God]"; saying: "The Lord gave and the Lord hath taken away. As it hath pleased the Lord, so is it done. Blessed be the name of the Lord."

They who read these pages must not be scandalized at what happened so unjustly to Father Paul. Our Divine Lord said to His disciples: "It is impossible that scandals should not come, but woe to him through whom they come." There were the scandals of His own betrayal, the false accusations and the desertion, in His own most desperate hour, of those to whom He gave the power to judge the twelve tribes of Israel. God permits these scandals only because He is infinitely able to bring good out of evil. Almighty God rewarded the faith of Job with a greater abundance than he possessed before his great trial. So, too, God greatly rewarded the faith of Father Paul in the ensuing days of his great trial.

When the tragedy struck Graymoor Father Paul was crushed. The labor of years crashed before his very eyes. But, like Job, he "sinned not by his lips; nor spoke he any foolish thing against God." He had the same promise from God that He gave to Abraham. And as Abraham did not ask God, when He told him to sacrifice his only son, Isaac: how then shall I be the father of a great nation? Neither did Father Paul question God. But for months he went about as in a daze, and even years later he could not think back on the incident without pain. Apparently the affair had its effect on his health also, for in her diary, under date of June 1, 1916, Mother Lurana wrote:

Such a beautiful day. A great peace seems to encompass the whole world and, like the hush before the battle, my own soul also. Indeed I am summoning all the foundations and pillars of my faith to reassure myself; for tomorrow Father will undergo his operation. It will, I think, be a serious one. It seems such a dreadful thing to strike down a man in apparently excellent health (for Father has slowly gotten back the ground he lost in the shock of a year and a half ago). He seems utterly unconcerned; went to a baseball game with some of the Brothers and boys, and this evening expects to greatly enjoy their debate on the question of "Women's Suffrage."

Of course word of what had happened reached the Archbishop. Even if it had not, it would have had to be reported to him. When summoned to the chancery and asked for an explanation, Father Paul was able to give very little explanation. However, the unpleasant affair was eventually thoroughly understood by the ecclesiastical authorities, much to the relief of Father Paul. He then set to work at rebuilding his community with new enthusiasm. He was a changed man after it was all over; and to his intimate friends this change was very obvious. It was not a gradual change but one which took place almost overnight. It was particularly noticeable in the tighter hold he took on the reins of the community. The discipline became stricter, and recalcitrants soon discovered that he could be a severe disciplinarian. The benevolent indulgence with which he had treated their infractions of the rules in former days was replaced by stern measures calculated to bring to the fore the character of his authority. He meted out penances that frequently seemed to be hard and unreasonable. But they had the desired effect. A healthful community life was soon in evidence. The best proof of the fact is that candidates who then

came to the Society had greater stability, and many of them persevered.

Many outsiders learned of the desertion at Graymoor. They knew,
too, of the grief and heartache it had caused Father Paul. Yet when
they saw him on infrequent occasions—unless they were his inti-
mates—they could discern no visible change in him. The same peaceful expression which was characteristically his remained through this
ordeal, as always. Not one word of complaint or even apology, for
that matter, escaped his lips. Some attributed this silence, this reluctance to speak of what had happened in the community, to embarrassment. But these persons did not know Father Paul as he really
was. Frankness was one of his most lovable qualities and he could
speak of the most delicate subjects with such guilelessness that one
knew at once it was a manifestation of his simplicity. Few realized
that in this instance the reason behind his reserve was something entirely different from what was imagined. That reason was his deep
sense of loyalty to the Society of the Atonement. He remained
serene because his trust in God had not wavered; his confidence in
the future of his community was not shaken. Father Paul believed
that the day would come when his friars would be as numerous as
the sands of the seashore and the stars in the heavens.

One important decision he made after the tragedy was to accept no
preaching engagements which would take him away from Graymoor
for more than one night. For almost twenty years he had carried a
burden that was almost too much to ask any man to bear. But the
circumstances were such that he had no alternative. His one companion of Anglican days, Brother Anthony, did what he could to lighten
the load. In caring for the many homeless men who were always
knocking at the friary door for food or a place to sleep he did all
that one could reasonably expect of him. Father Paul's great need for
years was priests of the Society to share some of the offices which he
discharged single-handed—Superior, novice master, teacher, editor,
chaplain.

After his conversion, his reputation as having been one of the best
preachers in the Episcopal Church became known among the Catho-

lic clergy, and many of them tried to obtain his services for parish missions. His background made him particularly desirable for missions to non-Catholics. He welcomed these invitations and responded to as many as was physically possible, even though it meant absences from the friary for long intervals at a time. Paramount in his mind, once he became a Catholic, was the idea of continuing to work for the conversion of his non-Catholic brethren. He did not want to lose contact with them. He wanted them to know that in "going to Rome" he had not abandoned them.

Preaching these missions to Protestants provided an outlet for his zeal. Archbishop Farley, who became a Cardinal of the Church with sixteen others—among whom was Monsignor Falconio—in 1911, invited Father Paul to give a mission for non-Catholics. He began it in St. Patrick's Cathedral on Laetare Sunday in 1914. The diocesan paper, the *Catholic News,* in an item with the headline: "Lenten Crowds at the Cathedral," and dated March 28th of that year, stated:

The course of lectures for non-Catholics delivered every evening during the past week by the Reverend Paul James Francis, of the Society of the Atonement, attracted to the edifice congregations that numbered almost three thousand persons each evening. The center aisle was reserved for non-Catholics, many of whom presented invitation cards at the door. It is estimated that nearly one-third of those who attended the lectures were non-Catholic.

The daily New York papers of March 26th reported an amusing incident which occurred during the mission. On the previous evening three clergymen wearing Roman collars entered the Cathedral and were met by one of the ushers. Not recognizing them, the usher explained to the visitors that all the seats were already taken. He then offered them three backless stools at the door. It was not until later, when one of the priests of the Cathedral came down the aisle to the back, that the usher discovered who the clergymen were. One was the Reverend Doctor William Hughes, Vice-President of Cathedral College; another was Monsignor Patrick J. Hayes, the Chancellor of the Archdiocese; and the third was Cardinal Farley. The news item concluded with the observation: "Cardinal Farley evidently enjoyed the situation more than anyone else, save possibly his two companions."

Father Paul learned of the incident the next day at dinner. Writing of it to the Community at Graymoor, he said:

Last night the congregation overflowed into the aisles and there were fully three thousand people present. . . . I did not know until dinner today that His Eminence sat for a whole hour in the rear of the Cathedral and heard both the regular instruction on THE MOTHER OF GOD and the sermon on CHOICE BETWEEN LIFE AND DEATH. . . . It was one of my most animated sermons, and I gave that description of Satan's Council of War in Hell, and his delight at the proposal of one of his satellites to go into the world and preach the gospel of PROCRASTINATION.

Father Paul was a preacher of the old school. Like the convert, Newman, he drew heavily from Scripture both for his texts and his examples. By his ingenuity he succeeded in making a seemingly dull incident in the Old Testament take on life and meaning. Moreover, he had the happy faculty of being able to reach each of his hearers as if he were talking to him personally. During this mission at St. Patrick's Cathedral he wrote to Mother Lurana:

I had the happiness this morning of being approached by a Catholic layman who, eleven years ago, was drawn away from the Church by the apostate Father O'Connor; and who accounts it a mercy of God that he accepted the invitation I had printed in the newspapers. The poor man came trembling with nervous fear, and went away with some of the joy of the Prodigal's welcome in his heart. I hope to reconcile him formally before the Mission is over.

Mother Lurana's diary is a rich source of information for the period. Her custom, from the very beginning of the Society's foundation, was carefully to record each evening the happenings of the day. We thank God that she was able to see the importance of this task. Because of her faithfulness in recording all events we have almost a day-by-day account of the activities of Father Paul. Her diary tells that the year 1914 was an extremely busy one for him. He gave one mission after another, hardly finishing at one place when

Father Paul and a Group of Friars

At Catholic University in Washington, D. C. The Apostolic Delegate to the United States, the Most Reverend Amleto Cicognani, is seated to the right of Father Paul.

A Group of Sisters of the Atonement

Sant' Onofrio al Gianicolo

Church of the Equestrian Order of the Holy Sepulchre of Jerusalem.
The Graymoor Friars are the custodians of this church in Rome.

he was already preparing to go to a new appointment. Besides missions, he was in great demand as an occasional preacher and lecturer. He delivered the sermon on the Feast of St. Patrick in 1914, at the invitation of Cardinal Farley. The following month he lectured to a woman's club of the Cathedral parish in Baltimore. During Holy Week he was in Far Rockaway, Long Island, preaching the Three Hours service.

One of the most successful missions was the one he gave in Holy Angels' Church in Chicago. The Auxiliary Bishop, Bishop McGavick, was the pastor of the church. The parish bulletin spoke highly of Father Paul's forcefulness as a preacher, and attributed the many spiritual fruits that resulted from the mission to his preaching. It stated:

The Mission to non-Catholics—conducted by Father Paul James Francis, is a pleasant memory in the parish. Seldom has any mission ever been given that made a profounder impression. The church was crowded every night, and on the last night many had to be sent away, much to their disappointment. Fully two-thirds of the attendance was non-Catholic. The discourses of Father Paul should do much to destroy prejudice, bringing about good will, and finally lead people to the Church. The results, too, were very gratifying. *Fifty-seven joined the instruction class, forty-three at this writing have been received into the Church and most of the rest will be received.* . . . A notable circumstance in connection with the Mission was the wonderful effect which the Missionary's sermon on the Real Presence had on the audience. They appeared overpowered or spellbound, and sat motionless in the pews and made no effort to leave the church until the lights were being put out. They seemed to feel that they were truly in the Divine Presence.

Is it any wonder that Father Paul was in demand everywhere? But when tragedy struck Graymoor he was compelled to decline any invitation which meant his being away for any length of time. He had to rebuild the Society; and, in rebuilding it, he was determined to stand guard himself. Father Paul sowed the seed of his Society again, but this time not on rocky ground; for now he well knew that such seeds, "when trouble and persecution come, at once fall away." Rather, he sowed in good ground to yield a hundredfold; and lo! it did.

Chapter XVIII

EVENTFUL YEARS

WHEN the Society of the Atonement was received into the Catholic Church, Graymoor was solitude, silence and peace. There was just a little frame friary on the summit of the mountain; and St. John's Church and the Sisters' convent at the foot of the Mount. One who knew it then wrote, thirty-five years later:

Graymoor in its early days was the abode of holy poverty; and, of course, Father Paul was Graymoor, all of it, its raison d'être, its heart, its soul. Graymoor had not become fashionable. The ubiquitous pilgrim had not discovered it and despoiled it forever of some of its primitive charm and simplicity. There were no winding drives, no house of studies, none of the things now deemed so necessary for a thriving community.

The physical development of Graymoor began almost immediately after the Society of the Atonement became Catholic. St. John's-in-the-Wilderness was completely renovated at the personal expense of Archbishop Farley. The work done added greatly to the beauty and strength of the building which, after the vicissitudes of thirty years of an interesting history, had become rather rickety. It was dedicated for Catholic services by the Most Reverend Thomas F. Cusack, who was assisted by seven priests, in October, 1910. The master of ceremonies was the Reverend Joseph P. Donahue, who is now an Auxiliary Bishop of the New York Archdiocese.

The next important development on the Mount of the Atonement was the erection of St. Francis' Chapel, which for almost forty years has remained the community chapel of the Friars. Famous as this chapel is, its architect is far more famous; for he is recognized as one of the world's greatest church architects. He is also the most eminent of Father Paul's converts.

Work was begun on the chapel on St. Patrick's Day, March 17, 1911. It was dedicated to St. Francis on the Feast of the Chair of

St. Peter at Rome, January 18, 1912. It was in this chapel that Father Paul praised God many hours each day as he chanted the Divine Office or knelt in silent prayer in his choir stall.

The original architect of St. Francis' chapel was John Cyril Hawes. Before the chapel was completed another famous architect and eminent convert, Mr. Carlton Strong—who was once president of Father Paul's *Anglo-Roman Union*—also worked on the plans.

Before coming to Graymoor, John Hawes was a clergyman of the Church of England, laboring in the Bahamas. Before leaving the Bahamas he had built six stone churches in two years, acting not only as architect but also working as mason and carpenter.

Father Paul received John Hawes into the Catholic Church on St. Joseph's Day, 1911. In gratitude to God for his conversion to the Catholic Church he drew up the plans for St. Francis' Chapel, and then returned to England.

Today John Hawes is one of the world's most famous men. He is the Right Reverend Monsignor John Cyril Hawes, a prelate of the Catholic Church. He is better known as Father Jerome, the Hermit of Cat Island in the Bahamas. On Cat Island Father Jerome wears the gray habit of a Franciscan friar because he has always loved St. Francis and the Franciscan way of life.

After many years as a Catholic priest in Australia, he returned to what he considers the most beautiful of all places—the Bahamas. There may be seen the fruits of his labor as an Anglican, considered architectural gems, and also the beautiful Catholic churches he has designed since he returned there as a Catholic priest. Plans for a new cathedral which will command the entrance of the harbor of Nassau have been drawn by him.

In coming to Graymoor, John Cyril Hawes found the gift of the Catholic Faith; and, in leaving, he left a trace of his genius on the Mount of the Atonement—the Caput et Mater of the Friars of the Atonement, the beautiful chapel of St. Francis.

In the same year that St. Francis' Church was dedicated Father Paul saw another dream of his realized. On May 21, 1912, Bishop Cusack broke ground for St. John's minor seminary. The following year, on the Feast of the Nativity of Our Blessed Lady, September

8, 1913, the school was opened. There were only four students in attendance. But Father Paul showed no discouragement in his writing in *The Lamp*. The God of Abraham seemed to be testing Father Paul's faith in the Covenant Promise; but that faith never wavered. "We have four young men to start with, in the new House of Studies," he wrote, "and others will be coming soon, we trust, and these should have plenty of good milk to drink. It is time the Friars had a cow. Who will give us one for our lads?"

The following year (1914) Father Paul wrote:

It is a great joy to us to record from time to time the growth of our Apostolic School which means so much for the future of our institute. We now have, besides the two novices, seven scholastics. . . . If the school keeps on growing at the present rate it will be only a short time when we shall have to be enlarging the building."

Father Paul's faith was, "the substance of things to be hoped for, the evidence of things that appear not." Despite the small number of students for the priesthood in St. John's, ground was broken for a new addition on June 5, 1914.

The following year (1915) St. John's seminary was filled with novices and scholastics, but it was then that tragedy struck Graymoor through the perfidy of one of its own members; and St. John's House of Studies was left desolate. With the exception of two students who remained loyal to Father Paul, the Society, as far as membership was concerned, was set back fifteen years, and Father Paul had to begin all over again. That testing of his faith in God's promise, *"Surely blessing I will bless thee; and multiplying I will multiply thee,"* continued for another ten years. In 1920 two friar clerics were ordained to the priesthood; but they also left the Society eventually.

In the meantime, the physical development of Graymoor kept up a rapid pace. In 1916 a large administration building was erected on the Mount of the Atonement. Adjacent property had been acquired for an industrial farm. On July 18, 1916, Mr. Floyd Keeler, a convert to Catholicism, arrived at Graymoor with his wife and three children to take charge of the farm. He was formerly an archdeacon of the Anglican diocese of Salina, Kansas. One of his children became a Sister of the Atonement. Mr. Keeler appears again, in this story, in Chapter XIX.

The two most important developments of the Society of the Atonement during the ten years between 1915 and 1925 were: the establishment of a major seminary adjacent to the Catholic University of America at Washington, D. C.; and the establishment of the Graymoor Press at Peekskill, New York.

The property which Father Paul acquired in Washington, D. C. for the establishment of a major seminary was known as the "Robinson Property." It consisted of thirty-three and one-third acres, and the Robinson family called it "The Vineyard." Graymoor purchased this magnificent property in the spring of 1923; and then it became the major seminary of the Friars of the Atonement. It solved the problem of providing for those who, having finished the course of studies in St. John's and the novitiate training, were prepared to go on for higher studies.

Father Paul, in the June, 1923, issue of *The Lamp,* explained the new development by stating with his characteristic faith:

. . . We have acquired title to "The Vineyard," a tract of thirty-three acres of land adjacent to the grounds of the Catholic University. Here again we see the finger of God. As the youngest member in the Religious Family of the Catholic Church in America, the Society of the Atonement was necessarily late in following the older Religious Communities in establishing their Colleges as the spokes of a wheel around the hub of the Catholic University proper.

The other Religious Orders and Congregations being first upon the field had the opportunity of selecting the choicest sites for their various monasteries, seminaries, novitiates, houses of study and college buildings. It has become more and more difficult from year to year for late comers to secure suitable grounds near the University, and the price for valuable land has risen accordingly. Nevertheless, as Divine Providence reserved the Precious Name of the Atonement for our Holy Society, born in the Religious Family of the Catholic Church 'out of due season' as it were; a Reservation all the more astounding when it is taken into account how prominent and central a place in Catholic theology is occupied by the Atonement; so it was only by an extraordinary intervention, as we regard it, of Divine Providence that one of the very choicest tracts of land adjacent to the Catholic University was held in reserve for the Friars of the Atonement. Only time can tell what educational buildings will be erected on these thirty-three precious acres, and what enormous influence they will exert in the future world-wide expansion of our Holy Society.

It is natural that the Father Founder of the Atonement institute should be given, by the Holy Spirit, a larger pre-vision of what is involved in the coming of the Friars to establish their educational center in connection with the Catholic University at Washington than to the rank and file of our Atonement Army; but, having received the vision, it is our obligation as your leader to inspire every soldier with that same vision, and to arouse your interest and support in the Great Enterprise.

Twenty-seven years after Father Paul wrote the above words all his predictions were fulfilled. The "pre-vision" of his "Great Enterprise" can be seen in reality today; for on the "thirty-three precious acres" there stands today, besides the *Atonement Seminary of the Holy Ghost*, a mammoth high school built by the Most Reverend Patrick A. O'Boyle, Archbishop of Washington, D. C.; the major seminary of a group of Oriental Catholics and a large Retreat House for women under the direction of the Sisters of the Atonement.

After the final negotiations for the Robinson Property were completed, Father Paul wrote in *The Lamp*:

I regard this as one of the most important forward steps the Society of the Atonement has taken in recent years. It is very difficult to measure the immensity of this new departure, and the possibilities which will, we trust, develop from it under the directing Hand of God. Certainly, we have never made so large a financial venture in the history of the Society of the Atonement. . . . It was only by degrees that we were able to adjust our own minds to the magnitude of the purchase; but, little by little, it became more evident to us that God willed it so and that certitude strengthens the faith of the Friars that the money to pay for the property will be forthcoming in due season. The brick mansion of the Robinson Family stands in the centre of the spacious grounds, supplemented by a cottage and stable. These buildings with some over-hauling will serve the immediate needs of the Society in providing a lodging-place for our clerics while studying theology at the Catholic University of America.

A solemn high Mass was celebrated by Father Paul in the former Robinson Mansion on September 16, 1925. The building was dedicated as *The Atonement Seminary of the Holy Ghost* with only

one Friar priest and five Friar clerics in residence. But Father Paul
was radiantly happy that day as he received the good wishes of the
Superiors of all the religious houses affiliated with the University. His
little community was insignificant compared with the number in the
massive seminaries that surrounded *The Atonement Seminary of the
Holy Ghost*, but God's promise was now beginning to be fulfilled
and Father Paul was grateful. He had four priests, five clerics; and
St. John's, once deserted, was now filled with worthy aspirants. Besides St. Joseph's House, a novitiate to accommodate thirty novices,
was under construction on the Mount of the Atonement.

At that time he wrote:

Not until Graymoor was linked up with the Central Power House of
Rome and the current which electrifies the Vicar of Christ was trans-
mitted to the spiritual dynamos of St. Paul's Friary on the Mount of the
Atonement and St. Francis House in Graymoor Valley, did the Covenant
promise of Almighty God really begin to be fulfilled—slowly at first, but
more strikingly as the years went on.

The second most important development in this period of the Society's history was the establishment of *The Graymoor Press* in the
city of Peekskill, approximately five miles from the Mount of the
Atonement. In 1921 Father Paul purchased a former music con-
servatory and converted it into a modern printing establishment.

Since that time *The Graymoor Press* has been expanded several
times and equipped with the most modern machinery. Its staff of
seventy persons send *The Lamp* and other Catholic literature each
month to all parts of the world.

During these eventful years in the life of Father Paul, when he
became a world-wide figure because of his many projects, men with
whom he had been associated in the Anglican Communion had attained positions of renown in the Episcopal Church.

The Reverend Paul Matthews, who preceded Father Paul as head
of the Associate Mission in Omaha, and who was the son of the
Honorable Stanley Matthews, Associate Justice of the Supreme Court
of the United States, became the Episcopal Bishop of New Jersey in
1915. The Reverend Irving P. Johnson, who offered the position of
Superior of the Associate Mission to Father Paul, became the Bishop

of Colorado in 1917. Dr. Sheldon M. Griswold of Hudson, New York, who recommended Father Paul for the position, became the Bishop of Chicago. When a former Anglican friend jocosely said to Father Paul: "Well, had you remained in the Anglican Church you, no doubt, would have become a bishop with a fine mitre to wear," Father Paul answered: "I am quite satisfied with my skullcap."

Chapter XIX

THE-UNION-THAT-NOTHING-BE-LOST

SECOND only to *The Church Unity Octave*, the founding of the missionary society know as The-Union-That-Nothing-Be-Lost is the greatest glory of Father Paul's life. Chronologically it precedes the Octave.
The telling of its foundation has been deferred because it was not
until the Society was Catholic that it became fruitful.

On the feast of St. Thomas, December 21, 1904, Father Paul
woke in his cell at five o'clock in the morning, hearing in his soul
the words; "Gather up the fragments that remain, that nothing be
lost." He at once recalled that these words had been spoken by
Christ to His disciples in the wilderness, after a multitude of five
thousand men had been fed by Him when He had multiplied the
five barley loaves and two fishes. In obedience to the command of
Christ, twelve baskets of food were gathered up by His disciples.

The thought that came to Father Paul, as he was putting on his
habit, was: "If the Christians of America could be trained to save
for the Foreign Missions, the fragments which they carelessly throw
away, or the many millions they waste and squander in ways that do
not profit, an army of missionaries, sufficient to conquer the heathen
world, could be supplied with all the material assistance needed for
their campaign of missionary conquest." And again the whispering
voice said to him: "You will have to wait seven years for this to be
accomplished."

So began the foundation of a great "ammunition base" which
Father Paul later established as *The-Union-That-Nothing-be-Lost*. He
planned it as a missionary society which would supply all the material
necessities for the front-line trenches, where the Soldiers of Christ
fight against the evils of the world for the salvation of the souls of
men. Shortly after the inspiration came to him he drew up the Rule

and Constitution of *The-Union-That-Nothing-Be-Lost*. He then made a diligent and persevering effort to enlist members in the Union among Anglicans; but his effort was a futile one.

Seven years later, in December of 1911, two years after the Society of the Atonement entered the Catholic Church, the Rule and Constitution of the Union was submitted to the Auxiliary Bishop of New York, Bishop Cusack, for his blessing and sanction. The Bishop said that he hesitated to bless it because the Rule was so perfect he feared that the Friars would find no one to live by it, and consequently it would be of no material gain to them in their good work. That answer came as a keen disappointment to Father Paul. At Mass the next morning, as he held the Eucharistic Christ in his consecrated fingers, before receiving Holy Communion, Father Paul prayed in these words: "Dear Lord—if *The-Union-That-Nothing-Be-Lost* is a creature of my own imagination, I beg you to dismiss it utterly from my mind; but if it comes as an inspiration from You, My God, please give me some tangible proof of it."

A few days later that prayer was answered in the person of a shabby-looking old man who came to St. Paul's Friary asking to see Father Paul. When Father Paul entered the small waiting room, seeing the visitor, he thought that this man was another of the many poor, homeless men who came to the Friary for food and shelter. Introducing himself as John Reid, from Waterbury, Connecticut, he then told Father Paul the story of his life. His life's story would never be considered interesting enough to be printed in the daily newspapers, but Father Paul saw in this man the answer to his prayer of a few days ago, and the very embodiment of *The-Union-That-Nothing-Be-Lost*. John Reid's parents had left him a plot of rocky land in Waterbury; and for years he had worked hard to make it productive. The produce of this small farm he sold, spending the minimum of the money he realized from it on himself in order that he might give the maximum to God. In coming to Graymoor to see Father Paul whom, he said, he considered a Christlike priest, he had ridden on street cars part of the way and walked the rest. For food he had with him a few sandwiches.

John Reid, in that conversation, asked Father Paul how he could establish a burse for the education of poor boys for the priesthood. Father Paul then told him of his desire, so long unfulfilled, of erecting in connection with the Friary a small seminary where poor boys could be educated for the priesthood. To Father Paul's amazement, John Reid offered to send five thousand dollars, when he returned to Waterbury, towards the erection of the college. It seemed almost unbelievable that this shabby man, so lean and emaciated looking, should have five thousand dollars. Did he really possess the money or was he just a visionary? Father Paul insisted that he remain at the Friary overnight before starting his journey home. A few days after he left Graymoor, John Reid sent a letter to Father Paul. It contained a bank draft for five thousand, two hundred dollars. Father Paul asked himself: "Why the two hundred dollars extra?" John Reid had only promised five thousand. Then Father Paul, who saw the Hand of God in all things, saw the extra two hundred dollars as an outward sign of God's approval of The-Union-That-Nothing-Be-Lost. The five thousand dollars represented the five barley loaves and the two hundred dollars represented the two fishes of Christ's great miracle in the wilderness. John Reid's letter was dated December 21, 1911, exactly seven years after Father Paul heard the voice telling him to "gather up the fragments."

From that day forward those five thousand, two hundred dollars began to multiply like the five barley loaves and two fishes. Father Paul enlisted thousands of members in his missionary union. From persons everywhere came donations small and large to be sent to missionaries the world over of almost every religious order whose appeals for financial help he printed in The Lamp. These donations represented the sacrifices Catholics were making while inflamed with a desire to see the world conquered for the Sacred Heart of Jesus.

In 1918 The-Union-That-Nothing-Be-Lost was incorporated under the laws of the State of New York, with the following object: "A missionary and charitable organization cooperating with the Society of the Atonement and having for its two-fold object corporal works of mercy and the salvation of souls. In furtherance of these ends it enjoins upon its members becoming self-denial and a holy simplicity of living, in conformity with their state of life, that nothing be lost which might be employed in extending the Kingdom of God or in ministering to the sick and poor."

Later, as a subsidiary of *The-Union-That-Nothing-Be-Lost*, came the *Rock of Peter Foundation;* an organization which, through the annuity plan, has built a trust fund the income from which goes on increasingly erecting churches, schools, hospitals and other charitable institutions. Since its foundation *The-Union-That-Nothing-Be-Lost,* has distributed to missionaries throughout the world millions of dollars. Every month funds go to foreign missionaries laboring in Europe, China, Japan, Africa and the Islands of the Sea. Through his *Union-That-Nothing-Be-Lost* Father Paul dotted the pagan world with churches where Christ is adored by people who once groped in darkness. The Union has ransomed thousands of pagan children in the Orient. It has educated, and is educating, hundreds of poor boys for the priesthood. It has alleviated the suffering of hopeless lepers doomed to a living death in the leprosaria of the world. It has done these and a thousand other spiritual and corporal works of mercy known only to the recipients of them, and to God.

Men whom the world calls dreamers, with apparently little practical sense according to the standards of the world, have been mankind's greatest benefactors. Life for us all is fuller and richer because they dreamed their dreams and gave of themselves to bring their dreams into the world of reality. In doing so they made the world a better place to live in. Father Paul was a dreamer. He dreamed wonderful dreams, such as the Unity of all Christians. *The-Union-That-Nothing-Be-Lost* was another dream of his. Its realization was made possible when men like John Reid found their souls aflame with a fiery zeal, enkindled as it was from the great conflagration of charity that was Father Paul. Father Paul was Charity personified. He was holiness in action. He walked the earth but he lived above the stars. Those who had the privilege of being intimately associated with him found in him what books, however learnedly written, cannot fully convey.

In John Reid, who later became a member of the Third Order and took the name of Brother Philip, T. S. A., Father Paul found a kindred soul. He was the living ideal of the Missionary Union.

And, as always happens in a pagan world whose philosophy is "dog eat dog," this lover of Christ was persecuted. John Reid wanted to share in the Atonement of Christ by his self-denial, and the worldlings called him a "fool." They also called him the "Miser of Waterbury." Father Paul often told stories about John Reid's parsimony. Some of them were amusing. There was one he often told about John's little tallow candle. It lasted for ages. John used it only when a visitor came to the door at night. He would light the candle to see the face of his caller, but once inside and seated with his guest John would blow out the candle and chat in the dark. But, as might be supposed, John had few callers. So his candle lasted.

John Reid's neighbors could not understand why his house was always in darkness. They did not know that for those who love God there is no darkness. He reigns for those who would find him in the shadows of a Sanctuary Lamp. John Reid died on January 30, 1922, on his eighty-second birthday. The money for the burial was demanded before the "miser's" body would be touched. After the funeral his neighbors hunted for John's cache of gold, but there was none. The money he earned through the sweat of his brow on his small farm had long since been put into a burse for the education of poor boys for the priesthood.

In a letter which Father Paul sent to John Reid in 1916, and in which he addressed him as, "My beloved son," there is a postscript which reads, "as you know, July 30th, the Seventh Sunday after Pentecost, is the twenty-third anniversary of our receiving the name and Scripture texts of the Society of the Atonement, and the sixteenth anniversary of its foundation on this holy mountain. I hope you will be able to receive Holy Communion on that day; and I am enclosing a bit of red ribbon which you will be very glad, I am sure, to wear with the enclosed medal of *The-Union-That-Nothing-Be-Lost*. I would send you a gold one, but I know you would object to that. Your golden crown and ornaments have been laid up at the right hand of the Great Judge, to be awarded after death."

The foundation stone of *The-Union-That-Nothing-Be-Lost* was the *Self-Denial* made by Catholics for the world-wide missions of the Church. Father Paul set the Fourth Sunday in Lent as the beginning of a week of Self-Denial by the members of the Union for the Missions. On that Sunday the Gospel, read in all Catholic Churches, is St. John's account of Our Lord's feeding the multitude by the multiplication of the loaves and the fishes. For the friars and students at Graymoor it was a week of "extra fasting." On the Fourth Sunday a card was placed on each one's plate listing the various items of food on the menu for the coming week—which was sparse to begin with. Whatever each one denied himself was checked off on the card. During that week Father Paul ate one meal a day. At the end of the week the saving of food through this Self-Denial by the community was credited to *The-Union-That-Nothing-Be-Lost* for distribution to the missions.

To illustrate how this special collection was allocated Father Paul explains the distribution for the years 1914 in *The Lamp* as follows:

"This year we propose to divide the Self-Denial week offering into three parts: the first part will be sent to China; the second part will be devoted to missionary work in the home field; and the third part we hope will be large enough to provide a scholarship for one of our boys in St. John's House of Studies." In the final accounting that year, the foreign missions sharing in one-third of the Self-Denial week were:

Father Leo Ting for work at Kin-Kwa-Fu, China.
Father Leo Ting, for building fund of Church of the Sacred Heart, Chu-Chow, China.
Sister Mary Louise, for Japanese orphans.
Bishop Everaerst, West Hupeh Vicariate, China.

Those sharing in the one-third for the home missions were the following groups:

The Ursulines of Alaska.
Club work among boys in New York.
Catholic Medical Mission Propaganda.
Franciscan Church of Our Lady of Pity, the Bronx, New York; to help enlarge school for Italian children.

Father Ting, mentioned in the disbursements above, in a letter of gratitude from Chu-Chow, China, wrote to Father Paul:

I, your servant, and my Christians whom you help, will not fail to pray to the good God to heap spiritual and temporal benedictions on you in return for all you have done for your poor Brothers here.

I am happy, my Very Reverend Father, to be able to tell you that now, thanks to the fruits produced by your collections, we are about to begin preparatory work for the erection of our future Church of the Sacred Heart. . . . This confidence with which you have inspired us, and your generosity in the past, allows us to rely on your zeal to sustain us and to finish that which your charity has allowed us to begin.

In the May, 1914, issue of *The Lamp* Father Paul tells of the *Catholic Medical Mission Propaganda* listed above, which later developed into what is known today as the *Catholic Medical Mission Board*:

On Good Friday, 1913, when conducting the Three Hours Service in St. Denis' Church, Yonkers, we remember pleading rather vehemently the cause of Foreign Missions, while preaching on Our Lord's brief cry, "I thirst."

After the service I was introduced to a young Catholic physician of Yonkers, Dr. Paluel I. Flagg, whose heart was already aflame with the fond ambition to go as a missionary into the Foreign Field. Since then, the great and noble thought of organizing a propaganda that will send trained physicians, as well as Priests and Sisters, to China, India and Japan, has gripped Dr. Flagg's soul; and recognizing only too well the importance of such an idea we gladly place our columns at his disposal.

In the same issue of *The Lamp* a letter to Dr. Flagg from the Archbishop of Madras, India; J. Aelen, was published. The Archbishop wrote:

In answer to your letter of the 17th of October, I have to state that there is a great demand in the foreign field for medical missionaries, and I think you cannot do better than start a Catholic Mission Propaganda among American physicians.

Above all, let me beg you most earnestly to train medical women, whom we want so very much in India.

The influence of the American Protestant missionaries is mainly due to the medical women, who are in charge of hospitals and have access to the gosha women of the country in time of sickness, but who will on no account allow men.

Courage, for you are doing a grand work, for which I have been longing for years, so strongly am I convinced of its necessity.

In June, Dr. Flagg wrote to Father Paul:

I know that you will be glad to hear that your article on the "Catholic Medical Missionary Propaganda" has already borne fruit. A Doctor Rouchel, of Croghan, New York, wrote and offered to assist in the expense of sending a woman M. D. to India. In the same mail came a notice of a vacancy in the Catholic Medical Mission at Rawal Pindi, and an application for help from a Dr. Lamont, who is willing and eager to go to India if only the passage money can be found and small immediate expenses met. I have placed these two ladies in communication with each other and pray that God will bless the common interest.

Father Paul appealed in *The Lamp* for funds, medical literature and medical supplies to further Dr. Flagg's project. The Dr. Lamont whom Dr. Flagg mentions was a Doctor Margaret Lamont, of Ashcroft, B. C., a convert from the Church of England. She was the first woman physician to set out for the mission fields under the Catholic Medical Mission Propaganda. She sailed on the *Empress of Japan*, July 23, 1914, from Vancouver. China was selected, rather than India, for her field of labor. Part of her diary appeared in the October issue of *The Lamp* in 1914. The Reverend M. Kennelly, S. J., wrote Father Paul from Shanghai of her arrival there. He told of the difficulty she was having with the language. "Meanwhile," he wrote, "she must be helped with funds and provided with a small medical library and surgical outfit. The venture, in the beginning may be rather slow and trying and will require the exercise of Christian patience. This has been the fate of all Catholic works. We are really proud that China has been chosen as the first field for Catholic medical work in the Far East."

The Macmillan Company published a book in 1925 with the title *Catholic Medical Missions*. The author is Mr. Floyd Keeler, a scholarly convert to the Catholic Church from the Episcopal ministry. A daughter of Mr. Keeler's is now Sister Isabelle of the Society of the Atonement. This volume relates the beginning of what later developed into the *Catholic Medical Mission Board*. It also reveals the assistance Father Paul gave to the founding of the medical organization.

The preface of the book is written by the Reverend R. H. Tierney S. J. who states:

He [God] inspired a New York physician with zeal for His Father's House, and, as usual, in times of crises, that zeal was kindled in apparently a most casual way, and took the most practical of all forms, a Catholic Medical Mission Propaganda. Dr. Paluel I. Flagg, the apostle of hospitals in mission fields, had suffered a great bereavement, and one day while in search of a sandal-wood crucifix, the Angel of Grace led him from the Society of the Propagation of the Faith, Boston, to the newly established Catholic Foreign Mission of America, at Maryknoll, Ossining-on-Hudson. There, for the first time, he was brought to realize the need of proper medical knowledge for those who devote themselves to work in foreign lands.

He immediately began to give courses in "first aid" to prospective missionaries. But so small a work did not satisfy his zeal, and in April, 1913, he went to South America. En route he stopped at Porto Rico, saw the late Bishop Jones, and aroused his interest in medical missionary work. Later he called at Curacao in the Dutch West Indies, where there is a large leper asylum, and in the fall of 1913 he was back at Maryknoll to continue his work under the kindly eye and kindlier direction of the Very Rev. James A. Walsh, founder of the Foreign Mission Society of America. But the doctor had apparently learned the spiritual adage of the monks of early days: "Not to go on is to go back." Be that as it may, he went on. He got in touch with missionary bishops throughout the world, offered prizes for the best essay on the subject nearest his heart, the "Catholic Medical Missioner." He attended the American Medical Association Convention held in Atlantic City, in June 1914, but, unfortunately, found little encouragement and comfort there.

About this time, late spring, 1914, Dr. Flagg, cherishing ever increasing hope for the success of his work, changed the name of the society he had founded to *Catholic Medical Mission Society*, and immediately thereafter explained his design to the Rev. Paul James Francis S.A., the founder of Graymoor-on-Hudson. This zealous Father, ever ready to help any good cause, invited Dr. Flagg to make use of the "Lamp," a monthly magazine, for the purpose of making his work better known to the world. Maryknoll, meanwhile, continued to benefit by the medical instructions given to prospective missioners. From that day forward, the success of the work seemed assured. A woman physician, Dr. M. Lamont, recently converted to the Faith, volunteered to go back to China where she had already practiced medicine among the natives. Father Walsh, of Maryknoll, who through the years has been a tower of strength to Dr. Flagg, sponsored the cause, and Father Paul James Francis furthered it through his magazine, with the result that Dr. Rouchel of Croghan, N.Y., paid Dr. Lamont's passage to China and supplied her with a small sum for maintenance.

The Catholic Medical Mission Society became the medical mission branch of *The-Union-That-Nothing-Be-Lost*. Eventually it became the *Catholic Medical Mission Board*, whose director since 1929 has been the Reverend Edward Garasché, S. J. This organization, which sends quantities of medical supplies to missionaries all over the world, had a humble beginning in a storage loft at 25 West Broadway in New York City. There the Sisters of the Atonement began to assist Father Garasché in 1929. On December 3, 1930, the present headquarters at 8 West 17th Street, New York, of the *Catholic Medical Mission Board*, was dedicated. Father Paul and Mother Lurana were present for the great event. After its establishment, Father Paul became a member of the Board. He also continued the campaign for the "Purchase and Maintenance Fund" of the new medical mission headquarters with appeals written by Father Garasche.

In 1934 Father Garasché promoted the establishment of a new religious community of Sisters, known as the *Daughters of Mary, Health of the Sick*, whose motherhouse is "Vista Maria" at Cragsmoor, New York. The Foundress of this community was formerly a Sister of the Atonement—Sister Angela, S. A. So from the chance meeting of Father Paul with the zealous Dr. Flagg developed, through *The Lamp* and *The-Union-That-Nothing-Be-Lost*, another great work in the Catholic Church.

The author, in his research work for this volume, has had the pleasure of being a guest of Dr. and Mrs. Flagg at their estate "Lisieux" in Yonkers, New York; and also of having the privilege of celebrating Mass in their private chapel. The late Cardinal Hayes gave the privilege of having his own private chapel to Dr. Flagg in appreciation of his work in organizing the *Catholic Medical Mission Society*. Almighty God has greatly blessed Dr. Flagg and his charming family of twelve children. He is today head of the Society for the Prevention of Asphyxial Death.

Father Paul had a great love for the medical missions of the Church. Each month funds were sent to hospitals and orphanages throughout the world. Besides the funds distributed after the Self-Denial Week appeal, funds were sent every month to missionaries everywhere who appealed through *The-Union-That-Nothing-Be-Lost*.

Father Paul became the almoner between benefactors of Graymoor and missionary Bishops, Priests, Brothers and Sisters. The name of Father Paul became as well known in Alaska, Uganda, Kottayam, Uppinangardi, Rome, Madras, Constantinople, Yokohama, Borneo, Putamaya, Champion Reefs, Mysore and Abyssinia as it was in Garrison, New York. Not one appeal was ignored, even if it came written on a postcard in Chinese. And whatever came in for a missionary was sent in full each month. The bookkeeper was not allowed to deduct even the postage.

The indefatigable zeal of Father Paul for the spread of the Kingdom of Christ upon the earth was contagious. How else can the generous response, time and again, of the members of his missionary Union to appeals by missionaries be explained? Through thirty years thousands of missionaries appealed to Father Paul for aid. And his pleas for them through *The-Union-That-Nothing-Be-Lost* brought millions of dollars for the expansion of the missionary endeavors of the Church. *The Lamp* readers sent checks to erect churches in China, Japan, India and Africa without ever having met Father Paul. While he was appealing for Father Ting in China, the following letter came on June 20, 1914, from Libertyville, Ohio:

THE LAMP

I have been watching you since you began to sputter and am now convinced that you are destined to illuminate the United States of America and shoot your rays to all English-speaking people on the globe.

Yesterday I read all your June number with great interest. The result of all this is the enclosed check which I hope and believe will please you and Father Ting and, better still, Our Dear Lord. Going along with this is an earnest prayer for *The Lamp* and Father Ting. I think this is the way you want it.

(signed)

C. C. COPELAND

In 1920 Father Paul had two priests of the Society ordained. One he sent immediately to the Texas missions. He was the first Friar of the Atonement in the mission fields. But Father Paul never became discouraged because he did not have Friars to send to the missions. That was God's Will for him and he accepted it. He found, however, a vast outlet for his love of the missions in his Missionary Union. Father Paul was the missionary who stayed at home and yet accomplished great things as a lone priest for the Missions of the Church.

In 1922 he was sending nine thousand dollars a month to the mission fields. But the banner year for *The-Union-That-Nothing-Be-Lost* was 1924 when more than two hundred and eighteen thousand dollars were collected. That year some of the funds were sent to the Most Reverend Isaias Papadopoulos, Assessor of the Sacred Congregation for the Oriental Church in Rome for Russian Relief. In April of 1924, His Beatitude Emmanuel Thomas the Second, Chaldean Patriarch of Babylon, in a letter to Father Paul said:

I thank you and your eminent committee for all the generous efforts to save the Chaldean Nation, sorely stricken by war. I am firmly convinced that these efforts will contribute effectively to give new life to this ancient Nation, formerly so great and flourishing that it was able, in its zeal and devotion, to carry the standard of Christ the Redeemer even to the farthest parts of China. And it will be no small glory for our benefactors of America, that through their generosity this nation may be raised from the ruins and set again in the path of progress, for the greater glory of God and the saving of souls redeemed by the Precious Blood. What embarrasses me most, in these days, is the state of my poor clergy, whose situation is most difficult by reason of their poverty . . . for you will realize that the priest is the most important instrument in the work of restoring our Christian communities. In return for these benefactions of your committee besides my fervent and continued prayers, those of my clergy and my orphans . . . I have today . . . offered the Holy Sacrifice of the Mass that Our Lord may grant you all the happiness a Christian heart may desire on earth, and crown with abundant prosperity your noble and generous nation.

Previously, the Abbé Naayem, a Chaldean priest, had arrived at Graymoor to establish the *Chaldean Relief Mission*. Later, in reporting at the office of *The Propagation of the Faith* in London, he told English journalists: "I cannot tell you how much I owe to the goodness of Father Paul. Had it not been for *The Lamp* and its invaluable help the Chaldean mission would never have got known in the U. S. A. But thanks to the steady sympathy and valuable publicity given by this great American journal, my work has won many friends in the states."

In 1928, Father Paul wrote:

And now the Union has scored its first million of contributions for the extension of the Kingdom of God at home and abroad; and is reaching out for greater achievements in support of the missionary work, not only of the Friars of the Atonement but of other Catholic missionaries who are laboring for the conversion of the Heathen, whether it be in Asia or in Africa or in the Islands of the Sea.

Relieving Bishops, Priests, Sisters and Brothers of financial burdens was a great joy to Father Paul. And throughout the world his name was revered and blessed by those who looked to him for aid. The appeals coming from missionaries became so numerous that he condensed them in whole pages of *The Lamp*. They came from members of almost every Religious Order, Society and Congregation in the Church; among the list of recipients of gifts from Graymoor, each month through the years, the array of designating initials are:

O.F.M.	C.S.C.	S.M.A.
O.S.F.	O.C.D.	O.S.A.
M.I.	O.M.C.	C.S.Sp.
O.S.B.	M.S.C.	O.F.M.,Cap.
C.M.	R.C.M.	M.H.M.
C.C.R.	O.M.I.	O.I.C.
S.V.D.	P.C.	C.P.
O.P.	M.M.	I.H.M.
T.O.R.	S.C.	O.C.S.O.
S.J.	O.Praem.	
T.O.C.D.	S.C.J.	

Besides these there were Cardinals of the Church, and many Most Reverends, Right Reverends, Very Reverends and Reverends of the secular clergy benefiting through *The-Union-That-Nothing-Be-Lost*. Also there were many hospitals, schools and orphanages that Father Paul helped to support through his Missionary Union. His favorite charities were the Convents of Carmelite nuns and those of the Poor Clares, especially the ones at Assisi and Rome.

The statement of monies distributed by *The-Union-That-Nothing-*

Be-Lost for the second quarter of 1929 covers two pages of fine print in *The Lamp*. The missions are grouped under the headings:

Africa—China—Europe—India—Holy Childhood Association—Japan—Korea—Near East and Asia Minor—Philippine Islands—Medical Mission Branch—The United States—Miscellaneous Missions.

This was all accomplished by one priest—Father Paul. In the late twenties the subscribers of *The Lamp* reached 165,000. God blessed the work of Father Paul beyond his fondest dreams. God blessed him because he was ever striving to be the personification of all that is good. He was strength, peace, tranquility, charity and faith. Father Paul was what happens when human nature is elevated and ennobled by Divine Grace. While he was building in the mission fields he was also building at Graymoor. But building stopped at Graymoor when the missions were in need. Some of his Friars who were not gifted with his deep faith saw this as a failing in him. They reminded him that "charity begins at home." But he knew that one must sow to reap and, as usual, he was right. For Graymoor today reaps in rich blessings what he sowed in the sweat of his brow for love of God and his fellow men. "God will never default in paying dividends," he often said, "if we only trust Him."

Apropos of this faith of his in God, Brother Fidelis, S. A., who was for many years treasurer of *The-Union-That-Nothing-Be-Lost*, and who is now the "Dean" of the Graymoor Friar Brothers, tells an interesting story. The Foreign Missionary Society of England, who are known also as the *Mill Hill Fathers*, were month after month among the recipients of Father Paul's benefactions; not just a few of them but many of them. One of their number was Bishop Biermans, Vicar Apostolic of Kampala, Uganda. Father Paul was always appealing for funds for him. In *The Lamp* he would caption an appeal: "Bishop Biermans of Uganda must have a seminary," or, "Twenty-three hundred dollars needed by Bishop Biermans for priests' passage from England to Uganda."

In 1923 Father Paul began a Tithe Club of *The-Union-That-Nothing-Be-Lost*. In announcing the new organization to the members of the Union he wrote: "We have long had under consideration the starting of a tithe-paying branch of *The-Union-That-Nothing-Be-Lost*, to be made up of those members of our Missionary Union who will set aside systematically at least one-tenth of their income from month to month, or year to year, as the Lord's Tithe, to be used for religious or charitable purposes." Whatever funds came in not designated for any specific charity were put into this Tithe Club, named in honor of St. Anthony. Moreover, one-tenth of the Community Fund was also put into it for needy missionaries.

One day an appeal came from Bishop Biermans to Father Paul for five thousand dollars to pay the passage of ten priests from England to Uganda, where they were badly needed. They were waiting in London to sail but were without funds. *The-Union-That-Nothing-Be-Lost* account as well as the Community account was practically exhausted, but the St. Anthony tithes amounted to well over four thousand dollars. Brother Fidelis had hoped to borrow the money from this account to pay the more pressing bills of the community, and then reimburse the Tithe account later from community funds. When Father Paul learned of the sad state of the financial affairs of the community he said to Brother Fidelis: "Let us make an Act of Faith in God and put everything we have into the Tithes and send the passage money to the Mill Hill Fathers. I am sure that St. Anthony will not only be pleased but will see to it that we will not want." So the five thousand dollars was cabled immediately to London, and the missionaries started for Uganda. Father Paul's faith was greatly rewarded, for not only were the most pressing bills paid but nearly all the financial obligations of the Society were satisfied within a month.

Father Paul set a goal each year to ransom one thousand pagan babies through the Holy Childhood Association of his Missionary Union. Some years he was able to ransom as many as six hundred. His appeals for these children were very tender—as were all his appeals for missionaries. Month after month articles were headed similarly to the ones for Bishop Biermans: "Resolved; that we build a new church for Father Collins in Sour Lake, Texas"; "Will Father Arnold Witlox, C. M., of British East Africa, Ask in Vain?"; "An Appeal for a Chapel"; "Poor Clares (of Rome) Close to Starvation";

"An Old Missionary in Southland who Needs Help"; "Food for the Starving"; "Father Rossi, S. J., Needs a Motor Boat in the Yukon"; "Uganda Missionary Needs Five Hundred Dollars to Build a School."

Having a sense of humor, Father Paul entitled one appeal from an Irish Priest, whom he was helping in Africa: "Irish Wit in Africa." The letter read:

VERY REVEREND AND DEAR FATHER SUPERIOR:

I think you will be inclined to say, when you see my letters, as Pat said when he saw the judges come into the court, "these things are only sent to try us."

However, so far you have passed a favorable judgment on them and many good friends and benefactors have come forward to pay the costs. Still I think some good friends ought to feel; Well, as that troublesome son of Erin has appealed to us so often, it is about time that we appealed to him to buy a pair of wings and join the angels, or, as they would say in Ireland, "to hold his whist." But as nobody has made that appeal to my generosity I take it that they want some more Irish melodies composed and written in the wilds of Africa to the tune of "St. Patrick's Day."

Good old Tom Moore told us all about the "Meeting of the Waters," and though I was on the spot many times where he wrote that song, it never occurred to me at the time to compose one on "How to Make Ends Meet." However, I have had many inspirations on that soul-stirring topic since then and, faith, the storms out here are mighty heavy. The "night of the big wind would not hold a candle to them." While some carry off the roof of my house others howl around the ruined habitation of my purse with plaintive wail. It is all right in Avoca, but, faith, it has no charm at all in a mud cabin in Africa.

But those storms and hurricanes and cyclones that whistle round me, and an empty purse, sets me a'thinking and . . . many a poetical thought inspires me about catechists and children and church and other buildings to build, and I hope that, as I am not much of a musician myself, some charitable souls will come along to the tune of "Brighter Days for old Ireland"—and for me. And as the good tropical rains pour down unstintingly into my house, so may showers of heavenly blessings pour down abundantly upon you and all my good benefactors.

(signed)   (Rev.) MICHAEL NEVIN
Kisumo P. O., B. E. Africa

Father Nevin must have kissed the Blarney stone before he left Ireland. Whether he did or did not his humorous appeals brought him checks month after month from Father Paul, which were sent by members of his Missionary Union. The volume of mail pouring into Graymoor was stupendous. How Father Paul was able to cope with it is a mystery. A short note from J. L. B. of Detroit read: "Enclosed is five dollars. . . . Kindly see that it is given to the Fund for the Conversion of the Jews."

Nor were all the members of the Missionary Union Catholic. One non-Catholic lady, Mrs. M. L. D., Salem, Mass., wrote:

I am enclosing ten dollars and will you please forward five of it to Sister Mary Bernadine of Jesus at Chefoo, China. My husband and I are very much impressed by her letters in *The Lamp*, and in fact by all the appeals, but as we cannot give to all will concentrate on one or two to give what we can. I am not a Catholic, but who knows, maybe sometime. Reading material like *The Lamp* is responsible for much good in unexpected, out of the way places, for instance myself. One cannot go on so thoughtless and indifferent after reading the magazine, full of the self-denials and sacrifices of the missionaries. I sincerely hope for you a successful year, so that you may carry on the good work.

After the first World War when the Near East was prostrate and starving, Father Paul pleaded for the relief of the frightful misery. The Greeks, the Armenians and the thousands of Russian refugees who had escaped the Bolshevik horrors of Crimea and fled to Constantinople were aided by Father Paul through the Most Reverend George Calavassy, Bishop of the Greek Catholics at Constantinople. Bishop Calavassy later sent the Right Reverend R. Barry-Doyle to Father Paul for help.

The result of that visit to America was the founding of *The Catholic Near East Welfare Association*, to which Chapter XXI is devoted.

The letters from priests laboring in the Near East to Father Paul after the first World War were heart-rending. One wrote: "I went to my Bishop for help, but he too is destitute. He said to me, 'Write to Father Paul in America; he will help you.'" The plight of Christians in the Near East at that time was appalling.

In the December issue of *The Lamp* of 1921 Father Paul printed, "An Appeal in Behalf of Unfortunate Armenia." It was from the Armenian Patriarch of Cilicia, Paul Peter XIII Terzian. The appeal tells the story of a crucified people and their frightful sufferings. The letter read:

Among the belligerent nations Armenia has been the worst sufferer both during and since the war. Bathed in the blood of its hundreds of thousands of martyrs, Armenia stands now destitute and devastated.

Shall we revert to the massacres of 1915, which continued until 1921? And the butcheries perpetrated in the Caucasus and in Cilicia under the very eyes of the European Powers? The number of Armenians massacred or systematically annihilated is conservatively estimated at 1,000,000. Almost the entire Armenian population of Asia Minor has been wiped out. Twelve of our dioceses are entirely destroyed. Our religious establishments and schools have been laid waste. Thousands of orphans of both sexes are now homeless and in most abject destitution, not to mention those who are starving.

The task of reorganization which confronts us is gigantic. Conscious of our limitations and the utter lack of means to undertake it, we feel almost discouraged; but we know that God Almighty is with us and that in a civilized Christian country like America we have charitable friends and Fellow-Catholics, both Clergy and Laymen, who are only too anxious to relieve our sufferings and help us reconstruct our Armenian Patriarchate so sorely tried and humiliated. To them we send this appeal, this cry of distress coming from the heart of the shepherd of an unfortunate fold, with the firm trust that it will find an echo in the hearts of our Catholic Brethren in America.

Some of Father Paul's methods of raising money for the missions through his Missionary Union were ingenious, and rather amusing on occasions. For instance, he portrayed an Irish priest—who was building a church in County Monaghan, Ireland, with a heavy debt to pay —as a priest with a great load on his back. The huge load was labeled "160,000 shillings of debt."

Another method Father Paul used in *The Lamp* was the picture of a clock, which would register one million dimes or one hundred thousand dollars. He used this method when he began the building of St. Anthony's Shrine at Graymoor; and for debts on other Graymoor properties, such as the Major Seminary in Washington, adjacent to the Catholic University of America.

During the years that Father Paul labored so untiringly for the spread of the Kingdom of God upon the earth two public attacks were made on his fund-raising by members of the clergy in the United States. One appeared in the *Acolyte* (since "ordained" the *Priest*) in the May 30, 1931 issue. The *Acolyte* was a magazine widely circulated among priests. The other attack appeared about the same time in the *Mentor*, the parish bulletin of the Catholic Church of the Nativity, Brooklyn, New York. Both attacks were devoid of any semblance of Christian charity. The author again reminds those who read these pages that they must not be shocked at these happenings. While the Catholic Church is Divine because of its establishment by Christ, and the Indwelling of the Holy Spirit Who keeps it from error in faith and morals, the instruments God uses to continue the great work of Man's Redemption are human, and therefore subject to all human failings. The sanctity of the Saints consisted in their constant striving to rid themselves of these imperfections so that they could be like unto God through the life of sanctifying grace, which is God's own Divine life in the soul.

Intimate friends of Father Paul among the members of the clergy and hierarchy both in the United States and abroad urged him to answer these charges. But, like so many other crosses he had borne, he spiritualized the pain they brought to him, offering it to the Eternal God for the salvation of the souls of men. Father Paul was too busy with positive things to bother with such nonsense. Moreover, his generous soul would never allow him to engage in a controversy that involved the sordid.

When the author began this biography he knew of these charges against Father Paul. At first it was his intention to ignore them as Father Paul had. For he remembered a story told him by a missionary bishop some years ago, who said: "When I am rebuffed in other dioceses as I plead from rectory to rectory for my poor diocese, I always advise the pastor who rebuffs me to see a doctor; for I have found that irritability in a priest is often occasioned by an existing ulcer. Ulcers," he continued, "are nasty things, and they are the unhappy lot of the intellectuals. Priests, as a whole, are charitable almost to a fault, and I dislike seeing one of them sick." It was good advice, and the author intended to follow it until, in the research work for the writing of this volume, he found that the attack in the *Acolyte* was filed as a public document in the library of the Catholic University of America at Washington, D. C.

This article is probably on file in the libraries of other Catholic colleges and universities and particularly in the private libraries of priests. Therefore it cannot be ignored. A biographer of Father Paul who would ignore it would be doing an injustice to his memory.

The article is entitled "Out of the Mouth of Sucklings." It is a scathing diatribe not only on Father Paul, but on others whom the writer refers to as "promotors of shrines." Eminent Catholic newspapers also come under the hammer of the harangue, notably the *Denver Catholic Register* and the *Catholic News* of New York, for carrying advertisements on shrines. The "Ulcer Theory" of the author, given above, may be discounted by a reason which the *Acolyte* writer himself gives for his article when he wrote:

Let the more glaring specimens furnish the condemnation. We select the *Denver Catholic Register*, because of its geographical position it has a wide circulation, and because this circulation is, for the most part, in small and poor parishes where the contributions of the faithful are sorely needed at home. For many months, we might say years, the Register has carried the adds (sic) of these shrines.

In his article in the *Acolyte* the writer refers sarcastically all through it to Father Paul as "The Shepherd of Graymoor." Unintentionally in writing of *The Lamp* he paid it a great compliment when he wrote: "*The Lamp* is the house organ of the Graymoor activities. Like the British Empire, the sun never sets on it." Continuing, the article reads: "Besides all this it [*The Lamp*] advertises for eighth-grade boys to enter the Order. A rather tender age at which to decide a boy's vocation." Here, of course, the learned writer seriously erred; for Father Paul, in fostering vocations and training youths for the Priesthood at a "tender age," was following the mind of the Catholic Church through the ages; and, in particular, the Council of Trent. There are minor seminaries of many religious orders and dioceses in the United States, and throughout the rest of the world, which receive candidates for the priesthood after the eighth grade.

The *Catholic Encyclopedia,* under: "Seminary—Admission and Dismissal of Students," states:

"Let those be received," says the Council of Trent (1545-1563), "who having been born in lawful wedlock, have at least attained their twelfth year, and are able to read and write passably, and whose naturally good disposition gives token that they will always continue in the service of the Church." It is the wish of the Council that the children of the poor should be preferred. Today an ordinary grammar school instruction is required for admission into the preparatory seminaries. Parents and parish priests are urged to encourage and to help boys who by their intelligence and piety give hope that they are called to the Priesthood. (Council of Baltimore No. 136)

The article in the *Acolyte,* in referring to St. Christopher's Inn at Graymoor where homeless men are fed, clothed and sheltered; and in referring also to *The-Union-That-Nothing-Be-Lost,* further states: "Granted that 69,207 meals and 23,055 lodgings were given in 1929, does not Graymoor get free labor in return to build the plant? Granted also that money is sent for foreign missions and home needs, the main thing is a grand shrine which will serve to draw the thousands mentioned. . . ."

Quite evidently, the writer of the article had never seen Graymoor. To begin with, the Inn is open day and night to the homeless of every race and creed. A man can find a bed and food, and leave the next morning without doing any work whatsoever—as many do. Those who do work, repair the roads or take care of the lawns. These men, in the main, when they come to the Inn, are too physically and mentally exhausted for any strenuous labor. Furthermore, the Inn is supported by the alms of the poor, who work themselves, every one of whom would be reluctant to support a project that fosters idleness. Only in an exceptional case is a man allowed to stay more than two weeks. While the Friars make no pretense at rehabilitating these men, a stay of two weeks is usually sufficient to put them on their feet again, exposed as they are to everything that is conducive to physical, mental and spiritual rehabilitation. A clean bed, good food, the service of a resident physician and the spiritual consolation of friar priests are at the disposal of any homeless man who seeks the shelter of the Inn. The charge of exploitation has never been heard from one of them since the Inn was founded. On the contrary, their expressions of gratitude would fill volumes.

In regard to the so-called "grand shrine" of which the writer of the article in the *Acolyte* wrote, it was Father Paul's great desire to build on the Mount of the Atonement a Shrine to St. Anthony. This he was able to begin in the early twenties. The Graymoor community grew so quickly after it was begun that Father Paul's plan for this "grand shrine" had to be abandoned, as being inadequate to accommodate even the community. To this day it remains unfinished. The "grand shrine" consists of a small crypt chapel, which can seat seventy-five persons at the most. In the entrance to this crypt chapel is the tomb of Father Paul. The upper part of the "grand shrine" has never been finished; and the crypt chapel is now used for the celebration of Mass by the Friar Priests resident at Graymoor. Services for the many pilgrims who come to Graymoor are held each Sunday on the lawn. On days when rain comes suddenly, the largest available chapel—The Little Flower Oratory—is used. This accommodates three hundred persons. The remaining pilgrims find shelter either in the outside cloister or in the cafeteria, being deprived entirely of attending the Benediction service.

When the crypt chapel was being built some of the Brothers Christopher (homeless men) did work on it under the supervision of a Graymoor priest. This work was entirely voluntary, and whatever was saved by these men in labor was credited to the Inn for their support.

A pilgrim chapel is now being constructed at Graymoor to accommodate one thousand persons. This is a simple chapel, modeled after an airplane hangar; and it is a far cry from a "grand shrine." Furthermore, it is not being constructed by the "free labor" of the homeless men, but rather by a New York construction company.

While Father Paul was sending millions to the home and foreign missions only the barest and most necessary accommodations were built at Graymoor for his community; and so it remains today for all the world to see. Whoever comes to Graymoor to see majestic and beautiful buildings is disappointed. Whoever comes to find the things that endure "unto life eternal" is not. Besides offering these spiritual gifts, however, the friars always offer to show to visitors God's beauty in the surrounding hills from an observation gallery built of wood over the crypt chapel of the so-called "grand shrine."

Another item the writer in the *Acolyte* took exception to was Father Paul's use of a clock for fund raising. The first time Father Paul used this method, however, was not to build on the Mount of the Atonement, but rather to wipe out a debt which lay heavily upon the Poor Clares in Assisi. The Abbess, Carmela Reattelli, had appealed to Father Paul for 30,000 lire ($6,000). In commenting upon the appeal editorially Father Paul wrote: "For the love of God and St. Francis we cannot turn to it a deaf ear."

The clock to raise funds for the Poor Clares appeared in *The Lamp* in the April, 1912, issue. It was a twelve-hour clock, and each hour represented five hundred dollars. In the November, 1912, issue of *The Lamp* Father Paul printed a list of religious, priests and prelates in the United States and Canada who had contributed to this great work. The list covered two full pages in small type. Numerically, the Franciscans of the United States led all the rest.

The Cardinal Protector of St. Clare's Basilica in Assisi was Father Paul's loyal and devoted friend, His Eminence Diomede Cardinal Falconio, the former Apostolic Delegate to the United States. While, in later years, the writer in the *Acolyte* and the Pastor of the Church of the Nativity in Brooklyn seemed very disturbed by Father Paul's method of fund raising, Cardinal Falconio and the saintly Pope Pius X assumed quite a different attitude as they blessed Father Paul for restoring one of the most famous shrines in Christendom. The following letter from Cardinal Falconio tells the story:

To the Rev. Paul James Francis, S. A.

REVEREND AND DEAR FATHER:

By *The Lamp* which you kindly sent to me, I learn with pleasure of the interest which you are showing in collecting funds for the restoration of the Church of St. Clare in Assisi. For this zeal in co-operating for the restoration of such a monument of Christian art, you and the contributors truly deserve our best thanks. St. Clare's Church in Assisi is the cradle and mother Church not only of all the Sisters who profess the Rule of the Second Order of St. Francis, but I may say of all the Franciscan Sisters throughout the whole world who recognize St. Clare as their spiritual mother and the foundress of the great Franciscan Order of women. It is in this temple where the remains of St. Clare are venerated and where thousands of pilgrims come to admire the wonderful work accomplished by Divine Providence through this faithful and holy Virgin.

Perhaps it will be of some interest to you to know that Our Holy Father has such veneration for this sacred historical building that He has been pleased to raise it to the rank of a Basilica Minor, and for the proclamation of this important pontifical document which confers such dignity and honor on St. Clare's beautiful temple, he has been pleased to select me as His Legate, and appointed me Protector of St. Clare's Convent and Church. The Brief is dated August 9th and was promulgated in the Church of St. Clare, now a Basilica, on the Feast of the Assumption of Our Blessed Lady, the 15th instant, amidst the joy of a vast multitude of people and the concurrence of all ecclesiastical and civil authorities. In such a solemn occasion I made it my duty to inspect personally the building and indeed I had to admire the beautiful colossal lines of this vast monument of Christian art, but my heart sank at seeing the great damage done by the inexorable hand of time. Here in Italy our ancestors full of faith and generosity left to the world the rich inheritance of this and other monuments of Christian art, but times have changed and in order to keep this wonderful work standing we need the help of generous Catholic souls and all of those who know and admire whatever is beautiful and grand in Christian art.

Yesterday I had the honor of a private audience with the Holy Father. He was highly pleased in hearing of the great interest which you were taking in the restoration of St. Clare's Basilica and requested me to inform you that He most willingly and lovingly bestows His blessing upon you and upon all the contributors.

Yours in Christ,
D. CARD. FALCONIO

Piazza Cavour 17, Roma
August 25, 1912

Father Paul used this (the clock) method again in June, 1920; not to build on the Mount of the Atonement, but rather to help wipe out a huge debt which lay heavily upon the shoulders of the parish priest and the parishioners of the Catholic Church in Peekskill, New York. In this campaign for funds his clock was to register one million dimes or one hundred thousand dollars. Graymoor had absolutely no responsibility in this affair, and yet Father Paul helped to shoulder it out of his love for things Catholic.

At a Month's Mind Mass, celebrated for the soul of the Reverend Richard H. Tobin, whose health had broken under the strain of the enormous debt he had inherited in assuming the pastorship, Father Paul, in a sermon, told the story of that project. Fortunately the sermon is preserved, but even if it were not, the pages of *The Lamp* have the entire history of the Peekskill project. In this sermon, Father Paul unwittingly gave an insight into his own magnificent character. The sermon is replete with his characteristic faith, hope, charity and vision. His text was taken from Psalm 115:15—"Precious in the sight of the Lord is the death of His Saints." The sermon read:

Almost a month ago amid a vast assemblage of Clergy and laity, packing to the doors this Guardian Assembly, we were present at the Holy Sacrifice of the Mass offered up for the repose of Richard Hartnett Tobin, Priest, and the sermon on that occasion was delivered by an old friend of his, Father Michael Reilly, formerly on the Apostolic Mission Band of the Archdiocese, and at present pastor at Woodlawn, New York City. The text which the preacher so happily chose was the words of Our Blessed Lord—"Unless the grain of wheat fall into the earth and die, it remains alone. But if it die, it brings forth much fruit." And the text I have selected from the Psalms of David will serve as a continuation of the same beautiful theme.

Undoubtedly the Great High Priest of our profession, Jesus Christ, was primarily thinking of Himself, when He used the figure of the grain of wheat.

He was looking forward, even as He spoke, to the consummation of His own ministry and Life in this world. It was not enough for Him to have become Incarnate, to take our flesh into union with the God-head and live as the Son of Man among men, going about and doing good, speaking as never man spoke the words of eternal wisdom. His mission on earth could not be fully accomplished except through death, so He was the grain of wheat that was to fall into the ground and die in order that it might bring forth much fruit, and that He might multiply after His own likeness those who would represent Him in the world, living the same life, animated by the same spirit and dying in one form or another the same sacrificial death.

In his well known lectures on Immortality, Mr. William Jennings

Bryan relates how when he was in Cairo, Egypt, he found there a few grains of wheat that had lain in the sarcophagus of an Egyptian mummy for 3,000 years. As he held them in his hand, he thought that if those few grains of wheat, instead of abiding alone, had been planted in the ground and died, out of them would have sprung up, "first the blade, then the ear, then the full corn in the ear." And if the sickle of the harvester had been brought into play and their progeny in turn had been planted in the earth, to go through the same mystery of death and resurrection through successive years, then at the present time the superabounding fruit of those few grains of Egyptian wheat would be sufficient to feed the teeming millions of the world.

This illustration, I trust, will help you to understand better Our Lord's meaning: How He willed to be Himself the initial grain of wheat, which fell into the ground on Calvary's field and died that He might not abide alone, but that through His death and resurrection He might multiply and increase the children of His Atonement every one of them a reproduction, more or less perfect, of His own likeness. And while this is true of all the faithful members of His mystical body, the Church, He wills it should be preeminently true of His Priests. To them He imparts by the Holy Ghost, His own eternal priesthood after the order of Melchisedech.

The priest is often called an "Alter Christus," another Christ. It is not only that he daily stands at the Altar and re-presents before the Almighty Father in Heaven the oblation of Christ upon the Cross, when He made an Atonement for the sins of the whole world; but in all his life as a pastor of Christ's sheep and a physician of souls, his calling and profession is to live and move and have his being among the people as another Christ, living the life He lived, going about doing good, consoling the sorrowful, ministering to the poor and the sick, and, if need be, laying down his life in sacrifice for the sheep of his flock, as so many of the priestly shepherds, following in the steps of the Good Shepherd, have done in the Christian centuries past.

Now Father Tobin in the twenty-four years of his priesthood followed closely in the steps of the Divine Shepherd. He was every inch a priest in all his utterances and in all his conduct, as you yourself can testify, among whom he exercised his ministry during the past twenty-one years. He never forgot that he was the Priest of Jesus Christ, and truly he had the spirit of his Master. There is a very old saying: "As a man thinks, so he is." Father Tobin so meditated from early youth upon what the Priest of Christ should be, that he became more and more what he thought, and we do not believe any of you in his presence ever forgot that he was just what he professed to be—a priest forever after the order of Melchisedech.

God knows the weakness and infirmity of our human nature, how we shrink from sacrifice, bodily mortification, toil and pain, how we draw back in horror from death. He knows that if we are left to ourselves the very best of us would never follow hard after Him in the way of the Cross.

As the sculptor has in his mind certain ideas of beauty as he stands before the block of marble and with chisel and mallet chips it here and there until at length he shapes the stone into a statue of wonderful symmetry, so does God by His own hand cut and shape his priests into likenesses of Himself, provided, like, Isaac, they are willing to be bound and laid on the altar of sacrifice.

Father Tobin made the necessary oblation of himself to the Divine Will and God did not spare or withhold the sacrificial knife. Indeed his life was a living death, because the process of death was always working within him, though he knew not until a few days before the end what the nature of the malady from which he suffered really was. He went on uncomplainingly, patiently bearing the cross of pain and suffering day by day. He was often so weak when he got up in the morning that it took a heroic sacrifice of his will to dress and go to the Church to say his daily Mass. Yet if we touched only on this martyrdom of physical pain we would not, after all, describe what was the heaviest cross Divine Providence laid upon the willing shoulders of this young and gifted priest.

What constituted the cross of Father Tobin's priesthood, more even than the secret disease which sapped his strength and caused him such acute physical suffering, was the Guardian Building, this mammoth structure erected by his predecessor, Dr. Curran. Dr. Curran was a large man in every sense of the word, in bigness of body, bigness of heart, bigness of thought, nobility of soul and spirituality. When he walked with the majesty of a king along the streets of Peekskill it was a sight worth seeing, the courtly grace and dignity with which he returned the salute of his fellow citizens, who tipped the hat in passing, Catholic and non-Catholic, out of respect for his sacerdotal character and majestic personality. Yet the doctor, while living and even after his death, has been criticized innumerable times, as a dreamer and visionary, who to his own physical undoing and the misfortune of his parishioners, erected in the village of Peekskill a monster parish building outclassing anything of its kind in even New York, the biggest city in the world.

Yet I challenge today the justness of this criticism and I venture the contrary opinion that time will prove a providential purpose in the erection of the Guardian Building which will show that Divine Wisdom inspired the vision and directed the hand of Dr. Curran.

But, be that as it may, no one will dispute the fact that, as the mantle of Elias fell upon the shoulders of Eliseus, so the burden of the Guardian Building fell upon the frail shoulders of Father Tobin, partially and increasingly during the last years of Dr. Curran's rectorship, and completely after his death, and indeed it was a burden that undoubtedly hastened the death of his predecessor and Father Tobin could not have borne up under it as long as he did unless he had been supernaturally sustained. I know no figure in history or fable that could be better employed or describe this burden than that of Atlas carrying the Globe upon his shoulders. Nobody but one who stood in the same place could exactly understand the terrible mental strain, the anguish of soul, the constant appeal to God for help which must have been experienced by Father Tobin during those long weary years when it fell to his lot to meet the interest payments on "The Guardian" which were continually coming due. Beside the mortgage debt he had to face an endless succession of notes, which with the inexorable exactness of the almanac kept summoning him to the bank on a certain date. And no sooner was one payment made than the next interest day immediately stared him in the face and this went on month by month and year after year and with the revolutions of the calendar the burden of debt never grew one whit less. This then was the secret cross which he carried, most of the time with a smiling countenance, and yet it was not altogether a secret one, for he was compelled to repeatedly announce to you from the altar that these notes had to be met, and that he could not make payment except through your alms. So you shared in his sacrifice, as children share their earnings with their parents in their need.

Now, my dear friends, that was the way of the cross he trod until he reached the hill of Calvary in his painful death, and all the while he was being formed more and more to the likeness of his Master.

Nor must we fail to take note that the hand of God was with him every step of the via dolorosa and never for so much as a single moment abandoned him. Our Lord always somehow enabled him to make every payment on those notes so constantly falling due, like an endless chain, one link after another.

It was in connection with the Guardian debt that I first came to intimately know your late Pastor; for twenty years I knew him more or less by reputation, and to some degree personally, but it was not until two years ago last June that Father Tobin one day surprised me by making his first visit to the summit of the Mount of the Atonement. He alighted from the automobile, and I met him at the Friary door. We went into the chapel together and he said: "Father Paul, I came to ask that I might enlist the assistance of *The Lamp* to help me meet this great burden of debt on the Guardian Building. Owing to the

Knights of Columbus war drive and other extra financial demands made upon my congregation I found myself at my wit's end to know how to make the next payment, when a few days ago I asked the people, as a last resort, to join me in a Novena to the Sacred Heart, and as I stood this morning at the altar saying Mass, Our Lord seemed to tell me to go to you, so I am here."

I replied: "Father Tobin, God knows we have burdens of our own and appeals enough already in *The Lamp*, but if the Sacred Heart sent you to Graymoor there is nothing for me to do but to help you as best I can."

Father Tobin's first appeal in *The Lamp* fell flat, it brought very little response. Then we hit on the project of BUILDING A MILE OF DIMES. It was Father Tobin's idea, not mine. I simply adopted it as the best method of appealing to our people, and you know how the readers of *The Lamp* all over America responded to that appeal. Prior to Father Tobin's death, over One Hundred Thousand Dimes had been contributed. Not long ago the first reduction on the principal of the Guardian debt was made by a draft on the Mile of Dimes. I speak intimately with you because I know that I am speaking to the parishioners of your late Pastor, and I feel that I have entered into partnership with you in carrying on this big task, where Father Tobin laid it down in obedience to a Divine Summons. You know that some months ago a theatrical company wished to purchase the Guardian Building and to convert it into a college or gymnasium for the education of actors and actresses for the stage. It was at a critical stage in those negotiations that Father Tobin and I had an important conference on the subject. We found that we were one in the belief that Our Lord did not permit Dr. Curran to build the Guardian that it might ultimately become a theatrical seminary; so we agreed to do our utmost to save this splendid edifice for God and the Church. As a result of our conference Father Tobin submitted to the Archbishop a proposition something like this: A united effort to be made in five years' time to wipe out the entire remaining debt of Four Hundred Thousand Dollars; the whole Archdiocese to assume the responsibility of raising a million and a half of dimes in that period of time, provided the Congregation would raise a million and a half, and *The Lamp* one million dimes in addition to the one hundred thousand its readers had already contributed. His Grace, the Archbishop, did not see his way clear at the time to adopt this plan on behalf of the Archdiocese; but he was sympathetic to such a degree that *The Lamp* volunteered to do its share in any case.

Now, my dear friends, you naturally want to build a monument to Father Tobin and Dr. Curran. You do not have to go far afield to seek some appropriate memorial. You have it right here in the Guardian Building. Let it stand here for generations as the concrete expression of that spirit of sacrifice which burned as a bright flame in the priestly hearts of these two men. We all know that they really gave their lives for this building, the one to erect it and the other to preserve it from going into secular hands. That burden is upon you and I feel a portion of it rests also upon my shoulders. Let us co-operate in carrying this Mile of Dimes on to completion, even as it was originally conceived and figured out in the brain of Father Tobin. Without any doubt, when he gets to Heaven, and indeed I trust he is there already, he will not forget the Guardian Building, nor those who contribute to his Mile of Dimes. We know also that the debt on the Guardian lay heavily upon the mind and heart of His Eminence Cardinal Farley, and no doubt he is praying in unison with Dr. Curran and Father Tobin before the throne of God for the success of this holy enterprise and to obtain a rich reward for all who co-operate on earth for its complete success.

Remember that all the sacrifices you have already and will hereafter make on behalf of this Guardian Building are intrinsically precious in the sight of God. There is nothing which counts with God so much as sacrifice. Even were this building actually to pass out of the hands of this Congregation, which God forbid, into secular control it would not have been in vain that it was erected, because it compelled both Pastor and people to make sacrifices and give alms which otherwise you might not have done to the same degree of loving generosity. I tell you, very often in the Providence of God the word "sacrifice" is spelled with the dollar sign ($), especially has this been so in the history of Church extension in America, even as today in the Propagation of the Faith among the pagans of Africa and Asia, an American dollar placed in the hands of a Foreign Missionary has the purchasing value of an immortal soul. The more you spell sacrifice with the dollar sign in helping to pay off the debt on the Guardian Building that it may stand here in the center of Peekskill a glorious monument sacred to the memory of Dr. Curran and Father Tobin, the more treasure will be yours in Heaven, and the more cordial greetings these two Holy Priests will give you when you arrive at the gates of Paradise, as I trust everyone of you will in God's good time; there to understand, with a vividness we can never experience on earth, the meaning of the Psalmist's words: "Precious in the Sight of the Lord is the death of His Saints."

The Guardian Building was built by the Reverend Dr. Curran as the school and recreation hall of the Catholic Church of the Assumption in Peekskill. Eventually Peekskill's population grew until it became a city. With its growth the Catholic population increased so that not only was the Guardian Building retained by the Church; but a new parish had to be established recently to take care of an ever-increasing Catholic population.

Father Paul promised that if the drive for one hundred thousand dollars for the Guardian Building went over the top by the Feast of the Assumption, August 15, 1921, he would send the surplus to the Poor Clares at Rome to help provide them with a worthy monastery. On the Feast of the Assumption of Our Lady, 1921, the clock struck twelve—one hundred thousand dollars had been raised to save the Guardian Building. Moreover, the drive went "over the top" with such velocity that Father Paul was able to send five thousand dollars to the Poor Clares in Rome for a new monastery directly across from the Vatican gardens.

In 1922 Father Paul had a clock running in *The Lamp* for the building of a magnificent church at Baguio, Philippine Islands. In November of that year a letter came from the Very Reverend A. Van Zuyt, Provincial of the Belgian Mission Fathers in the Islands. "As for the Church of Our Lady of the Atonement," Father Van Zuyt wrote, "I send you, enclosed, the latest picture. . . . The old chapel has been demolished and all the services are now held in the new church, in the 'Cathedral' as they say here. . . . As you see, the first and most necessary work to be done is to finish the towers."

In commenting on the letter Father Paul wrote in *The Lamp*:

We have resolved to conclude our 1922 campaign for a united offering of one hundred thousand dollars as a special appeal to all our readers on behalf of Our Lady's Church in the Philippines. It will come to our readers during Advent, and we hope that the response will be so unanimous that Clock number seven will score the completion of its task by January 1, 1923. Meantime we will welcome any immediate contributions which we can send to Father Van Zuyt.

During the year 1923, approximately eight thousand dollars were sent to this priest in the Philippines through *The-Union-That-Nothing-Be-Lost.*

When the Republic of Portugal was set up in 1910 the Catholic Church suffered greatly under the new government. The Patriarch of Lisbon, Antonio Cardinal Bello, appealed to Father Paul in a pathetic letter for help in 1922:

I ask you to excuse me for writing, yet I am confident that in your generosity and magnanimity you will forgive me.

I am an old man and broken-hearted because of the many persecutions we have all suffered in this country since the setting up of the Republic in 1910, which seems to have one purpose, namely, to destroy our Faith, our Seminary, and everything that has upon it the seal—Catholic.

Portugal is the most unfortunate country in the world at the present time . . . . my dear Father, we all know in Europe how generous America is . . . . On this general knowledge I base my confidence that the Catholics of your big nation will help us as much as they can and save us from utter ruin. Again I implore you in the Name of God to come to our aid and help us . . . and we invoke the blessings of Almighty God upon you.

Father Paul's comment in *The Lamp* was: "When a Cardinal of the Holy Roman Church and a Venerable Patriarch of one of the most ancient and distinguished cities of the world is constrained by unspeakable adversity to make an appeal . . . it certainly ought not to go unheeded." And so in the ensuing months offerings came to Graymoor for Cardinal Bello, and these were forwarded to him in Lisbon.

When Mother Anna Dengel founded the *Society of Catholic Medical Missionaries* Father Paul took a keen interest in her work. He had met Mother Dengel for the first time at a meeting of the Catholic Medical Mission Board when he was a member of it. Father Paul, in January, 1938, appealed in *The Lamp* for five hundred thousand bricks to erect a motherhouse for the Medical Sisters in Washington D. C.—prior to that time he had been helping them. When he died in February, 1940, Mother Dengel wrote to the Superior at Graymoor:

This is to express to you and your community our great sympathy in your bereavement and assure you of our prayers. Our little Society owes a deep debt of gratitude to your venerable founder—because from the very beginning he was in sympathy with our work and gave it moral and also financial support. We also feel his loss and like you— we must hope that he will help us in Heaven.

The author, in his research work for this volume, contacted Mother Dengel in Philadelphia, Pennsylvania, and asked her to write down her recollections of Father Paul. In accordance with that request she sent a charming letter dated August 25, 1950, which reads in part:

In accordance with your request I am jotting down some of the things that I remember about Reverend Father Paul.

I first met him in New York at a meeting of the Catholic Medical Mission Board held at Manhattanville (College), I think it was in 1926. I remember that he stood out definitely as being interested in medical missions.

Before starting our Society I saw that there was an empty house behind the Vineyard (the Graymoor major seminary at Catholic University, Washington, D. C.) I asked Father Paul if he would kindly allow us to occupy the empty house. He wrote that it was impossible but that he would help us in another way. So when we rented a house . . . Father Paul gave us twenty-five dollars per month for several years towards the rent. This was a big help to us.

I visited Graymoor on about 1926. . . . On that occasion Father Paul took us all around and showed us particularly the little place where *The-Union-That-Nothing-Be-Lost* was founded. Father Paul gave us a lot of time. He was most genial, kind and simple. One felt quite at home with him. I had several encouraging notes from Father in the course of years. A few months before his death he sent for me. . . . He had heard that I was in Washington.

Knowing that Father had great influence in Rome, I asked him: "would you please ask the Holy Father to simplify the habit of Sisters?" To my surprise, Father Paul seemed quite horrified. He said, "I would never do that." You can imagine how I felt.

I shall never forget Father Paul. His personality was unique, so genial, so practical and so holy . . . When we started our Society, very few people sensed the meaning of medical missions. Father Paul did. I count it as a great privilege to have known Reverend Father Paul and I hope he is continuing to keep an eye on the medical mission movement in which he was so very interested.

Sitting at his desk in a small convent nestled in the foothills of the Catskills, Father Paul knew the conditions existing in the farflung mission fields of the Church through the tremendous correspondence that he carried on with missionaries everywhere. To his tiny office came bishops and priests from all over the world with their problems, and in Father Paul they found a friend who understood. He did not merely say: "That is sad, Your Excellency (or Dear Father), I shall have the Graymoor community remember you in their prayers." But he also said: "Now let me see how much is in the treasury, perhaps we can solve this problem of yours and send you back to your people with a light heart." Everyone who came in contact with him went away richer, depending upon what they asked of him—spiritual or material aid.

Reading through the vast correspondence of Father Paul with missionaries, and the record of all that he accomplished for the missions, one is reminded of St. Paul's words: "I can do all things in Him who strengthens me." A large volume could be written on this one project of his life's work.

The Friars of the Atonement continue this missionary work of Father Paul. Since his death ten years ago disbursements to domestic and foreign mission fields have amounted to almost two million dollars. A staff of Friar Brothers are constantly working on these accounts. Father Paul's instruction that not even the postage be deducted from these offerings is still in force. The financial reports of the past ten years since Father Paul died do not vary much. Taking 1946 as a typical report for one year, the author found that $180,417.25 was disbursed through *The-Union-That-Nothing-Be-Lost*. Funds went to Africa—British West Indies—Canada—China—Germany—Greece—Holland—Honduras—India—Ireland—Italy—Lebanon—Palestine—Philippine Islands—Porto Rico—Turkey—South America—the United States.

Pope Benedict XV in 1919 indulgenced the recitation of a beautiful prayer which Father Paul composed for the members of *The-Union-That-Nothing-Be-Lost*. It is also one of the evening prayers said by the Friars of the Atonement wherever they are gathered together throughout the world. To those of us who had the privilege of living with the gentle Friar who composed the prayer, it brings back memories of him as he knelt, with outstretched arms, before the Eucharistic Christ enthroned on a marble altar, praying:

O Lord Jesus Christ, Who commandest Thine Apostles to gather up the fragments that nothing be lost, give us the grace to waste nothing, but to use all our time, talent, substance and opportunity for the greater Glory of God, the good of our neighbor, and the salvation of souls; and all for love of Thee, O Most Sweet Lord Jesus Christ, Who with the Father and the Holy Ghost livest and reignest God world without end. *Amen.*

Chapter XX

THE OCTAVE EXTENDED TO THE UNIVERSAL CHURCH

THREE MONTHS after the conversion of the Society of the Atonement to the Catholic Church, the *Church Unity Octave* was observed under Catholic auspices with the blessing of the Archbishop of New York, and the Apostolic Delegate to the United States, Monsignor Falconio. In a letter to Father Paul, dated November 29, 1909, Archbishop Farley said:

You have my cordial approval and blessings on every effort to se-cure prayers by means of *The Lamp*, during a Church Unity Octave, as your letter describes it, for the return of all Christians to Unity under one visible head, the successor of St. Peter, the Vicar of Christ on earth; and I feel with you that your reception and that of the community of Graymoor into the Church has been the outcome, in God's mysterious way, of the many prayers offered up in the past for this union of Christians.

The Apostolic Delegate wrote:

I am happy to learn that an appeal has been made through *The Lamp* for special prayers to be offered from the Feast of the Chair of St. Peter's at Rome to St. Paul's Day—namely from the 18th to the 25th of January, for the return of all Christians to the unity of the Church under the one Supreme Pastor, the Successor of St. Peter, the Vicar of Our Lord and Savior Jesus Christ. I have no doubt but that your appeal will be responded to by all sincere Christians. . . . I consider it my duty to join my prayers with yours in order that God in His great mercy may be pleased to bring about the desired Union.

In January, 1910, a letter came to Father Paul from Rome, stating that on December 27, 1909, His Holiness, Pope Pius X, "with his whole heart had blessed the said Father Paul, the 'Institute of the Society of the Atonement' and its work. The Holy Father, more-over, gave a special blessing to the Octave of Prayer for Unity and wished it great success." The letter was signed by the Reverend T. M. Brandi, S.J., editor of the *Civiltà Cattolica*.

For the next six years Father Paul propagated the Octave through personal letters to Bishops and Religious Superiors and through the pages of *The Lamp*. In view of the fact that the Octave was founded originally in the Episcopal Church the spread of the observance of the Octave in the Catholic Church was phenomenal. Bishops were most cordial in their acknowledgements of Father Paul's letters, and most of them blessed the Octave. Religious Orders and Congregations were enthusiastic in the observance of the Octave and helped to spread the devotion among the laity. Besides the Archbishop of New York and the Apostolic Delegate the other notable members of the hierarchy to approve and bless the Octave were: the Most Reverend Regis H. Canevin, Bishop of Pittsburgh, Pennsylvania; Archbishop Blenk of New Orleans, Louisiana, who in a pastoral letter commended the Octave observance to all his clergy and people; Bishop Schrembs of Cleveland, who as Ordinary of Toledo, Ohio, commanded that it be observed in all the churches of his diocese; Bishop Conaty of Los Angeles, California; and Bishop Grace of Sacramento, pioneers of the development of the Octave in the Western part of the United States. Cardinal Bourne of Westminster and Cardinal Logue of Ireland also endorsed and blessed the Octave.

The approval and blessing of so many bishops led to the next great step in the advancement of the observance of the *Church Unity Octave*—its official extension to the Universal Church. Cardinal Farley petitioned Rome for the decree of official recognition of the Octave as a form of prayer for the Universal Church. Cardinal Merry del Val, who was at that time Prefect of the Congregation of the Holy Office, sponsored the petition in Rome. Finally on February 25, 1916, His Holiness Pope Benedict XV, by a Papal Brief, extended its observance to the Universal Church; and at the same time enriched it with Indulgences, Plenary and Partial. The English Translation of the Brief is:

In every age it has been the concern of the Roman Pontiffs, our predecessors, and likewise it concerns us very much, that Christians that have, unfortunately, withdrawn from the Catholic Religion should at length be recalled to us as a forsaken Mother. For in the Unity of the Faith the foremost characteristic of the truth of the Church shines forth, and it is thus that the Apostle Paul exhorts the Ephesians to preserve the unity of the spirit in the bond of peace, by proclaiming that there is "One Lord, one Faith, one Baptism." (Ephesians IV—5) With a glad mind, therefore, we have heard from the Society which is called "of the Atonement," established in New York, that prayers have been proposed to be recited from the Feast of the Chair of the Blessed Peter at Rome to the Feast of the Conversion of St. Paul, in order that this aim of Unity might be obtained from the Lord, and at the same time we rejoiced that these prayers, blessed by Pope Pius the Tenth, of recent memory, and approved by the Bishops of America, have been circulated far and wide through the United States. And so, in order that the prayers above mentioned may be offered to God everywhere and with abundant fruit of souls and thus the desired end may be more easily attained, we, having also consulted our Venerable Brethren, the Cardinal Inquisitors General of the Holy Roman Church, mercifully grant and bestow in the Lord a Plenary Indulgence and remission of all their sins to each and all the faithful of Christ in the world, of either sex, who from the 18th day of the month of January, the Festival of the Chair of Blessed Peter of Rome, until the 25th day of the same month, on which the conversion of St. Paul is commemorated, shall recite every year once a day the prayers which are subjoined and on the last day of this Octave, truly penitent and confessed and refreshed with Holy Communion, shall visit any Chruch or Public Oratory and there say these prayers to God for the concord of Christian Rulers, the extirpation of heresies, the conversion of sinners and for the exaltation of our Holy Mother the Church. Moreover we also grant permission in virtue of which confession may be made and Holy Communion received, and the visit be made in order to gain the aforesaid Plenary Indulgence, on the Feast of the Chair of Blessed St. Peter in Rome. Furthermore, to these same faithful, who, with at least a contrite heart, say on any of the eight days named these prayers, we grant an indulgence of two hundred days from the penances imposed upon them or owing by them in any other way, according to the usual form of the Church. We mercifully grant in the Lord, that all these indulgences, remissions of sin and relaxation of penances may be applied in behalf of the souls of the faithful of Christ detained in Purgatory. This present letter shall be in force forever, anything to the contrary notwithstanding. The prayers, however, which are to be recited for the Unity of the Church during the Octave we have ordained, as above, are to be as follows and lest any changes might creep into them, we have decreed that a copy of them be kept in the archives of the Apostolic Briefs. (These prayers are given in Chapter XIII)

Given at St. Peter's, Rome, under the Seal of the Fisherman, the 25th of February, 1916, the second of Our Pontificate.

P. Cardinal Gasparri
Secretary of State

(These indulgences were renewed by Pope Pius XII through the Sacred Penitentiary Nicolà Cardinal Canali in 1946.)

With the promulgation of this Apostolic Brief of Benedict XV the Octave was raised from a private devotion to rank with the approved prayers of the whole Catholic Church. This Brief of the Holy Father gave a tremendous impetus to the observance of the Octave. Without this official sanction and blessing the Octave would have remained a private devotion subject to the approval of individual bishops. With Rome's approval it became a universal prayer, proper for the entire Church.

The soul of Father Paul was filled with joy and gratitude to God for His goodness towards the Octave. Nine years before, on October 26, 1907, the *Living Church* (whose editor had once called Father Paul an "erratic priest") in an article written on the book *The Prince of the Apostles* said:

We have a large sympathy with the dreamers of iridescent dreams. And a mirage does represent a far distant reality. The dreamers are the prophets of better times to come when men of other generations shall be able to realize what these could only dream of.

But from the beginning Father Paul's "dream" of the Reunion of Christendom was not something illusory. It was the prayer of Christ— "That they all may be One." Father Paul prayed, worked, sacrificed, preached, wrote and suffered to bring about the realization of the words of Christ: "Other sheep I have that are not of this fold. Them also I must bring, and they shall hear my voice, and there shall be one fold and one Shepherd." Christ was the Prophet of "better times to come." "One fold and one Shepherd" is *His Will* and so it must come to pass.

The labor of Father Paul, and the work of "men of other generations" shall bring to reality the prayer of Christ. And the iridescence of their "dreams" shall be seen in reality as men of every race and color gather around the *Chair of Peter at Rome* in Unity of Faith. This is the raison d'être of the Society of the Atonement.

Father Paul, with new enthusiasm and hope, now that the Octave was extended to the Universal Church, began immediately to send letters to all the Catholic Bishops of the world asking them to observe the Unity Octave in their dioceses. These letters were sent out by Mother Lurana and the Sisters under Father Paul's direction and signature. Even with their help, considering the tremendous correspondence of *The-Union-That-Nothing-Be-Lost* and other activities, it was a most remarkable accomplishment for one priest.

When he was asked, in a letter from a reader of *The Lamp*: "Why an Octave: why not a Novena?" he answered: "The fitness of an Octave beginning with a festival in honor of what God Himself has constituted the Centre of Catholic Unity, viz., The Chair of Peter, and ending with the feast of the Conversion of the great Apostle to the Gentiles, is so obvious that it needs very little exposition. When the Founder of Christianity prayed for the Unity of His disciples the reason He gave was 'That the world might believe.' We are, therefore, to begin with Unity that we may end in the Conversion of the whole world—The Chair of Peter stands for the first; St. Paul, the missionary convert, stands for the latter. Then, too, an Octave, as in music—it is the scale of harmony—may very well typify harmony and unity among Christians."

On December 15, 1920, Father Paul sent a letter to Cardinal Dougherty of Philadelphia requesting him to propose a resolution at the next meeting of the American Bishops to be held in Washington, D. C., which, if passed, would guarantee their support of the Octave. Father Paul asked that the Bishops, "take corporate action toward securing a general participation of everybody in praying for Unity during the Octave, so that its observance will come to be in time as much a matter of Catholic usage as the Rosary devotions during May and October." The Bishops received the resolution on September 22, 1921. The next day Cardinal Dougherty wrote the following letter:

Cardinal's Residence
1723 Race Street
Philadelphia
September 23rd, 1921

MY DEAR FATHER PAUL:

At a meeting of the Bishops yesterday morning, I presented a resolution that the Unity Octave be held throughout all the dioceses of the United States. It ws unanimously adopted by the Hierarchy. With best wishes, I remain

Very faithfully yours
D. CARDINAL DOUGHERTY
Archbishop of Philadelphia

The action taken by the Holy See toward the *Church Unity Octave* prompted the hierarchies of many of the European countries to prescribe the annual observance of the Octave in all the dioceses of their respective countries. Among these were the Bishops of England, Ireland, Scotland, Belgium, France, Poland and Italy.

Father Paul, in the meantime, was asking the Bishops of the Catholic Church throughout the world to sign a petition which was to be presented to the Holy Father at Rome asking him to make the observance of the Octave *Obligatory* upon the Universal Church.

In October, 1922, the Hierarchy of Greece, Constantinople and Asia Minor, among whom were the Most Reverend Demetrius Cadi, Melchite Patriarch of Antioch; the Most Reverend John Naslian, Bishop of Trebizond and Vicar General of the Patriarchate of the Armenian Catholics; the Most Reverend George Calavassy, Ordinary of Constantinople and all Greece, addressed a petition to His Holiness Pope Pius XI, asking him to render the *Church Unity Octave*, through Apostolic Letters, Obligatory upon the Universal Church. This request could not be considered until a similar one was presented by the Catholic Hierarchy of the West.

As Father Paul was seeking the signatures of prelates for his petition thousands of letters poured in and out of Graymoor. In the spring of 1925, Father Paul sailed out of New York for the Eternal City. He had four objects in mind: first, since it was a Holy Year, he went as a pilgrim to gain the jubilee indulgence; secondly, having great devotion to The Little Flower, he wanted to be present for her canonization; his third object was to present in private audience with Pope Pius XI the petition regarding the *Obligatory* observance of the Octave. The fourth object was to secure, through the Sacred Congregation of the Oriental Church, the consolidation into one Papal Society of all Near East agencies operating in the United States. This object was crowned with success beyond his most sanguine hopes in the Catholic Near East Welfare Association.

He carried with him two lists of the names of persons who had signed the petition. The first list was composed of the signatures of more than two hundred high-ranking ecclesiastics throughout the world. The second list was composed of the signatures of five thousand priests, religious and lay people. These he humbly presented to the Holy Father in a private audience on May 15, 1925. During his private audience Father Paul begged the Pope to make the *Church Unity Octave* of: "obligation on the faithful everywhere, in the same manner as are the prescribed devotions to the Blessed Virgin during the months of May and October." The Holy Father received his petition most graciously and assured him that every consideration would be given to the request. To expedite matters, he instructed Father Paul to leave a formal request in writing, together with all the documents, with the Cardinal Secretary of State.

When Father Paul returned to Graymoor from Rome he continued his crusade for the support of the Hierarchy and the Religious Superiors for the *Church Unity Octave*. In September, 1927, Father Vincent McNabb, O.P., of London, wrote to him:

Few have worked as you have worked for an understanding with our separated brethren. In His own days He who inspired and upheld you will reward you. One of the joys of my life has been to have worked by your side in the narrow field of reconciliation.

In answer Father Paul wrote:

I wish your viewpoint and spirit were more in evidence, rather, there is often-times a positively hostile attitude towards those good men in the Anglican body who are trying to work out its redemption. Many of them, as we know, recognize that such redemption involves ultimately a return for the Anglican prodigal to his Father's house.

On May 10, 1927, Father Paul wrote to Cardinal Merry del Val, who was the Archpriest of St. Peter's Basilica:

. . . That which I particularly desire . . . is to see the Feast of the Chair of St. Peter at Rome exalted to the same dignity throughout the Universal Church that it enjoys in the Basilica of St. Peter. . . . In the Roman Calender the feast of the Basilica of St. John Lateran takes precedence of rank over St. Peter's, the former being a double of the Second Class, while the Basilica of St. Peter is only a Major-Duplex. Would not the exaltation of the Feast of the Chair of St. Peter at Rome to the rank of a double of the First Class serve not alone to emphasize the Supremacy of the Apostolic See, but redound to the greater glory throughout the world of St. Peter's Basilica? When, on the occasion of the canonization of the "Little Flower," the Holy Father entered St. Peter's, elevated above the multitude in the gestatorial chair, I prayed that she would use her powerful intercession with Almighty God to elevate the dignity of the Feast of the Chair of Peter that all men might better understand that the Divinely constituted center of Christendom is nothing else than the Holy Roman See.

In January, 1928, reporting the progress of the Octave, Father Paul wrote:

The Octave is sweeping ahead throughout the world and gaining momentum as it goes. There are now about nine hundred and fifty (prelates) who have signed the petition, including three of our four American Cardinals. Cardinal Van Roey has just made it of obligation throughout Belgium; and a Jesuit Father wrote that he had distributed 280,000 leaflets; and similar word is coming from all over the world. The leaflet of approved prayers has been translated into many languages: Hindu, Malay, Arabic, French, Italian, German, Dutch etc.

The most ardent supporters of the Octave in Rome were the members of the Society of Jesus. The Very Reverend Francis Rauch, S.J., of the German and Hungarian Pontifical College, was the liaison officer between Graymoor and both the Papal Secretariate and the Sacred Congregation of Rites. Another indefatigable worker was a priest of the Ruthenian Pontifical College. To this priest Father Paul wrote on March 30, 1929:

Be sure to keep in step with Father Rauch, even when he may be marking time. . . . Much depends upon the influence and support of the

General of the Jesuits, as in the case of the Catholic Near East Welfare Association. When it seemed almost defeated it was the support of the Jesuit General who moved the Holy Father to make it his own Pontifical Society.

The Most Reverend Michel d'Herbigny, of the Oriental Church, advised Father Paul: "For the success of *the Church Unity Octave,* it seems important and perhaps necessary that there be a procurator and a procure of your own Congregation at Rome." This, of course, was impossible at the time. Father Paul explains why, in a letter dated February 2, 1929, to Father Rauch, S.J.:

We have not, as you know, any Priest of the Society of the Atonement to act as procurator in Rome to see this matter through; nor have I one that I am able to send. You know our Institute is still young, and although our seminary is full and ordinations are coming from year to year, still the few older Fathers must stay at their posts at Graymoor and Washington. Therefore, I am requesting you to act for me. . . . This is a great work, dear Father, but I know you have it all so much at heart that you will not fail me. . . . As you said, it will indeed crown my life's work. Let me hear the good news soon that you . . . are getting things in hand, and that you will present the petition and accompanying document to the Sacred Congregation of Rites.

The spiritual sons of Father Paul recognize the fact that they owe a great debt to the spiritual sons of St. Ignatius Loyola for their great loyalty and devotion to Father Paul in his old age, and to the Octave in its youth. For these kindnesses may the Jesuits be forever blessed.

Father Paul's petition to the Holy Father read:

Petition Concerning the Church Unity Octave

Most Holy Father:

The undersigned, Paul James Francis, Superior General and Founder of the Society of the Atonement, at Graymoor, in the Archdiocese of New York instituted, humbly prostrate at the feet of Your Holiness, humbly sets forth and with filial devotion asks that which follows concerning the Octave of Prayers for the Unity of the Church. This same Octave took its humble beginning in our Community even before, through the mercy of God, we were received all at one time, into the bosom of the Church. Also later by the Supreme Pontiff Pope Pius X it was praised, and was again commended by Pope Benedict XV, and by him subsequently enriched with indulgences.

It is now observed increasingly each year in nearly all parts of the Catholic world with fervor and piety, *from the Feast of the Chair of Saint Peter at Rome, January 18th, to the day of the Conversion of Saint Paul, January 25th, inclusively.* The intention of this pious observance being that all wanderers may return to the Unity of the Church and all unbelievers be led to the light of the Gospel, which intention, as all know and rejoice, is pleasing to Your Holiness.

In order that this pious practice may in the future be more universally and firmly established, and by that means its end more efficaciously obtained, very many of the holy Bishops throughout the world to the number of twelve hundred, and more particularly the Hierarchy of the United States by unanimous vote in Washington assembled on November 14, 1928, giving voice to their desires most ardently hope that Your Holiness confirming and supplementing the Apostolic Brief of Pope Benedict XV *"Romanorum Pontificum"* dated February 25, 1916, by your supreme Apostolic Authority will deign not only to commend this Octave of Prayers to the Universal Church by some solemn document, but also to prescribe in what way it may be everywhere observed. Among the petitioners are twenty-five Cardinals, headed by His Eminence, our Cardinal Archbishop of New York, many Superiors of Religious Communities and their subjects, with almost innumerable of the faithful of Christ.

Therefore, fortified by the prayers of so many petitioners and by them asked to present the same in their name, not less than in my own and those of my associates, to the Apostolic and Infallible Chair of Peter, with confidence I approach the Supreme Vicar of Christ on earth, who labors with indefatigable solicitude for this, that there may be one Fold and one Shepherd, and to him we dare spread forth these most humble prayers:

1. That the Feasts of the Chair of Saint Peter at Rome (18th January) and of the Conversion of Saint Paul (25th January) be raised to a double rite of the Second Class for the Universal Church, so that in no place and at no time may it be omitted.

2. That from the 18th to the 25th of January it may be permitted to priests every day, except Sunday, to celebrate the votive Mass *Ad Tollendum Schisma*, according to the same general rule that it is permitted to celebrate a Mass of the Feria in Lent *ad libitum* when there does not occur a feast of the first or second class.

3. That during the Octave in all Masses not that of *Ad Tollendum Schisma*, or a Requiem Mass, a prayer of the same votive Mass (*Ad Tollendum Schisma*) is to be added as *imperata pro re gravi.*

4. That in the Divine Office at Lauds and at Vespers for the whole Octave all be bound, whether privately or in choir, to add the proper prayers of this Octave, as below, according to the manner of a privileged octave whose commemoration is never to be omitted. These proper prayers are:

(These prayers are given in Chapter XIII)

5. That the same prayers, either in Latin or in the vernacular, be publicly recited after private (Low) Masses celebrated during the Octave, either in place of the customary prayers or after them; and the same be inserted before the *Tantum Ergo* as often as Benediction of the Most Holy Sacrament is given within the Octave.

6. It is strongly recommended that there be Exposition of the Blessed Sacrament throughout the day once within the Octave in public churches and in oratories of Religious Communities, the Ordinary approving.

7. That to the indulgences by Pope Benedict XV, through the aforesaid Apostolic Brief *"Romanorum Pontificum"* already conceded, Your Holiness deign to add fuller spiritual graces, namely:

(a) that a Plenary indulgence, not only once but twice within the Octave may be granted, that is, on both the Feasts of the 18th and the 25th of January;

(b) that the prescribed prayers being recited, there not only be conceded an Indulgence of two hundred days as often as they are performed within the Octave, but one hundred days at any time during the year.

That in this most auspicious fiftieth year of Your Priesthood, wherein even now, the world applauding, has occurred unhoped for triumph in the Chair of Peter, Your Holiness would deign benevolently to receive and benignly to hear these most humble prayers in order that more quickly there may become

"ONE FOLD AND ONE SHEPHERD"

On the Feast of St. Anthony, June 13, 1929, the petition signed by over twelve hundred prelates of the world was presented to His Eminence Cardinal Laurenti who, at that time, was the Pro-Prefect of the Sacred Congregation of Rites, substituting for Cardinal Vico who was sick and infirm. The petition was signed by Cardinals, Patriarchs, Archbishops, Vicars-Apostolic, Supreme Heads of Religious Congregations and rectors of the Seminaries in Rome. This list of Bishops was larger than the list of Bishops who petitioned the Holy Father to institute the Feast of Christ the King.

Those who presented the petition to Cardinal Laurenti were the Father General of the Third Order Regular (Franciscan), the Very Reverend Arnaldo Rigo, and Father Rauch, S.J. The Cardinal received the two priests very cordially and then said: "You ask a difficult thing."

However, he expressed the hope that the Holy Father would do something in the matter; perhaps recommend the Octave in a more solemn Brief or Encyclical. But he doubted the idea that the Pope would make the Octave "binding for the whole Church" since that would be without precedent, having no parallel in the history of the Church.

Father Rauch then mentioned the October devotions. "Something of this kind may be obtained," the Cardinal replied, "but, of course, even Leo XIII never speaks of an obligation, while the present petition goes further; for instance, the Commemoration in Vespers and Lauds as obligatory." The Cardinal then handed all the documents to his secretary, Monsignor Mariani, to be studied by the Consultors of the Sacred Congregation of Rites. And so the matter rested.

What Father Paul asked of Rome was most unusual—to make the observance of the Octave obligatory upon the Universal Church. Rome has ever been reluctant to change or to add to the liturgy. A history of the development of the May Devotions, The Sacred Heart Devotions and the October Rosary Devotions proved that they were not *prescribed* by Papal Authority for all dioceses until the devotions had assumed an importance sufficient to warrant the attention of the whole Church. In matters of this kind the *Vox Populi* (Voice of the People) is important. The May Devotions were the most rapid of the three in their spread. However, several centuries had to elapse before the Sacred Heart Devotions and the custom of reciting the Rosary in common during the month of October developed from permitted to prescribed forms of prayer.

Father Paul understood all these facts, but the response of the Bishops of the world to the observance of the Octave after the Society of the Atonement became Catholic so greatly encouraged him that he sought to have the Octave a prescribed form of prayer for the more speedy reunion of Christendom.

The decision of the Sacred Congregation of Rites was finally given in June, 1930, through Monsignor Carinci, who was then the official Secretary of the Sacred Congregation of Rites. The substance of the decision was that Father Paul was to institute a new, more intense and far-reaching campaign before it could become *obligatory*. This would entail a great harvest of testimonies from every Bishop, every parish, every religious house, as well as the intense and insistent acclamation and voice of the Faithful in every country throughout the world.

When Father Paul received the decision of Monsignor Carinci he was in the sixty-eighth year of his life. He had labored twenty years on the petition. Graymoor's achives were already bulging with thousands of letters, data, witnessings, details and proofs in various languages testifying to the growth of the Octave through those years. A monumental work had been done. It would have been impossible for him to undertake the campaign all over again and on a larger scale.

On July 24, 1930, a priest in Rome at the Ruthenian Pontifical College wrote to Mother Lurana urging her to advise Father Paul to begin the campaign again. In answering his letter she tells of existing conditions at Graymoor when she writes:

First, Father (Paul) has not the men to delegate for such an extensive and prolonged affair. . . . As Father grows older every moment of his time is taken up with the increasing responsibilities and active duties of his growing congregation. . . . And as the Institute is still young we have not anyone . . . who can be told to go ahead and manage the affair, nor do I think it would be completed in an average lifetime.

Father Paul bowed his head to the decision from Rome. It was the Will of God for him. He continued to spread the Observance of the Octave by correspondence with Bishops and through the pages of *The Lamp*. Though so many Bishops did sign the petition, a few were reluctant to sign because of the obligatory aspect. The Archbishop of Liverpool, England, wrote in January, 1926:

I was one of the first, if not the only English Bishop, to promote the Church Unity Octave some years ago when I was Bishop of Northampton. You may, therefore, credit me with sincere devotion to the object you have in view and no less sincere friendliness to your own particular organization. But I object on principle to imposing *as an obligation* on the whole Catholic world this or any other form of private devotion. . . . The surest way, in my opinion, to kill such a movement as yours is to trust to the calendar, instead of working it up year by year as you do now. . . . I trust, therefore, that you will recognize that Bishops may have respectable reasons for refusing to sign your petition. As a matter of fact it is much easier to sign anything . . . than to write long explanations, such as this, for declining.

Father Paul sent back a gracious letter from which we give the following excerpt:

It is that very "trusting to the calendar" that I do fear, and the waning enthusiasm of the succeeding years of a purely human propaganda. I, therefore, come, as many other founders have come before me, to the feet of the occupant of Peter's Throne to crave of Christ's Vicar the security and permanence for this Octave (the burden of which I believe God has placed upon my shoulders) that he alone can give.

When Father Paul founded the *Church Unity Octave* in the Episcopal Church there did not exist the various ecumenical movements for Christian Unity that exist today among non-Catholics. However, with the development of these, after the Society of the Atonement became Catholic, there arose the danger of Father Paul's Octave becoming identified with, or at least confused with these new movements for the Unity of Protestant bodies. Then, too, the title *Church Unity Octave* postulated ambiguity, and also misapprehension, about the very Unity of the Catholic Church itself, which has always been hers by her divine institution—One Lord—One Faith—One Baptism.

To distinguish the Octave founded by Father Paul from other ecumenical movements for Unity, the Sacred Congregation of Rites at Rome in 1927 gave it a sub-title—*Chair of Unity Octave*.

Since then the original title has been eliminated entirely and it is now known exclusively as *The Chair of Unity Octave*. The *Catholic Universe* (London) remarked editorially in 1928 that the new title of the Octave lifted it above any possibility of misunderstanding. But, of course, from the beginning Father Paul and the Graymoor community understood it in its true Catholic sense. From here on, in this book, the Octave, therefore, will be referred to by the author only as *The Chair of Unity Octave*.

Though the Octave today is not *obligatory* it is nevertheless observed universally. The fruits of this yearly observance of the Octave is known to God alone. The individual conversions which may be the fruit of it will be unknown until that day when we will no longer see "through a mirror in an obscure manner." The results of the Octave observance have been illustrated in letters of missionary bishops in many parts of the world. One of these letters, from Bishop Francis Roche, S.J., Latin Bishop of Tuticorin, South India, reads:

It is significant that nearly every year immediately after the . . . Octave, there is a good harvest of souls. Some time back, nearly all Protestants in the village of Seduramalingapuram joined the Catholic Church. There were only four families adamant. Wonderful to say that at the end of January these four families have become Catholics, so that the whole village which was once Protestant is today entirely Catholic. The village is now called Sesurajapuram, the village of Jesu Raja.

The myriad of prayers which ascend to God each year for the reunion of Christendom are powerful and bring down an abundance of God's Grace upon the intentions of the Octave. But on whom the Grace falls as a result of these prayers we cannot say with certainty.

We do know, however, that there have been *corporate* submissions of religious bodies to the Catholic Church since the Octave began, and that there is reliable evidence presented by members of these groups which give a certain amount of credit for their conversions to the observance of the Octave.

In relation to the *corporate* submission of groups to the Catholic Church, it must be remembered that other influences were at work helping to bring about the conversion of these religious bodies. For instance, an investigation of Papal Claims might well have been the cause of these conversions. The fact remains, however, that most of these groups were in correspondence with Father Paul before the final step of entrance into the Catholic Church was taken by them.

Father Paul always referred to the *corporate* reception of the Society of the Atonement as, "the first fruits of the Octave observance."

However, the Right Reverend Edward Hawks of Philadelphia disagreed with Father Paul, pointing to the *corporate* reception of the seven Companions of the Holy Savior on May 27, 1908, as the "first fruits of the Octave observance."

The history of other notable *corporate* receptions is briefly given here. The Anglican Benedictine monks of Caldey, England, founded in the last decade of the nineteenth century by Aelred Carlyle, were *corporately* received into the Catholic Church in December, 1912. Twenty-nine monks were received at one time, and two at a subsequent date. The Benedictine nuns of St. Bride's Abbey, Milford Haven, Wales, followed the example of the Caldey monks and were received *corporately* during the winter of 1913.

Dom Aelred Carlyle had corresponded for many years with Father Paul before the submission of his community to Rome. In 1908 he visited Graymoor and pledged his support of the Octave. Both the monks and nuns had observed the Octave from its very beginning. In a letter written to Father Paul in 1913, the Superior of Caldey said that he attributed the grace of his community's conversion in "large measure" to the prayers of the Octave.

On March 4, 1936, Brother Joseph, Founder of The Servants of Christ the King, at Frensham in Surrey, England, wrote to Father Paul:

> The event which you forecast in a letter to me some three years ago, and for which I know you have been praying, has come to pass. You have taken such a kindly and charitable interest in our development that we are confident that you will do all you can to help us in the future. . . . We hope to be received before Easter, but already the Bishop has allowed a priest to come and say Mass for us and our household.

The Servants of Christ the King were received *corporately* into the Catholic Church in the spring of 1936.

During the Octave observance of 1937, Mother Cecelia Mary, Foundress of The Sisters of the Love of Jesus, in the Anglican Church of Canada, invited Archbishop Duke of Vancouver to visit their convent in that city to discuss their corporate submission into the Fold of Peter. The nine members of the Sisterhood were *corpo-*

rately received on August 24, 1937. Mother Cecelia had been corresponding with Father Paul for four years before their conversion. They, too, had been faithful in the observance of the Octave.

The conversion of Mar Ivanios, Jacobite Bishop of Bethany (India); his suffragan, Mar Theophilos; scores of priests and hundreds of lay people in the fall of 1930 astounded the whole Christian world. When the number of converts reached the ten-thousand mark in 1931, it was even then accounted a *corporate submission* of a small minority of the South Indian Jacobite Church.

The following letter from Archbishop Mar Ivanios was recently received by the Author:

The Most Rev. Dr.
Archbishop Mar Ivanios, O.I.C.
Metropolitan of Trivandrum
Trivandrum
Travancore State
India

October 4, 1950

REVEREND AND DEAR FATHER GANNON:

I write to acknowledge with thanks the receipt of your letter dated September 18, 1950. The news that Father Paul and the entire Congregation of the Franciscan Friars of the Atonement founded by him as well as the Sisterhood of the Atonement founded by Mother Lurana under the inspiration and guidance of Father Paul, made their submission to the Catholic Church brought a thrill to my mind. At that time I was in the dissident Orthodox Jacobite Church. The Movement of the Church Unity Octave sponsored by Father Paul was known to me then. I observed it in the Monastery and in the Convent of Nuns which I founded in the dissident Church without any personal knowledge of, or correspondence with, Father Paul. A daily prayer for the Re-union of Christendom was introduced by me in my Monastery and Convent. God answered these prayers and guided me and the two Religious Congregations over which I was the Abbot to seek communion with the Holy See. On September 20, 1930, I made my submission to Pope Pius XI. The Religious Congregations followed me into the Catholic Church. Soon after these, I paid my respects in person to His Excellency Archbishop Mooney [now Cardinal Mooney of Detroit, Michigan] at Bangalore, who was then Apostolic Delegate to East Indies. At that time, I mentioned to His Excellency that I was expecting several priests (many of whom were my pupils formerly at the Seminary or at the University) to follow me into the Catholic Church and financial assistance would be needed to provide for the maintenance of these priests. His Excellency himself wrote to Father Paul recommending my needs. . . . The maintenance of the Sisters who had followed me into the Catholic Church was provided by the regular remittances of Mother Lurana. In this manner the financial difficulties incidental to the Re-union Movement at its early stages were solved by the generosity of Father Paul and Mother Lurana.

The Octave of the Church Unity appealed to me from the very beginning as the one essential thing to heal the wounds caused by schism in the mystical Body of Christ.

I am thankful to you for giving me the occasion to bear testimony to the spiritual greatness of Father Paul. You may remember that I visited Graymoor in 1947 and celebrated a Pontifical Requiem Mass for Father Paul and another Mass for Mother Lurana. God bless you.

Yours in our Blessed Lord,
MAR IVANIOS
Archbishop of Trivandrum

To: Rev. David Gannon S.A.
Franciscan Friars of the Atonement
Graymoor, Garrison, N. Y.
U.S.A.

The number of Jacobite converts in 1943 was eighty thousand. They are, therefore, the most important fruits of *The Chair of Unity Octave*.

The above communities who were received *corporately* into the Catholic Church attribute in no small way their conversion to the *Chair of Unity Octave* which Father Paul founded. These conversions are the great splendor of the Octave of Prayer and the living testimony of the efficaciousness of its observance. The Octave is our rainbow of hope for the conversion of the noble English nation and all the other nations of the earth.

It is most important to point out here that the *Universal Week of Prayer for Christian Unity*, observed at the same time that *The Chair of Unity Octave* is observed *is not identical with the prayer* movement founded by Father Paul. Because of the danger of its identification with Graymoor's Octave, which has been sanctioned and approved by four Popes, we give its history here. This movement for

Unity, among others, is the reason why the title of the Octave was changed from the *Church Unity Octave* to the *Chair of Unity Octave*.

The rapid growth of *The Chair of Unity Octave* among Catholics, Anglicans, Orthodox and a few Lutherans was bound to lead to some deviation from its original intention—*The Unity of all Christians under the See of Peter*—unless stress was constantly laid on this underlying theme of the Octave. Some persons, zealous in the work of propagating the Octave, and anxious to include even those Christians who had a violent antipathy to the Papacy, felt that it would be wise to make some change in the purpose of *The Chair of Unity Octave*. They thought that by generalizing its purpose and omitting the acceptance of the Petrine Claims much good would result. Then Protestant and Orthodox Christians would be more willing to pray for Christian Unity, having as the aim of their prayers, "the reunion of Christians in the manner best pleasing to Christ," rather than, "reunion under the authority of the Successor of Saint Peter," the Pope of the Catholic Church.

On the face of it, especially since all Catholics know that the manner of reunion "best pleasing to Christ" is identical with "reunion under the authority of the Successor of Saint Peter," and since it also meant that millions of non-Catholics could take part in it by prayer this idea seemed a good one. But the danger of this new, so-called "broadened form" of the Octave's observance lies in the fact that the doctrinal foundation of *The Chair of Unity Octave* is completely destroyed. There was nothing in the thesis of these ostensibly sincere men to cause an Orthodox believer to deviate from his belief that Christian Reunion would come when all men accepted the Orthodox concept of the Church with its theological and liturgical position. The new idea of prayer for unity would not disturb sincere Presbyterians from hoping that some day all Christians would accept Predestination as a doctrinal certainty. Even Quakers might join in the new prayer movement in the hope that the world would accept their brand of the openness of the heart to the promptings of the Holy Spirit as the basic rule of Christian life. This movement can never be identified with *The Chair of Unity Octave* conceived by

Father Paul at Graymoor, which has as its foundation-stone a firm belief in the Roman Primacy as the *sine qua non* of Reunion.

This watered-down prayer octave was instituted by a French Catholic priest and an emigré Russian Orthodox theological student. The Abbé Paul Couturier, professor of the College de Chartreux in Lyons, France, had become interested in the Russian Orthodox community in Lyons as early as 1925. He was a man of wide sympathies and broad understanding who realized that at his own doorstep was an example of a sturdy Christian group, faithful to most of Christ's teachings, but separated from the visible fold of the true Church of Christ. Impressed by the piety of the Russian exiles and the devotion of their priests, he became "fired with the desire to work for the union of the Russian Church with the Holy See."

In 1927 the Abbé came in contact with Serge Bolshakoff.

Though the Abbé Couturier was brilliantly educated and had read much, he was not acquainted with *The Chair of Unity Octave* until the summer of 1932. On a visit to the Benedictine Priory of Amay in Belgium, a member of the community explained it to him. In the following January he introduced its observance in Lyons. So as not to repel the Russian Orthodox and the French Protestants, the good Abbé observed the Octave on an ecumenical tone. He conferred with Serge Bolshakoff, and the two of them hit upon a solution that would leave no room for suspicion on the part of the Orthodox and Protestants. They decided on an octave of prayer during the same time that the Catholic Church celebrated *The Chair of Unity Octave*. In their octave, however, all Christians could join without making the doctrinal postulates required of those who would pray that all Christians be united under the authority of the Pope. So, in June, 1934, the "Universal Week of Prayer for Christian Unity" was conceived.

Orthodox co-operation with the Octave in this form was immediate. In an article entitled "The Church Unity Octave in the Orthodox Church," which Father Paul published in *The Lamp* of December, 1936, Serge Bolshakoff tells how the Octave came to be observed in the Orthodox Church. The Octave was solemnly observed in the Monastery of Petseri in Esthonia in 1935, with the full approval of Archbishop Nicholas; and in the St. Kirik Monastery in Bulgaria, with

Archbishop Damian presiding and preaching on the need of visible unity between East and West. In 1935 the Orthodox parishes in Lyons received permission from the Metropolitan Eulogius, their Ordinary in Paris, to observe the Octave. The National Synod of the French Reformed Church (Calvinist) approved the new form of the Octave in 1935; and it was observed in many of their parishes in 1936. In 1940 the *World Conference on Faith and Order,* an international inter-Faith group to which nearly all the Protestant denominations belong, approved the Octave in this new form, as the official time for prayers for Christian Unity on the part of all who call themselves believers. At present the period from January 18th to January 25th is being observed by large numbers of non-Catholic Christians in all parts of the world as a time for prayer for that kind of Christian Unity that is "best pleasing to Christ."

The *World Conference on Faith and Order* met in Edinburgh in August, 1937. In the "Affirmation of Unity" the Conference pathetically declared:

Our unity is of heart and spirit. We are divided in the outward forms of our life in Christ, because we understand differently His will for His Church. We believe however that a deeper understanding will lead us toward a united apprehension of the truth as it is in Jesus.

We humbly acknowledge that our divisions are contrary to the will of Christ, and we pray God in His mercy to shorten the days of our separation and to guide us by His Spirit into fulness of Unity.

We desire to declare to all men everywhere, our assurance that Christ is the one hope of Unity for the world in face of the distractions and dissensions of this present time. We know that our witness is weakened by our divisions. Yet we are one in Christ and in the fellowship of His Spirit. We pray that everywhere, in a world divided and perplexed, men may turn to Jesus Christ Our Lord, who makes us one in spite of our divisions; that He may bind in one those who by many worldly claims are set at variance; and that the world may at last find peace and Unity in Him; to whom be glory forever.

In his correspondence with the Abbé Couturier and Serge Bolshakoff, Father Paul agreed that there was much to be said in favor of any form of prayer which would mean that millions of people were praying for that Christian Unity which would "be pleasing to Christ." As a man of prayer and a firm believer in the power of prayer, he would do nothing to hinder prayer on the part of earnest non-Catholics for that solution to the unity of Christians that would "be pleasing to Christ."

Father Paul believed that this was the prudent attitude to take towards the week of prayer, "watered down" as it was from the original—*The Chair of Unity Octave.* For he reasoned that when men pray sincerely to God for that which is "pleasing to Christ" they ask that God's Will be done. Father Paul also reasoned that the Unity of Christians which is most "pleasing to Christ" is a United Christendom with the Successor of St. Peter at its head. The storm of controversy which raged around him as an Anglican for years was caused by his adamant stand on this one point. And as a Catholic leader he had no desire to hold out to non-Catholics the hope that Rome might change in her attitude on the method by which Christian Unity was to be attained.

However, by a strange coincidence, as the author was writing this chapter on Father Paul's life, the profound Encyclical letter *Humani Generis* of Pope Pius XII was promulgated on August 21, 1950. This Apostolic letter puts forth in no uncertain terms the attitude that is to be taken by the Catholic Bishops of the Universal Church as well as Catholic theologians and philosophers in regard to ecumenical movements such as the *Universal Week of Prayer for Christian Unity.*

This Apostolic letter firmly upholds the "teaching authority of the Church" in contradistinction to "some false opinions." It warns against the distortion and watering down of Catholic truth in a vain attempt to present it in a more palatable form to those not of Catholic faith.

In the Encyclical letter the Pope discusses present day philosophical, theological and scientific trends both inside and outside the Church, and issues this warning: "Let no Christian, whether philosopher or theologian, embrace eagerly or lightly whatever novelty happens to be thought up from day to day, but rather let him weigh it with painstaking care and a balanced judgment lest he lose or corrupt the truth he already has, with grave danger and damage to his Faith."

The letter is characterized by such terms as "aberrations from the truth," "imprudent zeal for souls," "erroneous philosophy," "advocates of novelty" and "conjectural opinion."

In this new Encyclical letter the Holy Father in condemning "false opinions which threaten to undermine the foundations of Catholic doctrine," warns against, and gives the answer to, the so-called "Eirenic Theology" when he states:

Another danger is perceived which is all the more serious because it is more concealed beneath the mask of virtue. There are many who, deploring disagreement among men and intellectual confusion, through an imprudent zeal for souls, are urged by a great and ardent desire to do away with the barrier that divides good and honest men; these advocate an "eirenism" according to which, by setting aside the questions which divide men, they aim not only at joining forces to repel the attacks of atheism, but also at reconciling their differences in dogma.

And as in former times some questioned whether the traditional apologetics of the Church did not constitute an obstacle rather than a help to the winning of souls for Christ, so today some go as far as to question seriously whether theology and theological methods such as with the approval of ecclesiastical authority are found in our schools, should not only be perfected, but also completely reformed, in order to promote the more efficacious propagation of the Kingdom of Christ everywhere throughout the world among men of every culture and religious opinion.

Now if these only aimed at adapting ecclesiastical teaching and methods to modern conditions and requirements, through the introduction of some new system, there would be scarcely any reason for alarm.

But some through enthusiasm for an imprudent "eirenism" seem to consider as an obstacle to the restoration of fraternal union, tenets founded on the laws and principles given by Christ and likewise of the institutions founded by Him, or which are the defense and support of the integrity of the faith, and the removal of which would bring about the union of all, but only to their destruction.

These new opinions whether they originate from a reprehensible desire of novelty or from a laudable motive, are not always advanced in the same degree, with equal clarity nor in the same terms, nor always with the unanimous agreement of their authors. Theories that today are put forward rather covertly by some, not without cautions and distinctions, tomorrow are openly and without moderation proclaimed by others more audacious, causing scandal to many, especially among the young clergy and to the detriment of ecclesiastical authority.

Though they are more cautious in their published works, they are more open in their writings intended for private circulation and in conferences and in lectures. Moreover, these opinions are published not only among members of the clergy and in seminaries and religious institutions, but also amongst the laity, and especially amongst those who are engaged in teaching youth.

In theology some want to reduce to a minimum the meaning of dogmas and to free dogma itself from terminology long established in the Church and from philosophical concepts held by Catholic teachers, and to return in the explanation of Catholic doctrine to the way of speaking used in Holy Scripture and by the Fathers of the Church.

They cherish the hope that when dogma is stripped of the elements which they hold to be extrinsic to Divine Revelation, it will compare advantageously with the opinions of those who are separated from the unity of the Church and that in this way they will gradually arrive at a mutual assimilation of Catholic dogma and the tenets of the dissidents. . . . Finally let them not think, indulging in false "eirenics" that the dissident and erring can happily be brought back to the bosom of the Church if the whole truth found in the Church is not sincerely taught to all without corruption or diminution.

This new Encyclical letter is, in that part of it which is concerned with the *Reunion* of Christendom, an elaboration of the Instruction to Local Ordinaries on the *Ecumenical Movement* issued on December 20, 1949, by the Supreme Congregation of the Holy Office which reads in part:

The Catholic Church takes no actual part in "ecumenical" conventions and other assemblies of a similar character. Yet as numerous pontifical documents show, she has, despite this fact, never ceased, nor will she ever cease to pursue with deepest concern and promote with assiduous prayers to God every endeavor to bring about what was so close to the Heart of Christ the Lord, viz., that all who believe in Him, "may be made perfect in one." Indeed she embraces with truly maternal affection all who return to her as the only true Church of Christ. Hence any plans and enterprise which, with the consent of the ecclesiastical authority, have been undertaken and are being carried out to enlighten converts properly in the faith or to impart a more thorough instruction to those already in the Church, can never be sufficiently approved or given too much encouragement. . . .

Certain attempts that are being designated by diverse names in different countries, have hitherto been made by various persons, either individually or in groups, to effect a reconciliation of dissident Christians with the Catholic Church. Such initiatives, however, do not always rest upon correct principles, although inspired by the best of intentions, and even when sprung from sound principles they do not avoid besetting particular dangers, as past experience has shown. For this reason this Supreme Sacred Congregation, which has been charged with the care of defending and preserving intact the deposit of faith, has seen fit to call to mind and enjoin what is here set forth. . . .

Bishops will not allow recourse to a perilous mode of speaking which engenders false notions and raises deceitful hopes that can never be fulfilled. Such would be, for example, the allegation that what is in the Encyclical Letters of the Roman Pontiffs about the return of the dissidents to the Church, or about the constitution of the Church, or about the Mystical Body of Christ, need not be so rigorously taken, inasmuch as not all things are of faith, or, what is worse still, in matters of dogma not even the Catholic Church is already in possession of the fullness of Christ and hence others are still in a position of contributing towards its perfection. . . .

The whole and entire body of Catholic doctrine is, therefore, to be proposed and explained. Nothing embraced in the Catholic truth concerning the true nature and means of justification, the constitution of the Church, the Roman Pontiff's primacy of jurisdiction, and the only real union effectuated by a return of the dissidents to the one true Church of Christ, must be passed over in silence or cloaked under ambiguous language. Non-Catholics may certainly be told that, in returning to the Church, they will forfeit none of the good that the grace of God had hitherto wrought in their souls, but that the return will bring this to its perfection and final consummation. Yet this must not be represented in such a fashion as to create in them the impression that by their return they are making a contribution to the Church of something essential that she lacked in the past. All this must be truly set forth clearly and intelligibly for the double reason that they are really seeking the truth and that outside of the truth no true union can ever be attained.

These two documents; the Instruction of the Holy Office and the Encyclical letter of Pope Pius XII, express the mind of the Catholic Church, the true Church of Christ; and also the attitude to be taken by all her members in regard to the *Ecumenical Movement*. The only *Reunion* the Catholic Church is interested in is the return of all the "other sheep" to the one Fold of Peter under his Successor who is the Vicar of Christ on earth.

In his article of December, 1936, (in *the Lamp*) Serge Bolshakoff, who at that time was the Prior of the Orthodox Confraternity of Saint Benedict, wrote:

. . . For the Confraternity the Octave is the prayer for the rapprochement between Eastern and Western Christians with a view to restoration of their former Unity and of deliverance of Christendom from the advancing forces of Antichrist in various disguises. The way of rapprochement and of reunion is not defined but left to the Providence of God, Who knows incomparably better than men when and how to restore it.

Serge Bolshakoff then goes on to tell of his efforts to have an article, written by the Abbé Couturier published in the Orthodox press. "The Editors were reluctant," he wrote, "to give space for the exposition of the Octave and ideology by a Roman Catholic Priest until some influential Church authority expressed its conviction on the orthodoxy of the Octave." (At this time three Roman Pontiffs had blessed *The Chair of Unity Octave*).

Serge Bolshakoff's article further stated:

For the same reason tentative efforts to introduce the Octave into the Orthodox Churches of Central Europe failed. The Confraternity decided then to obtain the judgment on the Octave of some influential ecclesiastical authority. Accordingly, the President of the Confraternity requested the annual plenary Synod of Russian Bishops abroad, held at the Patriarchal Palace, Sremski-Karlovtci, in Jugo-Slavia, to express an opinion on the Octave. The Synod, after careful consideration, found the observance of the Church Unity Octave, as it is interpreted by the Confraternity, permissible in the Orthodox Church, and left the Diocesan Bishops the freedom to observe it or not, according to individual judgment.

The Octave "as it is interpreted by the Confraternity" is "the Reunion of Christians in the manner best pleasing to Christ." Father Paul, in establishing the Octave, also established "the manner best pleasing to Christ"; that is, "Reunion under the authority of the Successor of Saint Peter." The same Peter to whom Christ said: "Thou art Peter and upon this rock I will build my Church."

The danger of the watered-down prayer Octave can be found in Serge Bolshakoff's own words when he wrote in the V*oice of the Church* (February, 1942) "quite a number of Anglicans and Orthodox, including a number of eminent persons, thought I was trying to convert the Catholics to the Orthodox Church."

However, *The Chair of Unity Octave*, founded by Father Paul, continues to march on, observed by greater numbers and more universally each year. In the United States the most celebrated observance of the Octave takes place in the National Shrine of the Immaculate Conception on the campus of the Catholic University of America. Each year sermons on the intentions are delivered by outstanding and scholarly preachers. Bishops, priests, clerics and religious from more than thirty seminaries attend the evening services. In this way, priests and future priests from all parts of the world are acquainted with the aims of the Octave. Many Catholic and non-Catholic laymen also attend. The Divine Liturgy of the Oriental Church is celebrated on the Sunday within the Octave—a glorious manifestation of the universality of the Catholic Religion, which knows no bounds of race or tongue or color.

In Rome, the Eternal City, where the Friars and Sisters of the Atonement are now established, the observance of the Octave outshines every other observance of the Octave throughout the world. In 1950 the observance took place at the Gesù, the centrally located, spacious and beautiful church of the Jesuits. Publicity was given prior to the observance in the *Osservatore Romano* and on the Vatican radio. Seven Cardinals and one Archbishop presided at the different services. The sermons were broadcast to the world over the Vatican radio. The Octave was opened by the Cardinal Protector of the Sisters of the Atonement, Nicolà Cardinal Canali, Grand Penitentiary of the Roman Church and President of the Pontifical Commission for the Government of the State of Vatican City. The Octave was closed by an old friend of Graymoor, Pietro Cardinal Fumasoni-Biondi. On the second day of the Octave observance when Eugenio Cardinal Tisserant presided, the students of the various Oriental Rite colleges walked in the procession of prelates and priests in full vestments to attend Cardinal Tisserant, who is Secretary of the Sacred Congregation for the Oriental Church. There in the center of Christendom pilgrims from all lands knelt to pray for the realization of the dream of Christ, "That all may be One."

Only forty-two years before Father Paul, "the erratic priest," had begun the Octave of Prayer on a lonely mountain known only to a few as Graymoor. But he prayed with faith, and through the telescope of his deep faith he saw the fruits of his prayer in Rome, Washington, Travancore, Paris and Yokohama. For faith was the foundation stone of Father Paul's edifice of sanctity; and God, seeing the beauty of that edifice, further adorned it with the priceless souls of men.

On the second page of the first edition of *The Lamp*, in February, 1903, he wrote these magnificent words, while still an Anglican:

Is then Christian Unity a visionary dream? Will the prayer of the Son of God never be answered? Was He a lying Prophet when He foretold the time of its fulfilment, saying: "Other Sheep I have which are not of this fold (the one Catholic and Apostolic Church) them also I must bring and there shall be one fold and one Shepherd." Let who will deride or shake their heads in doubt saying: "Heresy and schism have gone too far; the seamless robe of Christ is too much torn to tatters ever to be mended; the reunion of Christendom is utterly out of the question; Rome is too proud and unbending; England is too self-satisfied: the East too orthodox; Protestantism too much enamoured of letting everybody do and think just as they please. They never can and they never will come together. Christian Unity is hopeless!" Our answer is, God's Will is Omnipotent; the Fiat of the Most High must prevail; the prayer of Jesus Christ has got to be answered; the Almighty Father would never refuse the dying request of His Only begotten Son; sooner or later every petition of Christ will inevitably be granted. Were the mountains of difficulty to be surmounted a thousand times higher and vaster than they are, God is able to cast them into the sea. Faith serenely rests her case with Him.

Yet even Faith must "Tarry the Lord's leisure" for with God "a thousand years are but as one day." Patience must be allowed plenty of time to do her work perfectly. She cannot and will not be hurried, the fabric is exceedingly delicate, the pattern most elaborate; the Robe of Unity she is weaving for the Son of God will be of matchless beauty. And it is the work of many generations and Hope with smiling countenance kneels and prays, being quite happy and content to wait. And Love, standing between the two, looks over the shoulder of Patience and cheers her on, saying: "Be of good courage, my sister, He, the desire of all nations, will come and will not tarry and behold His reward is with Him."

Chapter XXI

"WILLINGLY DO I BEAR WITNESS"

When the cornerstone of "The Little Flower Memorial" on the Mount of the Atonement was laid on July 19, 1926, by the Papal Legate to the Chicago Eucharistic Congress, John Cardinal Bonzano, many Bishops, priests and laymen wondered how Father Paul was accorded this signal honor by a Cardinal who had many more important things to do and places to visit during his short stay in the United States. Patrick Cardinal Hayes, who accompanied the Papal Legate to Graymoor, in introducing Cardinal Bonzano, said:

"Many wonder, and probably nobody knows, how Father Paul was able to obtain a visit from the Papal Legate which many practically under the very eaves of the Archiepiscopal Cathedral have been unable to do."

Prior to Cardinal Hayes' introduction of Cardinal Bonzano, Father Paul had taken the Papal Legate on a tour of the Mount of the Atonement and, standing beneath the Corpus Christi cross, Father Paul said to him, as they looked down into the valley, "Does it not remind Your Eminence of Assisi?"

Cardinal Bonzano had previously been Apostolic Delegate to the United States and was an old friend of Father Paul's. Moreover, he was, since he had returned to Rome, greatly impressed with Father Paul's work for the world-wide missions of the Church, particularly those of the Near East. To show his personal appreciation of Father Paul's work he accepted an invitation to lay the cornerstone. Before sailing for Italy Cardinal Bonzano wrote to Father Paul: "I am glad to know that my visit to Graymoor was a source of pleasure to you. To me it was no less gratifying, and I can assure you that it will forever remain permanent in a cluster of delightful recollections of my visit to the United States for the Eucharistic Congress."

An account of this memorable occasion is left to us by Mr. J. A. M. Richey, an associate editor of *The Lamp* who signs the account "Saul." He used the pen name "Saul" because he had once been a persecutor of Father Paul. The preacher on the occasion was the Right Reverend Monsignor Barry-Doyle who in his sermon said:

"Father Paul, Founder of the Society of the Atonement, a branch of the Seraphic Family of St. Francis, has conferred upon me a singular honor. . . . I have the great honor and coveted distinction of speaking before the Cardinal Legate of the Eucharistic Congress, and also an opportunity of offering to the Father Founder and to the Friars of the Atonement the warmest congratulations of their numerous friends, not only throughout the length and breadth of the United States, but in every part of the Catholic world." In the conclusion of his sermon Monsignor Barry-Dole turned to Father Paul and said:

FATHER PAUL: This day marks a most glorious event in the history of the Society of the Atonement and in your own history too. In the opinion of many it is a reward for your burning charity to all in distress and your constant zeal for the support of God's Kingdom in the hearts of men. In the mysterious, exotic Orient where I spent some years, and in the Near East, where I also labored, your charity, your deeds of compassion have made hearts, crushed with crimson sorrow, and souls, blasted by the fire of race hatred, realize that Christ still lives in the hearts of men. *Willingly do I bear witness* to the magnificent things you have helped us to make possible in Constantinople, in Athens, on the Plains of Marathon and around the shores of the Aegean Sea! I rejoice with you today. Graymoor and the Society of the Atonement started in silence and obscurity; today it is known in every part of the Catholic world. . . . Nor does it need a prophet's vision to visualize a saintly Friar of the Atonement, weary and old at the service of God, telling a young Novice that the Little Flower Building is his most sacred heritage because, long, long ago, at the request of the Father Founder, the cornerstone was laid by His Eminence, John Cardinal Bonzano, a Prince of the Sacred House of Peter the Fisherman and a Legate of the great and glorious Pius the Eleventh, the Pope who established the Feast of Christ the King and raised the Little Flower to the altars of the Church!

Monsignor Barry-Doyle who paid this great tribute to Father Paul on a red-letter day in Graymoor's history was the co-founder with Father Paul of what is today known as the Pontifical Society of *The*

Catholic Near East Welfare Association. The Monsignor was born in Wexford, Ireland, and was ordained a priest at St. John's College, Waterford. When the First World War broke out he was one of the many priests who joined the army to minister to Roman Catholic troops. He was wounded once and shell-shocked twice. General Harrington, in an address at a public reception in Constantinople, proclaimed Monsignor Barry-Doyle the most distinguished Chaplain in the British Army. In recognition of his untiring and ceaseless work among the troops he had received decorations from almost all the Allied Governments. After the armistice Monsignor Barry-Doyle was stationed at Constantinople, where he became thoroughly familiar with the complex conditions at the Dardanelles and the Golden Horn.

Father Paul's interest in the Oriental Church dates back to his Anglican days. In those days he believed in the *Corporate Reunion* of the Anglican Church with Rome, as well as in the validity of Anglican Orders. From the years 1903 to 1909 he constantly held out hopes to Anglicans for *Corporate Reunion*, always pointing to the fact that Rome never hesitated to acknowledge the valdity of the orders received by priests in the schismatical churches of the East, even though some of these churches were infected with Christological heresies.

After his reception into the Catholic Church his chief means of contact with Eastern Catholics was *The-Union-That-Nothing-be-Lost.* It was through letters from Catholic prelates of the Eastern Rites in need of alms that many lasting friendships developed between Father Paul and the Bishops of the Oriental Church. The correspondence he carried on with these prelates is tremendous. The deepest friendship he developed among them was with Monsignor George Calavassy of the Byzantine Rite, who later became Bishop of Constantinople and all Greece.

After the First World War when the Near East lay prostrate, Greek, Armenian and Russian refugees fled to Constantinople by the thousands to escape from the Bolshevik horrors of Crimea. Pope Pius XI then ordered Bishop Calavassy to proceed to the United States to explain to the American Hierarchy and to American Catholics the sad plight of the people of the Near East, and also

the immense importance of the *Reunion* Movement of the Orthodox
Greeks with Rome. The Bishop was to seek financial assistance for
helping the people and also for the erection of churches, seminaries
and schools in Constantinople and Athens. These were needed for
the Orthodox Greeks who desired reunion with the Holy See.

It was impossible at that time for Bishop Calavassy to leave Constantinople, so he and the Apostolic Delegate prevailed upon Monsignor Barry-Doyle to plead the cause of the Near East in the
United States.

The Monsignor was instructed by Bishop Calavassy to contact his
old friend Father Paul immediately on his arrival in America. He arrived at Graymoor on November 25, 1922, and stayed four
days; during which time a plan for fund-raising was mapped out
by Father Paul. Two weeks later when the December *Lamp* was
published Father Paul graciously introduced Monsignor Barry-Doyle
to *The Lamp* readers, and then made the bland announcement that
a campaign was now under way to raise *one million dollars* for Near
East relief. The announcement was rather breath-taking, for in those
days this was considered a huge sum of money. But Father Paul said
that the Holy Father needed it for the people of the Near East and
if the half million people who read *The Lamp* would send two
dollars, Monsignor Barry-Doyle could leave promptly and lay the
million dollars at the Holy Father's feet. Furthermore, if the
165,000 subscribers to *The Lamp* would each send ten dollars, Monsignor Barry-Doyle could lay almost two million dollars at the feet
of Pius XI. "Letters," he wrote, "addressed to the Monsignor care
of *The Lamp* will be forwarded to him at any time." To Father
Paul, who had faith in human nature and a deep and lasting faith
in God, the solution of the Monsignor's problem was as simple as
that. At the same time Graymoor was inundated with appeals from
missionaries all over the world and money was badly needed at
Graymoor for housing facilities for a fast-growing community. Immediately under the appeal for the Monsignor was one for bread for
Bishop Calavassey's seminarians. "Now is the hour of Constantinople's greatest need. Bishop Calavassy's Greek Seminarians are
hungry and must be fed. . . . There must be thousands of *The-*

Union-That-Nothing-Be-Lost Self-Denial envelopes lying on the writing desk, table, or in the drawers of our *Lamp* readers. Just take one of these and write Constantinople Bread League across the face of it and insert an offering."

So the drive for the Near East was on and month after month Father Paul pleaded for the stricken people of Greece and Constantinople. In February, 1923, Bishop Calavassy wrote to Father Paul: "For the sake of God do all you can to alleviate my heavy burden! . . . You can imagine how heart-breaking it is . . . when thousands of starving people are appealing to me, as to their Father, for bread!" The next month he wrote: "More than half of the expenses for the maintenance of our Missions, Schools, Nuns, Seminary and clergy was afforded by *The Lamp* and *The-Union-That-Nothing-Be-Lost*, which proves how beneficial is your work to the Church and to the cause of Reunion. . . . Thanks to your assistance we have been able to increase the number of our Sisters, of our Seminarians and of our Clergy . . . to build a new chapel, to enlarge our school buildings, to bring the number of our students to 540 and to receive into the Church 335 converts." Monsignor Barry-Doyle wrote in *The Lamp* that same month: "The recent victory of the Turks over the Greeks and subsequent events have given additional trouble and anxiety to Bishop Calavassy. . . . The awful conditions in the East today will, if taken in the proper spirit by all practical Catholics, prove one of the greatest blessings for the Christian people of the Orient."

Meanwhile, the Monsignor was touring the United States and Canada on a lecture tour. He spoke in such places as the ballroom of the Plaza Hotel and Carnegie Hall in New York, the Metropolitan Opera House of Philadelphia and to more select gatherings in the town houses of Clarence Mackay of New York and Thomas McKean of Philadelphia. Cardinal Dougherty was an ardent supporter of the Monsignor and he also had the support of every member of the Hierarchy in America. In the January, 1924, issue of *The Lamp*, Father Paul wrote: "The gross receipts from the Monsignor's lectures, and contributions sent to his fund through the medium of *The Lamp* and *The-Union-That-Nothing-Be-Lost* during 1923, have totaled more than forty thousand dollars."

In 1924 the work was incorporated under the title *The Catholic Near East Welfare Association*, with headquarters at 277 Park Avenue, New York City. The President named for the incorporated association was Monsignor Barry-Doyle. Father Paul was vice-president and also a member of the Board of Directors, whose chairman was the Most Reverend M. J. Hoban, Bishop of Scranton, Pa. After the incorporation *The Lamp* readers were instructed to send their contributions to the headquarters in New York. However, even with the new arrangement, over sixteen thousand dollars was sent to Bishop Calavassy that year through *The-Union-That-Nothing-Be-Lost*. Before Father Paul left for Rome in 1925, Monsignor Barry-Doyle sent him a letter in which he said: "Again I thank you from my heart for all you have done for the cause of the Church in dear Greece. I know when you kneel at the feet of the Holy Father in Rome when you present your pilgrims to him you will ask His Holiness to continue to bless my efforts."

In the fall of 1925 the Monsignor went to Rome and presented to the Holy Father a full report of *The Catholic Near East Welfare Association*. He also had important conferences with Cardinal Gasparri; the Papal Secretary of State, Cardinal Merry del Val and Cardinal Tacci, Secretary of the Sacred Congregation of the Oriental Churches. To all these great personages the Monsignor told of the enormous help of Father Paul and *The Lamp*. "Very few American Catholic periodicals," he wrote Father Paul, "are as well known in Rome as *The Lamp*."

During the time that Monsignor Barry-Doyle toured the United States and Canada seeking relief for the Near East there was a Benedictine priest touring American cities for practically the same purpose. He was the Reverend Augustine Count Von Galen. Father Von Galen's brother became the famous Bishop Clement Von Galen of Muenster, who resisted Adolf Hitler's persecution of the Church in Germany. In 1946 Pope Pius XII raised Bishop Von Galen to the Sacred College of Cardinals. As a resident of Vienna, Austria, Father

Von Galen was deeply moved by the sad plight of the Russian refugees of that city, and conceived the idea of forming a society to aid them. He named his society *The Catholic Union,* and with the permission of his superiors he began to organize his work in several centers. The aims of *The Catholic Union* were to relieve the distress of the refugees of Vienna as well as to reunite them with the Catholic Church by the education of Eastern priests who would eventually be apostles of unity to their own races. Father Paul also sponsored the work of Father Von Galen, whose work had received the special blessing and approval of the Pope Pius XI. Among others who aided the work of *The Catholic Union* were the students of the College of St. Elizabeth, Convent, New Jersey. On May 15, 1926, they sponsored a program at which the Russian Baroness Catherine de Hueck spoke. The Baroness was an indomitable and faithful Catholic who had escaped the first Bolshevik massacres, come to America, and here, after years of hardship, had been able to found and maintain large Catholic centers which she calls "Friendship Houses." In these she carries on her work against the evils of Communism.

It became evident that Monsignor Barry-Doyle and Father Von Galen were working for practically the same end; and that two societies occupying the same field might readily tend to overlap in their efforts and produce confusion in the minds of the people. So a plan was drawn up to combine these two societies, and this plan was submitted to the judgment of the Holy See. When Father Paul went to Rome in 1925, this was one of the objects of his visit.

After a careful consideration of all phases of the matter, it was decided, in the fall of 1926, that the work should be enlarged in scope and placed under the immediate direction of the Holy See and the American Hierarchy. In an official Letter Pius XI directed that, "in view of the personal interest hitherto manifested in *The Catholic Near East Welfare Association* by His Eminence Patrick Cardinal Hayes, it seemed well that he should be designated as Protector of the enlarged association, for which the title *The Catholic Near East Welfare Association* will be sufficient to express adequately the general purpose and scope of these two unified organizations." The letter further declared that "the title includes also *The Catho-*

lic Union and the purpose for which that Society has hitherto labored."

The Holy Father conferred the honor and responsibility of being President of the new organization upon the Reverend Edmund A. Walsh, S. J., Regent of the School of Foreign Service and Vice-President of Georgetown University. Previously when the Russian people were starving Pius XI organized a relief mission and sent Father Walsh as his personal representative to Russia as head of this mission.

On September 29, 1926, a meeting of the new association was held in New York. Its purpose was to put into effect the will of the Holy Father and the action of the American Hierarchy at their meeting in Washington. In the absence of the first President of the Association, Monsignor Barry-Doyle, who was ill, the Vice-President, Father Paul, presided until the election of Father Walsh, S.J. as President. When the new President took the chair Father Paul was again elected as Vice-President. The other officers elected were laymen. Cardinal Hayes accepted the position of Protector of the Association. The Board of Directors consisted of William Cardinal O'Connell, Archbishop of Boston, Chairman; Patrick Cardinal Hayes, Archbishop of New York; Denis Cardinal Dougherty, Archbishop of Philadelphia; Most Reverend John Joseph Glennon, Archbishop of St. Louis; Most Reverend Edward J. Hanna, Archbishop of San Francisco; Most Reverend Michael John Hoban, Bishop of Scranton; Most Reverend Thomas F. Lillis, Bishop of Kansas City.

At the meeting of the American Hierarchy in 1927 the following resolution was passed:

The Hierarchy of the United States in conference assembled express their full approval and adoption of the program of the Holy See providing for the unification of all societies now working in the United States of America for Russia and the Near East. The resultant organization, *The Catholic Near East Welfare Association, Inc.*, shall be the sole instrumentality authorized to solicit funds for Catholic interests in those regions and shall be so recommended to the entire Catholic population of the United States simultaneously in all dioceses on a given Sunday, the date to be arranged in consultation with the respective Ordinaries.

In the November, 1926, edition of *The Lamp* Father Paul wrote:

Under the blessing of God enormous results ought to follow . . . now that the Holy Father has created *The Catholic Near East Welfare Association* into a Pontifical Society and at the will of the Supreme Shepherd all the Cardinals, Bishops and Priests of America will henceforth both sanction and support it. As for the Catholic faithful of our country there is no question of their following where their shepherds lead the way . . . for the proper carrying on of this enormous work that has to do with the return of one hundred and fifty million stray sheep of Orthodoxy to One Fold under One Shepherd.

The Friars and Sisters of the Atonement, since the death of Father Paul, continue to aid the Christians of the Near East through their Bishops and also through *The Catholic Near East Welfare Association* which has for its President, Francis Cardinal Spellman. The Right Reverend Thomas J. McMahon, National Secretary, in a letter to the Mother General of the Sisters of the Atonement, on February 7, 1944, stated:

My sincere thanks to you and all for your generous stringless gift to the Near East. It will do untold good for our poor missionaries.

Dear Father Paul was one of the founders of this Association. This is another reason why I revere his saintly memory.

May God bless you all. May He inspire you to follow closely in the footsteps of your Father Founder and Mother Foundress.

The Most Reverend George Calavassy, having heard that Father Paul's biography was to be published, wrote from Athens, Greece, to Graymoor under date of October 22, 1950:

I am so glad that you are soon going to publish the biography of Father Paul. I am sure that it is going to be a most interesting and inspiring biography.

No doubt, the chapter on *The Catholic Near East Welfare Association* will show how broad-minded Father Paul was and how zealous he was for the *Cause of Reunion.*

He certainly was co-founder of the Association and its Vice-President. Very often in his letters Monsignor Barry-Doyle recognized that his success in organizing his work was mainly due to the interest and assistance of Father Paul. For instance, in his letter of February 14, 1923 to me, he wrote: "Father Paul, who has been wonderfully helpful and kind, has

sent to Bishop Papadopoulos (in Rome), as a result of my efforts, about
$3000 for you and more is coming in daily. . . .

"Father Paul has been more than kind and encouraging to me; in fact,
my entire success, so far, is due to his extraordinary zeal for your work
and his esteem for you personally. . . . It will not be child's play to
collect the million dollars, in fact it will involve much work and
thought, but as Father Paul has promised to cooperate with me and advise me, I feel confident of success."

The work begun by Monsignor Barry-Doyle and Father Paul is today a great Pontifical Society, very dear to the heart of Pius XII as
it was to the heart of Pius XI. Like Monsignor Barry-Doyle it, too,
bears witness "to the magnificent things" Father Paul accomplished
in "Constantinople, in Athens, on the plains of Marathon and around
the Aegean Sea."

Chapter XXII

THE MUSTARD SEED BECOMES A TREE

St. Mark the Evangelist, explaining the teaching method of the Savior of the World, says: "And in many parables He spoke to them, according as they were able to understand it; but without a parable He did not speak to them. But privately He explained all things to His disciples." These words of St. Mark come immediately after the words of Christ, in chapter four, in which He likens the Kingdom of God to a grain of mustard seed; the mustard seed which "becomes larger than any herb, and puts out great branches, so that the birds of the air can dwell beneath its shade."

To prevent the slow growth and expansion of the Society of the Atonement from discouraging his Friars, Father Paul often spoke privately to them of God's Covenant with him. In those conferences he often said that the seventeen members of the Society who were originally received into the Catholic Church were the "mustard seed" which would become a great tree. In the last ten years of his life, beginning with the year 1930, Father Paul saw the "mustard seed" grow up and put forth its branches. By that time the original two Friars and five Sisters had multiplied many times over.

Not only was St. John's minor seminary filled to capacity, but part of the new large friary also had to be turned over to the students for sleeping quarters. *The Atonement Seminary of the Holy Ghost* in Washington, after being enlarged, was also filled. In September, 1935, Father Paul wrote in *The Lamp*:

There are in the Society of the Atonement now twenty-one Priests, forty Professed Clerics, eight Cleric Novices and fourteen Tertiary Brothers. This fall we expect an enrollment of over seventy students in our preparatory college. Of the one hundred and sixty-five members of the community one hundred and eighteen are studying for the Priesthood. Forty of these students attend the Catholic University at Washington, while the rest pursue their courses under our own faculty at Graymoor.

A year later Father Paul gave the habit of the Friars of the Atonement to nineteen young men. At that ceremony, after reminding those who had received the habit that they now wore the armor of the Militia of Jesus Christ and that they should be ever ready to do battle against the hosts of Antichrist who were spreading over the earth, he said: "Today in lands that were once predominantly Catholic, priests and religious are being brutally murdered for professing Christ. And perhaps you, too, may one day experience a martyr's death at the hands of those among whom you labor."

Yes, the grain of "mustard seed" was fast becoming a great tree. One year later, on the Feast of the Assumption, August 15, 1937, Father Paul, before a vast concourse of people assembled on the lawn of the friary, gave the habit of his Society to twenty-six young men. The following day, seventeen of the nineteen who had received the holy habit the year before were professed in religion by making the temporary vows of Poverty, Chastity and Obedience.

Two months later, Father Paul wrote in *The Lamp*:

Our Preparatory Seminary, which we call St. John's Atonement College, opened according to custom on the Feast of the Nativity of the Blessed Virgin, that being the thirty-seventh anniversary of the breaking of the ground for St. Paul's Friary, the first building to be erected upon our Atonement Mountain. The students came in on the flood-tide . . . the new students outnumber those who were graduated last June. Consequently the College is in the same condition as all our Community buildings, viz., crowded to capacity. The necessity of enlargement confronts the Friars in every direction. Not only the College, itself, must be enlarged, but the Friary, the Novitiate, the house occupied by Tertiaries; and a larger St. Christopher's Inn project themselves upon our attention.

Extraordinary as the sudden growth of the Friars was, the development of the Sisters in the valley was even greater.

Thirty-nine years before these developments Father Paul had been tempted to give up the idea of founding the Society of the Atonement. The Omnipotent God, through His Holy Word, had reassured Father Paul with the words of the Covenant He had made with Abraham: "Surely blessing I will bless thee; and multiplying I will multiply thee." Like Abraham, after Father Paul had "patiently endured he obtained the promise."

But before Father Paul "obtained the promise" he had to suffer much through misunderstanding, false accusations, loneliness, dire poverty and the desertion of those he loved and trusted. Then there was the keen suffering of the disillusionment which came when he faced the dazzling light of truth, and found that the seemingly secure life he had known as an Anglican clergyman would be destroyed by his own trumpet proclaiming that truth.

But he was a man of great faith and courage. From boyhood he had known that God had a special work for him to do, and he kept the goal ever before him. When the world he had known as an Anglican clergyman crumbled around him, Father Paul began to build a new one on the firm Rock of Peter. When great trials came to him in the Catholic Church his faith in God's promise never wavered, and he lived to enjoy the reward of his faith and his labor.

During the time that the "mustard seed" was becoming a great tree, tragedy again struck Graymoor. On April 15, 1935, at 6:15 A.M., the Mother Foundress of the Society of the Atonement, Mother Lurana Mary Francis, S.A., passed to her eternal reward. The eulogy was preached by a faithful friend of Graymoor, Monsignor Lavelle, whose text was taken from Proverbs: chapter 31, verse 10: "Who shall find a valiant woman? Far and from the farthest coast is the price of her."

In a letter to the Rosarians the following month Father Paul wrote:

Having the name of the Atonement she [Mother Lurana] was called by God to be an atoning victim in union with the Crucified. At the commencement of her religious life she saw herself as a slain lamb and this vision of the night was particularly fulfilled in her last long illness extending over many months, during which time to an extraordinary and striking degree she was conformed to the image of the Lamb slain upon the cross. Unable to take food or drink without experiencing great nausea, she passed through a long period of fasting almost as absolute as that of Our Lord in the wilderness. She once spoke of her body as a "pain factory" and truly such it was. For a time one particular part of the body would be subjected to excruciating pain; and when it became almost unendurable it suddenly shifted to some other portion of the body, until almost every organ or member was involved in the sufferings of the crucified. But the sufferings of Mother Lurana were not entirely physical; during the thirty-six years of her life as a Religious at Graymoor she was called upon to pass through many periods of great mental strain, not the least acute of which served as an introduction to her last illness.

So passed away one whom Father Paul called "The Handmaid of the Lamp." While he occupied the center of the stage in the movement for Christian Unity she remained hidden in the wings of the world-wide theatre, watching with keenest interest every scene and act of the great drama. She gave her whole-hearted support to the Friar-Preacher, and when *The Lamp* was finally published, it was Mother Lurana who made it possible for Graymoor's luminary— *The Lamp*—to shed its light throughout the world. Her name will ever remain among the great ones in the work for Christian Unity.

Two weeks after Mother Lurana's death another great epoch in Graymoor's onward drive for Christian Unity began. On Sunday afternoon, April 28, 1935, a radio program sponsored by Graymoor and known as the *Ave Maria Hour* began the dramatization of the lives of the Saints and the heroes of the Catholic Faith. The first broadcast was the dramatization of the life of St. Mary of Egypt. The story of this new Graymoor project, established to glorify the Mother of Christ—Our Lady of Unity—is a most interesting one.

The *Ave Maria Hour* was founded by Father Anselm di Pasca, S.A. He is today Graymoor's senior priest. Father Anselm was one of the two students who remained loyal to Father Paul when St. John's was left desolate in 1915. For that loyalty God greatly rewarded Father Anselm. His work in founding the *Ave Maria Hour* has brought renown to the true Church of Christ and the Society of the Atonement.

From his youth Father Anselm has had great devotion to the Mother of Christ. In 1919, during his theological studies at St. Bonaventure Seminary at Allegheny, New York, Father Anselm enlisted the aid of Mother Lurana in collecting all the musical compositions of the *Ave Maria* that were available.

In 1935 Father Anselm read *The Glories of Mary* by St. Alphonsus. It was then that the idea of broadcasting a religious program came to him. His first intention was to broadcast weekly novena devotions in honor of Our Lady, hoping that through the radio some notion of her power and love might become instilled in the hearts of non-Catholics. Father Paul, the devoted Knight of Our Lady, not only encouraged Father Anselm but he was thrilled at the idea of a weekly broadcast in her honor.

Many obstacles were placed in the way of the first broadcast but, strange to say, Father Anselm found the greatest supporter of his idea in the person of a Jew. Instead of a novena it was decided that the broadcast should dramatize the lives of the Saints. The thought that in the Catholic Church there were millions who knew little about the Saints and that outside her fold Saints seemed legendary figures, prompted Father Anselm to follow the advice of a non-Catholic.

Father Paul, relying on the never-failing Providence of Almighty God to pay for the broadcasts, gave permission to Father Anselm to start the work. But like so many other projects begun at Graymoor in a humble way, Father Paul did not realize at the time that this was the beginning of another great work in the Church.

The very first broadcast of the *Ave Maria Hour* brought results beyond the fondest hopes of Father Paul and Father Anselm. Letters from those who heard the first program proved that the lives of the Saints, dramatized on the air waves, would cause men to reflect on things eternal, men who had never seriously considered religious truths before. Many listened to the first broadcast out of curiosity and were deeply impressed by the significance of the drama. Non-Catholics were as enthusiastic in their praise of the program as were Catholics.

Father Paul and Father Anselm learned from the results of the very first broadcast that this novel means of bringing home to men aspects of the teachings of Christ, manifested as they were in the life of this humble saint—Mary of Egypt, was in conformity with Graymoor's work, "to reconcile sinners to Jesus Christ through the Precious Blood of the Atonement." Proof, if tangible evidence was needed, came to Graymoor in letters from souls who had been led to definite resolutions through hearing the story of the conversion of Mary of Egypt from a life of sin.

The success of the first broadcast of the *Ave Maria Hour* assured its continuance on the air waves. Month after month the number of radio stations broadcasting the *Ave Maria Hour* on a transcription basis increased. In a few years after its inauguration millions of people throughout the United States were listening to the *Ave Maria Hour* over more than one hundred radio stations.

Great quantities of letters came to Graymoor from radio listeners. Letters came from good Catholics, indifferent Catholics, lapsed Catholics, as well as from Protestants and Jews. Letters came even from those who professed no religion. The writers of these letters attested to the good of the program in reference to their personal lives. To each one of them the *Ave Maria Hour* had brought a message, and they were grateful for that message. The prayer of many was that the *Ave Maria Hour* would continue on the air, to bring new hope and inspiration to others like themselves.

The missionary value of the *Ave Maria Hour* became more apparent to the Friars of the Atonement as time went on. The program was heard in the homes of millions of people of every class of society in the United States. Among these were men and women who would never buy or read a Catholic newspaper, book or pamphlet; and still others who would hesitate to speak to a Catholic priest on the subject of religion. However, many of these, impressed by the example of the Saints, all of whom were Catholic, did not hesitate to write to Graymoor for information about the Catholic Faith. This led to a new development in Graymoor's world-wide work for the *Reunion* of Christendom—a correspondence course in religion.

Since the correspondence course began in 1941 thousands of non-Catholics have applied for the course, which consists of six lessons. After the fifth lesson the correspondent is requested to send the name of the pastor of the Catholic Church nearest his home. When the course is finished, a letter of introduction to that pastor is sent to the correspondent. A conservative estimate of the number who eventually enter the Catholic Church through Graymoor's correspondence course is given, by the priest in charge, as one-third of those who complete the course.

One correspondent who had finished the course in 1942 did not enter the Church until 1949. Writing to Graymoor after her reception she stated: ". . . Because of the fact that convictions of a lifetime are not overcome in a day, I have waited until now although I regret having waited so long."

Today, fifteen years after the first broadcast, the *Ave Maria Hour* is heard over four hundred radio stations throughout the United States, Canada, Alaska, China, India, Hawaii, Panama and the Philippine Islands. Most of these stations carry the program on a sustaining basis.

In 1938, a young actor, who was a convert to Catholicism from the Anglican Church, came to the *Ave Maria Hour* studio in New York. There he met Father Paul. Later he entered the Society of the Atonement and studied for the priesthood. Today, as Father Terence Cummings, S.A., the young convert priest is the Director of the *Ave Maria Hour*.

During these years of growth and expansion when the "mustard seed" became a tree, Father Paul never relaxed his indefatigable labors for the spread of Christ's Church upon the earth. As the years piled up so did his many responsibilities and activities.

Years before the American people became conscious of the perils of Communism Father Paul saw the danger of this new materialistic philosophy of life. He was well acquainted with the horrors inflicted upon the Christians of the Near East by the Bolsheviks, through the correspondence he carried on with Catholic Bishops everywhere.

As early as May, 1923, he wrote in *The Lamp*: "Let us make no mistake concerning the animus of the Soviet Regime; nor should we be blind to the fact that the same Prince of Darkness who has got his grip so effectively upon the Sovietized masses of Russia, plans to control our American Democracy as well." To the day of his death Father Paul strove to awaken the American people to the danger of the *Red Peril* by his gifted pen and tongue.

In a meditation which he gave to the Friars extempore on the thirty-fourth anniversary of the founding of *The-Union-That-Nothing-Be-Lost*, December 21, 1938, he said: "I am the only connecting link between the founding of *The-Union-That-Nothing-Be-Lost* and our present development. There is no one on the mountain today who was here thirty-four years ago. I occupy the same cell that I did when the inspiration of founding the missionary union came to me. I cling to that cell because of what happened that morning, and I will probably end my days in it, if the Communists do not give me a crown of martyrdom."

In developing the theme of the meditation he showed that *The-Union-That-Nothing-Be-Lost* through the years had been a bulwark against the spread of Communism as it maintained the missionaries of Christ. "The more we cut down expenses running Graymoor," he said, "the more we shall have to support the missions. . . . So that principle of economy, the consecration of every faculty, every power, every opportunity, all the time God gives us must be utilized in the fight against Communism. Go and preach the Gospel to every nation. For it is by preaching and speaking the Word that the Children of the Atonement are generated. They must know Christ to embrace Him and be saved."

Chapter XXIII

THE BROTHERS CHRISTOPHER

THE READER of these pages in his relations with other men, either in business, in trade or in the professions, may recall the story of a man eminently successful financially and socially, who "cracked up" and suddenly disappeared, after being driven to the wall by financial disaster, marital troubles, the curse of drunkenness or a great sorrow.

The reader may also remember that for a time he was spoken of, either in the homes of his former friends, in the directors' meeting, on the golf course or in the club bar; and always the discussion ended with the question, "I wonder what ever became of him?" Perhaps that man was at some time or other, or even now is, a guest at St. Christopher's Inn at Graymoor, an institution founded by Father Paul for homeless men.

Because of the human interest element of this particular work at Graymoor it has been the subject of almost countless magazine and newspaper articles through the last fifty years. So much publicity has been given to this work by reporters and writers who saw human interest angles to it that, unfortunately, this publicity has obscured in the minds of many the primary work of Father Paul's life and the Society of the Atonement—the Reunion of Christendom.

It is unfortunate that this false impression of Graymoor's work has been so widely circulated. St. Christopher's Inn, from the beginning, has been merely another expression of the Charity that burned in the great heart of Father Paul for all men. The author has given this phase of Graymoor's work a separate chapter to make clear the important point that *this is not the primary work* of the Friars of the Atonement, but only an incidental charity associated with their great and larger work, the At-One-Ment of all men in Christ. It is further written to reveal how Father Paul helped these homeless men because he understood the dignity of the human personality, animated as it is by a priceless and immortal soul.

It is the hope of the Friars at Graymoor that, after the publication of this volume, this point will be cleared up in the minds of many who labor under an illusion; and that as far as Graymoor's primary work is concerned "the cart" will cease "pulling the horse" in their conception of Graymoor's primary work.

While this work at St. Christopher's Inn has been a source of much heartache, headache, disappointment and downright chagrin at times to the Friars, it has also been the source of many blessings and graces. The name which Father Paul gave to these men, Brothers Christopher (Christ-Bearers), is the key to the ideal upon which the work was founded and continues.

Despite the fact that the work has a seamy side, working as the Friars do with the dishonored as well with as the dregs of humanity, many men have responded to what the Inn has to offer for their spiritual and physical rehabilitation and this has been a consolation to the Friars.

This human consolation, however, is not the motive underlying the work, for Father Paul made no pretense at that rehabilitation for which organizations like *Alcoholics Anonymous* strive. The underlying motive of the work is to hear Christ say to the Friars and Sisters of the Atonement on the last day: "Come, Blessed of My Father, take possession of the Kingdom prepared for you from the foundations of the world; for I was hungry and you gave me to eat; I was thirsty and you gave me to drink; I was a stranger and you took me in; naked and you covered me; sick and you visited me. . . . Amen I say to you, as long as you did it for one of these, the least of My brethren, you did it for me."

Thousands of men have found hospitality at the Inn through the years. The work began when men coming along the highway asked for food at the convent or friary. In the early days this feeding of strangers was a real sacrifice to the members of the Society who had no abundance of food for themselves. But being lovers of the poor like their great Exemplar—St. Francis—they shared what they had, remembering the words of St. Paul to the Hebrews, "Let brotherly love abide in you, and do not forget to entertain strangers; for thereby some have entertained angels unawares."

A lady visitor to Graymoor in 1910 in recording her impressions wrote:

> . . . When we reached the other side [of West Point] there were three of the Graymoor Sisters in the quaintest old country wagon. . . . They gave me such a sweet loving welcome and we started for Graymoor. . . . By and by we reached the quaint medieval-looking little convent—everything so rustic and so poor—just as St. Francis would have loved to see it. . . . There were three other guests. One of the things that touched me was the way they treat everyone to the same fare—there is no difference for tramps or us—and there are always tramps there, winter and summer—and they welcome them all and call them "Brothers Christopher." . . . One old man, an Irish Catholic, stayed two winters with them and died a most beautiful death blessing the "Graymoor Franciscans."

The housing of these men started when Father Paul with the assistance of a few Brothers Christopher cut down some trees on the mountain and built a chicken house from these logs. Not long after, Father Paul on a visit to Washington saw, in one of the government buildings, a photograph of the log cabin in which Abraham Lincoln was born. He decided then and there that the log cabin he had built with the help of the homeless men was worthy of a nobler destiny than that of housing chickens. When he returned to Graymoor the chicken house became the first St. Christopher's Inn.

As Father Paul expressed it: "the hens moved out and the men moved in." The work expanded through the years and larger quarters were built. The financial disaster of 1929 was followed by an economic depression that brought hundreds of homeless men to Graymoor. The present Inn was built during these difficult times. It is a spacious building accommodating more than one hundred men, but in winter it is not large enough for all who seek its hospitality. Often it is filled in summer also by those happy troubadours who follow the sun and who have it marked on the map of their "circuit" for a night's stay.

Through the years have come white and Negro, Catholic and non-Catholic, Jew and Gentile, for no man is ever turned away. There is a room kept open at night in the basement of the Inn where a stranger can find a cot and a blanket. This is called the "dugout" by

the men. A resident of the "dugout" is ever hopeful to be graduated
to the dormitory upstairs, which happens when some occupant there
leaves for greener pastures.

These men come from all walks of life. The Inn has housed former business executives, doctors, lawyers, architects, musicians, writers
and artists; as well as men who were electricians, carpenters, plumbers
and technicians in many other fields. They come to the Inn as men
without hope, weary in soul and body, hungry, shabby and friendless,
asking for food and shelter, clothing, and to be left alone. Many of
these men endure the keen suffering born of the remorse which comes
with the conviction of "what might have been," which gnaws at the
conscience of a man who cannot forget that, through human weakness he has dishonored his own humanity.

While the Friars abide by the instruction of St. Paul, "to entertain
strangers; for thereby some have entertained angels unawares" in the
hope that there are always a few angels among the men, the fact remains that they have entertained convicts unawares. Graymoor is not
a great distance from Sing Sing Prison. A few who found prison life
uncomfortable have escaped from it and sat like angels in the Inn
only to have their peaceful repose interrupted by the State Police.

It was suggested once to Father Paul, much to his horror, that
each man coming to the Inn be fingerprinted. This request he, of
course, refused. Each man is asked his name and the name and address of his nearest relative or a friend in case of serious illness or
death. Beyond these no other questions are asked. There is a guest-
book in the "dugout" where a man who stops for a night's rest may
write his name and address. The author was amazed to find, in
glancing through it, how many persons by the name of Jones and
Smith are homeless in the United States. One overnight guest signed
the name of the President of the United States. The author was
tempted to take a cross-section of the given addresses to verify their
authenticity, but then remembered that his sanity might be questioned if he were found visiting vacant lots and warehouses. This
artlessness on the part of Father Paul in placing a guest-book in the
"dugout" shows his Franciscan simplicity and his faith in men, which
were two of his most charming virtues.

Some men have sought the peace of the Inn to escape a nagging wife, which was better than trying to drown their sorrows at the corner tavern; but Father Paul always sent these men back home with the admonition that not even the peace of the Inn may "put asunder" . . . "what God has joined together."

Distraught wives and parents have begged the Friars to take into the Inn an alcoholic problem in the home. While the Friars are ever striving to alleviate human misery, and do all they possibly can for sick people, the Inn is not a hospital, and that is where a person suffering from over-indulgence in alcohol should be sent.

Neither is St. Christopher's Inn a home for the aged. Some women who could no longer tolerate the "smelly old pipes" of their fathers-in-law in their immaculate living rooms have offered to pay the Friars for taking care of these old men with their "smelly old pipes"; but they were referred to homes for the aged.

Then there was the old man who years ago had given Father Paul one hundred dollars for a bed in the Inn; after his wife died he arrived one day at the Inn and announced that he had come to occupy the bed in his declining years. Father Paul in establishing the Inn meant it to be a place for transient, homeless wayfarers. He never intended it as an old man's home. To cater to persons who have the money to pay their way in some other institution would be to defeat the purpose for which Father Paul established the Inn.

At least ninety per cent of the men who seek the hospitality of the Inn are victims of an unbridled passion for alcohol. It is what has brought about the downfall of most of them. Father Paul, during his whole life, never touched either alcohol or tobacco. He was constantly preaching to others to give up the use of these two creatures and thereby make atonement for the abuse of them by men. Yet he was kind and charitable to these men. Each man got his weekly quota of tobacco. As an Anglican clergyman he prevailed on some men to take "the pledge." The Father Director of the Inn today never asks a man to take "the pledge." Remembering "the pledge" he has broken is no help to a man who tries once again to root out the besetting passion of his life. He must root out an evil as he sowed and nurtured it—day by day. The victory of today is the hope and the courage for the victory of tomorrow.

While Father Paul never made any pretense at rehabilitating these men, many of them have taken new hope and re-established themselves after a stay at the Inn. For there a man finds everything spiritual and material conducive to restoring confidence in himself for a new start in life. Only God knows the exact number of the "Inn's Alumni" who have conquered the despair and discouragement which had beset their lives.

When Father Paul was raising funds to build a new St. Christopher's Inn in 1924 a feature article on the Inn appeared in the *New York Sunday World* of August 10th; the article was an appeal for funds for the new Inn. The author wrote the article in gratitude for Father Paul's hospitality to him when he was destitute. Father Paul in commenting on the article in the *World* stated:

It was written by a college graduate, a Protestant newspaper reporter, and a European correspondent during the world war, who was so shot to pieces, not by the cannonading of the Central Powers, but by the too incessant tipping of the bottle that for some time he sought refuge in St. Christopher's Inn.

Perhaps it will not be amiss to insert here a few paragraphs from the article, which is a strange mixture of "jungle jargon" and the language of the lecture hall. These extremes of culture may be found any day in the Inn's dining hall. The article read in part:

. . . However, there is one solace for these weary knights of the road. They can rest and feed up at St. Christopher's Inn, Graymoor. About midway between New York City and Poughkeepsie is this veritable sanctuary, a refuge about as near to heaven in more ways than one as they could wish for . . . No matter what the wayfarer's religion, age or condition of life and person, upon his arrival at the mountain top he is welcomed by a tall, sunbrowned friar in sandals. From that moment he is known as a "Brother Christopher" and the home, the woods, the fields and the gardens are his. . . . In the . . . years since Father Paul built the Inn . . . no man has been turned away from the place hungry, weary or shoeless. Should he arrive early in the mornng or late in the night, even though he be a professional tramp or hobo, he is welcomed and his immediate needs attended to. He is offered a steaming platter of nourishing food and a bed and blankets for much needed sleep; if he needs tobacco or cigarettes they are his for the asking. No questions are asked other than his needs and plans for the following day. If he chooses to stay he may count on "three squares and a flop." . . . Many weary days tramping the roads have been the lot of most of these men and they are seldom in condition to do any hard work. So they are given work in the gardens or in one of the many buildings. . . . The atmosphere of the Holy Mountain has an interesting effect on the men. . . . None of the hard-boiled old-time tramps used their usual blasphemy, without which their efforts at connected conversation seemed difficult. . . . Back in 1909 Father Paul . . . built for the wayfaring men, who came knocking at the monastery door in increasing numbers, as word was passed along among the fraternity of the highways that food and lodging were given to strangers, because in each poor man who came the Friars saw a representative of the Savior of mankind.

A good many other men like the author of the above article, after a stay at the Inn, have re-established themselves in society. At the Inn there is a beautiful chapel which was built by the men themselves. However, Religion was never forced on any man by Father Paul. But as the earth drinks in the warmth of the sun, a man staying at the Inn exposed as he is to kindness, understanding and the things of God, cannot help but learn the eternal truth: God made man to love Him and serve Him and to be happy with Him always. Conscious of this truth a wayfarer soon realizes the worth of the human soul and the dignity of the body which contains it. A full stomach, a clean body, respectable clothes, and a comfortable bed, Father Paul knew to be good mediums in helping a man to lift his head again. Father Paul kept no case histories because to him a man was more important than his history. He fostered the Brother Christopher work to give glory to God through Christian Charity and to contribute to the greatness of America by fostering good citizenship.

For years the Brother in charge of the men's dormitory was an Irishman, Brother Mark, a member of the Third Order of St. Francis. As he woke the men each morning at 6 A.M., he would say to those he knew were Catholics: "The Grace of God is waiting for ye in the Chapel if ye'll accept it." But whether they did or not no one remained in bed, if he were well, for Brother Mark said, "The

Lord will never be able to accuse me of letting men sleep while Mass was being celebrated." The body of Brother Mark rests today in the Graymoor cemetery close to the thirty-three Brothers Christopher who died without relatives and were buried by the Friars through the years.

One of these was a man who came to Graymoor and gave his name as "Kelly." Whether that was his right name or not no one ever knew. He took care of the Sisters' gardens and lived in a room over the garage on their property. Kelly stayed and stayed tending the flowers which he loved. After twenty-four years he died. His funeral was especially beautiful. The Friars sang a High Mass and the Sisters walked up the mountain to the Inn to attend the Mass and pray for his soul. It was impressive and beautiful, just as "Kelly" wanted it to be.

Under another cross in the Graymoor cemetery lies the body of a man whom everyone at Graymoor called "The Incinerator Man" because that was his job while he lived at the Inn—tending the incinerator. The story of this man's life prior to his coming to Graymoor was buried with his bones. What it was no one knew. Nor did anyone ask about it.

In the weeks that the Incinerator Man was a guest at the Inn he had faithfully carried out his task of burning the waste paper and refuse which accumulated around the monastery each day.

On May 29, 1948, the Friars wended their way down the mountain to the graveyard escorting the body of Brother Philip, S.A., who after many years of faithful service in the Vineyard of the Lord died of cancer. When the hearse passed by, the Incinerator Man, apparently well, doffed his hat. But in two hours the hearse was back again for the Incinerator Man, who had died suddenly from a heart attack.

Close by the incinerator was a small hut in which the Incinerator Man found shelter from inclement weather while his fires kept devouring the refuse. Its bare furnishings consisted of a table, a stove, a chair and a small but lovely shrine of the Blessed Mother. Here the Incinerator Man said nine Rosaries a day while his fires kept burning. His prayers were for the benefactors of the Inn, World Peace, the

Friars and other intentions which only he and God knew. He was a daily communicant and never missed the evening devotions. What this one man found at St. Christopher's Inn for the salvation of his immortal soul justifies the existence of the Inn for all time; and only God knows how many others who have sought shelter at the Inn through the years have found something infinitely more precious than food and shelter at Graymoor. They found it only because the Christlike Father Paul could pierce through the veils of dishonored humanity to the human soul which he knew could be transformed by the indelible charm of divine grace. Christ in the human soul was the Beauty which merited his love and because all men are potential Christophers (Christ-bearers) to Father Paul all men were important.

There were some who resented the name Father Paul gave to the Brothers Christopher. One of these persons sent the following letter in 1918 to *The Lamp*:

THE LETTER

DEAR EDITOR:

For years I have read and enjoyed *The Lamp*. 'Tis not an uncommon remark among Catholics to the manner born, that every convert to our holy faith has at least one eccentricity. There is more than a modicum of truth in the saying. What is your "eccentricity" then? 'Tis one that gets on my nerves; in fact, I often before felt like protesting against it. At last I've made up my mind to do so, and do it most emphatically. Why should you call hoboes or tramps "Brothers Christopher?" Doesn't that tend to cheapen the name of "Brother," a thing certainly not to be desired? Cut out "Brother Christopher" please, as applied to tramps. If I find it used in that sense any more I shall discontinue reading your Monthly. Besides, I know a real Brother of a Religious Order, an old friend of mine, who quit years ago taking *The Lamp* for the same reason. Cut it out, then I pray, 'tis most disrespectful—although not so intended—to our various noble Brotherhoods; it cheapens the name. Fancy a future edition of Soule's Synonyms giving "Brother Christopher" as a synonym for "Vagabond, bum, tramp," etc. Cut it out, please do.

Yours sincerely,

A HOOSIER

Quite evidently, from the terminology of the letter, the writer was Irish. But, Irish or not, he met his "Waterloo" in Father Paul, who, apparently very much shocked at the receipt of it, wrote:

The editor of *The Lamp* not long ago heard himself described as a pious man but eccentric. We have been wondering since wherein the eccentricity lay: we are very grateful to our "Hoosier" correspondent for having answered the question which might otherwise have remained unsolved. We wished to make the discovery in order to eliminate the eccentricity, if possible; but now that we know what it is, we have no desire to *"cut it out"*; on the contrary we are inclined to say with St. Paul, when Festus accused him of being eccentric to the verge of madness—I am not eccentric. Most Excellent Hoosier, but I use the language of our Lord and His Servant, St. Francis. I would to God that both in a little and in much, not only thou, but also all that read *The Lamp*, should become as eccentric as the Editor in the matter of the Brothers Christopher.

The zeal of our correspondent is of course to be commended in so far as he desires to protect the good name of those who bear the honored and sacred title of Brother in Holy Religion; but we maintain that these can suffer no more indignity by sharing the name of Brother with the least and the humblest in the Kingdom of God, though he chance to be a vagabond, and a social outcast, or the poorest of beggars, than has the Son of God in stooping to take our humanity into union with His Godhead and to call these very same "Hoboes" if you will, *His* brothers. If any one challenge us to give chapter and verse in support of this assertion, we refer him to the description given by our Blessed Lord of the Judgment at the last day, in the 25th Chapter of St. Matthew's Gospel: —*"Then shall the just answer Him saying: Lord when did we see Thee hungry and fed Thee, thirsty and gave Thee drink; and when did we see Thee a Stranger and took Thee in, or naked and covered Thee, or when did we see Thee sick or in prison, and came to Thee? And the King answering them, shall say:*—AMEN, I SAY TO YOU, AS LONG AS YOU DID IT TO THESE MY LEAST BRETHREN, YOU DID IT TO ME." There readily comes to mind in this connection the experience of St. Martin of Tours; one night before his Baptism, as he mounted guard in the Roman army, he was accosted by a "hobo" clothed only in his rags, and shivering in the frosty wind. Martin cleft his army coat in twain and wrapped the poor beggar in it; later on the same night he saw Jesus Christ wearing the other half of his army coat, and he heard him say: "This was given Me by Martin the Catechumen." Since our Lord, both by word and deed, has thus identified Himself with the Knights of the Road, it would be in our humble opinion, a queer kind of Brother in Holy Religion and a singular imitator of His Master who would begrudge to the beggar man or tramp the title of Brother Christopher.

No one has done more than St. Francis of Assisi to dignify the name of Brother as borne by the Religious; he always called himself Brother Francis and clung to that estate, although solicited by those high in authority to assume the dignity of the Priesthood; yet as St. Francis was always ready to give even his habit to anyone he met more poorly clothed than himself so he freely gave not only to beggars, but even to birds and beasts and inanimate creatures the loving salutation of Brother, Brother Leper, Brother Wolf, Brother Fire.

The letter of "A Hoosier" was not well received by the readers of *The Lamp*, one wrote:

I have just laid down *The Lamp* after reading what the Hoosier said. The Hoosier may be a tramp too some day: who knows? We are all tramping onward to eternity. Some like Lazarus and others like Dives. Over nineteen hundred years ago Our Blessed Lady and St. Joseph had to tramp looking for shelter where the infant Jesus might be born. His coming has made us all brothers, and even if the Hoosier does not like it, we will not worry; for brothers we are and brothers we will have to be.

Chapter XXIV

LIFE WITH FATHER PAUL

BECAUSE the holy Ones of God—His intimate friends who walk the earth—are so utterly normal in the abnormal surrounding of present-day materialistic civilization, they are often considered "eccentric" by the so-called "normal" people among whom they walk. A man who would speak to God by reading his prayer book or by saying the rosary as he rides in a crowded subway train on his way to work would be considered "queer" by some of his fellow travelers. The place for prayer is in a church, not a subway, and the time to pray is a Sunday morning provided a man is not too tired to go to church on Sunday. So the majority of the so-called "normal" people of the world think.

It has often been said that it is difficult to live with a Saint. Yet the Saints were the most normal people. Wherein, then, does the difficulty lie in living with holy people? The difficulty lies in the abnormalities and imperfections of those who find it difficult to live with holy people, who have already rid themselves of abnormalities and imperfections. A man in the subway reading a sensational newspaper which is nothing more than a "scandal sheet" will look askance at a fellow traveler reading a prayer book; but which of the two is using his intellect normally? God's purpose in giving man an intellect is that man might always seek and know and love the truth.

A religious in a convent or monastery who is still in the Purgative way of the spiritual life may consider another who has attained to the Unitive way difficult to live with simply because he keeps the rule of the community more perfectly. But the more normal of the two is the religious who lives more perfectly the life they both have freely chosen. To keep the commandments of God is to live normally and according to nature. It is when the commandments are broken that we have an abnormal condition of life.

The happiest Priests and Monks and Sisters and Brothers are those who keep the rule of their particular congregations minutely. Some deluded religious who thought they were not becoming Saints quickly enough have left their monasteries or convents for others with a stricter rule of life, without ever having tried to live normally, and as perfectly as possible, the rule of the first monastery or convent. The final result in many of these cases was a lost vocation. Every religious community offers to its members the reward of eternal life if they live the rule normally. Eccentricity or capriciousness, either in the world or in a monastery, is the fruit of a warped mind and a distorted sense of values. If the other man's fields look greener to some it is only because they have never given their own fields the chance to be normal by proper cultivation.

The charming part of life with Father Paul was that he was perfectly normal as he lived the Franciscan Rule of life which he had freely chosen. He acted as a normal human being whether he was playing croquet with his Friars, chatting with the rich in a magnificent drawing room, or consoling the poor in a hovel. He was just as normal saying the rosary in the subway, which he often did, as he was in choir chanting the Divine Office. He was just as normal and humble talking to a homeless man as he was when he spoke to the Vicar of Christ on earth, the Holy Father. There was nothing "eccentric" or "erratic" about Father Paul's sanctity. He always acted as a perfectly normal, human individual. He was "all things to all men" because he was ever conscious that his every thought, word and deed was a sanctified act by the daily consecration of his life to God. He had the "human touch" only because he was so constantly "in touch" with the Divine.

Father Paul spoke of God, Our Lady of the Atonement and the Saints as a man speaks of his father, mother and friends. To include the heavenly family in ordinary conversation was Father Paul's normal way of speaking just as it should be every Christian's. When a certain novice complained to him about some unpleasant task assigned by the novice master, Father Paul told him in a kindly way how the great St. Francis kissed the sores of lepers. He told the novice of the great humility of St. Francis not to embarrass the complaining novice but rather to show him that by the sanctification of unpleasant things Francis became a great Saint.

Those who spoke of Father Paul, both in the Catholic Church and outside of it, as "erratic," "eccentric" and "abnormal" were, as we have seen, persons who had never met him. He once attended a Catholic function and seated at the very same table was a priest who had attacked him in his parish monthly. The priest's name happened to be mentioned at the table, and Father Paul, not realizing that the priest was sitting there, said to the priests at his table: "My, my, I hope Father——soon turns me and *The Lamp* over on his gridiron for we are quite scorched on one side." By the charm of his personality and humor and the utter lack of any bitterness on his part, Father Paul turned what might have been an unpleasant experience into a joke. It was not until after he left the table that Father Paul learned that the priest who had attacked his life's work had broken bread with him. When he returned to Graymoor he told the story of the incident, much to everyone's amusement. Those who had the pleasure of knowing Father Paul knew him for the perfectly normal, supernaturalized, gentlemanly priest that he was. Those who had doubts about him seemingly never bothered to verify them.

Because he was so natural and so normal, however naïve at times, he was delightful to live with. To the day of his death he took part in every activity of the Friars and students. The older Friars knew that Father Paul had a cardiac condition and they were always on the alert, especially when he was no longer young, to spare him any extraordinary exertion. But like all active and busy men he would not spare himself. The author remembers particularly coming up the Mountain in 1939 and seeing, to his amazement, Father Paul, who was then seventy-six years old, in the hot sun playing tennis in his habit with three young seminarians. It took some real diplomacy to stop the game and convince Father Paul it had to be stopped not because of his health or his age or his ability to win, but because the sun was too hot for the students—which it was—not to speak of Father Paul.

The recreation hour was spent on summer evenings on the lawn playing croquet. Father Paul liked croquet but he disliked losing any game to his Friars. If he lost he pouted. Apropos of croquet there is a humorous incident in Father Paul's life which is another manifestation of his complete naïveté. In the summer of 1933, when Father Paul was not feeling well, he spent a few days at Long Beach, New York. His companion was another priest who had made an engagement with some friends to play golf at the Lido Club, but he had to leave for New York without being able to notify them. When they arrived Father Paul opened the door. The friends of the priest explained about the appointment for the game of golf. Father Paul told them what had happened, and then he asked, "What is the game of golf like?" When they explained the intricacies of golf, he said, "Why, it's just like croquet; will it be all right with you if I go?" They said that, of course, it would be a pleasure. So off they drove to the fashionable Lido Club, with Father Paul wearing a red flannel shirt, a cap, khaki trousers, suspenders and high top shoes.

When they reached the first tee and handed Father Paul a club to "tee off," he turned to them and said: "I forgot to tell you, I am a southpaw." So back to the clubhouse went one of the men, who happened to be a banker, for a bag of left-handed clubs. The caddie-master said that there was only one set there and it belonged to a member who probably would come out to play that day. "Give me the clubs," said the banker, "and tell him that Father Paul is using them." The caddie-master said, "This man doesn't know Father Paul; he's a Protestant." Finally the manager was sent for and to him it was explained that the famous Catholic priest, Father Paul, Founder of Graymoor, was waiting for a left-handed set of clubs to tee off on the golf course. The manager graciously took the responsibilty of lending the clubs, and Father Paul finally "teed off." In relating the story at Graymoor he said, "My golf companions were very courteous; they let me carry my ball over the water hazards." The story of Father Paul's first—and last—golf game has often been told in the Bankers' Club of New York. Aside from the hazardous episode of the left-handed golf clubs, Father Paul's golf companions have often said that it was one of the most delightful afternoons of their lives.

During the very trying days of the economic depression which gripped the United States during the nineteen thirties, Father Paul carried a heavy burden in trying to provide for a fast-growing community. A Jesuit priest spent some time at Graymoor as a guest of Father Paul during those trying days, and in an effort to divert Father Paul's mind from so many cares, the Jesuit prevailed upon him to learn how to play cards during the recreation hour. The game he learned we called "Five Hundred." At that time he also learned how to play chess. The older friars and the good Jesuit Father, knowing Father to be a "bad loser" always let him win. However, when he played with the novices on Wednesday evening, which he always did, he sometimes lost, which was something he did not like. Father Paul, as supreme head of Graymoor who had borne the burden and heat of the day before most of his friars were born, just could not endure losing in chess or cards or croquet to his friars. It was a human failing, but one found in many great men.

Neither did Father Paul like to see the students in the minor seminary—St. John's—or the Friars in the major seminary lose a baseball game to another seminary. For years there was a baseball game scheduled between St. John's minor seminary at Graymoor and the major seminary of the Foreign Mission Society of the United States—Maryknoll. The founders of both Societies were intimate friends.

For years the score did not vary much. It was usually Maryknoll 12, Graymoor 2. However, in May 1934, through some oversight in arranging the schedule Maryknoll found that they were booked to play another seminary on the same day that a game was arranged with Graymoor. Not to disappoint Graymoor, Maryknoll sent its second team for the game. The result was that for the first time in six years Father Paul's boys defeated Maryknoll.

Father Paul was so delighted that he gave the following account of the victory in the June, 1924, issue of *The Lamp*:

The Maryknoll team came to Graymoor for the annual baseball game on Wednesday, May 16. This game always stands out as the most important one of the season. For six years running the Maryknoll clerics have defeated the St. John's team. This year the tables were reversed. The battle on the diamond started at two o'clock and finished at half past four. It proved to be one of the most thrilling games we have ever witnessed, and the tension increased as the game drew to its conclusion.

At the start the St. John's boys had the lead with a score of four to one, but when Very Reverend Patrick Byrnes, Vice-President of Maryknoll and Father Francis Winslow, Assistant General, arrived on the ball ground during the fifth inning, their presence gave the Maryknoll boys a new lease on life, and they fought desperately from that time until the end to overcome the lead of the Graymoorians. When the ninth inning came the score was three to four in favor of Graymoor.

Peter Katsuno, our Japanese Pitcher, struck out two of the Maryknoll batters, and then the third one sent the ball sailing out into the right field and two men got their bases. Whether those men on bases would succeed in reaching the home plate thus giving the lead to the Mary-knollers was of supreme interest. Our Peter rose to the emergency, how-ever, and struck the third man out, thus giving the game to Graymoor.

Father Paul was seventy-one years old when he described the base-ball game so vividly in *The Lamp*. He held that same enthusiasm for all the student activities until he died six years later.

An interesting and amusing sequel to the story of the baseball game was told by the present Father General of Maryknoll, the Most Reverend Raymond A. Lane, fifteen years later, when he came to Graymoor on the occasion of its Golden Jubilee. In telling of the friendship that had existed between the Founders of Maryknoll and Graymoor, Bishop Lane recalled the story of the baseball game.

Bishop Lane was Rector of the Maryknoll Seminary at the time the game was played. When Bishop Walsh, the Founder of Maryknoll, read Father Paul's account of the game in *The Lamp*, he asked the Rector for a report on Maryknoll's defeat. When the circumstances were explained to him Bishop Walsh said: "I do not mind the de-feat as much as I mind Father Paul's publishing an account of it in *The Lamp*." Bishop Lane concluded the story by saying: "Wasn't it wonderful, that our two Founders, despite their preoccupation with many important affairs, and despite, or maybe because of, their evi-dent sanctity, always remained human enough to be keenly interested in the victories and defeats of the ball teams representing their schools?"

As Father Paul strove for perfection in this vale of tears, it was apparent to all who were closely associated with him that the one imperfection he struggled with was a quick temper, or the disposition to become angry. Sometimes in his sermons, as he condemned the evils of the day, his anger would flare up just as it did in his office when he was annoyed by some subject's infraction of the rule. But the inward struggle in the soul of Father Paul against this imperfection was so great that at times it manifested itself outwardly in the quivering of his lips. This particular imperfection of Father Paul is recorded because it is the desire of the author to present Father Paul as he really was. However, since the essence of perfection consists in love of God and the supernatural love of neighbor, and since Father Paul exemplified this charity throughout his whole life, this imperfection never marred the reflections of the divine perfection which men saw in him.

As he grew older, his Friars, knowing that he would not touch money, were careful in arranging for someone to accompany him wherever he went. But sometimes he would suddenly decide to go to New York from his office at the convent, and he would be gone before they knew it. To forestall his suffering humiliation, a commutation ticket on the New York Central Railroad from Peekskill to New York was kept in his coat pocket. This solved the train fare problem but it did not solve the subway or bus fare problem, which Father Paul begged from passers-by as he needed it. Before he asked anyone for his fare he always said one "Our Father." Even when he was given the fare by some kind person there was the problem of his not handling it. So he would have the person either drop the coin between the pages of his breviary or into an empty envelope. When the turnstiles were erected in the subways and on busses another problem was to get the conductor or agent to drop the coin in the slot for him. Fortunately, and by the Goodness of God, Father Paul met up with many Catholics, who saved him the pain of being rebuffed by those who would not understand.

On a trip to the Major Seminary in Washington Father Paul and his Friar companion stopped off at Philadelphia to see the Sisters who have a mission among the Negroes of that city. Resuming the journey, railroad tickets had to be bought from Philadelphia to Washington, and a telegram sent to the Washington Superior as to their arrival. Reaching the telegraph office the clock showed that there was very little time before the train left. Father Paul's companion asked him if he would write out the telegram, and before leaving for the ticket office he deposited a dollar bill on the counter. Later when Father Paul met him at the train he handed him a neat little yellow package. It contained the change from the dollar bill, which Father Paul had the attendant wrap in a telegram blank.

Because of his compliance with the private vow he had made never to touch money, Father Paul, particularly in his Anglican days when he constantly wore his habit, suffered many humiliations. Once, when he was an Anglican clergyman, he accosted a man to pay his subway fare. The man, looking on Father Paul in his habit, said: "Why, you lazy monk; I wouldn't give you a red cent!" The "lazy monk" at that time was doing enough work to keep four men busy.

In the last ten years of his life Father Paul was spared this humiliation by the constant vigilance of the Friars and the Sisters. Only once did he slip away and at that time, for some reason or other, he did not have even the commutation ticket. The station agents of the New York Central Railroad, however, took care of the situation and were later reimbursed by the Friars.

In a little book found after his death there is a record of an accusation of himself for having allowed a Friar to persuade him to take a taxicab instead of a street car, one hot day in Washington. They were visiting the major seminary at Catholic University shortly before Father Paul's death. The little book told the story of how twenty cents was spent unnecessarily through a permission Father Paul gave to the Friar.

The Poverello of Peekskill, as one writer called him when he died, ever strove to follow in the footsteps of the Poverello of Assisi. Cardinal Dougherty writing of Father Paul on October 16, 1945, stated:

. . . I was struck by his eloquence, the clarity of his discourse, and the ease with which he delivered it. One could not help being struck forcibly by his profound spirit of poverty in which he seemed to emulate the Poverello of Assisi; and this was not the only outstanding quality of St. Francis of Assisi that he strove to practice. He transferred from the thirteenth century to the twentieth century the religious fervor, which characterized the middle ages.

Even though some have written to the contrary, Father Paul in his intimate family life with his friars never made claim to having had "personal visions" of any kind. On November 10, 1926 in writing to a former Anglican associate he stated:

. . . It is indeed news to me that I had a "Vision of the Blessed Virgin Mary ordering me to hold on to the Book of Common Prayer." There must have been some confusion of ideas in this regard, because I have no recollection of ever having been favored with a vision of the Blessed Virgin in all my life and had such been the case I could hardly have ever forgotten it.

In later years, being constantly occupied with many big problems, Father Paul became forgetful of little things. He was constantly losing his breviary whenever he left Graymoor. He came in on the Long Island Railroad one day shortly before he died, and was met by one of the Friars at the station. "Well," Father Paul said with a smile, "I left my breviary on the train again." The Friar assured him that it was quite all right and that he would seek it in the "Lost and Found Department." "I went in there," Father Paul said, "to report the loss of my breviary, and I left my brief-case on the counter; so you will have to retrieve both of them." Once he walked off a Third Avenue elevated train, leaving his breviary, and that one was never recovered.

As Founder of the Society of the Atonement, Father Paul was the personification of the Society's Rule of life. Like most religious communities the Graymoor Friars rise at five A.M. No matter how quickly after rising the young Friars could reach the chapel, Father Paul was always already there kneeling before the Blessed Sacrament, a brown-robed figure before a white marble altar, illuminated by a flickering sanctuary lamp. The points for the half hour meditation, which always begin at five-thirty A.M., were often given extempore by Father Paul on some phase of the Atonement of Christ, or on some special graces which God had showered upon the Society of the Atonement. Often he would give a very "down-to-earth" meditation such as the ones he often gave on the difficulties of monastic life.

"If," he once said, "you think you will get used to rising at five o'clock in the morning and like it you are very much mistaken. I am over seventy and I have not gotten used to it yet. But the sacrifice you make pleases God and brings down His Mercy upon a sinful world; and console yourselves, for in Heaven there is no weariness. There we shall always be refreshed as we participate in the infinitely active life of the Blessed Trinity."

Father Paul loved the great feast days of the liturgical year. The great events in the life of Christ, the feast days of the Blessed Mother and the other patrons of the Society were days of special rejoicing. After the solemnization of the Divine Mysteries, the joy which exuded from Father Paul's own personality pervaded Graymoor through the day. At the noon and evening meals there was always some extra item of food, and talking was permitted during the meal; never, however, at breakfast, since the great silence which always begins at Graymoor after night prayers does not end until after breakfast. In the evening of a great feast day the students would put on a minstrel show or a debate, which Father Paul always attended with a deep interest. He liked the debates best since they helped to develop the talents of the future preaching Friars.

Father Paul particularly loved the Feast of the Transfiguration, celebrated on August 6th. On that feast day in 1934, after intoning the Gloria of the Mass, he stood before the tabernacle seemingly lost in the joy of the occasion, and instead of sitting down at the Sedalia he continued to sing in Latin with the choir, in his deep, resonant voice, the words of the Doxology, "We praise Thee, we bless Thee, we give thanks to Thee for Thy great glory." His particular love for the Feast of the Transfiguration can probably be explained by his many years of suffering. Father Paul knew that Christ gave to Peter, James and John a glimpse of heaven on Tabor, and that for those who love and serve Christ and suffer with Him there is to come the joy of an everlasting Tabor, so beautifully expressed in the hymn of the first vespers of the feast:

> All you who seek, in hope and love
> For your dear Lord, look up above:
> Faith may a glorious form descry

Lo! on the trembling verge of light
We see something divinely bright,
Immortal, infinite, sublime,
Older than chaos, space or time.

Father Paul conducted a perpetual novena to St. Anthony, whom he called "the Friars' Elder Brother." Each night he would read aloud the various petitions sent in and the names of the senders. Listed under the various requests were a long list of names. The author recalls Father Paul reading a particular petition for months which always brought a smile over the faces of the community. After the petitions had been read for health, employment, lost articles, success in examination, etc., he would look up at the image of St. Anthony and say, "and a husband for Nellie C." Finally, after praying for the request of "Nellie C." for months, Father Paul ended the list of petitions one night with the words, "and thanksgiving to St. Anthony for Nellie C. And now may she live happily ever after."

During the novena service he would speak with complete simplicity and naïveté which were characteristic of his whole life. During the years of economic depression which gripped the United States in the early thirties there was always a long list of petitioners asking St. Anthony's prayers for employment. At the end of the list Father Paul would occasionally say, "And do not forget the ten million others who are unemployed." During this particular period when the Friar priest in charge of the Administration Building was besieged by merchants who were insistent that food, coal and clothing bills be paid, he went one day to Father Paul and told him that the bills now amounted to over fifty thousand dollars. Father Paul's answer was, "Now, don't worry, for that is St. Anthony's job and he will see to it that the bills will be paid." "Well, Father," replied the priest, "I wish St. Anthony were here to answer the telephone and assure these insistent merchants of their money." Father Paul, with a beaming smile replete with faith and confidence, said: "I have him constantly on the heavenly telephone of prayer."

Pentescost Sunday in the year 1939 was a beautiful day. Thousands of pilgrims came to Graymoor. The afternoon devotions and the novena to St. Anthony was scheduled to be broadcast at three P.M. As usual. Father Paul was to give the sermon. The large bell in St. Francis' chapel was rung and the people began to gather on the lawn. Father Paul sat under a tree making the usual last-minute revisions in his sermon. Suddenly a strong wind started to blow and increased in strength every minute. Towards the west the sky began to darken and great black thunderheads to accumulate. The sky over Graymoor became darker. Brother Aelred, who had charge of the St. Anthony Radio Hour, wondered if the storm would hold off until after the broadcast. He stepped up to the microphone and asked the pilgrims to say some prayers to St. Anthony, asking his intercessory prayers before the throne of God that the storm pass over Graymoor. In a few minutes the sky became blacker and the wind was roaring. Brother Aelred began to move the microphone under the trees in the hope that if the storm did break during the broadcast the organist and choir could fill in after Father Paul's sermon, for if it rained there would be no Benediction of the Most Blessed Sacrament. When he had moved the second microphone Father Paul's voice came over the public address system from another part of the lawn.

"Now, see here, Brother Aelred," he said, "that is not the way to show your faith in St. Anthony. You asked the pilgrims to pray for his help, and you are not waiting to find out if he is going to give a favorable answer."

Brother Aelred was embarrassed and apologized, moving the microphones back where they had been.

It was then five minutes to three, the hour the program was scheduled to go on the air-waves. Having had experience in the field of radio before he became a Religious, Brother Aelred judged that the best decision was to telephone the radio station in New York that the broadcast was off; but, in the light of what had happened, he did not dare do it.

Three o'clock came, with the sky over Graymoor getting darker and the wind now a heavy gale—and the Saint Anthony Hour went on the air. The pilgrims seemed nervous, and the novices, singing the opening theme, had one eye on the music and the other on the clouds, which were now black. As the announcer began to speak there came a sudden blinding flash of lightning that struck the water tower dedicated to the Holy Ghost. The radio engineer was lifted out of his chair and the thousands of pilgrims sat stunned. Then the thunder roared and the lightning flashed and the wind was so violent that it seemed the trees would be uprooted. Finally the heavens opened and Graymoor was deluged with water. It seemed as if the floods of Niagara were inundating the earth. The pilgrims scattered in all directions, the radio engineer made a hurried "sign-off" and dashed for shelter, the choir and organist ran for the nearest cover. In a few minutes thousands of people seemingly disappeared off the face of the earth. Brother Aelred stood in the downpour, dazed. He thought he was alone until he saw Father Paul under the tree, still revising his sermon. Then he went up to Father Paul and said: "I am afraid we cannot have the broadcast, Father."

With that gracious, benign smile that was so characteristic of him, Father Paul said: "No, I guess not. What Sunday is this, Brother Aelred?"

"Pentecost," said Brother Aelred.

"That's right; and the signs of the Holy Spirit are wind, fire and water. We surely had the rushing of the wind, didn't we? And that lightning was certainly fire, wasn't it?" Then, stretching forth his hand in the heavy rain, he laughed and said: "We certainly cannot doubt the water, can we? Well, if the Holy Spirit wishes to show us His mighty signs on His great feast day, I guess He can take precedence over our powerful St. Anthony to do so."

Father Paul and Brother Aelred walked in the teeming rain and, with soaked habits, entered the Little Flower chapel where hundreds of pilgrims found shelter. Laying aside his prepared radio sermon he gave an impromptu one on the Holy Spirit with all the beauty and magnificence of his gifted tongue.

It was in an impromptu sermon that Father Paul was at his best. The obligation that radio stations placed on him to submit his sermons for approval before a broadcast greatly irritated him. Before a broadcast, or during one in a New York studio, he would sit in a corner revising a sermon that had already been submitted and approved. When a Friar companion would, with great tact, tell him that he was not permitted to change his sermon he would indignantly ask: "Who said so? Don't the radio people know yet that God owns the air waves, and that radio is a gift out of God's storehouse of treasures so that men may learn of Him?" Often he was cautioned that he would be cut off the air if he changed his sermon again. His answer was always his usual benign smile; and the following Sunday the same thing would happen. Where the things of God were concerned no man intimidated Father Paul. Had he lived under a persecutor of the Church he would have been among the martyrs.

[*Chapter XXV*]

OUR LADY RECEIVES A NEW TITLE

FATHER PAUL had a deep, tender and beautiful devotion to the Mother of Christ from his earliest years. In choosing the patrons for the Society of the Atonement, both he and Mother Lurana chose Mary as the Queen of the Friars and the Sisters. When St. Francis' convent was dedicated on October 4, 1899, to St. Francis of Assisi, the chapel was dedicated to Our Lady of the Angels. So it is called to this day. When the friary was dedicated on December 8, 1900, Father Paul announced to those present that the friary would be dedicated in honor of the dogma of the Immaculate Conception and that the building itself would bear the name of St. Paul.

On October 7, 1901, while the Society was in the Anglican Church, he and Mother Lurana established The Rosary League of Our Lady of the Atonement. The object of the League was to promote among Anglicans (Episcopalians) "an increase of true devotion to the Holy Mother of God, thereby helping to win back for our glorious Lady her 'Dowry' in the homes and hearts of American and English Christians, that Mary's English speaking Children may once more become renowned throughout Christendom for the love and honor they show to the Blessed Virgin."

Father Paul "lighted" *The Lamp* on the feast of Candlemas, 1903. In doing so he placed it under the special protection of "Our Immaculate Lady, Mary Queen of Heaven." In his first editorial he called her "the Lamp of Burnished Gold, who came into the Temple bearing the Light of the World."

In that first issue of *The Lamp* he enclosed a leaflet to the members of *The Rosary League*. A lady, a member of the Episcopal Church, had sent a letter which he printed in the leaflet. It read:

327

DEAR FATHER:

I thank you and the patient good Sisters for prayers for H————'s eyes. They are about all right now. How kind and good our FATHER is all the time and we are so unworthy. Oh, how I long to be real good. Pray that the LORD will help me to grow stronger each day. It is my constant prayer. G———— is so well and everyone remarks how fleshy she is. My heart overflows every minute with gratitude for such blessings from a kind and loving FATHER, and how little I do for Him. If I lived a thousand years it would be but a trifle.

Dear Father, will it be too much trouble to explain to me about using a Rosary when we pray. I cannot understand why we should do so. I cannot find anything in the Bible about it. And I feel it must be right when such a good and true man as you thinks it is.

Father Paul's answer to the lady was a masterpiece of exposition on the Rosary and the power of intercessory prayer. It shows his great love for Our Lady of the Atonement which increased with the years. To him the three great tragedies of the "Erastian Captivity" of the English Church were: the abolition of objective worship offered to Jesus Christ in the Holy Sacrifice of the Mass; devotion to the Mother of God; and obedience to Christ's Vicar enthroned in the Chair of Peter on Earth.

Nothing horrified him quite so much as the disrespect of some non-Catholics for the glorious Mother of Christ. In the August, 1905, edition of *The Lamp* he wrote: "There is no lie forged in hell more in conflict with the Will of God expressed in Scripture and Catholic tradition than the Protestant conceit that they honor Christ best who most ignore the existence of His Mother." Throughout his whole life Father Paul was the Blessed Mother's gallant knight, defending her prerogatives until she came at last to gather up his restless soul in the folds of the blood-red mantle he gave her as a symbol of the Precious Blood of the Atonement. His answer to the lady's letter was:

DEAR MRS. S————

Yes, you have much to be thankful for. Things looked very dark when your husband was taken from you but the God of the widow and fatherless has wonderfully cared for you and yours. You ask me to explain to you "about using a Rosary." You say you feel it must be right because I, whom you esteem beyond my deserts, think it is. This of itself would be a very insufficient ground of belief, but the case is vastly different when you think of the countless millions who have used the Rosary these past seven hundred years, among them thousands upon thousands of the holiest men and women Christianity has produced, glorious saints of God whose feet I am not good enough to kiss. If the use of the Rosary was not pleasing to God and a real blessing to those who devoutly "say their beads," these saints of God would long ago have found it out. We can hardly make a mistake in adopting for ourselves a devotion which Catholic saints with one consent have practiced through the course of almost seven centuries.

There is a great deal more contained in saying the Rosary than I have time to explain at this writing. Let me concentrate your thought on just one purpose of its use, viz:

The invocation of the Blessed Virgin and our asking her to pray for us.

This is one of the chief reasons why Catholics cling to their rosaries, it is the best known means of obtaining a share in the prayers and intercessions of the Holy Mother of God. If the Rosary had no other value or purpose attached to its use, this alone were enough to make it immensely precious.

Your letters to me show how great store you set upon prayer. You are not content to pray directly to God, but you invoke your friends to pray for you and yours. That your faith in the efficacy of intercessory prayer is well grounded what you write me about your little daughter G——— and your son H——— strikingly illustrates. Sometime ago you asked us to have the Friars of the Atonement and the Sisters pray for G———'s health, she was so thin and delicate. We did as you invoked us to do and now you write "G——— is so well and every one remarks how fleshy she is." A few weeks later you wrote asking the Graymoor intercessions for your son's eyes, which were in a very bad way. Once again God condescended to hear the prayers of a few poor sinners on earth and so you are able to return thanks, saying "H———'s eyes are about all right now."

With such an object lesson on the wonderful power of intercessory prayer before your eyes it ought to be a very easy matter for you to believe in calling upon the Saints in Heaven to pray for you and above all the Blessed Virgin Mary, whose prayers must prevail with God more than those of anyone else. If it is right to call upon me to pray for you, though fifteen hundred miles away, can it be any the less right to invoke the Blessed Virgin, whom God has crowned as Queen of Saints and Angels in Heaven.

You say you "cannot find anything in the Bible about it."

I on the other hand find a great deal in the Bible about it. For instance I find the Our Father in the Bible and the Hail Mary too. The saying of these is all there is to the Rosary, except the Creed and the Gloria and if these are not verbatim in the Bible, they are there in substance at least.

And while we are on the subject of the Bible let me tell you this: The Protestant says his religion is "the Bible and the Bible only," but there is a tremendous lot in the Bible to which both his eyes and ears are tightly shut. The Catholic accepts his religion (the Bible included) from "the Church of the Living God, the Pillar and Ground of the Truth" (1 Tim. 3:15), but when it comes to putting into practice what the Bible actually teaches, the Catholic is far ahead of the Protestant. Devotion to the Virgin Mary is a good illustration. The New Testament is full of Mary. To her God sends the Archangel Gabriel, "the Power of the Highest overshadows her," "the HOLY GHOST comes upon her," the WORD by whom the worlds were made becomes her babe and suckles at her breast; for thirty years Jesus is subject unto her in the home of Nazareth; the first miracle of His public career is performed at her request; she stands by His cross when the disciples save John have fled; one of the seven sayings of Jesus in his death agony is addressed to her, constituting her to be through eternity the mother of all, who should be redeemed by His Precious Blood. Before the last pages of Holy Scripture are written the veil that hides the glory of the unseen world from our eyes is lifted and "Behold a great wonder in Heaven; a woman clothed with the sun, and the moon under her feet, and upon her head a crown of twelve stars." She, whom the HOLY GHOST declared long before should be called "Blessed among women," is exalted as Mother of GOD to be the great wonder and admiration of the heavenly hosts. A queen, whose robe is the sun, her footstool the moon, her diadem the stars. The Catholic recognizing the grace and majesty wherewith GOD has been pleased to endow the Mother of the Incarnate WORD pays homage where homage is due, being much more fearful of falling short of what GOD expects of mortals in honoring the Mother of His Only Begotten Son, than of honoring her too much. The Protestant, true to his name, almost entirely ignores the existence of the Blessed Virgin, except to impeach her virginity and stainless conception, to insist that she was a sinner like the balance of humanity, and to falsely accuse Catholics of making a goddess of her and rendering her idolatrous worship.

Take as your guiding principle in relation to the Blessed Virgin the famous saying of St. Francis of Assisi, "Fear not to attribute to Mary all that is not repugnant to her dignity as Mother of God," and then you will not have any conscientious scruples about becoming a member of the Rosary League and doing what you can to restore "Mary's Dowry" to our glorious Mother in Heaven.

In the early editions of *The Lamp* long articles appeared on "The Invocation of the Blessed Virgin and the Saints"; "The Assumption of the Blessed Virgin Mary"; "The Church of England and the Immaculate Conception."

In December, 1904, *The Lamp* carried a full-page picture of Our Lady under the title, *The Immaculate Conception*. The editorial written by the Anglican Father Paul stated:

If there is one country in Christendom more than another which should celebrate with devotion December 8th, the Festival of the Immaculate Conception of the Blessed Virgin Mary, that country is England. The Anglican who pays scant respect to the Holy Mother of God; never says a Hail Mary; has no use for the Rosary; and rejects as false the dogma of the Immaculate Conception, is recreant to the oldest and most hallowed traditions of the Anglican Communion.

There was a time when England's devotion to the Blessed Virgin won for her a foremost place among the domains of the Queen of Heaven; and even now after those three centuries of dreadful apostasy preceding the Oxford Revival, during which the English people did their utmost to dethrone and degrade the Mother of their God, England still retains that ancient title which differentiates her from other nations, as in a peculiar and pre-eminent degree, the dowry of the Blessed Virgin, for if any one at any time in any part of the world should speak of "Mary's Dowry" every well instructed Catholic would at once understand him to refer to England. . . .

That this dogma is no new thing, invented by Pope Pius IX, no one ought to know better than those who call themselves English Catholics. The greatest theological champion the dogma ever had . . . was an Oxford professor, who flourished six hundred years ago, The Franciscan doctor, John Duns Scotus.

The previous month in *The Lamp* Father Paul wrote a learned article on *The Assumption of the Blessed Virgin Mary* which shows his great love for the Mother of God. He wrote:

The cause of Catholic reunion demands, primarily, a reasonable and candid explanation of differences of view. We Anglicans are much too ready to consider our own point of view and to expect others to give way to us. The fact that the Festival of the Assumption of the Blessed Virgin Mary was struck out of the Anglican calendar in the Book of 1549, has caused the majority of us to pay little heed to a doctrine which is firmly held by the majority of Christians in the world at the present time. . . .

The Theological reasons for accepting the doctrine of the Assumption are overwhelming in their cogency. It is unthinkable to any devout and reverent mind that our Lord would permit the body of His Mother, which He had hallowed by His Incarnate Life, to become food for worms in the corruption of the grave. . . .

As the instrument of the Incarnation, moral and physical, the Blessed Virgin is above angels and archangels. She is the first of created beings. It is revealed to us in Holy Writ that Enoch and Elijah were translated to Heaven with their bodies preserved from the corruption of the grave. Can we conceive that Enoch and Elijah, and Moses also, whose body was preserved to appear with Elijah at the transfiguration, were accorded a privilege which was denied to our Blessed Lady. It is contrary to every sound theological reason to imagine such a thing for a moment. The immeasurable dignity of the Theotokos (Mother of God) places her next to our Blessed Lord in His Kingdom, and her glory and honor exceeds that of Enoch and Elijah. . . .

It would be contrary to the whole analogy of Divine Revelation to expect detailed historical evidence for the resurrection of the body of the Blessed Virgin by the power and love of her divine Son. Such a manifestation of His love for her is a sacred mystery of His Incarnation that immediately concerns what we reverently term His private relation to her, and not the public relation of His Incarnate Life to redeemed humanity in general.

The title, Our Lady of the Atonement (Domina Nostra *Adunationis*), which Father Paul gave to the Mother of Christ, was taken from the name of the Society he founded. The charming story of how he received the name is told in Chapter IV. In that instance, as an Anglican clergyman, he used the King James edition of the Bible. Had Father Paul used the Douay version of the Bible he would not have found the word *Atonement* in Romans V:11, but rather the word *Reconciliation*. The *Catholic Encyclopedia* states that *Atonement* is an English term, "almost the only theological term of English origin."

St. Thomas More is said to be the first English writer to make use
of the word *Atonement*. In his unfinished history of Richard III
(1513) he gave it to mean an open reconciliation of enemies. Later,
the word was used in Catholic and Protestant theology. The word is
found today in both the Douay and King James versions of the Old
Testament as the equivalent of expiation. In the King James version
of the New Testament the word *Atonement* is used as the equivalent
of reconciliation. Although the word *Atonement* does not appear in
the Douay version of the New Testament, it has been introduced as
a footnote in the Westminster version in connection with Romans
V:11, which contains the Central Text of the Society of the Atonement: "We joy in God, through Our Lord Jesus Christ, through
Whom we have now received the Atonement."

When Father Paul was received into the Catholic Church he was
careful in seeing that the original name of the Society was preserved;
for the word *Atonement* itself, separated into the three words *At-
One-Ment* was the key to the Society's work—the *At-One-Ment*
of all men in Christ. UT OMNES UNUM SINT (that all be one) has
been printed on every page of *The Lamp* for almost a half century.

Some difficulty arose, however, when Pope Benedict XV extended
the *Chair of Unity Octave* to the universal Church in an Apostolic
Brief on February 16, 1916. In referring to the Society of the
Atonement he used the word "Expiationis" (Expiation); and for a
time the Society was so designated in Rome. Father Paul in correspondence with the Papal Secretary of State succeeded in having
the name of the Society officially recorded at Rome as the *Societas
Adunationis* (Society of the Atonement). Pope Benedict XV, in
granting certain indulgences to the Society of the Atonement on
April 10th, 1919, used "*Adunationis*."

It seemed that the matter was finally settled. But in the crusade
to make *The Chair of Unity Octave* obligatory upon the Universal
Church the word "expiationis" appeared again in certain documents
Father Paul received from important personages in Rome. In answering one of these letters to the Jesuit Fathers at Rome Father Paul
wrote:

Feast of St. Michael, 1929

Reverend Anthony Rauch, S.J.
Pont. Collegio Germanico ed Ungarico
Via S. Nicola da Tolentino 8
Roma (30) Italia

MY VERY DEAR FATHER:

It was with great joy that I received your letter written on the Feast of the Patronage of St. Joseph, containing the re-drafted petition to the Holy Father. I have gone over this carefully, made a few verbal changes and I have written to the Secretary of our Cardinal asking for an opportunity to present the same to His Eminence, trusting that he will attach his signature to the document. As soon as this is done I will forward the same to you without further delay. I regard it as auspicious that it arrived in my hands on the first day of May, the month of Our Lady of the Atonement (Domina nostra *Adunationis.*)

I presume the reason why the Jesuit Father substituted the word *"expiatione"* was because the Society is so described in the Brief of Pope Benedict XV, but I believe that was the work of His Eminence Cardinal Merry del Val without referring the matter to us, and His Eminence was not aware that we had adopted the word "adunatio" as the Latin equivalent of the Society's name in English. There are several reasons for this:

(1) It was desirable that "S.A." should be the initial letters of our Society, whether in English or in Latin. The word "expiatio" therefore, would not do.

(2) The Latin "adunatio" etymologically is exactly the same as the English "atonement", the root words being *ad* and *unus*, in English *at-one.*

(3) God has very clearly impressed the vocation of unity on our holy Society, the Church Unity Octave itself being one of the evidences of this truth, consequently it may well be called the "Society of Unity." It was through Our Lord's sacrifice on the cross that an at-*one*-ment, or reconciliation, was made between God and man, and the union of God and man in the person of Our Lord Jesus Christ at His Incarnation was through Our Lord made possible for the elect by His sacrifice on Calvary. The central text of our Institute, which contains the word "atonement" is this: "We joy in God, through our Lord Jesus Christ, by Whom we have now received the atonement." (At-*one*-ment) *Reconciliatio* is the vulgate word, which the King James version (from which our name was originally derived) translates Atonement in Rom. 5, 11: "We joy in God, through Our Lord Jesus Christ, by Whom we have now received the Atonement."

(4) As you will note, the verb *"Adunare"* appears twice in the Canon of the Mass, as expressing the unity of the faithful in God and with each other, namely in the "Te Igitur"—"quam pacificare, custodire, *Adunare,* et regere digneris toto orbe terrarium . . ." And then again in the prayer, which is the Oratio of the Church Unity Octave, "Domine Jesu Christe . . . pacificare et Coadunare digneris." The same word occurs, also, in two of the prayers of Holy Week (Prayer after the Passion in the Mass of Good Friday and after Prophecy X in the Mass of Holy Saturday).

(5) As an evidence that the word has already been recognized by the Holy See as part of the title of our Institute, I am sending you a copy of certain Indulgences granted through Bishop Papadopoulos, on April 10, 1919, where you will notice that "adunationis" is used in both the name of the Society and, also, of Our Lady of the Atonement. I trust this will be sufficient to satisfy the Jesuit Father who prepared the original draft that the word "adunationis" is the proper one to appear in this petition.

In answer, Father Rauch, S.J., wrote to Father Paul:

. . . Indeed the word "expiatio" will not do. Your lengthy and charming explanation of "At-one-ment" given in your St. Michael's letter has fully satisfied me.

In all official documents from the Holy See to Graymoor, the title *Societas Adunationis* is used and the Queen of Graymoor is known there as *Domina Nostra Adunationis.* The people of Rome call Our Lady of the Atonement—"the American Madonna."

Father Paul wrote a letter each month to the members of the Rosary League. He always stressed the power of the Rosary. After the Society of the Atonement became Catholic he wrote to the members of the League:

. . . When the Holy Father took our institute under his sovereign care it was with the understanding that the Friars and Sisters of the Atonement were to labor in concert for the reconciliation of Anglicans and other non-Catholics to the Holy See, the conversion of sinners and the extension of Christ's Kingdom in heathen lands. This is far too vast an apostolate for any Society of human beings whatsoever to carry on with even the smallest success unless supernatural assistance in given them, and grace from Almighty God, as every Catholic well knows, is poured down from on high in answer to prayer. . . .

Without prayer we can do nothing and the design of the Rosary

League is to surround the Society of the Atonement with an army of faithful auxiliaries, who recite the prayers of the Society . . . because we think Our Lady herself desires to be invoked and honored under this new name; and that she will grant special favors to those who have recourse to her under the salutation of Our Lady of the Atonement.

In the March 1910 issue of *The Lamp* the editorial was on *The Atonement*. Father Paul wrote:

There came to us only yesterday from a Capuchin Father at Rome, a late addition to the hundreds we have received of a similar nature from all parts of the world since the Society of the Atonement was received into the Catholic Church. But amid his congratulations and good wishes and the prophecy of "great and noble work for the souls of men," he interjects: "Of course you will have your trials. They are the sign manual of God's special love." In the same way we have been admonished to expect the cross by veteran servants of God, writing us not only from the Eternal City, but from the Northland and the Southland, from the Orient and the Occident, from Jesuit Father and Carmelite Nun, from the learned and the lowly, from the humblest mission priest to the most exalted ecclesiastic. The explanation is that all true Catholics from the least unto the greatest, are trained for heaven by Jesus Christ in the school and discipline of the Cross, and all therefore look for it as the badge and seal of every holy enterprise.

God forbid that the Children of the Atonement should ever be strangers to the passion and crucifixion of Jesus Christ. From its very inception every member of the Society has been required to wear the crucifix, either openly upon the breast, if he or she has assumed religious vows, or secretly about the neck, if pursuing the secular walks of life. The very name, Atonement, is a perpetual reminder of the Cross. Our Lord hanging there in mortal agony; our Lady standing by, the sword, foretold by Simeon, piercing her heart; this is the central scene in the mystery of the Atonement, around which all else revolves. . . .

What is the Atonement, and why should "the sign manual of God's special love" be the Cross? Divide the word, according to its etymology, and you have At-One-ment, and note how by this simple analysis is revealed the purpose and the end of the Atonement. That man might be united with God and that this union in its perfection and its bliss might be perpetuated through eternity. That is why Jesus suffered and was crucified and why Mary became Our Lady of the Atonement.

In 1919 Father Paul appealed to the Holy Father, Benedict XV, for Apostolic recognition to the Graymoor custom of invoking the

Mother of Christ under the title of Our Lady of the Atonement. The Holy Father not only gave Apostolic recognition to the name but extended rich indulgences to the members of the League. A plenary indulgence was granted to them under the usual conditions, on the Feast of the Most Holy Rosary and also on the Feast of Our Lady of the Atonement.

With these plenary indulgences came partial ones of three hundred days each for the recitation of prayers Father Paul composed for the members of the League. The first was the Three-Fold Salutation to Our Lady of the Atonement:

THE THREE-FOLD SALUTATION

We salute thee, Holy Mary, Daughter of God the Father, and entreat thee to obtain for us a devotion like thine own to the Most Sweet Will of God.

We salute thee, Virgin Mother of God the Son, and entreat thee to obtain for us such union with the Sacred Heart of Jesus, that our own hearts may burn with love for God, and an ardent zeal for the Salvation of Souls.

We salute thee, Immaculate Spouse of God the Holy Ghost, and entreat thee to obtain for us such yielding of ourselves to the Blessed Spirit, that He may, in all things, direct and rule our hearts, and that we may never grieve Him in thought, word, or deed.

The second indulgenced prayer reads:

THE DAILY PRAYER OF ALL THE CHILDREN OF THE ATONEMENT

O God, Who has prepared for those who love Thee, such good things as pass man's understanding, pour into the hearts of the Children of the Atonement such love towards Thee that we, loving Thee in and above all things, may obtain Thy promises which exceed all that we can desire, through Jesus Christ Our Lord. *Amen.*

The third indulgenced prayer was the morning offering composed by Father Paul:

THE MORNING OFFERING

O my God, I offer Thee today my prayers, works and sufferings in union with the Sacred Heart of Jesus and the Immaculate Heart of Mary with the intention wherewith our Great High Priest pleads His Atonement in Holy Mass, in thanksgiving for Thy favors, in Atonement for our offences, for the petitions of all our associates and especially for the Sanctification and Increase of the Children of the Atonement, the Unity of Christians and the Conversion of the World, through Christ Our Lord. *Amen.*

In his monthly letters to the Rosarians we find the depth of Father Paul's strong and virile spirituality. He constantly warned them against the temptations of the world, the flesh and the devil. He asked them time and again to sacrifice the baubles of the world and lay away treasure in heaven by helping to spread the Kingdom of Christ through the world-wide missions of the Church. He cautioned them against immodesty in dress, and often his innate humor manifested itself when he ventured into the field of women's finery.

The money spent by women on cosmetics irritated him very much. The statistics which told what Americans spent on tobacco, liquor, rouge, lipstick and perfume made him sad. "Imagine," he would say, "what our missionaries could have done with that money." Once when he learned that some women were paying forty dollars for one hat he was shocked. Writing to the Rosarians he said: "Such a hat must be a very heavy burden on a woman's head and conscience, if she knows that with that forty dollars she could have saved nine Chinese babies from being devoured by dogs, and through the instrumentality of Catholic Sisters saved for eternity through the Holy Childhood Association."

Father Paul both in his sermons and in his writings inveighed against immodesty in dress and manners. Painted lips and painted fingernails he abhorred. "Beauty parlors," he said, "are transforming our decent Catholic women to look like modern Jezebels." In his August, 1924, letter to the Rosarians he wrote: "I say we need a crusade for reform in dress, reform in manners, reform in pursuits, and a change from the worship of the creature to the Creator; a re-study of St. Paul's epistle to the Romans, in which he affirms that to be spiritually minded is life and peace in Jesus Christ; but to be carnally minded is death, and that all they who sow to the flesh shall to the flesh reap corruption."

Father Paul set the high ideal of Sainthood before the Rosarians, whom he called, and always addressed as: "Beloved Sons and Daugh-

ters of the Atonement." "As Sons and Daughters of the Atonement,"
he wrote to them, "we are a royal family, princes and princesses of
the House of David. The King of Kings is Our Elder Brother
and the Queen of Heaven is Our Mother. We should never forget
this but act always as becomes our royal blood and divine lineage."

He stressed this family aspect of the Royal Family of Christ in
the following magnificent letter he addressed to the Rosarians in
the August, 1920, issue of *The Lamp*:

We are celebrating this month the glorious Assumption of Our Lady
of the Atonement into Heaven and she has taken her station at the
right hand of her Divine Son as the new Eve, the Mother of the Elect
Seed that are to reign with Christ as citizens of that new Kingdom
which he came on earth to establish and "of which there shall be no
end." Our individual salvation and share in the beatitude of the saints
on high should undoubtedly be a matter of paramount concern with us,
but we must not be self-centered and selfish even in "making our calling and election sure." Every Rosarian should be ashamed to enter
Heaven as a solitary pilgrim. The insatiable desire of Christ and Mary is
the salvation of souls, the increase and multiplication of the Children of
the Atonement . . . every one of us should be influenced with the same
desire.

Long ago God commanded the children of His election to "increase
and multiply." We know how "nature abhors a vacuum" and how God in
like manner abhors barrenness in His Elect. Do you recall how Our Lord
cursed the barren fig tree, because He came seeking fruit thereon and
found only leaves. I fear our Catholic layfolk do not realize this sufficiently.

Whether married or unmarried the vocation of every Christian in the
Lord is to increase and multiply the Children of Divine election. If God
calls any of you to the married state He wishes you to have large families in order that you may bring up sons and daughters in the practice
of the Catholic Religion so as to people Heaven after they die. If you
are not called to the married state, your virginity should be consecrated
to God, that in cooperation with the Holy Spirit and His Spouse, Our
Lady of the Atonement, you may be all the more fruitful on that account, even as the Psalmist says: "the barren woman hath many more
children than she that hath a husband."

In September, 1932, explaining the position of the Mother of
Christ in God's plan of Creation and Redemption, he wrote:

. . . The purpose for which Our Divine Redeemer offered Himself as a slain Lamb upon Calvary was to take away the sins of the world and restore that Unity, or at-one-ment, which flourished between God and our First Parents in the Garden of Paradise before the fall of Adam and Eve. But the unity with God which regenerate man is destined to enjoy forever in Heaven through the Incarnation and Atonement of Jesus Christ far transcends the intimacy which man enjoyed with his Creator in the state of primal innocency before the fall. . . .

When we, therefore, give to our Blessed Mother the title of Our Lady of the Atonement we mean: Our Lady of Unity. As she sits enthroned, as the Great Wonder of Heaven, wearing a crown of twelve stars, clothed with the sun, the moon her footstool, she presents to the universe the highest possible approach of a creature to intimate and exalted union with God. She is at one and the same time the most perfect and the most beloved Daughter of God the Father; she is the Mother of God the Son; and she is the Spouse of God the Holy Ghost.

But Our Lady of the Atonement is not alone the Mother of God, she is also the New Eve, the Mother of Redeemed Mankind; she is the center of the Family Unity for which Christ prayed, and willed might flourish among the Sons and Daughters of the Atonement. As the mother is the center of the home, binding together the love of her husband and of her children, so Our Lady of Unity cooperates with the Holy Ghost and the Sacred Heart of Jesus to bring about that blissful state of Unity which will constitute the joy of Heaven; and toward which the souls of men approximate upon earth in the measure and degree that they correspond to the vocation God has imposed upon His elect children, and which St. Paul expresses in his letter to the Romans when he tells them: "You are all called to be saints."

When, therefore, we address the Blessed Virgin Mary as Our Lady of the Atonement we think of her as the connecting link between ourselves and God, and while we gaze fondly upon her as Our Mother we should try to correspond with the work of the Holy Ghost, the Sanctifier, in our mind, heart and soul to make us like unto her as children resemble their parents.

Father Paul had a deep love for the Blessed Mother. He always saw her enthroned in power and majesty and glory just as St. John describes her in the Apocalypse as the Great Wonder of Heaven. Father Paul instituted a custom at Graymoor in which all the community knelt at her altar before leaving chapel after a religious exercise. At night before leaving the chapel he would kneel first before the Blessed Sacrament; then he would pray before the Shrines

of all the Patrons of the Society—St. Joseph—St. John the Baptist—
St. Peter—St. Paul—St. Francis—St. Anthony. On the way out of
the chapel he would kneel at the altar of Our Lady of the Atonement. There he gazed upon the image which he had himself designed—Mary clothed with the sun, having as her footstool the moon
and crowned with a diadem of twelve stars, holding in her arms the
Christ Child who holds a cross in His right hand. The robe Father
Paul gave her is blue and her mantle is blood-red, symbolic of the
Precious Blood of the Atonement. On each side of the figure are
two angels holding the instruments of the Passion—the lash—the
crown of thorns—the nails—the lance.

Like a child Father Paul knelt before his powerful heavenly
mother, day after day, pouring out his heart filled with problems that
often caused that heart to ache so terribly. He well knew that her
own heart had been pierced with a sword and she would understand,
and so she did. Father Paul loved the Lady to whom he gave a new
title, and she loved him; for the gifts he asked through the power
of her prayers for the Society of the Atonement God graciously
granted—and still does.

Chapter XXVI

EPILOGUE

THE FRIARS ON THE MARCH

IN WRITING the last chapter of the biography of Father Paul the author can say with St. John the Evangelist: "This is the disciple who bears witness concerning these facts, and we know that his witness is true." Never once throughout this whole volume has the author allowed his imagination to glamorize facts, and therefore he hopes that he has been able to avoid any criticism of this work as being "Pietistic." For it was never his intention to be either effusive or sentimental.

Father Paul was a strong man with a strong faith in God. His love for God and his fellow men was deep and true but never maudlin. His virtues were many and these virtues are attested to in the foregoing pages, not so much by the author as by others through documentary evidence. Being a child of Adam Father Paul had faults and failings. These the author related as he saw them. While there is always the temptation to overlook faults and failings in those whom we love, to do so in a work of this kind would be an injustice to the subject and the reader. Longfellow says: "Lives of great men all remind us we can make our lives sublime."

However, who will not strive bravely to emulate the great Ones of the human family when he knows that they too had to overcome not only great trials but also human failings, perhaps exactly like the ones he himself is striving to overcome! The Saints became what they are by striving to imitate other holy persons who had gone before them. Men courageously cultivate the habits of virtue when they see good habits in others; but those who would light the coals of virtue from the fire of other men's virtues often realize that beneath the brilliant fire from which they take their light are burnt-out ashes of inordinate desires which have long since been consumed on the altar of renunciation.

Father Paul labored all his life to become like unto Jesus Christ Who was Infinite Perfection Incarnate. His was a life of renunciation and suffering which he undertook with joy in order to share in *The Atonement* made by Christ for the sins of the world. Father Paul labored incessantly for the spread of the Kingdom of God on earth. Rarely was he ill. In this respect Almighty God was especially good to him. Those who knew him for the indefatigable worker that he was realized that it was graciously kind of God to take him quickly. They could never imagine Father Paul as an invalid. Invalidism would have been the heaviest of all his crosses. Now that the shock is over and the wound has healed those who loved Father Paul know that God's way of taking him quickly was a great blessing. Faith always sees the cross of yesterday as a blessing in the light of today.

Funeral services were conducted for Father Paul on Monday, February 12, 1940. The Little Flower Chapel was much too small to accommodate the great throng of clergy and laity who came to Graymoor for the ceremony. The Pontifical Requiem Mass was celebrated by the Most Reverend Stephen J. Donahue, Auxiliary Bishop of New York. The Most Reverend Eugene J. McGuinness, Bishop of Raleigh, N. C., now Bishop of Tulsa and Oklahoma City; and the Most Reverend Louis La Ravoire Morrow, Bishop of Krishnagar, Bengal, India, were also in the sanctuary.

The Friars, in selecting a priest to preach the Eulogy, chose a long-standing, loyal and true friend of Father Paul and the Society of the Atonement—the Very Reverend Ignatius Smith, O. P., Dean of the School of Philosophy at the Catholic University of America. In establishing the major seminary of the Society at Washington, Father Paul had sought the aid and counsel of Dr. Smith. Because of the friendship which existed between St. Francis and St. Dominic, the Franciscans and the Dominicans have, through the centuries, maintained close bonds of friendship. In the Very Reverend Dr. Smith, the spiritual son of the noble Dominic, Father Paul found a good friend, and so he has remained to the Friars of the Atonement to this day. In delivering the Eulogy the Very Reverend Dr. Smith said:

The winds sing a dirge on the Mount of Graymoor. In the valley there is peace but a numbing sorrow. The angels of God in the heavens above us rejoice that the soul of a saint has come home to the Father. Humanity here is bowed under sorrow that shows in tears streaming down loving faces, not tears of rebellion but from hearts left so lonely by the death of a father and friend. The message of God, in the call of the grim reaper, has called from our midst the soul of Father Paul Francis. To honor his work, to pray for his peace, to console his spiritual family we gather here before his mortal remains, scarcely realizing that he is gone. The Friars of the Atonement, Priests, Brothers and Students, are stunned by the trial and the loss that they suffer. The Sisters, both here on the Mount and out on the far flung firing line of Catholic work inspired by Father Paul Francis, are hallowing their grief with their prayers of devotion. The Brothers Christopher, the constant object of his tender affection, are mute in the sorrow imposed by the death of this apostle of charity. Away from these legions who watched o'er his body are thousands of tertiaries, a hundred thousand members of the Rosary League and of the Union-That-Nothing-Be-Lost who have learned both to love this champion of the church and to lean upon him for spiritual consolation. And scattered over the world from Rome to China, from the Yukon to the Amazon, are hundreds of thousands of men, women and children, high ecclesiastics and humble laity, Protestants, Catholics, Jews and infidels to whom he has appealed and whom he has helped. The Church, the Nation and the ranks of humanitarians have lost an international leader. A place has been left vacant that will never be filled. . . .

Father Paul Francis lived to see his work grow to tremendous proportions. There is no time for me to mention the growth of the Society of the Atonement in physical equipment and resources under his leadership and through his untiring efforts and prayers. Suffice it to say that this bleak and desolate mountain has been turned into a little populous and attractive city of God with numerous buildings and activities, while at the same time bleak and barren hearts and souls have been made attractive and fruitful with the manifold graces of God brought to them through the example and intercession of this other Christ who went about always doing good. Father Paul Francis lived to see the houses of the Friars and of the Sisters established in New York, Philadelphia, Washington, Texas, British Columbia, Northern Alberta, Ireland, England, Assisi and Rome. Into the Catholic Church, when he brought the Society of the Atonement, he led two Friars, five Sisters and ten Tertiaries. He lived to see his number grow, within thirty years, under the Sacramental power of the Catholic Church to one hundred and seventy Friars, two hundred and thirty Sisters and one thousand Tertiaries. During the same time he enrolled in the Rosary League and the Union-That-Nothing-Be-Lost one hundred thousand persons. Rivalling this numerical and physical growth of the works inspired by God in the mind and the life of this saintly apostle of poverty, was the growth of the recognition extended to his undertakings by the authorities of the Church. In 1909 the Church Unity Octave was sanctioned and blessed by Pope Pius the Tenth and in 1916 it was extended to the Universal Church. In nineteen hundred and twenty-one, the Catholic Hierarchy decreed that it should be established in the various dioceses of the United States. In this way the work as well as the name of Father Paul has become known in every city, town and hamlet of the nation, confirming the fame and advancing the labors of this genial ascetic for the salvation of souls through the radio with the Ave Maria hour and other programs to turn the mind and the heart of the nation heavenwards. Truly this was a marvelous career that could have been achieved only by one with a very unusual character.

Only to a few persons, and at rare intervals, does Almighty God give the abundant qualities of mind and heart bestowed on Father Paul Francis. He was almost prophetic in his vision of the future. It is difficult not to believe that he received special enlightenment from the Holy Ghost in most of his projects. They proved to be loaded with the wisdom of another world while the wise of this world thought them to be foolish. He had a confidence in God that could come only from a mind thoroughly illumined by the light of an extraordinary faith. With a contempt for personal possessions and a vow never to touch money, he joined an astute shrewdness with worldly affairs that would have made him a most successful business man. From the depths of his intelligence came a concept of human nature and the dignity of human personality that created in him and in everything around him a spirit of democracy that preaches to the nation. This same mind brought him closer and closer, day by day, to God because of its power to penetrate the meaning of God's word and the application of the Gospel to the daily life of this generation. With such a mind we would expect to find, naturally, the qualities of a great heart. We are not disappointed. Neither was our Church. Neither was God.

We have known that from his earliest days he was passionately devoted to the salvation of the souls of men and to the unity of Christians. Out of these passions grew his love for the Church of Jesus Christ and his restless, ceaseless, soul-exhausting efforts for the preservation and propagation of the faith. Out of this love grew his deep reverence for the office and the person of the Pope as Vicar of Jesus Christ on earth and his reverence for the successors of the Apostles in the members of the

Catholic Hierarchy. Standing out supreme among the great qualities of his magnanimous heart was courage. It was something of which ordinary men, lay and clerical, stood in awe. It can be explained only when we know of his constant and consuming sense of the living presence of God at all times and everywhere in everything he thought and did. It can be explained, this supernatural courage, only when we understand that here is a man who took Jesus seriously, and lived Him literally, and was eternally conscious of the Divine Providence of the Omnipotent Creator and Preserver of this universe. One cannot speak of the heart of Father Paul without referring to the magnetism that was a vivid reflection of the divine attractiveness which drew to him the thousands who are proud to claim him today as their spiritual father and who are left spiritual orphans by his sudden death. I need not speak again of the spirit of practical charity by which he gave life to the spiritual and corporal works of mercy and through which so many thousands have been made more comfortable in body and in soul. I might ask you who knew him longest and lived with him most closely to speak for the more concealed qualities of heart which he manifested so constantly with you of the community.

Though Father Paul was your Founder, spiritual guide and Father General, he was the leader in the practice of the virtues on which the religious life is erected. He entered in holy competition with the youngest and strongest of you in the practice of mortification and heroic self-denial, asking no exemption for his age, seeking no dispensation because of position. And he led all in the sacrosanct rivalry for God's Approval. Deep down in the foundation of his spirituality was the bedrock of humility, the humility that is possessed only by great souls who know how to be courageous in defeat as well as sober and poised in the midst of remarkable success. The career and the character of Father Paul are beautifully matched in their federation for the extension of God's glory and the promotion of human happiness. This you have learned. This all of us have learned. I would like to suggest that the entire nation may learn from the career and character whose merits will be even more appreciated as the future becomes the past, and whose help from above to you, his sons and daughters, will be even more faithful and effective than it was before.

He teaches us that religion can be made most attractive when the instincts of a gentleman are supernaturalized. He teaches us that religion and that men can be best induced to live the works of religion by Apostles who really live it themselves. He teaches us that the sternest and most exalted standards of Christian ascetics are not impossible for attainment by those that work in partnership with Christ the Lord. He has done a tremendous service to the citizens of this country who are concerned about social security and the permanence of living by showing to us the real security and permanence that comes to us from the realization of the existence, presence and providence of the God of men and of nations. He has done a tremendous service to the social thinking of the nation by proving to all that unity and peace in every society and in all society are best obtained by the organization of each individual through the orderly arrangement of mind over body and of God over all, through the suppression of self and the unstinted love of neighbor and of God. He has shown that under the direction of the authorities of our Church and under the lease of grace which this Church alone is capable of invoking from God, that good works can be made better and great works can be made heroic.

We thank God for having given to this world Father Paul. We give him back to God reluctantly but submissively. We know he will not forget us. We promise that we will remember him by prayers for the repose of his soul and by the perpetuation of the vineyard which he planted. May his soul rest in peace.

When the mortal remains of Father Paul were laid to rest, the Friars of the Atonement found a Father, a wise Counsellor and a great friend in the Archbishop of New York—His Eminence Francis Cardinal Spellman. Were it not for the gracious direction of Cardinal Spellman serious mistakes might have been made by those who had to shoulder the tremendous burden of carrying on the work of Father Paul, unacquainted as they were with the vastness of that work. The Cardinal took a keen interest in Graymoor and devoted much of his invaluable time to its welfare. He became so interested in the life work of Father Paul that he offered to write the foreword to his biography.

The most important development of the Society of the Atonement since Father Paul's death has been the establishment of the Friars of the Atonement in Rome. The most cherished ambition of Father Paul was to see a house for his Friars established in the city of Rome where the Vicar of Christ resides. In 1938 he sent three student Friars to Rome to study under the Dominican Fathers at the "Angelicum College." The Friars, not having a house of their own, resided with the Christian Brothers. In June, 1940, because of the war raging in Europe, the three Friars were forced to return to Graymoor.

On August 15, 1945, Pope Pius XII by the Motu Proprio "Cum Ordo Equester" gave to the Equestrian Order of the Holy Sepulcher of Jerusalem the use of St. Onofrio's (St. Humphrey's) church on the Janiculum Hill in Rome. The Cardinal Patron of this ancient Order is Nicolà Cardinal Canali. On June 18, 1946, he sent the following letter to Graymoor from Vatican City:

I am pleased to inform you that the Supreme Pontiff, having received the proposal made by the Order of the Knights of the Holy Sepulcher of Jerusalem, has deigned to entrust to the Franciscan Friars of the Atonement, whose Mother House is located in Graymoor, Garrison, N. Y., U. S. A., the sacred officiation and religious services in the Church of S. Onofrio on the Janiculum in Rome, which has been assigned by the Motu Proprio of the above reigning Pontiff Pope Pius XII dated August 15, 1945, to the Order of the Knights of the Holy Sepulcher of Jerusalem, and has granted to the undersigned Cardinal every faculty for subsequent arrangements. . . .

With most cordial congratulations for this especial testimonial of particular benevolence on the part of the Holy Father towards the Congregation. . . . I am

Sincerely yours in Christ,

N. Card. Canali

This new development in the history of the Society of the Atonement was something that Father Paul had worked and prayed for through many years. The realization of his dream came six years after he died. Before the final approval given by the Holy Father, the matter had to be approved by four Cardinals of the Church. The first authorization was graciously given by Francis Cardinal Spellman, Archbishop of New York. The late Emanuel Cardinal Suhard, Archbishop of Paris, whose titular church it was, and the late Francesco Cardinal Marchetti-Selvaggiani, Vicar General of His Holiness, had also to give their approval. The Knights of the Holy Sepulcher were represented by Nicolà Cardinal Canali.

In July, 1946, the Friars returned to Rome to establish headquarters in the center of Christendom at St. Onofrio's, one of

Rome's most beautiful churches, a church which is five hundred years old. There they study and carry on the work of Christian Unity throughout Europe. One of the Friars, writing to Graymoor, recently stated:

Those who met Father Paul never tire of telling us about his visits to Rome. The Spanish Third Order Regular Franciscans keep, as relics, all the letters he ever sent them. Father Paul stayed at their monastery at the Church of San Giovanni Decollata at Rome. Father Schilling, a Friar Minor who once escorted Father Paul about Rome, often stops us on the way home from classes to say a word about him. Cardinals and Bishops speak of him with respect and reverence, while the Poor Clares of Assisi refer to him as "il santo fondatore" (the Holy Founder). What is here at Rome is merely the fulfillment of Father Paul's work and charity.

In recalling God's promise to him in the *Covenant Text*, Father Paul often said that his Friars would be seen in the courtyards and marketplaces of foreign lands. That dream of his, so far as the Orient is concerned, came true when in 1948 a large territory of the Diocese of Yokohama, Japan, was offered for them to labor in by His Eminence Pietro Cardinal Fumasoni-Biondi, Secretary of the Sacred Congregation of the Propaganda. Again Francis Cardinal Spellman approved and blessed this new missionary project of Graymoor. On January 9, 1949, he personally came to Graymoor to attend the Departure Ceremony and bid Godspeed to the first contingent of six Friar Priests and two Friar Brothers who were leaving to establish the Society in Japan.

Cardinal Spellman ended his profound sermon with the words:

Your simplest act will be a consecrated act, great with the greatness of a Love Divine, as daily you labor for the aged, the incurable, the foundling, the homeless, the neglected and the sick. You will ask no questions of any man but from world's end to end wherever human beings are in need you will minister unto their misery, to alleviate sorrow, physical suffering and spiritual sickness, for the missionary asks not who calls, but where he is needed. And today as I beg God's mercy, protection and consolation for your loved ones, I pray His blessings upon yourselves and all your works, as valiantly you go out to labor in the mission fields of Japan to bring the God-Man to dwell within the hearts of men, and peace within their souls.

The mission territory assigned to the Friars in the Diocese of Yokohama is sixty miles long and twenty-five miles wide. There are millions of souls in it. Soon after their arrival, Bishop Thomas Wakida dedicated the principal mission house of the Friars. It is known as "Graymoor-in-Japan." This name was well received by the Japanese and by the Americans in the Army of Occupation who, when visiting the Friars, speak of "going to Graymoor." That would have delighted Father Paul had he lived.

In the first contingent leaving for Japan were two Japanese Friar Priests who as children attended the mission of the Sisters of the Atonement in Vancouver, British Columbia. Later under the guidance of the Sisters they were received into the Catholic Church, and later came to Graymoor to study for the priesthood. One of these Japanese priests is the Regional Superior of all the Graymoor missions in Japan.

On St. Francis' Day, October 4th, each year Friars leave for Japan. It is "Departure Day" at Graymoor, when there is a commingling of sorrow and joy; the joy which every missionary experiences as he sets out for a pagan land; and the sorrow his parents and family and friends experience in seeing him go.

St. John's Atonement Seminary which was built with the original offering of John Reid, the first member of *The-Union-That-Nothing-Be-Lost*, had, at Father Paul's death, already become inadequate to house the many worthy young men seeking admission to the Society. In 1948 the Friars found an old, abandoned college at Montour Falls, New York, which had for years been operated under Protestant auspices as a fine school. It is today known as St. John's Atonement Seminary, and it is able to accommodate one hundred and fifty-two students.

The Montour Falls Foundation is perhaps the most interesting development in the whole history of the Society of the Atonement, other than Graymoor itself. When the Friars found the abandoned Baptist school it was a shambles. Not having been occupied for six years, vandals had practically destroyed it. However, the foundation and walls were strong and sound, and being offered to them for a small sum of money the Friars bought it.

Father Paul always said that the Society of the Atonement would fulfill the words of Isaias: "And the places that have been desolate for ages shall be built in thee. Thou shalt raise up the foundations of generation and generation: and thou shalt be called the repairer of the fences, turning the paths to rest." He incorporated those words into a series of prayers, said every day by the Society of the Atonement, which are known as, "The Occasional Offices of the Society of the Atonement."

After the Friars had received the permission and blessing of the Most Reverend James E. Kearney, Bishop of Rochester, to establish a house in his diocese, and also the sanction and blessing of Francis Cardinal Spellman, they began to realize they had a "desolate" place to rebuild. As for the repairing "of the fences"—they were beyond repair. But they accepted the work as a challenge to their faith and courage, and after two years of hard work it developed into a fine minor seminary for students for the priesthood.

As this book goes to press another foundation has been made at Valley Falls, Rhode Island (near Providence). The Friars acquired this property from the Cistercians of the Strict Observance—popularly known as the Trappists—who had occupied the property for fifty years. This spacious property will be used as the Novitiate of the Society of the Atonement; and the name will be changed from Our Lady of the Valley to Our Lady of the Atonement. This transfer came through the gracious permission of His Eminence Francis Cardinal Spellman and Bishop Russell J. McVinney of Rhode Island.

Since the death of their beloved Founder, Father Paul, the Friars of the Atonement have been "on the march," inspired by the magnificent example that Father Paul set before them. They are now established on three continents of the globe, laboring among the four races of the earth—white—black—yellow—red. Houses have been established in Rome, Italy; the Archdioceses of Vancouver B. C., New York and Washington, D. C.; also in the dioceses of Ogdensburg and Rochester, New York; Raleigh, North Carolina; the diocese of Amarillo, Texas; of Nelson, British Columbia; and the diocese of Yokohama, Japan.

There are over one hundred Friar Priests, fifty Friar Brothers, and one hundred and twenty seminarians studying for the priesthood. The Sisters of the Atonement, the Spiritual Daughters of that valiant woman Mother Lurana number three hundred and fifty Sisters. They have recently opened their fiftieth mission.

So closes the story of Father Paul's life, a story of a man's love for God and his fellow men. Father Paul not only knew and loved Christ, but he also lived Christ. In living Christ he proved to the world that "the foolishness of God is wiser than men, and the weakness of God is stronger than men." Father Paul rested his faith "not on the wisdom of men, but on the Power of God." "He went about doing good" so that men might look up to God, the Infinite Good, and know the peace which is the reward of those who are in *At-One-Ment* with *Him*.

INDEX

Acolyte, the, adverse criticism of Father Paul in, 239–245

"Adunationis" (of the Atonement), 332; use of word by Pope Benedict XV, 333; letter to Father Rauch, S.J. concerning, 334–335, and reply, 335

Aelen, Most Rev. J., Archbishop of Madras, India, his letter to Doctor Paluel Flagg, 227

Aelred, Brother, S.A., incident of storm at Pentecost, 324–325

Aitkens, Very Rev. F. E., Episcopal Dean, 132; member Anglo-Roman Union, 134

Alberta, 5

Amelia, Sister, S.A., attends Father Paul's ordination, 197

American Catholic, Anglican periodical, article on conversion of Father Sargent, 173–174

American Ecclesiastical Review, review of *Prince of the Apostles,* 137

Angela, Sister, S.A., foundress Daughters of Mary, Health of the Sick, 230

Angelicum College, Rome, three Atonement Friars sent to, 347

Anglicans, condolences from, 9–10; Father Paul calls upon to repudiate Reformation, 96–97; Father Paul's lifelong love for, 103; some reject, some accept Papal letter "Apostolicae Curae," 107–109; sensation among, created by *Prince of the Apostles,* 137–139; Octave was Father Paul's last work as, 142 *et seq.;* Monsignor Benson on, 195–196

Anglican Orders, *see* "Apostolicae Curae"

Anglo-Roman Review, of Paris, rebuked by Pope Leo XIII, 107–108

Anglo-Roman Union, foundation of by Father Paul, 103, 132–134; *New York Herald* editorial on, 133–134

Anselm, Father, S.A., founded Ave Maria radio hour, 297

Anthony, Brother, S.A., convert from Judaism, 10; formerly Ferdinand Wallerstein, 82–83; conversion, career and death, 89–90; in 1920 still only Friar-Brother, 201–202

Apologia pro vita sua, 32n.

"Apostolicae Curae," Pope Leo XIII letter on Anglican Orders, 17, 107 *et seq.*

Archdeaconry meeting (Anglican Diocese of Long Island), 98–103; comment on in *Living Church,* 104

Associate Mission (Anglican Order in Omaha), Father Paul joins, 39; leaves, 50; Father Howard leaves, 75–76

Assumption, The, Father Paul writes on, 328–332, 339–341

Atonement (At-One-Ment), Children of God redeemed by the, 10; search for name of new Society and discovery of, 34–36; equivalent "At-One-Ment," 36; quote from *Catholic Encyclopedia:* "almost only theological term of English origin," 332; "At-One-Ment," keynote to work of Society of the Atonement, 333 *et seq.*

At-One-Ment with Him, 352

Atonement, Sisters of the, hear of death of Father Paul, 4; condolences to from Holy See on death of Father Paul, in letter from Cardinal Canali, 9; suggested as Second Order of Society of the Atonement and resolve of Mother Lurana to found, 43; their house at Assisi today, 44; Father Paul predicts future, at dedication of first convent, 66–69; "Non nisi te Domine," motto of, 69; St. Francis patron of, 74; Father Paul chaplain for, 77; Miss Buxton, convert becomes member of, 81; they take possession of new convent, 85; valiant work for *The Lamp*, 119–121; in Ireland, 150; send Peter's Pence to Rome, 151; received into Catholic Church, 159–164; lawsuit filed against, 168 *et seq*.; Miss Chadwick refuses to join plaintiffs against, 174–177; Father Paul on lawsuit, 181; correspondence with James Dempsey, attorney for, 181–184; petition in behalf of to Bishop Greer, 185–186; note on their convent in 1909, 214; letter of thanks to from National Secretary Near East Welfare Association, 292; Mother Lurana, foundress of, dies, 296–297; reference to, by visitor in 1910, 304; Negro mission in Philadelphia of, 319; in 1940 there were 230 members of, 344–345; in 1950 there were 350 members of, 352

Atonement, Society of the, Father Paul founder of, 3; Cardinal Tisserant's letter of condolence to, 6–7; Cardinal Canali's letter from the Holy See to, 9; Catholic League of England's (Anglican) letter to, 9–10; name originated, 35; Father Paul receives the Atonement Texts, 35–36; vocation of, 49; Father Paul chooses Graymoor as the home of, 61; Father Sargent derides plan for founding, 72; choice of heavenly patrons for, 74; Father Paul receives deed to Graymoor in name of, 82–83; *Church Standard* calls them "ecclesiastical squatters, 84; type of habit of determined upon, 87; "Francis" the family name of, 89; "corporate reunion" the early vocation of, 91–92; in 1901 small size of, 97; *Rose Leaves from Our Lady's Garden* the first publication of, 97–98; reference to later corporate reception of, 115–116; "That they all may be One," the basic prayer of, 134; Fa-

ther Paul's letter to Cardinal Falconio requesting reception into the Catholic Church and the Cardinal's answer thereto, 156–158; influence of *The Lamp* towards corporate reception of, 159; Cardinal Merry del Val later tells Father Paul of circumstances leading to corporate reception, 159; Monsignor O'Keeffe appointed instructor of, 159; Monsignor Conroy instructed to receive, 160; reception of into the Church, 161; announcement in *The Lamp* of the reception, 161–162; article in *New York Times* concerning reception, 162–164; "Tabor," 164; lawsuit against Sisters of the, 168 *et seq*., Chapter XV; Rev. Paschal Robinson, temporary chaplain; other chaplains, 191–192; Archbishop Farley confirms 13 members of, and supplies funds for *The Lamp*, 192–193; serious threat to future of, Chapter XVII; dedication of St. Francis' Chapel in 1912, 214–215; administration building erected, 216; property in Washington, D.C., acquired for Atonement seminary of the Holy Ghost, 217–219; Graymoor press acquired, 219; inspiration and foundation of Union-That-Nothing-Be-Lost, 223 *et seq*., Chapter XIX; promotion of Catholic Medical Mission Board by, 227 *et seq*.; disbursements to missions since 1940 by, 254; advocacy of Octave, Chapter XX, and blessing of Pope Pius X, 256–257; cornerstone of Little Flower Oratory laid, 284; campaign for Near East Relief, 286; and its growth into Catholic Near East Welfare Association, 286–293; slow growth of Society until about 1930, 294; rapid growth of by 1935, 294; beginning of Ave Maria Hour, 297; and its growth, 297–300; St. Christopher's Inn, Chapter XXIII; in 1940 there were 170 Friars and 230 Sisters in, 344–345; establishment of, in Rome, 347; in Yokohama, 349–350; at Montour Falls, N. Y., 350; at Valley Falls, R. I., 351

INDEX

Attwater, Donald, editor, *Catholic Dictionary*, 126n.

Ave Maria, Catholic periodical, errs on "Infallibility," 110–111; approves Octave, 141

Ave Maria Hour, 4; founded by Father Anselm, 297; development of, 297–300; direction of, by Father Terence, 300

Baker, Edward Ignatius, member Graymoor community corporately received, 161

Barnes, Father, rector St. Barnabas' Episcopal Church, Brooklyn, welcomes Father Paul, 95

Barney, John W., of *Wall Street Journal* and convert, member Anglo-Roman Union, 134

Barry-Doyle, Rt. Rev. Monsignor Richard, Bishop Calavassy sends to Father Paul for Near East relief, 237; preaches at Graymoor, 285–287; his visit to the United States, 288–293; Bishop Calavassy quotes letter of, 288; confers with Cardinals Tacci and Merry del Val, 289

Baxter, Sister Isabel, member Graymoor community corporately received, 161

Bello, Antonio Cardinal, Patriarch of Lisbon, Portugal, appeals for and receives aid from Graymoor, 252

Benedict XV, Pope, indulgences prayer for Union - That - Nothing - Be - Lost, 254; extends observance of Church Unity Octave to the Universal Church in 1916, 257–259; Brief, "Romanorum Pontificum," 265–266; uses word "Adunationis," 333; recognizes title "Our Lady of the Atonement" and extends indulgences, 336–337

Benson, Monsignor Robert Hugh, Father Paul quotes, 195–196

Beresford, Rev. Dr. C. H., Honorary Secretary Catholic League (Anglican), Father Paul's letter to, 143–144

Bernardone, Francesco, *see* St. Francis of Assisi

Bethany, Congregation of Jacobite Monks, corporately received, 115; in Mar Ivanios' letter, 272–273

Biermans, Bishop of Uganda, help from Father Paul, 234

Blecke, Father Edward, O.F.M., arranges for affiliation of the Society of the Atonement, 160; instructs Graymoor community, 196; accepts life vows of Father Paul, Brother Anthony and clothes Brother Francis, 201–202

Blenk, Archbishop of New Orleans, blesses Octave, 257

Blessed Vincent Pallotti, *see* Pallotti

Bolshakoff, Serge, Russian refugee in Lyons, France, collaborates with Abbé Couturier on revised Octave prayer, 275–277, 280–282

Bonzano, John, Cardinal, lays cornerstone of Little Flower Oratory, 284

Boston Pilot, the, Catholic periodical, comment of Graymoor's corporate reunion, 165

Bourne, Cardinal, of Westminster, blesses Octave, 257

Bourne, Rev. James H., professor at Nashotah Seminary, 130; convert, 119, 130

Boyer, Rev. Charles, S.J., editor *Unitas* and Prefect of Studies and Dean of the Theological Faculty, Pontifical Gregorian University, Rome, 149

Brandi, Rev. T. M., S.J., editor of *Civiltà Cattolica*, letter from, with blessing from Pius X, 257

Brine, Rev. Charles Le V., castigates Father Paul, 118

British Columbia, mission house in, 5, 351

Brooklyn Citizen, the, quotes Father Paul's sermon, 95–97

Brothers Christopher, origin of name, 4; criticism of, in *Acolyte*, 242; story of, Chapter XXIII, 302 *et seq.*

Brothers of Penance (Third Order Secular of St. Francis), *Foreword*

Buchanan, W. A., vice-president Anglo-Roman Union, 134

Burnett, Father, C.P. (Anglican), member Anglo-Roman Union, 134

Buxton, Miss Mary, meets Mother Lurana, 80; convert, and becomes Sister Mary Clare, S.A., 81

Byrnes, Very Rev. Patrick, vice-president of Maryknoll, 318

Cabot, explorer under English flag, *Foreword*

Cadi, Most Rev. Demetrius, Patriarch of Antioch, letter to Pope Pius XI, petitioning Octave be made obligatory, 261

Calavassy, Most Rev. George, Bishop of Greece, tribute to memory of Father Paul, 7–8; sends Monsignor Barry-Doyle to Father Paul, 237; letter to Pius XI petitioning Octave be made obligatory, 261; appeals to Graymoor in urgent need, 287–288; letter of thanks to Graymoor, 292–293

Caldey, Benedictine Monks of, corporately received, 115, 271

Cammack, W. M., president Anglo-Roman Union, 134

Canali, Nicola, Cardinal, *dedication page*; letter from, in tribute to Father Paul, 9; renewal of indulgences for Church Unity Octave, 257–259; his blessing and observance of Octave in Rome during 1950, 282; Patron of the Order of the Holy Sepulcher of Jerusalem, 348; his letter to Graymoor on custody of St. Onofrio's Church by the Society of the Atonement, 348

Canevin, Most Rev. Regis H., Bishop of Pittsburgh, blesses Octave, 257

Canon XIX (Anglican "open pulpit"), 125, 126 *et seq.*

Canterbury, Archbishop of, reply to papal bull, 108–109

Carinci, Most Rev. Alfonso, Secretary Sacred Congregation of Rites, 268

Carlyle, Dom Aelred, Abbot of Caldey, 271

Carr, Viola, companion of Mother Lurana, 63

Catholic Courier of Rochester, N. Y., tribute to Father Paul, 6

Catholic Dictionary, Donald Attwater editor, definition of Modernism, 126n.

Catholic Encyclopedia, reference "Pallotti," 148; quotation on "Seminary," 241; reference to "Atonement," 332

Catholic League, England (Anglican), condolences of, on Father Paul's death, 9–10; Father Paul's correspondence with, 143–145

Catholic Medical Mission Board, initiative of Dr. Flagg, 226 *et seq.*; aid from Graymoor, 228; story of, in Keeler's *Catholic Medical Missions*, 228 *et seq.*; Father Garasché, S.J., director of, 230; Mother Dengel M.D., 252–254

Catholic Medical Mission Propaganda, *see* Catholic Medical Mission Board

Catholic Near East Welfare Association, 3; founding of, 237; pilgrimage of Father Paul to Rome to establish, 262; Father Paul and Monsignor Barry-Doyle co-founders of, 285 *et seq.*; Cardinal Spellman president of, 292

Catholic News, the, reports Father Paul's preaching mission at St. Patrick's Cathedral, 211; criticized by *Acolyte*, 240

Catholic Standard and Times, Philadelphia, Monsignor Hawks' tribute to Father Paul in, 6

Catholic Union (later Catholic Near East Welfare Association), relief organization of Father Count Von Galen, 289–290; aided by St. Elizabeth's College; Baroness Catherine de Hueck, 290

Catholic Universe, the, England, notes change in name of Octave, 269

Catholic University, 5; Father Paul speaks at, 103; Atonement Seminary adjacent to, 217–219; in 1930, 40 students of Society of the Atonement at, 294

Catholic university in Japan, 123; influence of *Rose Leaves* and *The Lamp* in establishing, 124

Cecelia Mary, Mother, foundress Sisters of the Love of Jesus (Anglican), and convert, 271–272

Chadwick, Julia Halsted, finds deserted chapel in wilderness, 59 *et seq.*; champions cause of Sisters in letter to *Living Church*, 175–177; the single lay defendant in suit against Sisters, 181–185; her conversion and death in Florence, Italy, as Catholic, 186

Chair of Unity Octave, in *Foreword*; name "Church Unity Octave" changed to, 269; "Universal Week of Prayer for Christian Unity not identical with, 273–274; watered-down version of, started by Abbé Couturier and Serge Bolshakoff, 275 *et seq.*; in 1950 gloriously observed in Rome, 282; intentions of the Octave, *see* Chapter XIII, 142 *et seq.*

Chaldean Relief Mission, thanks for help by Father Paul, 232

Chu-Chow, China, mission aided by Graymoor, 226

Churchman, The, Episcopal periodical, 18; urges "Protestant Federation," 131

Church Standard, the, of Philadelphia, attacks Father Paul, 117–118, for "Protestant Federation," 131

Church Unity Octave, Father Paul the founder of, 3; "inspirer of and initiator of," eulogies concerning Father Paul by Monsignor Hawks and Cardinal Tisserant, 6–7; Father Paul speaks at Catholic University on, 103; development of, 136 *et seq.*, Chapter XIII; reference in Dr. Smith's eulogy to Father Paul, 345; *see also* Chapter XX, "The Octave Extended to the Universal Church."

Cicognani, Amleto, Apostolic Delegate, condolences from, 5

Cistercians (Trappists), transfer of property to Society of the Atonement, 351

Civiltà Cattolica, letter in, announces blessing of Father Paul and the Society by Pope Pius X, 257

Clairborne, Rev. W. E., attack on, and answer to, by Father Paul, 172–173

Coleman, Leighton, Episcopal Bishop of Delaware, dedicates St. Francis' House, 84–85; Father Paul takes vows before, 89; in 1900 dedicates St. Paul's Friary and his conversation

with Father Paul, 94–95; resigns his position as Visitor to Graymoor and considers deposition of Father Paul, 121–122; his death, 153

Communism, in 1923 Father Paul warns against, 300–301

Companions of the Holy Savior (Episcopalians), 129–130

Conaty, Bishop, of Los Angeles, blesses Octave, 257

Conroy, Most Rev. Joseph, Bishop of Ogdensburg, receives Society of the Atonement into the Catholic Church, 160–162

Copeland, C. C., Libertyville, O., letter from, 231

Corbould, Rev. W. Robert, president Catholic League (English Anglicans), letter of condolence from, 9–10

Corporate Reception *or* Corporate Submission, *see* Corporate Reunion

Corporate Reunion, Father Paul's emphasis on, 91, 98, 106; etymology of, 113; Father Paul's early ideas on, 113; Father Paul's later change of position on, 114 *et seq.*; Dr. Lloyd's belief in, 123; "Open Pulpit" movement vitiates idea of, 125; impossibility of, between Anglicanism and Holy See, 134–135; "England and the Holy See" advocates, 136–137; Father Paul's plea to Monsignor Falconio for, 155–158; *The Lamp's* influence in effecting, 159; Church receives Society of the Atonement corporately, 162–164; other groups admitted, 270–273; as affecting sects in schism, or dissident, 286–287

Corpus Christi Cross, at Graymoor, 81–82

Correspondence Course, Graymoor's for non-Catholics, 299–300

Couturier, Abbé Paul, a revised form of the Octave prayer started by, 275 *et seq.*; *also see* Bolshakoff

Covenant, the, origin and hymn of, 54–58, *also see* Chapter VI; God's promise of, recalled, 349

Cree, Mary Margaret, member Graymoor community corporately received, 161

Cummings, Father Terence, S.A., director Ave Maria Hour, 300

Curran, Rev. Dr., former pastor at Peekskill, N. Y., in sermon of Father Paul, 247–250, originator of Guardian Building, 250

Curtis, Georgina Pell, author of *Beyond the Road to Rome*, quotes Father Paul, 117, 117n.

Cusack, Most Rev. Thomas F., Auxiliary Bishop of New York, consulted by Father Paul, 203–204; St. John's Church dedicated by, 214; ground broken for St. John's Seminary by, 215; fears that too perfect a Rule is demanded for Union-That-Nothing-Be-Lost, 222

Daughters of Mary, Health of the Sick (Sister Angela), 230

David, Father, *see* Gannon, Rev. David, S.A.

Davis, Mr. Joseph, meets Father Paul, 78–79; supplies shack as "friary," 85

Davis, Rev. Mr., temporary chaplain to Sisters, 62, 85

Declaration of Independence, *Foreword*

De Hueck, Baroness Catherine, 290

Delahunt, Very Rev. Angelus, S.A., Father General Society of the Atonement, 12

De Lisle, Ambrose Phillipps, Catholic scholar, 16, 16n.

De Maria, Rev. Joseph, P.S.M., biography of Pallotti, 146–148

Dempsey, James, Peekskill, N. Y., attorney for Sisters, 181 *et seq.*

Dengel, Mother Anna, M.D., founder of Society of Catholic Medical Missionaries (later Catholic Medical Mission Board), interest of Father Paul in work of, 252; her 1940 tribute to Father Paul, 252–253; letter from, August 25, 1950, 253

Denver Catholic News, criticized by *Acolyte*, 240

d'Herbigney, Most Rev. Michel, Oriental Church, letter from, 264

Dimond House, first home of Sisters, 64–65, 179

Doane, William Croswell, Episcopal Bishop of Albany, 40, 42

Donahue, Most Rev. Joseph P., at dedication of St. John's Church, 214

Donahue, Most Rev. Stephen J., Pontifical Requiem Mass celebrated for Father Paul, 343

Dougherty, Dennis, Cardinal, letter from Father Paul requesting support of American hierarchy for Octave, 260; favorable reply from, 261; director in Catholic Near East Welfare Association, 288–291; in 1945 writes of Father Paul, 320–321

Drain, Rev. Patrick, pastor at Cold Spring, N. Y., Graymoor in his parish, he assists in corporate reception, 162

Drexel, Mother Superior, Sisters of the Blessed Sacrament, 129

Duke, Archbishop, of Vancouver, corporately receives Sisters of the Love of Jesus, 271–272

Dunwoodie Seminary (St. Joseph's), testimony from, as to Father Paul's theological soundness, 71; Father Paul's life at, 193–195

Ecumenical Movement, Pope Pius XII on, 279–280

Edith, Mother, Superior Sisters of Mary, Peekskill, N. Y., convert, 129

"Eirenic Theology," Pope Pius XII on, 278–279

Elliot, Alice May, finds deserted chapel, 59; Mother Lurana visits, 62; letter to Mother Lurana, 66; plaintiff in lawsuit against Sisters, 63, 179–180, 185; conversion and death at Graymoor, 187; Father Paul's memorial to, 187–190

Elmendorf, Rev. Augustine, member Anglo-Roman Union, 134

Emmanuel Thomas the Second, Patriarch of Babylon, letter of thanks to Father Paul, 232

England and the Holy See, book by Rev. Spencer Jones, 136–137

Evans, Sister Amelia, member Graymoor community, corporately received, 161

Everaerst, Bishop, China, beneficiary of Graymoor, 226

"Expiationis," early variant of "Adunationis" (Atonement), 333–335

Falconio, Diomede, Cardinal, O.F.M., 78; as Apostolic Delegate consulted by Father Paul on submission of Society of the Atonement, 153, 155–159; introduces Father Paul to Archbishop Farley, 159; becomes Cardinal, 211; Protector of St. Clare's Church (Basilica) at Assisi, and letter from him to Father Paul, 243–244; his letter approving Church Unity Octave, 256

Farley, John, Cardinal, as Archbishop of New York, Mother Lurana interviewed by him, 152; Father Paul meets, 159; makes arrangement for reception of Graymoor community, 159–161; authorizes Father Blecke to receive Graymoor vows, 202; becomes Cardinal, 211; invites Father Paul to preach mission at St. Patrick's Cathedral, 211–213; St. John's Church, Graymoor, renovated by, 214; blesses Church Unity Octave, 256; petitions Rome for Octave's extension to Universal Church, 256–257

Father Paul, Foreword; death of, 3; radio announcement of death, 5; letters of condolence from: Apostolic Delegate Cicognani; Rt. Rev. Edward Hawks in Catholic Standard and Times; the editor Catholic Courier, Cardinal Tisserant, Bishop Calassy, 5–8; Cardinal Canali's letter of condolence from the Holy See, 9; Catholic League of England (Anglican) letter of esteem from, 9–10; obedience to Rev. David Gannon S.A. to write life of, 12; his birthplace at Millington, Md., January 16, 1863, 22; his boyhood, 22–24; student days, 25–26; Episcopal deaconate, 27; presbyter, 28; begins publication of Pulpit of the Cross, 29; life at Kingston, N. Y., 28–38; receives Atonement Texts, 34–36; at Associate Mission, Omaha, 39–50; correspondence with Mother Lurana, 42, 45–46; investigates Roman Catholic claims, 46–47; leaves Omaha, 50; visits Mother Lurana at Warwick, N. Y., and the "Covenant" is made, 52–58; enters Order of the Holy Cross, Westminster, Md., 55; first visit to Graymoor, 61–62; letter on dedication of St. John's-in-the-Wilderness, 67–69; studies with Order of the Holy Cross, 70–73; letter to Mother Lurana on style and habit of the Society, 75; leaves Order of the Holy Cross to serve as chaplain for Sisters of the Atonement, 77; visits Franciscan monastery, Washington, D. C., 77–78; arrival at Graymoor to stay and gives it name of Mount of the Atonement, 78–79; receives money for purchase of Graymoor from Dr. Taylor, 80–81; takes legal possession of Graymoor, 81; Corpus Christi Cross, 81; "The Palace of Lady Poverty," 85–86; habit of the Society decided upon, 86–88; professed in religion by Bishop Coleman, 89; in 1900 advocates "corporate reunion," 91; his championship of "Jure Divino," 95; announces his Catholic position to Bishop Coleman, 94; Brooklyn Citizen article on, 95–97; establishes Rosary League and publishes magazine Rose Leaves, 97; Archdeaconry meeting of Episcopal diocese of Long Island, 98–104; founds Anglo-Roman Union, 103; "He Lights The Lamp," Chapter XI; his change on corporate reunion, 114; New York Herald article on, 121–122; Bishop Coleman resigns as Visitor to Graymoor, and threatens deposition of Father Paul, 121; his friendship with Dr. Lloyd of Japan, 123–124; his editorial on "Open Pulpit," in The Lamp, 130–131; New York Herald article on Anglo-Roman Union, 133–134; he allows no gates at Graymoor, 135; his conception of a worldwide movement of prayer—the Church Unity Octave, 136 et seq. in Chapter XIII; collaborates on

Prince of the Apostles, 138; his idea of Church Unity Octave, while he is still Anglican, approved by Cardinal O'Connell, 141; correspondence on Octave with Catholic League, England, 143–145; magazine *Unitas* proclaims him founder of Chair of Unity Octave, 149; pays Peter's Pence to Rome, 151; visits Monsignor O'Keeffe, 152; visits Cardinal Gibbons, 153; letter from Bishop Kinsman, 154–155; visits Monsignor Falconio (later Cardinal), requesting reception into Church, 155–157; request granted, 158; his later interview with Cardinal Merry del Val, 159; meets Monsignor Falconio and Archbishop Farley, 159; received into Catholic Church, 160–161; accused by Rev. W. H. Van Allan of obtaining money under false pretenses, and his answer, 169–170; his defense by former opponent, Rev. J. A. M. Richey, 170–173; comment in *Lamp* on lawsuit against Sisters, 181–182; receives support of Hamilton Fish leading to settlement of suit, 185; his Memorial to Miss Elliot, 187–190; he is temporarily a layman, 191; student at Dunwoodie Seminary, 193–195; ordained priest, 197; protests in *Lamp* about prejudice against Graymoor, 201; professed in religion by Father Blecke, O.F.M., 201–203; consults Bishop Cusack about Father Francis, 203; comments on Father Francis' departure, 204–205; letter from Monsignor Hawks, 206–208; preaches in 1914 in St. Patrick's Cathedral, 211; letter to Mother Lurana, 212; preaching missions in Baltimore, Far Rockaway, Chicago, 213; St. Francis' Chapel dedicated, 215; St. John's Seminary opened, 216; purchase of property for Atonement Seminary of the Holy Ghost at Washington, D. C., and its development, 217–219; Graymoor Press established, 219; inspiration and growth of the Union-That-Nothing-Be-Lost, 221 *et seq.*; arrival of John Reid and his story, 222–226;

Rock of Peter foundation, 224; letter from Father Ting, China, 226; initial letter from Dr. Flagg and its consequences, 228 *et seq.*; Catholic Medical Mission Board and its development, 228–230; letter from C. C. Copeland, 231; letters from Chaldean Church, 232; various Religious Congregations benefitted by, 233; circulation of the *Lamp* as edited by, 234; Brother Fidelis on difficulties of raising funds for missions, 235; Monsignor Barry-Doyle's mission to, 237; and founding of Catholic Near East Welfare Association, 237 *et. seq.*; appeals from Armenia to, 238; *Acolyte* and *Mentor* criticize his methods, 243–244; his aid to the Guardian Building, Peekskill, N. Y., 245–251; sends aid to Poor Clares in Rome, and to church at Baguio, Philippines, and to Cardinal Bello, Patriarch of Lisbon, 251–252; aid to Mother Dengel for motherhouse in Washington of Catholic Medical Sisters, 252; Pope Benedict XV indulgences his prayer for Union-That-Nothing-Be-Lost, 254; his Church Unity Octave under Catholic auspices, 256, Chapter XX; Pope Pius X blesses him and Octave, 256; numerous prelates bless Octave, 257; Pope Benedict XV by Papal Brief extends observance of Octave to Universal Church, 257; *Living Church* (Anglican) in 1907 approves Octave, 259; his letter to Cardinal Dougherty requesting support for Octave, and favorable report to, 260–261; his audience with Pope Pius XI concerning Octave's obligatory observance, 262; active aid from Society of Jesus, 263; his formal petition to Pope Pius XI, 264–266; Sacred Congregation of Rites recommends new campaign to make Octave obligatory, 268; no confusion as to meaning of Octave at time of its founding in January, 1908, but in 1927 it is officially changed to Chair of Unity Octave and henceforward so known, 269; his ideas on corporate submission and corporate reception, 270; letter of Archbishop Mar Ivanios, India, to Rev. David Gannon concerning Octave, 272–273; he publishes in *Lamp* the form of Octave observed in non-Catholic communions, 275; his words on Christian Unity in 1903, 283; Cardinal Bonzano visits and writes to, 284; Monsignor Barry-Doyle's tribute to in 1926, 285; co-founder of Catholic Near East Welfare Association, 3, 285; Bishop Calavassy sends Monsignor Barry-Doyle to, 287; vice-president Catholic Near East Welfare Association, 289; last ten years of his life show very rapid growth of Society of the Atonement, 294; his letter on death of Mother Lurana, 296–297; he sponsors Ave Maria radio hour, 297; his early stand against Communism, 300; his primary work, the reunion of Christendom, 302; derivation of the name "Brothers Christopher," 4, 303; founding and growth of St. Christopher's Inn, Chapter XXIII; his attitude towards rehabilitation of drunkards, 307; article concerning, in *New York World*, 307; his characteristics of sanctity, 314; his experiment with golf, 316; interest in baseball, 317–318; eschews money, 319; denial of any personal visions, 321; innate simplicity, 323; his lifelong devotion to Our Lady, Chapter XXV, 327; establishment in 1901 of Rosary League, 327; his funeral and Dr. Smith's sermon, 343–347; his ambition to establish house in Rome realized in 1946, 348; his prediction of vast expansion of Friars' mission fulfilled, 349; his Society established in Japan, 349

Fay, Sigourney, professor at Nashotah Seminary, 130

Fidelis, Brother, S.A., describes difficulties of fund-raising for missions, 235

Fish, Hamilton, residence at Garrison, N. Y., 184; champions cause of the Sisters, 184–185, 188; senior warden,

St. Philip's Episcopal Church, Garrison, 185

Fitz, Rev. R. J., member Anglo-Catholic Union, 134

Flagg, Dr. Paluel I., meets Father Paul, 227; letter to Father Paul, 228; story of, in Keeler's *Catholic Medical Missions*, 228–229; establishes Catholic Medical Mission Propaganda with support of Maryknoll, Very Rev. James A. Walsh and Father Paul, 229–230; author visits with, and his family, at "Lisieux," Yonkers, 230

Foundation Day, December 15, 1898, originated, 63–64

Fox, Father Matthew, O.F.M., welcomes Father Paul to Franciscan monastery, Washington, 77–78

Francis, Father, defection of, 10; account of his defection, 202–208; forgiveness of, by Father Paul, 208

Fumasoni-Biondi, Pietro, Cardinal, at 1950 observance Chair of Unity Octave in Rome, 282; offers Society of the Atonement missionary field in Japan, 349–350

Gannon, Rev. David, S.A., author *Father Paul of Graymoor*, title page; Foreword; receives obedience to write, 12; visits Dr. Flagg, 230; letter from Mother Dengel, M.D., 253; letter from Archbishop Mar Ivanios, 272–273

Garasché, Rev. Edward, S.J., director Catholic Medical Mission Board, 230

Garrison, N. Y., address of Graymoor, 5; residence of Miss Chadwick, 59; St. Philip's Episcopal Church at, 180; residence of Hamilton Fish, 184–185

Gasparri, P., Cardinal, as Papal Secretary of State forwards Brief extending Octave to Universal Church, 257–259; confers with Monsignor Barry-Doyle, 289

Geare, Brother George (Rev. John Holwell Geare), convert, tertiary brother, and death, 81–82

General Theological Seminary (Protestant Episcopal), Rev. Joseph Newton Wattson attends, 13–19; students of who became Catholic, 20; Father Paul enrolls and graduates at, 25–26

Gibbons, James, Cardinal, his advice to Father Paul, 107; Father Paul visits, 152–153

Gibson, Elizabeth Monica, member community corporately received, 161

Gladstone, William Ewart, English statesman, attempts settlement of Anglican Orders, 108

Glennon, Most Rev. John Joseph, Archbishop of St. Louis, director Catholic Near East Welfare Association, 291

Grace, Bishop of Sacramento, blesses Octave, 257

Gray, Rev. A. Z., rector Episcopal church, Garrison, N. Y., name "Graymoor" derived from, 60; builds original chapel, 175–176

Graymoor, 3, Chapter VII et seq.; origin of name, see Gray

Graymoor Press, established, 219

Greer, David H., Episcopal Bishop of New York, Graymoor petition addressed to, 185–186

Griswold, Rev. Sheldon M., rector Episcopal church, Hudson, N. Y., 37; Episcopal Bishop of Chicago, 220

Guardian Building, Peekskill, N. Y., payment of debt on, 245–251

Halifax, Lord, attempts settlement question of Anglican Orders, father of recent ambassador, 136n.; writes Preface to book by Rev. Spencer Jones, 136, 137

Hanna, Most Rev. Edward J., Archbishop of San Francisco, director of Catholic Near East Welfare Association, 291

Hawes, Rev. John Cyril, eminent architect and convert, 215

Hawks, Rt. Rev. Monsignor Edward, tribute to Father Paul, 6; professor at Nashotah (Episcopal seminary), 118–119; convert, 130; friend of

Graymoor in adversity, 206–207; on corporate reception, 271

Hayes, Patrick, Cardinal, Father Paul preaches for, 103; as Monsignor hears Father Paul preach, 211; at laying of cornerstone of Little Flower chapel, 284; Protector of Catholic Near East Welfare Association, 291

Hazelhurst, George, member Anglo-Roman Union, 134

Hecker, Rev. Isaac, Redemptorist, later Paulist, 20

Hennepin, Father, Franciscan pioneer in America, Foreword

Hoban, Most Rev. M. J., Bishop of Scranton, chairman of directors, Catholic Near East Welfare Association, 291

Holy Angels Church, Chicago, mission at, conducted by Father Paul, 213

Holy Childhood Association, Graymoor ransoms pagan babies, 235

Holy Cross, see Order of the

Holy Cross, chapel at Kingston, N. Y., 33; Father Paul returns to preach at, 51

Holy Ghost, Atonement Seminary of the, (The Vineyard) Washington, D. C., 217–219; in 1930 filled with students, 294

Holy Sepulcher, Equestrian Order (Knights) of the, Cardinal Canali Patron of, 348; St. Onofrio's, Rome, their church, and Friars of the Atonement at, 348–349

Hostel, Our Lady's, Graymoor, occupied by Professed Sisters, 182

Howard, Father, succeeds Father Paul as Superior, Associate Mission (Anglican), Omaha, 47–48; leaves Mission, 75–76

Hughes, Most Rev., Archbishop of New York, 18

Hughes, Rev. Dr. William, vice-president Cathedral College, hears Father Paul preach, 211

"Humani Generis," encyclical letter of Pope Pius XII, 277

Huntington, Rev. James, O.S., Superior of Order of the Holy Cross (Anglican), 70; sympathy with Father Paul, 73, 76

Immanence, Heresy of, 125
Ireland, mission house in, 5
Italy, Society of the Atonement church in, *see* St. Onofrio's

Jacob, Brother Paul, *see* Anthony, Brother
Jacobite Monks, *see* Bethany Congregation of
Jacobite Sisters, corporately received, 115
Japan, Emperor of, employs Dr. Lloyd, 123; receives Bishop O'Connell, 124
Japan, Society of the Atonement missionaries to, 349–350; a Catholic university established in, 124
Jerome, Father, *see* Hawes, John Cyril
Jessup, Rev. Charles A., friend of Father Paul, 98–99
Johnson, Rev. Irving P., visit to Father Paul, 37; Episcopal Bishop of Colorado, 219
Jones, Rev. Spencer (English Anglican), author *England and the Holy See*, and lifelong friendship with Father Paul, 136–137; collaboration with Father Paul on *The Prince of the Apostles*, 137–138; various comments on this book, 138–139; letters from Father Paul to, on Church Unity Octave, and his replies, 144–146
Joseph, Miriam Irene (later Sister Miriam, S.A.), member Graymoor community corporately received, 161
"Jure Divino," foundation of the Papacy, 92; favorite theme of Father Paul, 95

Katsuno, Peter, seminarian and baseball player, 318
Kearney, Most Rev. James E., Bishop of Rochester, gives permission for Montour Falls Foundation, 351
Keeler, Rev. Floyd, convert, 216; author of *Catholic Medical Missions*, 228
Kennelly, Rev. M., S.J., letter from China about missions, 228
King, H. M., member Anglo-Roman Union, 134

Kingston, N. Y., Father Paul's ministry at, 28–38; revisits, 51
Kin-Kwa-Fu, China, mission aided by Graymoor, 226
Kinsman, Dr. Frederick Joseph, Episcopal Bishop of Delaware, his decisive letter to Father Paul; his conversion, lifelong connection with Graymoor and death, 153–155
Knights of the Holy Sepulcher, *see* Holy Sepulcher, Equestrian Order of

"Lamentabili," papal decree, 126
Lamont, Dr. Margaret, volunteers for foreign missions, convert, 228–229
Lamp, The, Father Paul editor of, 6; *Rose Leave from Our Lady's Garden*, precursor of, 124; starts publication February, 1903, 104–124 *et seq.*, Chapter XI; derivation of name, 105; inadequate explanation of "Infallibility" in, 110; "Ut omnes unum sint"—at top of every page, 117; *Church Standard*, Rev. C. LeV. Brine and Father Richey criticize, 117–119; devotion of Mother Lurana to, 119–121; voice of pro-Roman minority in the Episcopal Church, 121; Dr. Lloyd writes for, 123, 139; editorial on "open pulpit," 130–131; advocates reunion of Christendom, 136; editorial on *England and the Holy See*, by Spencer Jones, in, 137; publishes *Prince of the Apostles*, 138–139; announces first observance of Church Unity Octave, 140; "Catholic" writing of Father Paul in, 150–151; importance of, in furthering reception of Society of the Atonement into Catholic Church, 159; announcement of reception of Society of the Atonement into Catholic Church, 161-162; Church desires continuation of, 162; approval of some Anglicans of continuation of, 167; disapproval of others, i.e., Rev. Dr. Van Allan, Rev. W. S. Clairborne, 168–173; Father Paul's editorial on lawsuit against Sisters, 181–182; Memorial to Miss Elliot, 187–190; Archbishop Farley supplies funds for, 193; Father Paul quotes

Father Benson, 195–196; protest against prejudice of some clergy, 201; articles on major seminary in Washington, 217–219; staff of at Graymoor Press, Peekskill, 219; publicizes Catholic Medical Mission Board, 227; in 1920's has circulation of 165,000, 234; appeal for Armenia, 237–238; use of "clock" for raising funds by, 238; unfavorable comments by *Acolyte* on, 239–240; appeal for Poor Clares, Assisi, and Cardinal Falconio's gratitude, 243–244; story of Guardian Building, Peekskill, N. Y., 245–250; appeal for church in the Philippines, 251; asks help for Cardinal Bello, Portugal, 252; appeals to build motherhouse for Catholic Medical Missionaries (Mother Dengel), 252; voices requests of Archbishop Farley, Monsignor Falconio, many bishops, for publicizing Church Unity Octave, 256; Bolshakoff's letter in, 275; Father Paul's letter of 1903 on Christian Unity, 283; account of cornerstone laying, Little Flower Oratory, 285; campaign for one million dollars for Near East Relief, 287–288; account of creation in 1926 of Catholic Near East Welfare Association by Pope Pius XI, 292–293; growth of Society of the Atonement by 1935, 294; Father Paul's letter on Mother Lurana's death, 296–297; Father Paul writes against Communism in 1923, and 1938, 300; discussion of Brothers Christopher in, 310–312; letter to Rosary League in first issue of, 327; Father Paul writes on Our Lady and her Assumption, 331–332; and of Our Lady of the Atonement, 336–340

Lane, Most Rev. Raymond A., Father General of Maryknoll, tells story of baseball game with Graymoor, 318

Laurenti, Cardinal, petition for Octave presented to, 266–267

Lavelle, Rt. Rev. Monsignor, friend of Graymoor, 186; preaches at Mother Lurana's funeral, 296

La Curon, Father, Franciscan pioneer in America, *Foreword*

Lee, Alfred, Episcopal Bishop of Delaware, 19; makes Father Paul deacon, 27

Leo XIII, Pope, declares Anglican Orders invalid, "Apostolicae Curae," 107; letter of rebuke to Cardinal Richard, 108–111; Father Paul proclaims supreme, 122

Lester, Sister Edith, member Graymoor community, received corporately, 161

Lillis, Most Rev. Thomas J., Bishop of Kansas City, director Catholic Near East Welfare Association, 291

"Little Flower," canonization of, Father Paul's pilgrimage to Rome to be present at, 261–263; his comments on, 263

Little Flower Oratory, Graymoor, its limited capacity, 242; cornerstone laid in 1926 by Cardinal Bonzano accompanied by Cardinal Hayes, 284; Father Paul's funeral service in, 343–347

Liverpool, Archbishop of, letter to Father Paul, 268–269

Living Church, the, Anglican periodical, comments on Archdeaconry meeting, 104; calls Father Paul "erratic priest," 121; reviews *Prince of the Apostles*, 139; comment on Father Paul, Dr. Lloyd and Rev. Spencer Jones, 139; tribute to Bishop Kinsman, 155; letters from J. A. M. Richey and Rev. W. E. Clairborne to, 171–173; Miss Chadwick's letter to, championing Sisters of the Atonement, 175–177

Lloyd, Rev. Dr. Arthur, Episcopal missionary to Japan, co-operates with Father Paul, 123–124; *Living Church* comment on, 139; contributor to *The Lamp*, 123, 139; pays Peter's Pence, 151

Locke, Florence Elliot (later Sister Mary Francis, S.A.), member of Graymoor community corporately received, 161

Logue, Cardinal, of Ireland, blesses Octave, 257

Lowndes, Rev. Arthur, co-plaintiff in lawsuit against Sisters, 175

Lurana, Mother, see Mother Lurana

Mackay, Clarence, patron of Catholic Near East Welfare Association, 288

Manning, Rev. John, champions Father Paul, 103

Marchetti-Selvaggiani, Francesco, Cardinal, authorizes Society of the Atonement at St. Onofrio's, Rome, 348

Margil, Father Antony, Franciscan pioneer in America, Foreword

Mariani, Monsignor, secretary to Cardinal Laurenti, 267

Mar Ivanios, Archbishop of Trivandrum, India, his Jacobite monks corporately received, 115–116; conversion of, 272; letter to author concerning Church Unity Octave, 272–273

Mar Theophilos, Suffragan Bishop in India, Jacobite Sisters corporately received, 115–116

Mary Angela, Sister, Episcopalian, meets Mother Lurana, 59; urges Franciscan foundation at Graymoor, 61

Maryknoll, Dr. Flagg at, 229; baseball games, 317–318

Mary Louise, Sister, aid from Graymoor for Japanese orphans, 226

Matthews, Rev. Paul, Superior of Associate Mission, Omaha, 37; later Episcopal Bishop of New Jersey, 220

McGarvey, Rev. William, convert, 26; Superior, Companions of the Holy Savior (Anglicans), resigns as rector St. Elizabeth's, Philadelphia; ordained priest, 129–130

McGavick, Auxiliary Bishop of Chicago, Father Paul preaches mission for, 213

McGuiness, Most Rev. Eugene J., Bishop of Raleigh (later of Oklahoma City and Tulsa), present at Father Paul's funeral, 343

McKean, Thomas, patron Near East Catholic Welfare Association, 288

McMahon, Rt. Rev. Thomas J., National Secretary Catholic Near East Welfare Association, his letter of thanks to Sisters of Atonement, 292

McMaster, James A., convert, and editor New York Freeman's Journal, 20

McNabb, Rev. Vincent, O.P., reviews Prince of the Apostles in American Ecclesiastical Review, 137

McVinney, Most Rev. Russell J., gives permission for transfer of Valley Falls, R. I., property to Society of the Atonement, 351

Mentor, the, parish bulletin, adverse criticism of Father Paul, 239

Merry del Val, Raphael, Cardinal, on dedicatory page; acknowledges Peter's Pence from Graymoor, 151–152; Father Paul his guest in Rome, and he tells of his plea to the Holy Father, 159; sponsors petition for university of Octave, 257; Father Paul writes to, 263; Monsignor Barry-Doyle confers with, 289

Milford Haven, Wales, Benedictine Nuns of, received corporately, 115

Missionary Union of the Clergy, see Unitas

Modernism, heresy of, 125 et seq.

Montour Falls Foundation, 350

Mooney, Edward, Cardinal, Apostolic Delegate to East Indies, meets Mar Ivanios, 272

Moore, Mr., Columbia University professor, builder of original St. John's Church; name "Graymoor" partially derived from, 60

Morrow, Most Rev. Louis La Ravoire, Bishop of Krishnagar, India, at Father Paul's funeral, 343

Mother Drexel, see Drexel, Mother

Mother Edith, see Edith, Mother

Mother Lurana, Foundress Sisters of the Atonement, 4; in Cardinal Canali's letter, 9; Father Paul's later letter to, concerning name "Atonement," 35; as Sister Lurana Mary White, her first letter to Father Paul, "Enter Mother Lurana," Chapter V, 41 et seq.; invited to Omaha, refuses, 47–48; Father Paul visits at Warwick, N. Y., and the "Covenant" is made, 52–58; correspondence with

Sister Mary Angela, 59, 61; Father Paul writes her about Graymoor, 63; her first winter at Graymoor, 63–66; letter to, from Father Paul on cornerstone laying of St. Francis' Convent, 67–69; Father Paul's correspondence with, and her decision on the style of habit of the Society of the Atonement, 73–75, 87; story of the purchase of Graymoor, 79–83; writes Bishop Potter on dedication of convent, Bishop Coleman substitutes, 84–85; Brother Anthony introduced by, 89–90; she considers Father Paul's advocacy of corporate reunion, 91–92; her devotion to, and work for *The Lamp*, 119–121; she sends *Rose Leaves* to Dr. Lloyd in Japan with important consequence, 123–124; her influence on book *Prince of the Apostles*, 138; pays Peter's Pence to Rome, 151–152; visits Archbishop Farley, 152; received into Catholic Church, 157–161; lawsuit filed against her and the Sisters, Chapter XV, 167 *et seq.*; her letter to plaintiff's attorneys, Zabriskie, Murray, Sage and Kerr, 177–181; correspondence with James Dempsey, her attorney, 182–184; letter of George Zabriskie to James Dempsey, 184; intervention of Hamilton Fish in behalf of, and his petition to Bishop Greer, 185–187; settlement of lawsuit, 186; attends Father Paul's ordination, 197; letter to, from Father Paul on "prodigal," 212; letter from Ruthenian Pontifical College, and her answer, 268; death of in 1935, 296–297; cofounder of Rosary League in 1901, 327; in 1950 her spiritual daughters number 350, and conduct 50 missions, 352

Naayem, Abbé, Chaldean priest, expression of gratitude for help from Father Paul, 232
Nashotah Seminary, Wisconsin, influence of *The Lamp* at, 118–119; its reaction to "open pulpit," 129–130; Mr. Richey on effect of *Lamp* at, 170–173
Naslian, Most Rev. John, Bishop of Trebizond, letter to Pope Pius XI petitioning Octave be made obligatory, 261
Nelson, Diocese of (Canada), 351
Nevin, Rev. Michael, Kisumo, Africa, letter of thanks to Father Paul, 236
Newman, John Henry, Cardinal, "Tracts for the Times," 13; active in Oxford Movement, 13–18; letters to Maria Giberne and T. W. Allies, 16–17; his reception into Catholic Church, 16–17; "Via Media," 30; *Apologia pro vita sua*, 30–31, 31n.; "genuine Catholicity of," 131
New York Freeman's Journal, McMaster, James A., editor of, 20
New York Herald, article in, April 20, 1903, 121–122; editorial on Anglo-Roman Union, 133–134
New York Sun, predicts Father Paul will be "Catholic," and his reply, 31, 150
New York Times, on Graymoor's reception into Catholic Church, 162–164
New York World, article in 1924 on St. Christopher's Inn, 307–308
Nicholson, Mrs. Sarah (formerly Miss Elliot), 59; Mother Lurana visits, 62; her lawsuit against Sisters and death at Graymoor as convert, plaintiff in lawsuit, 175, 185, 187–188; death in 1949, 187
Nuns, Jacobite, corporately received, 115; of Milford Haven, corporately received, 115

O'Boyle, Most Rev. Patrick A., Archbishop of Washington, 218
O'Brien, Judge Morgan J., counsel to Sisters of the Atonement, 186
O'Connell, William, Cardinal, embassy to Emperor of Japan, 124; approves Octave, 141; director Catholic Near East Welfare Association, 291
Octave, *see* Chair of Unity Octave, Church Unity Octave
Octave of the Epiphany, originated by Blessed Vincent Pallotti, 147–148

Ogdensburg, Diocese of, Bishop Wadhams, convert and first Catholic Bishop, 20; as Monsignor Conroy, Vicar General of, he receives Society of the Atonement in the Catholic Church, 160–162; house of the Society established in, 351

O'Keeffe, Monsignor C. G., pastor at Highland Falls, N. Y., instructor of Society of the Atonement prior to Catholic reception, 159–162

"Open Pulpit," 125 et seq., all of chapter XII

Order of the Holy Cross (Anglican), Father Paul goes to, 55; Father Paul studies with, 70–73; leaves, 76–77

Oriental Church, rites of, at Octave of Epiphany, 147; Bishops petition Pius XI for Octave, 261; letter from Bishop d'Herbigney, 264

Orthodox Jacobite Church, in schism, 116

Osservatore Romano, Bishop Calavassy's reference to, 7; publicity by, on observance of Octave, 282

Our Lady of Pity, Bronx, N. Y. Church, aided by Graymoor, 226

Oxford Movement, under John Henry Newman, 13–18; Dr. Taylor product of, 80; reference in Lamp to, 106

Pallotti, Blessed Vincent, notes on life of, by Father De Maria, 146–148; citation in Catholic Encyclopedia, 148

Papadopoulos, Most Rev. Isaias, receives funds from Graymoor, Bishop Calavassy thanks for help for, 293

Pascal, Brother, friend and confidant of Father Francis, 203–208

"Pascendi," papal encyclical, 126

Passionists, Father Paul's impulse to join, 54

Pellitzer, Sister Clara Francesca, member Graymoor community corporately received, 161

Peter's Pence, payment by Dr. Lloyd, 123; payment by Father Paul and Mother Lurana while still Anglicans, 151–152; acknowledged by Cardinal Merry del Val, 151–152

Pious Society of Missions, founded by Blessed Vincent Pallotti, 146

Pius IX, Pope, directed Father Hecker to found Congregation for the conversion of America, 20

Pius X, Pope, communication from Dr. Lloyd, 124; encyclical "Pascendi" and decree "Lamentabili," 126–127; prays for Graymoor's conversion, Chapter XIV; blesses Father Paul and Church Unity Octave, 256

Pius XI, Pope, receives letters from Oriental Bishops asking to make Octave obligatory, 261; Father Paul has private audience with, 262; Father Paul's comment on at canonization of "Little Flower," 263

Pius XII, Pope, in 1946 renews indulgences for Church Unity Octave, 259; encyclical "Humani Generis," 277; "Eirenic Theology," 278–279; on Ecumenical Movement, 279–280; creates Bishop Von Galen Cardinal, 289; authorizes services of Friars of the Atonement at St. Onofrio's, Rome, 348

Pontifical Gregorian University, see Unitas

Poor Clares, the Lady Clare, 44; Second Order of St. Francis, 74; favorite beneficiaries of Father Paul, 233; Abbess of, at Assisi, appeals for help, 243; letter from Cardinal Falconio announcing raising of their church at Assisi to rank of Basilica, 243–244; Father Paul sends $5000 to, at Rome, for a new monastery, 251; their veneration for Father Paul, 349

"Portiuncula," 156, 181

Portugal, see Bello, Cardinal

Potter, Henry C., Episcopal Bishop of New York, admits Father Paul as presbyter, 28; invited to dedicate St. Francis', obliged to decline, 84; sponsors Father Paul, 85; did not recognize St. John's Church prior to Father Paul's arrival, 177, 180

Poverello, the, see St. Francis of Assisi

Prescott, Oliver, student at General Theological Seminary, 13

Prince of the Apostles, the, collaboration by Father Paul and Rev. Spencer Jones, 137–139, see also Mother Lurana

Prior Ernest John, member Anglo-Roman Union, 134; he, and Emma Louise and Mallam and David, members Graymoor community corporately received, 161

Pulpit of the Cross, began publication, 29; revived at Omaha, 40

Purcell, Edmund Sheridan, author of *Life and Letters of Ambrose Phillipps de Lisle*, 16n.

Raleigh, Diocese of, Society of the Atonement established in, 351

Rauch, Very Rev. Francis, S.J., ardent supporter of Octave, 263; Father Paul's letter to, 264; presents petition for Octave to Cardinal Laurenti, 266–267; Father Paul writes to on "Adunationis," 334–335

Reatelli, Carmela, Abbess of Poor Clares, Assisi, appeals to Father Paul, 243

Reid, John, first member of Union-That-Nothing-Be-Lost, 222; later association with Graymoor, and death, 222–226

Religious Congregations, *Foreword*; benefitted by Graymoor, 233

Rhode Island, see Valley Falls, R. I.

Richard, Cardinal, Leo XIII's letter to, concerning *Anglo-Roman Review*, 108

Richey, Rev. J. A. M., professor at Nashotah Seminary, vigorously opposed to Father Paul, 118; convert and priest, 119; supports Father Paul while still at Nashotah, 170–173; associate editor of *The Lamp*, and article on cornerstone laying of Little Flower Oratory, 285; pseudonym "Saul," 285

Rigo, Very Rev. Arnaldo, O.F.M. with Father Rauch presents petition for Octave to Cardinal Laurenti, 267

Riley, Rev. James, vice-president Anglo-Roman Union, 134

Robinson, Rev. Paschal, O.F.M., in 1899 meets Father Paul, and is later Papal Nuncio to Ireland, 77–78; instructor to Graymoor community,

160–162; unofficial chaplain to Graymoor after its reception into Church, 191

"Robinson property," see Holy Ghost, Atonement Seminary of the

Roche, Bishop Francis, S.J., of Tuticorin, India, his letter to Father Paul, 270

Rochester, Diocese of, Society of the Atonement established in, 351

Rock of Peter Foundation, established, 224

"Romanorum Pontificum," 1916 Brief of Benedict XV, 265–266

Rosary League, established, 97; purpose of, to increase devotion to Our Lady, 327–331; letters from Father Paul to, 338–340

Rose Leaves, Graymoor magazine established in 1901, 97; its influence on Dr. Lloyd in establishing Catholic university in Japan, 124

Rouchel, Dr., of Croghan, N. Y., woman physician who paid expenses of first woman medical missionary to China, 228

Sacred Congregation of Rites, petition for Octave presented to, 268

Sacred Heart Messenger, adversely criticizes Father Paul, 111

St. Anthony's Shrine, 12; not "grand shrine," as *Acolyte* charged, 242; temporarily abandoned, 242

St. Clare's Church, Assisi, Mother Lurana visits, 44; Abbess of, appeals to Father Paul, 243; Cardinal Falconio, Protector of, and his letter to Graymoor, 243–244

St. Clement's Episcopal Church at Millington, Md., parish of Rev. Joseph Newton Wattson, 19; and rectory of, birthplace of Father Paul, 22

St. Christopher's Inn, 4; enlarged, 295 and Chapter XXIII

St. Denis' Church, Yonkers, N. Y., Father Paul pleads for missions and meets Dr. Flagg, 227

St. Elizabeth's Church, Philadelphia, parish of Rev. William McGarvey and home of Companions of the Holy Savior, 128–129

St. Elizabeth's College, Convent, N. J., raises funds for the Catholic Union, 290

St. Elizabeth of Hungary, chapel at Graymoor, 86

St. Francis of Assisi, his influence on Father Paul, 33–34; visit of Mother Lurana to tomb of, 43–44, 53; Mother Lurana's deep love of, 50; beginning of Father Paul's devotion to, 50–52; the Three Orders of, 74, 75, 75n.; his original refusal of Priesthood, 311–312; Cardinal Dougherty praises Father Paul as emulator of, 320

St. Francis' Chapel, begun 1911, dedicated 1912, 214–215; John Cyril Hawes and Carlton Strong, architects, 215

St. Francis' Convent, dedicated 1899, 84–85, 327; in 1900 community's vocation of Christian unity signed at, 93

St. Ignatius Loyola, see Society of Jesus

St. James' Church, Port Deposit, Md., Father Paul deacon at, 27

St. John Baptist Church (St. John's-in-the-Wilderness), discovery of, by Misses Elliot and Chadwick, 59–61; Mother Lurana's first winter at, 63 et seq.; Miss Chadwick's letter concerning, 175–177; in memorial to Miss Elliot, 187–188; renovated by Cardinal Farley, 214

St. John's Church, Kingston, N. Y., Father Paul's first Anglican parish, 28; Father Paul's career at, 28–38

St. John's Seminary, Graymoor, 4; built in 1913, 11; majority of students desert, 204–207; ground broken for and development of, 215–216; in 1915 filled to capacity, 216; in 1937 Father Paul writes of, 295

St. Joseph's Seminary, see Dunwoodie Seminary

St. Luke's Episcopal Church, Baltimore, 19

St. Mary's Hall, Burlington, N. J., preparatory school of Father Paul, 24

St. Onofrio's Church, Rome, Cardinal Canali protector of, 348; in custody of Society of the Atonement, 348–349

St. Patrick's Cathedral, Father Paul preaches at, 103, 211–212

St. Paul's (Episcopal) College, Tokio, Dr. Arthur Lloyd at, 123–124

St. Paul's Friary, Mother Lurana supplies money for, it is built and is dedicated by Bishop Coleman on December 8, 1900, 94; 37th anniversary of, 295

St. Philip's Episcopal Church, Garrison, N. Y., lack of interest in St. John's, Graymoor, 180; Hamilton Fish senior warden of, 185

St. Stephen's College, Annandale, N. Y., academic education of Father Paul at, 25

Salve Mater, by Bishop Kinsman, 155

San Damiano, Church of, Assisi, inspires restoration of St. John's, Graymoor, 61; Miss Elliot inspired by story of, 187

San Giovanni Decollata, Rome, Church of, Franciscan, 349

Santa Chiara, Assisi, see St. Clare's Church

Sargent, Rev. Harry R., seminarian and convert, 26; Novice Master, Order of the Holy Cross, 70–73; joins Church of Rome, letter in American Catholic on, 173–174

"Saul," pseudonym of Rev. J. A. M. Richey, 285

Scarborough, John, Episcopal Bishop of New Jersey, makes Father Paul presbyter, 28

Schilling, Rev. Godfrey, O.F.M., founder of Franciscan monastery in Washington, D. C., 77

Schrembs, Bishop of Cleveland and Ordinary of Toledo, blesses Octave, 257

Seabury, Episcopal Bishop of Connecticut, 18

Seabury, Dr., editor of the Churchman, 18

"Seminary—Admissions and Dismissals, regulations governing," in Catholic Encyclopedia, 241

Serra, Father Junipero, Franciscan pioneer in America, *Foreword*

"Servants of Christ the King" (Anglican Order), corporately received, 115, 271

Seymour, George F., Episcopal Bishop of Springfield, baccalaureate sermon, 26

Sister Lurana, *see* Mother Lurana

Sisterhood of the Holy Child, Mother Lurana receives education at, 41; enters and leaves Sisterhood, 41–43

Sisters of the Atonement, *see* Atonement, Sisters of the

Sisters of Bethany, London (Anglican), Mother Lurana enters novitiate and remains a year, 43–44

Sisters of the Blessed Sacrament, *see* Drexel, Mother

Sisters of St. Mary, Peekskill, N. Y., order of Sister Mary Angela, 59 and *see* Edith, Mother

Sisters of the Love of Jesus (Anglican), Archdiocese of Vancouver, corporately received, 271–272

Smith, Very Rev. Ignatius, O.P., eulogy at Father Paul's funeral, 343–347

Smyth, Dr. Newman, Congregational minister, editorial in *Living Church*, 132

"Societas Adunationis," officially recorded at Rome, 333

Society of Jesus, "Jesuits in Disguise," Chapter II, foremost supporters of Octave, 263; loyalty of the Society of the Atonement to, 264

Solanus, Father, O.F.M., attends Father Paul's ordination, 197

Spellman, Francis, Cardinal, author of *Foreword*, president Catholic Near East Welfare Association, 292; interest in Graymoor, 347; authorizes Society of the Atonement at St. Onofrio's, Rome, 348; preaches to first Atonement missionaries to Japan, 349; blesses Montour Falls foundation, 351; approves transfer of Valley Falls property, 351

Staunton, Rev. John J., Jr., Anglican missionary to Philippines, his letter to Father Paul, 116–117; convert, 116

Stigmata of St. Francis, grotto of at Washington, 77

Strong, Carlton, member Anglo-Roman Union, 134; co-architect St. Francis chapel, and convert, 215

Suhard, Emmanuel, Cardinal, Archbishop of Paris, authorizes Society of Atonement at St. Onofrio's, Rome, 348

Tacci, Cardinal, Monsignor Barry-Doyle confers with, 289

Taylor, Dr. John, English surgeon, brother-in-law of Miss Buxton, sends money for purchase of Graymoor, 80–81; a product of Oxford Movement, 80

Terzian, Paul Peter XIII, Armenian Patriarch of Cilicia, letter of appeal to Father Paul, 238

Thomas, His Beatitude Emmanuel, Patriarch of Babylon, letter of thanks for help from Father Paul, 232

Thompson, Rev. Walter (Episcopalian), in 1893 helps renovate St. John's Church, 176

Tierney, Rev. R. H., S.J., writes Preface to Keeler's *Catholic Medical Missions*, 228

Ting, Rev. Leo, contributions from Graymoor and acknowledgment, 226–227

Tisserant, Eugenio, Cardinal, tribute to Father Paul, 7–8; participation in 1950 Octave at Rome, 282

Tobin, Rev. Richard, pastor at Peekskill, N. Y., Father Paul's sermon on, 245–250

Tompkins, Justice, of New York State Supreme Court, rules against Sisters in lawsuit, 181, 186

"Tracts for the Times," *see* Newman

Trappists, *see* Cistercians

Union-That-Nothing-Be-Lost, 221 *et seq.*, Chapter XIX

Unitas, official publication of Unitas Association of Rome, edited by Rev. Charles Boyer, S.J., of Pontifical

Gregorian University, publishes 1950 resolution of Missionary Union of the Clergy urging increased effort for Chair of Unity Octave, 149

Ursulines of Alaska, mission aided by Graymoor, 226

"Ut Omnes Unum Sint" ("That they all may be one"); headline of every page of The Lamp, 117, 134, 259, 282, 333

Valley Falls, R. I., Cistercian monastery acquired as novitiate by Graymoor in 1951, 351

Van Allan, Rev. William Harman (Anglican), Father Paul preaches for, at Elmira, N. Y., 86; visit to Graymoor, 92; opposes Father Paul, 121; letter to Living Church, 169–170

Vancouver, Archdiocese of, Archbishop Duke corporately receives Sisters of the Love of Jesus, 271

Van Roey, Joseph, Cardinal, makes observance of Octave obligatory throughout Belgium, 263

Van Zuyt, Very Rev. A., letters from, concerning Church of Our Lady of the Atonement, Baguio, Philippine Islands, 251

Vaughan, Cardinal, doubts feasibility of corporate reunion, 114

Venard, Marie, member Graymoor community corporately received, 161

"Via Media," Cardinal Newman's original path, 31

Vico, Cardinal, pro-Prefect, Sacred Congregation of Rites, 266

"Vineyard, the," see Holy Ghost, Atonement Seminary of the

Voice of the Church, article by Bolshakoff in, 281–282

Von Galen, Rev. Augustine Count, Benedictine, also raising money for Near East Relief, 289–290

Von Galen, Bishop Clement, Cardinal in 1946, 289

"Vox Populi," important in change of liturgy, 267

Wadhams, Edgar F., Episcopal seminarian with Rev. Joseph Newton

Wattson, and convert and first Catholic Bishop of Ogdensburg, 20

Wakida, Most Rev. Thomas, dedicates Society of the Atonement mission in Japan, 350

Wallerstein, Ferdinand, see Anthony, Brother

Walsh, Rev. Edmund A., S.J., president Catholic Near East Welfare Association, 291

Walsh, Very Rev. James A. (later Bishop) of Maryknoll, sponsor of Catholic Medical Mission Board, 229; his interest in baseball, 318

Walworth, Rev. Clarence, seminarian with Rev. Joseph Newton Wattson, convert, pioneer Paulist, 20, 24

Ward, Maisie, author of Young Mr. Newman, 15n., 17n.

Warwick, N. Y., home of Mother Lurana, 45; visit of Father Paul to, there originating "Covenant," 52–55

Wattson, Rev. Joseph Newton, father of Father Paul, 13; at General Theological Seminary, Chapter II; later ministry, 19; influence on his son, 22–25; assists son at Kingston, N. Y., and death, 27–28

Wattson, Rev. Lewis Thomas, see Father Paul

Wattson, Mary Electa, mother of Father Paul, 22; later years and death, 39

Weber, Rev. Eugene, biographer of Blessed Vincent Pallotti, 147

Whitaker, Ozi William, Episcopal Bishop of Pennsylvania, 130

White, Miss Annie, sister of Mother Lurana, 43, 52, 63

White, Lurana Mary, see Mother Lurana

Whittingham, William F., Episcopal Bishop of Maryland, 19

Winslow, Rev. Francis, Assistant General of Maryknoll, 318

World Conference on Faith and Order (non-Catholic), "Affirmation of Unity," 276

Worthington, George, Episcopal Bishop of Nebraska, 37; Father Paul reports to, 40; Father Paul leaves, 47

Woywood, Rev. Stanislaus, O.F.M.,

78; helps write Franciscan Rule at Graymoor, 196.

Yokohama, Diocese of, Society of the Atonement established in, 349–350

Zabriskie, George, brings suit against Sisters after their reception into Catholic Church, 174; Mother Lurana's letter to, 177–181; in letters of James Dempsey, 183–184; in petition of Hamilton Fish, 185; resists settlement, 186; Chancellor of Episcopal Diocese of New York, 186

Zabriskie, Murray, Sage and Kerr, see Zabriskie, George